RESIDENTIAL SECURITY

AUSTRALIA
The Law Book Company
Brisbane * Sydney * Melbourne * Perth

CANADA
Carswell
Ottawa * Toronto * Calgary * Montreal * Vancouver

AGENTS:
Steimatzky's Agency Ltd, Tel Aviv;
N.M. Tripathi (Private) Ltd, Bombay;
Eastern Law House (Private) Ltd, Calcutta;
M.P.P. House, Bangalore;
Universal Book Traders, Delhi;
Aditya Books, Delhi;
MacMillan Shippan KK, Tokyo;
Pakistan Law House, Karachi, Lahore.

RESIDENTIAL SECURITY

JILL E. MARTIN, LL.M., LL.D. (Lond.)
Barrister,
Professor of Law,
King's College London

Second Edition

LONDON SWEET & MAXWELL 1995

First edition 1989

Published in 1995 by
Sweet & Maxwell Limited
183 Marsh Wall, London E14 9FT
Typeset by York House Typographic Ltd
Printed and bound in Great Britain by
Hartnolls Ltd, Bodmin.

**A catalogue record for this
book is available from
the British Library**.

ISBN 0-421-541504

P REFACE

When the previous edition of this book was published in
1989 the Housing Act 1988 had only recently come into
operation and there was no case law to illustrate and clarify
the assured and assured shorthold provisions of the 1988
Act and the substantial amendments made by the new Act
to the Protection from Eviction Act 1977. In the years since
the 1988 Act came into force there have been several
significant decisions in the higher courts on the civil action
for unlawful eviction and a body of case law and
commentary has begun to build up on the assured tenancy
regime. Meanwhile, decisions on the Rent Act 1977
continue unabated. These are significant in their own right,
in view of the large numbers of surviving protected and
statutory tenancies, and because the concepts they examine
are often relevant to assured tenancies under the Housing
Act 1988.

The structure of the book is similar to that of the previous
edition save that the chapter on restricted contracts and the
section on restricted contracts in Chapter 10 (rent control)
have gone. This reflects the fact that the more transitory
nature of restricted contracts has allowed them to be phased
out by the 1988 Act much more quickly than regulated
tenancies. In other chapters in Part II, on the Rent Act
1977, the emphasis is on matters which continue to give rise
to litigation or which remain relevant to assured tenancies.

Part I deals with licences and with the Protection from
Eviction Act 1977. The lease/licence distinction continues to
generate considerable case law. Particular mention should
be made of *Westminster City Council v. Clarke*, where the
House of Lords re-examined exclusive possession, and
Family Housing Association v. Jones, which rejected the view
that homeless persons enjoying exclusive possession are not
tenants under the *Street v. Mountford* principles. Of the cases
on the civil action for unlawful eviction, the most significant
are *Tagro v. Cafane* and *Jones v. Miah*, dealing with the
measure of damages and clarifying various points arising
from the 1988 amendments to the Protection from Eviction
Act 1977.

Part II deals with regulated tenancies under the Rent Act
1977. Many of the recent cases have some scope for
application to assured tenancies also. These include
Britannia Building Society v. Earl (paramount title of
mortgagee), *Killick v. Roberts* (rescission of tenancy), *Kaye
v. Massbetter* (company lets) and *Crago v. Julian*
(assignment). Recent cases on the grounds for possession, in
particular Cases 9 and 11, are too numerous to mention
here. Cases on rent registration have highlighted the
question of whether diminishing scarcity, brought about by

increasing numbers of dwellings to let on assured or assured
shorthold tenancies, should result in the "fair rent" being
increased to market levels.

Part III, on the Housing Act 1988, is expanded to deal
with the new case law, in particular *Panayi v. Roberts* and
Bedding v. McCarthy on the conditions for the grant of
assured shortholds, *Mountain v. Hastings* on recovery of
possession from assured tenants and *N. & D. (London) Ltd
v. Gadsdon* on the assessment of rent by the rent assessment
committee. On the legislative front, the accelerated
possession procedure applicable to shortholds and to certain
mandatory grounds for possession is examined. Both Part II
and Part III have been updated to reflect the replacement of
the rateable value limits with the high and low rent
exclusions by the Local Government and Housing Act 1989.
The forthcoming Family Homes and Domestic Violence
legislation, enabling cohabitants to seek occupation orders
and transfer of tenancy orders, is referred to in Bill form.

As with the previous edition, my aim has been to combine
a practical approach with a critical analysis, and to provide
ample references to periodical literature where points may
be followed up. The book is primarily intended for
practitioners, but will, I hope, be of use to students of the
law of Landlord and Tenant in university and professional
examinations.

The law is stated as at May 1, 1995.

Jill Martin
King's College London
May 1, 1995

C ONTENTS

TABLE OF CASES

TABLE OF STATUTES

TABLE OF STATUTORY INSTRUMENTS

I INTRODUCTION

After a brief historical outline, this Part will deal with two matters which are essential to an understanding of security of tenure.

Licences   The first is the distinction between leases and licences, where there have been many developments since the landmark decision in *Street v. Mountford.*[1] It should be added that the distinction is just as important under the Housing Act 1988 as under the Rent Act 1977.

Protection from   The second is the Protection from Eviction Act 1977,
Eviction Act 1977   which was substantially amended by the Housing Act 1988.

---

[1] [1985] A.C. 809.

1 HISTORICAL OUTLINE

The Rent Acts have been with us now for 80 years. This brief historical survey will show a story of piecemeal amendment and consolidation, with major legislation following a change of government, only to be reversed by a subsequent change of government.

As a temporary wartime measure, the Increase of Rent and Mortgage Interest (War Restrictions) Act was passed in 1915. At this time a far greater proportion of the population lived in private rented accommodation than is the case today,[1] with the growth of the public sector and owner occupation. Other Acts followed in the remaining years of the First World War. However, the end of the war did not bring with it any decrease in the housing shortage. The legislation was consolidated in 1920 by the Rent and Mortgage Interest (Restrictions) Act, which brought more properties into control by raising the rateable value limits. This Act, as its name suggests, restricted rents and the rates of mortgage interest and conferred security of tenure.

A measure of decontrol followed in the period between the wars as a result of legislation in 1923, 1933 and 1938, but this trend was reversed by the Rent and Mortgage Interest Restrictions Act 1939. The Acts of 1920 and 1939 dealt with what were known as "controlled tenancies", and survived until the consolidating legislation of 1968.

Furnished lettings

None of the legislation so far mentioned gave protection to furnished lettings. A separate code of protection for them was introduced by the Furnished Houses (Rent Control) Act 1946, creating rent tribunals having jurisdiction to fix the rent and to confer a measure of security of tenure.[2]

Regulated tenancies

The Conservative Government introduced significant decontrol in the Rent Act 1957, but most of the properties decontrolled by that Act were brought back into protection on a change of government by the Rent Act 1965, which introduced "regulated tenancies" and a new system of rent control involving the registration of "fair rents", assessed by the rent officer, with an appeal to the rent assessment committee.

This was followed by the consolidating Rent Act 1968, which included (in Part VI) the provisions on furnished

---

[1] Today's figure is about 6 or 7% nationally and 12% in London; Housing and Construction Statistics (Department of Environment) 1990; General Household Survey 1991; London Housing Survey 1992.
[2] This was amended by the Landlord and Tenant (Rent Control) Act 1949. The Housing Repairs and Rent Act 1954 permitted rent to be increased to reflect repairs, to encourage the latter.

lettings. These were known as "Part VI contracts" (and are now called "restricted contracts").

Conversion of controlled tenancies

The Housing Act 1969 provided for the conversion of some controlled tenancies to regulated tenancies, provided the property had the standard amenities and was in good repair. This was replaced by the Housing Finance Act 1972, a Conservative measure, which extended this process by providing for the phased conversion of all controlled tenancies into regulated tenancies according to their rateable values. However, a return to power by the Labour Party put an end to this process in the Housing Rents and Subsidies Act 1975.

The Labour Government introduced a major reform in the Rent Act 1974, bringing furnished lettings into full

Resident landlords

protection and excluding tenants of resident landlords. These tenants received the limited protection of the restricted contract code which had previously applied to furnished lettings.

Another consolidation followed in the Rent Act 1977.[3] This Act, like its predecessors, reveals the legislative method of simply lifting sections from previous Acts, sometimes without regard to their appropriateness to modern conditions. So, for example, section 101, dealing with overcrowding, was stated to apply only to premises "used as a separate dwelling by members of the working classes or of a type suitable for such use."[4]

Housing Act 1980

The Conservative Government returned to its policy of abolishing controlled tenancies in the Housing Act 1980. Those that remained were converted to regulated tenancies (or, if there was any business use, to tenancies within Part II of the Landlord and Tenant Act 1954). This affected approximately 200,000 properties.[5] A major feature of the 1980 Act was the introduction of security of tenure and the right to buy for local authority tenants. These provisions, now found in the Housing Act 1985, are outside the scope of this book, but other significant changes brought about by the Act in the private sector included the creation of shorthold and assured tenancies[6] and the reduction of the limited security of tenure enjoyed by tenants within the restricted contract code.

The next piece of legislation was the Rent (Amendment) Act 1985, but this merely amended one of the grounds for possession.[7]

[3] The Act does not apply to Scotland or Northern Ireland.
[4] The reference to the working classes was finally deleted by the Housing (Consequential Provisions) Act 1985, Sched. 2.
[5] See (1980) 253 E.G. 125.
[6] See below, pp. 77, 79. These "old-style" shorthold and assured tenancies are not the same as those introduced by the Housing Act 1988, below. They were designed to ease the shortage of private rented accommodation by encouraging landlords to let, but they enjoyed limited success.
[7] The Act was passed to reverse *Pocock v. Steel* [1985] 1 W.L.R. 229, below, p. 128.

The general scheme of the Rent Act 1977, as amended by the Acts of 1980 and 1985, was to provide security of tenure to the tenant and his family (by means of the statutory tenancy and the succession rules), subject to grounds for possession established by the landlord, and to provide financial security by controlling the rent level, coupled with a prohibition on premiums. The need for such legislation, of course, arises from the fact that the demand for affordable

Shortage of private rented accommodation

private rented accommodation for those who do not qualify for local authority housing but cannot afford to be owner-occupiers exceeds the supply of such accommodation. But the problem has always been to find the correct balance between protecting the tenant and providing an incentive to the landlord. The view of the present Government is that the Rent Act legislation was at least partly responsible for the shortage of private rented accommodation. Strict controls of rent coupled with security of tenure result in many landlords preferring to sell their property when it falls vacant, or simply to leave it empty, rather than re-let.[8]

Housing Act 1988

The latest legislation, the Housing Act 1988, attempted to reverse this trend by phasing out regulated tenancies under the Rent Act 1977 and by replacing them with assured and assured shorthold tenancies. Tenancies granted before the 1988 Act were not affected (except for some modifications to the succession rules).[9] The characteristics of assured and assured shorthold tenancies under the 1988 Act are that, while the basic principle of security of tenure remains, the grounds for possession are strengthened and the tenant enjoys minimal rights of succession and rent control. It was hoped that these measures, coupled with tax advantages,[10] would provide a sufficient incentive to landlords to let and would thereby ease the shortage in the private rented sector.

The years since the passing of the Housing Act 1988 have indeed seen an increase in the private rented sector. Figures from the Office of Population Censuses and Surveys revealed that in the two years after the Act the number of households in London living in private rented accommodation rose by 44,000.[11] Nationally there were 480,000 new deregulated lettings, but a similar number of Rent Act lettings ended.[12] Clearly, however, the increased supply of private sector lettings cannot be attributed solely to the effect of the 1988 Act. A significant factor has been

[8] The Empty Homes Agency, [1992] 07 E.G. 113, gives the figure of 768,000 empty homes in the public and private sectors. According to "Shelter", *The Times*, November 29, 1989, there were 579,500 empty homes in the private sector.

[9] See below, p. 143.

[10] The Business Expansion Scheme, which encouraged investment in assured tenancies. This tax relief was ended on December 31, 1993 by the Finance (No. 2) Act 1992, s. 38. See below, p. 191.

[11] *The Times*, February 26, 1992.

[12] Survey of the Association of Residential Letting Agents, *The Times*, August 18, 1992.

the slump in the property market, which has caused many owners to let because they have been unable to sell. Similarly, the large numbers of mortgage repossessions during the recession and the phenomenon of the "negative equity" have deterred many from becoming owner-occupiers.

2 LICENCES

Relevance of the distinction

The distinction between leases and licences, which has exercised the courts on countless occasions, has significance in many contexts. As far as statutory security of tenure is concerned, the definitions of a protected (or statutory) tenancy under the Rent Act 1977 and of an assured tenancy under the Housing Act 1988 do not include licences. A contractual licence may, however, be protected as a restricted contract[1] under the Rent Act 1977. Although outside the scope of this book, it might be added that licences can fall within the secure tenancy code in the public sector,[2] may also be protected under the agricultural holdings legislation,[3] but are excluded from the business tenancy code.[4]

Security of tenure

Protection from eviction

As will be seen in Chapter 3, the Protection From Eviction Act 1977 affords some protection to contractual licensees as well as tenants. So, for example, the criminal offences of harassment and unlawful eviction may be committed against both kinds of occupier; a licensee as well as a tenant may invoke the civil remedy introduced by the Housing Act 1988; the requirement of a court order for possession applies to tenants and licensees (subject to exceptions) under the 1988 amendments; and the four weeks' notice to quit rule is extended to licensees by the 1988 Act, again subject to exceptions. The general effect of the Housing Act 1988 is that the distinction between tenants and licensees is less significant than previously in the context of protection from eviction while the distinction is fully maintained in the context of security of tenure.

Other examples

In addition to the above, there are many areas of the general law where the distinction between tenants and licensees is important. So, for example, a lease is assignable unless there is a covenant against assignment, while a licence is not normally assignable. A lease may require to be granted by deed at law, whereas there are no formality requirements for the creation of a licence. A contract for a lease exceeding three years must be in writing[5] and will be registrable as an estate contract under the Land Charges Act 1972 in unregistered land or as a minor interest under the Land Registration Act 1925. These provisions are not applicable to licences. In certain circumstances a lessee paying no rent may acquire title under the Limitation Act 1980,[6] whereas a

---

[1] Provided it was granted before the date on which Housing Act 1988 came into operation. See below, p. 80.
[2] Housing Act 1985, s. 79(3).
[3] Agricultural Holdings Act 1986, s. 2.
[4] Landlord and Tenant Act 1954, s. 23.
[5] Law of Property (Miscellaneous Provisions) Act 1989, s. 2.
[6] s. 15(6); Sched. 1, para. 5(1).

licensee (whose licence has not been terminated) can never be an adverse possessor.[7] A licensor owes a duty of care to his licensee to keep the premises secure.[8] No such duty is owed by a landlord to a tenant. A licence is subject to an implied term of fitness for purpose,[9] but a lease contains no such term.[10] A licence, but not a lease, may terminate automatically on the occurrence of a future uncertain event.[11] More significantly, a lease is enforceable against third parties either as a legal estate or an equitable interest. A contractual licence, on the other hand, does not bind the licensor's successors in title, unless the circumstances are such as to give rise to a constructive trust.[12]

These issues, and others,[13] have given rise to the seemingly incessant flow of litigation on the distinction between leases and licences. The principles which determine the status of a residential occupier will now be examined.

Criteria for distinguishing leases and licences

Exclusive possession

It is well established that there cannot be a tenancy without exclusive possession,[14] and that the presence of exclusive possession, while indicative of a tenancy, may nevertheless be consistent with a licence. In other words, absence of exclusive possession is conclusive (the occupier must be a licensee), while the presence of exclusive possession is not conclusive either way. However, while a licence with exclusive possession is possible, it will exist only in a limited number of situations, as explained below.

Exclusive occupation

It is also important to distinguish exclusive possession (the right to exclude all others, including the owner) and exclusive occupation, which signifies something less than exclusive possession and leads to the conclusion that the occupier is a licensee.[15] A person may have exclusive occupation of a room although the owner has a right of access at all times. It is exclusive if the owner does not have the right to occupy the room himself or to permit a third

[7] *Heslop v. Burns* [1974] 1 W.L.R. 1241.
[8] *Appah v. Parncliffe Investments Ltd* [1964] 1 W.L.R. 1064.
[9] *Wettern Electric Ltd v. Welsh Development Agency* [1983] Q.B. 796.
[10] *Hill v. Harris* [1965] 2 Q.B. 601.
[11] *Tyler v. Royal Borough of Kensington and Chelsea* (1991) 23 H.L.R. 380 (licence until building works to another flat completed); *Norris v. Checksfield* [1991] 1 W.L.R. 1241 (service occupancy ends automatically on termination of employment). For the position as to leases, see *Prudential Assurance Co. Ltd v. London Residuary Body* [1992] 2 A.C. 386.
[12] *Ashburn Anstalt v. Arnold* [1989] Ch. 1.
[13] See *Bone v. Bone* [1992] E.G.C.S. 81 (abandonment).
[14] *London and North Western Ry. Co. v. Buckmaster* (1874) L.R. 10 Q.B. 70.
[15] But see *A.G. Securities v. Vaughan* [1990] 1 A.C. 417, below, p. 20, where Lord Templeton repeatedly refers to exclusive occupation as the characteristic of a tenancy. Similarly *Aslan v. Murphy* [1990] 1 W.L.R. 766.

party to do so. "A person has a right to 'exclusive occupation' of a room when he is entitled to occupy it himself, and no one else is entitled to occupy it."[16]

In the last century, the prevailing view was that exclusive possession was inconsistent with a licence.[17] From the middle of this century the principle emerged that exclusive possession was not conclusive. The determining factor was the intention of the parties, who were at liberty to create a licence where, although exclusive possession was conferred, no lease was intended.[18] The principles governing the distinction were re-examined by the House of Lords in *Street v. Mountford,*[19] where their Lordships reasserted the traditional view that exclusive possession raises a strong presumption of tenancy, rebuttable only by certain narrow "special factors."

The decision in *Street v. Mountford*

In this case the owner granted the defendant the right to occupy a furnished room under a document described as a licence. The "licence" included the following terms: "this personal licence is not assignable"; a "licence fee of £37 per week" was payable; the "licence may be terminated by 14 days written notice"; and "a licence in the above form does not and is not intended to give me a tenancy protected under the Rent Acts." It was conceded that the defendant had exclusive possession of the room. Subsequently she applied to have a fair rent registered, whereupon the owner sought a declaration that the agreement created a licence only. The Court of Appeal held that it was a licence, notwithstanding exclusive possession, because that was the intention of the parties. This ruling was unanimously **Hallmarks of** reversed by the House of Lords. It was held that where there **tenancy** is *exclusive possession* for a *term* at a *rent*, there is a strong presumption of tenancy rebuttable only by certain "special factors." The court should be concerned to inquire simply whether the occupier is a lodger or a tenant. It was reaffirmed that the label on the document is not conclusive: the legal consequences of the agreement are determined by

---

[16] *Luganda v. Service Hotels Ltd* [1969] 2 Ch. 209 at 219 (Lord Denning M.R.).

[17] *Lynes v. Snaith* [1899] 1 Q.B. 486. See also *Glenwood Lumber Co. Ltd v. Phillips* [1904] A.C. 405.

[18] See *Murray Bull & Co. Ltd v. Murray* [1953] 1 Q.B. 211; *Somma v. Hazelhurst* [1978] 1 W.L.R. 1014; *Aldrington Garages Ltd v. Fielder* (1978) 37 P.&C.R. 461; *Sturolson & Co. v. Weniz* (1984) 272 E.G. 326. These cases were overruled in *Street v. Mountford,* below.

[19] [1985] A.C. 809; see also [1985] All E.R. Rev. at 190 (P.J. Clarke) and 214 (P.H. Pettit); (1986) 83 L.S. Gaz. 1703 (N. Madge); [1985] 44 C.L.J. 351 (S. Tromans); [1985] Conv. 328 (R. Street); (1985) 48 M.L.R. 712 (S. Anderson). For reviews of subsequent cases, see [1986] Conv. 344 (S. Bridge); (1987) 281 E.G. 996 (D. Williams); (1987) 84 L.S. Gaz. 1639 (W. Hanbury). For the position in N. Ireland, see [1987] Conv. 56 (G. McCormack).

the effect of its terms. These "hallmarks of tenancy" will now be examined.

Exclusive possession   The distinction between exclusive possession and exclusive occupation has already been discussed.[20] As it was Lord Templeman's judgment in *Street v. Mountford* which emphasised the significance of exclusive possession, it is all the more remarkable that his Lordship in *A.G. Securities v. Vaughan*[21] should refer repeatedly to exclusive *occupation* as the hallmark of a tenancy. The other members of the House of Lords, on the other hand, spoke in terms of exclusive possession. Of course, exclusive possession does not require physical occupation. A tenant who sublets the whole nevertheless has exclusive possession as against the landlord. Lord Templeman had this in mind when defining exclusive possession as including receipt of rents and profits.[22] It should be added that exclusive possession can exist even though for less than 24 hours a day,[23] although in the residential context a restriction on the hours of use is likely to be held a sham.[24]

In order to determine the status of the occupier, the starting point will be a consideration of the terms of the **Terms of** document, which may expressly deny exclusive possession,[25] **document** although such a term on its own would not be conclusive. It is necessary to construe the document as a whole to see whether its terms are consistent or inconsistent with exclusive possession. In *Dellneed Ltd v. Chin*,[26] a case concerning business occupation, it was held that the grantor's express reservation of a right to enter for a particular purpose indicated that the grantee had exclusive possession. In *Dresden Estates Ltd v. Collinson*,[27] on the other hand, the presence of such a term was outweighed by other terms, in particular the grantor's right to move the occupier to other premises,[28] which was inconsistent with exclusive possession. The question whether terms which have the effect of preventing exclusive possession may be struck out as shams is discussed below.[29]

---

[20] See above, p. 8.
[21] [1990] 1 A.C. 417; below, p. 20.
[22] *ibid.* at 455. See also *Camden L.B.C. v. Shortlife Community Housing Ltd* (1993) 25 H.L.R. 330 at 347.
[23] *Graysim Holdings Ltd v. P&O Property Holdings Ltd* [1994] 1 W.L.R. 992 (market stall).
[24] See below, p. 28.
[25] See *Dresden Estates Ltd v. Collinson* (1988) 55 P.&C.R. 47; *Essex Plan Ltd v. Broadminster Ltd* (1988) 56 P.&C.R. 353; *Antoniades v. Villiers* [1990] 1 A.C. 417.
[26] (1987) 53 P.&C.R. 172; below, p. 30. Similarly in *Street v. Mountford* itself.
[27] See above. See also *Markou v. Da Silvaesa* (1986) 2 P.&C.R. 204; below, p. 28.
[28] Such a "mobility clause" was conceded to preclude a tenancy in *Westminster City Council v. Clarke* [1992] 2 A.C. 288, below.
[29] See below, p. 25.

Keys   Retention of keys by the owner is not conclusive, as it is not a requirement of a tenancy that the tenant should have exclusive possession of the keys.[30] Retention of a key for entry in emergency is not inconsistent with a tenancy, nor even where the key is retained to facilitate the provision of support services by the owner (a housing association).[31] On the other hand, where a key is retained by the owner in order to perform services such as cleaning, the occupier will be a lodger, as explained below.[32]

Hostel for   The House of Lords had occasion to revisit the question
homeless   of exclusive possession in *Westminster City Council v. Clarke*,[33] which concerned the occupation of a bedsitter in a hostel for the vulnerable homeless. As noted above,[34] it was conceded that the occupier was a licensee, but a licensee who enjoys exclusive possession has security under the Housing Act 1985.[35] The occupiers were supervised by a resident warden, who had a key to the rooms. The warden was supported by social workers and a council representative could enter at any time. The agreement provided that the occupier could be moved to a different room or required to share. There were restrictions on visitors and the occupier had to be in by 11 p.m. The council's policy was to supervise and rehabilitate the occupiers and then to move them to more permanent accommodation. It was held that the occupier did not have exclusive possession but was akin to a lodger. Exclusive possession would have been inconsistent with the council's purposes. Such a finding, resulting in security of tenure, would not have been conducive to the optimal use of the council's temporary accommodation for the vulnerable homeless. This was regarded as a special case because the agreement was designed not to avoid security of tenure but to enable the council to discharge its duties to the homeless. Its terms could not be used as a precedent by other landlords.

It will be recalled that *Street v. Mountford*[36] itself involved single occupation. It does not resolve the difficult problems
Multiple   of multiple occupation. Sharers may each have separate
occupation tenancies of parts of the premises, or they may be joint tenants, together enjoying exclusive possession of the whole, or they may be licensees, having no exclusive possession either individually or together. Of course, if the sharing term is a sham, it will not operate to prevent exclusive possession.

---

[30] *Aslan v. Murphy* [1990] 1 W.L.R. 766.
[31] *Family Housing Assocation v. Jones* [1990] 1 W.L.R. 779; below, p. 17; *cf.* *Westminster City Council v. Clarke* [1992] A.C. 288.
[32] Below, p. 13.
[33] [1992] 2 A.C. 288; [1992] Conv. 113 (J. Martin) and 285 (D. Cowan); (1992) 142 N.L.J. 281 (J. Driscoll); [1992] All E.R. Rev. 225 (P. Clarke). See also *Brent People's Housing Association v. Winsmore*, County Court (1986), noted [1988] 36 E.G. 20 at 22 (D. Williams).
[34] n. 28.
[35] s. 79(3); below, p. 17.
[36] See above, p. 9.

The problems of multiple occupation are dealt with separately below.[37]

Term   A tenancy requires a term,[38] which may be either fixed or periodic. As Lord Templeman explained in *Street v. Mountford*, the grant may be express, or may be inferred where the owner accepts weekly or other periodic payments from the occupier.[39] A tenancy may exist even though possession is limited to certain hours a day.[40] Similarly where property is sold at a discount in consideration of the vendor's right to reside rent-free for life.[41] Such an arrangement is treated by statute as a term for 90 years.[42]

Rent   *Street v. Mountford* appeared to assert that there could be no tenancy without a rent. The possibility of a rent-free tenancy, however, has long been recognised, and is included in the definition of a "term of years absolute" in the Law of Property Act 1925.[43] The question arose in *Ashburn Anstalt v. Arnold*,[44] where the occupier was let into possession for business purposes under a rent-free arrangement pending redevelopment. The agreement was **Rent not** held to create a lease even though the element of rent was **essential** missing. *Street v. Mountford* was regarded as holding that exclusive possession at a rent and for a term gave rise to a tenancy, but not that exclusive possession for a term without a rent could not do so. Nevertheless, the absence of rent, whilst not conclusive, is surely indicative of a licence in a case where there is no express intention to create a lease.[45]

Rent may take the form of periodical payments or a premium or both. Services may constitute rent at common law, although they must be quantifiable in money in order to constitute rent for Rent Act purposes.[46] Where they are not so quantifiable, it is likely that the occupier is a licensee.[47]

---

[37] See below, p. 18.
[38] *cf.* a tenancy at will, which has no term, either fixed or periodic.
[39] *Tower Hamlets L.B. v. Ayinde* (1994) 26 H.L.R. 631.
[40] *Graysim Holdings Ltd v. P&O Property Holdings Ltd* [1994] 1 W.L.R. 992 (market stalls).
[41] *Skipton Building Society v. Clayton* (1993) 66 P.&C.R. 223; [1993] Conv. 478 (L. Crabb).
[42] L.P.A. 1925, s. 149(6). The two-thirds discount was a "premium" within the subsection.
[43] s. 205(1)(xxvii).
[44] [1989] Ch. 1. This was overruled in *Prudential Assurance Co. Ltd v. London Residuary Body* [1992] 2 A.C. 386 so far as it held that a right to possession terminable by notice on an uncertain event was a "term". See also *Skipton Building Society v. Clayton*, above (consideration but no rent as such, which was in any event not required).
[45] See [1988] Conv. 201 at 203 (M.P. Thompson). See also (1988) 104 L.Q.R. 175 (P. Sparkes).
[46] *Montagu v. Browning* [1954] 1 W.L.R. 1039; *Bostock v. Bryant* (1991) 61 P.&C.R. 23.
[47] *Barnes v. Barratt* [1970] 2 Q.B. 657.

Lodgers Lord Templeman in *Street v. Mountford*[48] stated that:

Meaning of lodger

"An occupier of residential accommodation at a rent for a term is either a lodger or a tenant. The occupier is a lodger if the landlord provides attendance[49] or services which require the landlord or his servants to exercise unrestricted access to and use of the premises. A lodger is entitled to live in the premises but cannot call the place his own."

A lodger (assuming he does not share his room) may enjoy exclusive occupation,[50] but does not have exclusive possession. While a tenancy may, of course, exist even though the landlord provides attendance or services to the tenant, the point being made by Lord Templeman is that the occupier must be a lodger if the services are such that the owner requires access to the room in order to provide them, without the occupier being there to let him in.[51] So, for example, if the owner is responsible for the cleaning of rooms or the changing of bedlinen, the occupier will be a lodger. If, on the other hand, the owner is responsible merely for the collection of rubbish or used linen from outside the door, the occupier may be a tenant. In *Marchant v. Charters*,[52] the occupier of a bed-sitting room was a licensee where the owner cleaned the rooms daily and provided clean linen. In *Abbeyfield (Harpenden) Society v. Woods*,[53] the occupier of a room in an old people's home was a licensee. Both these cases were regarded as examples of lodgers in *Street v. Mountford*. It has been held, in the context of a business arrangement, that entry by the owner for the performance of services is not inconsistent with a tenancy where the services are performed pursuant to a separate agreement and not as landlord.[54]

Lord Templeman's words in *Street v. Mountford*, quoted above, convey the impression that an occupier who is not a lodger must be a tenant. This led the county court judge in *Brooker Settled Estates Ltd v. Ayers* to conclude that a woman sharing a flat with two others under a "licence" agreement must be a tenant because, no attendance or services being

Where no attendance or services

---

[48] [1985] A.C. 809 at 817–818. *cf. Bradley v. Baylis* [1881] 8 Q.B.D. 195.
[49] For the meaning of which, see below, p. 71.
[50] See above, p. 8.
[51] See *Markou v. Da Silvaesa* (1986) 52 P.&C.R. 204, holding also that the occupier cannot change his status by declining the services.
[52] [1977] 1 W.L.R. 1181. The result was approved in *Street v. Mountford*, although the reasoning was criticised.
[53] [1968] 1 W.L.R. 374.
[54] *Vandersteen v. Agius* (1993) 65 P.&C.R. 266 (owner providing ancillary services for osteopath tenant).

provided, she was not a lodger. The Court of Appeal[55] held that the absence of services did not automatically result in a tenancy. There could only be a tenancy if the occupier had exclusive possession, which was not necessarily so in the present case.

Shams   Of course, the fact that a document is called a "lodging agreement" does not conclusively establish that the occupier is a lodger. Its terms must be construed, and any sham terms disregarded. This is discussed below.[56]

Special factors rebutting the presumption of a tenancy   It will be recalled that the House of Lords in *Street v. Mountford* held that the right to exclusive possession for a term at a rent gave rise to a presumption of a tenancy which could be negated only by special circumstances. The examples given by their Lordships included absence of intention to create legal relations, and where the right to exclusive possession is referable to a legal relationship other than tenancy. These special circumstances will now be examined.

No intention to create legal relations[57] Prior to *Street v. Mountford* there was a well known line of cases (the "generosity factor" cases) holding that exclusive possession attributable to an act of generosity did not result in a tenancy. As Denning L.J. said in *Facchini v. Bryson*[58]:

> "In all the cases where an occupier has been held to be a licensee there has been something in the circumstances, such as a family arrangement,[59] an act of friendship or generosity, or such like to negative any intention to create a tenancy ... "

It is important to distinguish cases where the parties did not intend to create any legal relationship at all, and cases where special factors negative the intention to create a

---

[55] (1987) 54 P.&C.R. 165. A new trial was ordered. See, further, *A.G. Securities v. Vaughan* [1990] 1 A.C. 417 at 459, where Lord Templeman repeated the statement that an occupier who was not a lodger must be a tenant. Here, however, these words were prefaced by a proviso requiring exclusive occupation [*sic*].

[56] See *Markou v. Da Silvaesa* (1986) 52 P.&C.R. 204; below, p. 28.

[57] See Maudsley and Burn, *Land Law: Cases and Materials* (6th ed., 1992) p. 432. pointing out that intention is relevant to the question whether there was an intention to create legal relations but is not relevant in deciding what legal relation has been created.

[58] [1952] 1 T.L.R. 1386 at 1389–1390.

[59] This does not of itself prevent a tenancy; *Nunn v. Dalrymple* (1990) 59 P.&C.R. 200; *Ward v. Warnke* (1990) 22 H.L.R. 496.

tenancy, but some legal relationship is nevertheless created. Cases in this latter category will be dealt with below.[60]

Examples of "no intent to create legal relations" cases decided before *Street v. Mountford* and which survive that decision include *Marcroft Wagons Ltd v. Smith*,[61] where the landlord allowed the daughter of a deceased tenant to stay on for a few months at a rent. The inference will be more readily drawn in a case where the occupation is rent-free, as in *Cobb v. Lane*[62] (brother occupying rent-free was licensee and not tenant at will) and *Heslop v. Burns*[63] (friends of owner occupying rent-free were licensees and not tenants at will), although absence of rent does not inevitably point to a licence.[64] In *Errington v. Errington*,[65] on the other hand, where a father contracted to allow his son to buy the father's house on payment of the instalments of the father's mortgage, the son was held to be a licensee. This was a case where the exceptional circumstances negated the prima facie presumption of a tenancy, not one where there was no intention to enter into any legal relationship at all. A more recent example is *Sharp v. McArthur*,[66] where the defendant, who urgently required accommodation, was let into possession of premises which were for sale as a favour. It was agreed that the arrangement was terminable at a month's notice. The defendant was given a rent-book because he needed it as evidence of his outgoings for housing benefit purposes. The Court of Appeal held that the presumption of tenancy was rebutted, as there was no intention to create legal relations.

The difficulty with some of these cases where the occupier is paying rent is that, if intention to create legal relations is denied, presumably there cannot be a contractual licence.[67] Yet the occupier obviously is not a gratuitous licensee. It seem that the money paid could be treated as mesne profits, *i.e.* compensation for occupation other than under a contract.[68] Some of the earlier cases in fact seem to have been based on "no intention to create a tenancy" rather than "no intention to create legal relations." While the latter category is clearly suited to the "family arrangement" cases, it seems less appropriate in the commercial context, but *Street v. Mountford* does not draw this distinction.

Rent may be payable

Status of occupier

---

[60] Under "status of occupier".
[61] [1951] 2 K.B. 496. See also *Booker v. Palmer* [1942] 2 All E.R. 674; *Isaac v. Hotel de Paris Ltd* [1960] 1 W.L.R. 239.
[62] [1952] 1 All E.R. 1199.
[63] [1974] 1 W.L.R. 1241. (But exclusive possession doubted.)
[64] *Ashburn Anstalt v. Arnold* [1989] Ch. 1; above, p. 12.
[65] [1952] 1 K.B. 290.
[66] (1987) 19 H.L.R. 364. See also *Monmouth B.C. v. Marlog* [1994] 2 E.G.L.R. 68 (sharing of council house).
[67] See [1986] Conv. 39 (D.N. Clarke); Yates and Hawkins, *Landlord and Tenant Law* (2nd ed., 1986) p. 25.
[68] See the account of *Marcroft Wagons Ltd v. Smith*, above, in *Street v. Mountford*. See also *Westminster City Council v. Basson* (1991) 62 P.&C.R. 57.

It may be, however, that an occupier whose claim to a tenancy fails will be held a trespasser rather than a licensee. A third party who continues in occupation without the owner's consent after the tenant's departure may be a trespasser even where payments have been accepted by the owner, for such acceptance does not necessarily evince an intention to create legal relations.[69]

Possession referable to a legal relationship other than tenancy. The examples given in *Street v. Mountford*, which were not intended to be exhaustive, were occupancy under a contract for sale of the land, occupancy pursuant to a contract of employment (a service occupancy), or occupancy referable to the holding of an office.

Contract for sale   Looking first at the contract for sale exception,[70]this apparently refers to the case where a purchaser is let into possession between contract and completion. In *Bretherton v. Paton*,[71] the defendant approached the owner with a view to a letting. The owner declined but agreed to sell if the defendant moved in and put the premises into repair so that she could obtain a mortgage. There was no written agreement. Subsequently the parties failed to agree on the sale price and the owner sought possession. It was held that the defendant had a Rent Act tenancy. She had exclusive possession for a periodic term, paying the rates and a weekly sum described as towards insurance. Although neither party intended a tenancy, it did not fall within the exceptions to *Street v. Mountford*. May L.J. even stated that the situations referred to by Lord Templeman as cases where exclusive possession was referable to a legal relationship other than tenancy should not be regarded as exceptions. Presumably it might have been otherwise if the sale contract had been concluded. In *Javad v. Aqil*,[72] however, possession pending negotiations for a business lease (ultimately abortive) was regarded as a classic circumstance for the creation of a tenancy at will.[73] The issue was whether the occupier was a tenant at will or a periodic tenant and not whether he was a licensee. A tenancy at will does not confer security under the Landlord and Tenant Act 1954, Pt. II, although the position

---

[69] *Westminster City Council v. Basson,* above; [1992] Conv. 112 (J. Martin); *cf. Tower Hamlets L.B. v. Ayinde* (1994) 26 H.L.R. 631.

[70] See [1987] Conv. 278 (P. Sparkes).

[71] [1986] 1 E.G.L.R. 172. *cf. Isaac v. Hotel de Paris Ltd* [1960] 1 W.L.R. 239, where an employee occupying a hotel pursuant to "subject to contract" negotiations concerning the running of the hotel was a licensee. This was regarded in *Street v. Mountford* as a case where the parties did not intend to enter into legal relations until the negotiations were replaced by a binding contract. See also *Essex Plan Ltd v. Broadminster Ltd* (1988) 56 P.&C.R. 353.

[72] [1991] 1 W.L.R. 1007; [1991] 50 C.L.J. 232 (S. Bridge).

[73] See also *Heslop v. Burns* [1974] 1 W.L.R. 1241 (occupation prior to contract to purchase a classic case of a tenancy at will); *cf. Bretherton v. Paton,* above.

appears to be otherwise in the case of a residential tenancy at will.[74]

Option It has been held that occupation pending the exercise or expiry of an option to take a lease, conferring an immediate equitable interest in the land, is referable to a legal relationship other than a tenancy.[75] On the other hand, the existence of a contract for the sale of the goodwill of a business cannot be relied on to preclude a tenancy. Such a contract does not carry a right of occupation, and so exclusive possession will not be referable to the contract but will indicate a tenancy.[76]

Service occupier A service occupier is an employee who lives in his employer's property not for his own convenience but in order to facilitate the performance of his duties, even if his residence is not actually essential. Such an occupier will be a licensee, and this is so even though the anticipated duties have not yet been performed.[77] A school "house parent" living in a flat at the school will be a service occupier and hence a licensee, but it may be otherwise if he lives further away, even though in a property owned by the school.[78]

Homeless persons One question which has arisen is whether the grant of exclusive possession to a homeless person by a local authority (or other body) creates a licence only on the ground that the exclusive possession is referable to a relationship other than that of landlord and tenant, namely the relationship between a homeless person and the local authority which has statutory duties to house the homeless. It should be added that even a licensee may fall within the definition of secure tenancy within the Housing Act 1985,[79] but that accommodation for the homeless is excluded from security in certain cases.[80] It is now clear that this is not an exception to *Street v. Mountford* and that a homeless person to whom exclusive possession has been granted is a tenant. The Court of Appeal so held, with some misgivings, in *Family Housing Association v. Jones*,[81] even though the housing association retained somewhat greater rights than those usually retained by a landlord, and the accommodation was clearly intended to be temporary. The

---

[74] *Dunthorne and Shore v. Wiggins* [1943] 1 All E.R. 577.
[75] *Essex Plan Ltd v Broadminster Ltd*, above. (Held licensee even though continued in occupation after expiry of option. In any event, no exclusive possession.) See also rental purchase schemes below, p. 58.
[76] *Vandersteen v. Agius* (1993) 65 P.&C.R. 266.
[77] *Norris v. Checksfield* [1991] 1 W.L.R. 1241 (dismissed before duties commenced).
[78] *Royal Philharmonic Society v. County* [1985] 2 E.G.L.R. 109; [1986] Conv. 215 (P. Smith). See also *Whitbread West Pennines Ltd v. Reedy* [1988] I.C.R. 807.
[79] s. 79(3). Only a licensee with exclusive possession falls within this provision: *Westminster City Council v. Clarke* [1992] 2 A.C. 288. Since *Street v. Mountford* the subsection has limited scope because an occupier with exclusive possession will normally be a tenant.
[80] Sched. 1, para. 4. The intentionally homeless, for example, are excluded.
[81] [1990] 1 W.L.R. 779; [1990] Conv. 397 (J. Warburton).

problem here is one of balancing the needs of an individual homeless person with the rights of homeless persons as a whole to enjoy limited supplies of housing stock. This difficulty can be avoided by a finding that the homeless person does not in fact enjoy exclusive possession.[82]

No leasing power

Finally, Lord Templeman mentioned cases where the grantor had no leasing power, referring in particular to the case where a war-time requisitioning authority had no power to grant a tenancy.[83] Another example is where a local authority has restricted leasing powers.[84]

Object of charity

A further exception mentioned by Lord Templeman was the situation where the occupier enjoying exclusive possession was an "object of charity."[85] This has been little examined, and may overlap with the "no intention to create legal relations" exception.

Although it has been held that the categories of "special circumstances" capable of rebutting the presumption of a tenancy are not closed,[86] a narrower view was taken in *Camden L.B.C. v. Shortlife Community Housing Ltd.*[87] Millett J. held that if a right to exclusive possession had been granted in circumstances where there was power to grant a tenancy, an intention to create legal relations and no other relationship to explain the exclusive possession, there must be a tenancy. Having got to that stage, there was no room for any "special circumstance" to rebut the presumption of tenancy.

It should be added that the *Street v. Mountford* principles will determine the question whether an occupier of part of demised premises is the subtenant or lodger of the tenant.[88] Clearly an occupier claiming through the owner's licensee cannot have a tenancy as against the owner.[89]

Multiple occupation

"Unfortunately *Street v. Mountford* has not turned out to be a magic wand which enables the right answer to be found without anxious thought, and there are particular difficulties in cases involving multiple occupancy (there was a sole tenant in *Street v.*

[82] *Westminster City Council v. Clarke* [1992] 2 A.C. 288; above, p. 11.
[83] *Southgate B.C. v. Watson* [1944] K.B. 541.
[84] *Camden L.B.C. v. Shortlife Community Housing Ltd* (1993) 25 H.L.R. 330.
[85] *Street v. Mountford* [1985] A.C. 809 at p. 818. See *Brent People's Housing Association v. Winsmore*, County Court (1986), noted [1988] 36 E.G. 20 at 22 (D. Williams).
[86] *Dellneed Ltd v. Chin* (1987) 53 P.&C.R. 172.
[87] (1993) 25 H.L.R. 330; criticised in [1993] Conv. 157 (D. Cowan).
[88] *Monmouth B.C. v. Marlog* [1994] 2 E.G.L.R. 68 (court slow to infer subletting of part by council tenant).
[89] *Shepherd's Bush Housing Association v. HATS Co-operative* [1991] E.G.C.S. 134. A tenancy by estoppel may exist as between the occupier and the owner's licensee. See *Family Housing Association v. Jones* [1990] 1 W.L.R. 779.

Mountford) or where there is uncertainty as to whether exclusive possession has been granted (conceded in *Street v. Mountford*)."[90]

May be joint tenancy

Where two or more persons are sharing occupation, the proper conclusion may be that all together they enjoy exclusive possession and are accordingly joint tenants. Assuming that is not the case, another possibility is that each enjoys exclusive possession of his own room and is therefore a tenant of part of the property with ancillary rights over the kitchen and bathroom and so forth.[91] It may be, however, that no occupier enjoys exclusive possession of any part, in which case they will be licensees only.

Sharing device

Prior to the decision in *Street v. Mountford*, it was possible to deprive an occupier of any protection by the sharing device upheld by the Court of Appeal in *Somma v. Hazelhurst*.[92] Under this scheme two or more occupiers would sign separate documents, make separate payments and agree to occupy subject to the rights of each other (and, sometimes, of third parties) to share the accommodation. These "sharing licences," it was held, prevented any degree of exclusive possession. This decision was regarded as wrong in *Street v. Mountford* on the ground that the sharing term was a sham. The meaning of "sham," which is discussed separately below,[93] is very important in these sharing cases, but is not the only factor, because not all sharing terms are shams. The real question is whether the arrangement, shorn of any sham terms, gives the occupier exclusive possession.

In *Brooker Settled Estates Ltd v. Ayers*,[94] the defendant occupied a double bedroom in a flat containing two other single bedrooms, a kitchen and a bathroom. The owner ran this flat and two others to provide accommodation for single women working in London. The flat was advertised as a "Flat to share with two other girls." By a standard form agreement, the defendant was granted a "licence" to occupy the flat, sharing facilities with the existing occupants and those introduced from time to time. It was further provided that she did not have exclusive occupation of any part. The owner claimed that it was a licence because all occupants had access to all parts, and a right was reserved to put another person in the double room. As no services were provided, the county court judge, misinterpreting *Street v. Mountford*, held that the defendant, not being a lodger, must be a tenant.[95] The Court of Appeal held that there

Fact that not "lodger" not conclusive

[90] (1987) All E.R. Rev., p. 170 (P.H. Pettit). See also (1988) 104 L.Q.R. 173 (P.V. Baker).
[91] As to which see Rent Act 1977, s. 22, below, p. 63.
[92] [1978] 1 W.L.R. 1014. See also *Aldrington Garages v. Fielder* (1978) 37 P.&C.R. 461; *Sturolson & Co. v. Weniz* (1984) 272 E.G. 326; *cf. O'Malley v. Seymour* (1978) 250 E.G. 1083; *Demuren v. Seal Estates Ltd* (1978) 249 E.G. 440; *Walsh v. Griffiths-Jones* [1978] 2 All E.R. 1002.
[93] See below, p. 25.
[94] (1987) 54 P.&C.R. 165.
[95] See above, p. 9.

could not be a tenancy without exclusive possession, which was a question of fact. A new trial was ordered to determine whether the defendant did enjoy exclusive possession.

The matter next arose in *Hadjiloucas v. Crean*,[96]where occupiers shared a flat under individual "licences." A and B entered into agreements at the same time to occupy for six months and to share with one other, each being responsible for the whole rent. A left after two months and arranged **Where one** with the landlord that C should replace her. C left when the **occupant is** agreement expired. Subsequently the owner told B to leave **replaced** when she applied to the rent officer to fix a fair rent. The Court of Appeal held that in cases where the sharing term was not a sham, the correct approach was to consider the contractual terms against the factual matrix. The fact that the landlord was entitled to nominate a new occupant if an existing occupant left was an important consideration, but not decisive, because each occupant might have an individual tenancy of a separate part of the premises. In determining whether A and B were joint tenants or individual licensees, relevant factors included the joint approach by A and B to the owner; the fact that the agreements imposed joint and several liability for the whole rent on A and B; and the absence of any provision about what was to happen if A or B wished to leave prematurely. An obligation to accept a sharer of unknown identity at the time of signing the agreement would be inconsistent with a joint tenancy. While A's departure and replacement were not relevant in construing the agreement, their effect could not be ignored.[97] As these matters had not been properly considered, the case was remitted for a new trial. Lord Templeman has subsequently suggested[98]that the occupiers in this case (A and B) were joint tenants, because they applied for and enjoyed exclusive occupation [*sic*], adding that the sharing term was a pretence. In so far as this term was actually operated, it is difficult to see why it should have been so regarded.

Position The status of sharers has now been analysed by the House **analysed by** of Lords in *A.G. Securities v. Vaughan* and *Antoniades v.* **House of Lords** *Villiers*.[99] *A.G. Securities v. Vaughan* concerned a property consisting of four bedrooms, two living rooms, a kitchen and a bathroom. Four young men signed separate agreements at different times and upon different terms (*e.g.* as to rent).

---

[96] [1988] 1 W.L.R. 1006.

[97] If B was not consulted, this would cast doubt on a joint tenancy. If B had agreed, there could have been a surrender and regrant of a joint tenancy, but this would require a new tenancy agreement. If a joint tenancy, A would remain liable for the whole term if the substitution of C was ineffective.

[98] In *A.G. Securities v. Vaughan*, above.

[99] [1990] 1 A.C. 417 (joint appeals). See [1988] All E.R. Rev. 172 (P. Clarke); (1989) 48 C.L.J. 19 (C. Harpum); (1989) 105 L.Q.R. 165 (P.V. Baker); [1989] Conv. 128 (P.F. Smith); (1989) 139 N.L.J. 323 (R. Nobles); [1989] 11 E.G. 22 (S. Murdoch); *Legal Action*, March 1989, p. 21 (N. Madge); (1989) 52 M.L.R. 408 (J. Hill).

They had applied independently rather than as a group. The documents which they signed were described as licences, denied exclusive possession of any part, and required the occupier to share the property with a maximum of three other persons. Vacancies were filled as they occurred. When this happened there was a "pecking order" for the best rooms. There was no claim by an individual to be a tenant of his own room. This would have been possible only if a particular room, by agreement with the owner, was to be the exclusive domain of a particular individual, which was not the case here.[1] The issue was whether the four occupiers were individual licensees or joint tenants. The Court of Appeal, by a majority, had held that they were joint tenants, the reasoning being that whenever one occupier's agreement terminated, there was an implied surrender of the joint tenancy and a regrant to the remaining occupiers and the new sharer. Hence, it was held, the "four unities" of possession, interest, title and time were present. In reversing this decision, the House of Lords described this theory as "strange and unnatural,"[2] "entirely unreal,"[3] "somewhat startling,"[4] and as involving "the highest degree of artificiality."[5]

Surrender and regrant theory rejected

Lord Bridge added that "These rights and obligations having initially been several, I do not understand by what legal alchemy they could ever become joint."[6] As Lord Jauncey explained, the surrender and regrant theory was unworkable in view of the different rents and terms. If A's agreement expired and he was replaced by C, who entered into an agreement for six months, at a time when B had one month left of his six month agreement, would the joint tenancy between B and C be for one month or six months? Either answer would conflict with the individual rights of B and C. Further, the supposed surrender and regrant would not operate because of any act on the part of the surrendering grantee but because of the "chance advent of a stranger."[7]

The unanimous decision was that the four occupiers were licensees. Neither individually nor collectively did they have a tenancy of the whole or any part. They did not have exclusive possession, nor were any of the "four unities" present, which would be necessary to a joint tenancy. In

Joint tenancy requires "four unities"

---

[1] Lord Templeman at 455 said that each occupier would be a tenant of his room if he had exclusive possession of the room (which was not the case), sharing the common parts. In *Westminster City Council v. Clarke* [1992] 2 A.C. 288 at 300, however, his Lordship gave the more doubtful explanation that the occupiers in *A.G. Securities* did have exclusive possession of their bedrooms but were licensees because the bedrooms were not "dwelling-houses".

[2] [1990] 1 A.C. 417 at 472 (*per* Lord Oliver).

[3] *ibid.*

[4] *ibid.* at 473 (*per* Lord Jauncey).

[5] *ibid.* at 454 (*per* Lord Bridge).

[6] *ibid.* at 454.

[7] *ibid.* at 474.

substance and reality they were licensees, each intending to have individual rights, to be liable only for his own rent, and to have an arrangement which was terminable without reference to the others. They had no right to exclude the owner, who continued to enjoy the premises through his "invitees." It could not be said that they together had a single indivisible term consisting of an amalgam of the individual overlapping periods. The agreements reflected the true bargain, which was:

> "a sensible and realistic one to provide accommodation for a shifting population of individuals who were genuinely prepared to share the flat with others introduced from time to time . . . There was no artificiality in the contracts . . . "[8]

A similar conclusion was subsequently reached by the Court of Appeal in *Stribling v. Wickham*,[9] even though the three occupiers were friends who signed identical agreements on the same day. This was outweighed by the fact that each individual was liable only for one third of the rent and could give (or be given) 28 days' notice, and one had done so. The flat was suitable for use by a multiple and shifting population and was so used. In any event, the fact that the agreements were simultaneous would not be significant if they replaced earlier agreements which were not simultaneous.

The second case considered by the House of Lords, *Antoniades v. Villiers*,[10] concerned a cohabiting couple who applied together to rent a small flat comprising a bedroom, a bed-sitting room (containing a bed-settee), a kitchen and a bathroom. Each separately signed a "licence" in which the owner declared unwillingness to grant exclusive possession of any part. The "licensee" was to use the flat in common with the owner or other licensees permitted by the owner. The document, which was modelled on *Somma v. Hazelhurst*,[11] stated that: "The real intention of the parties in all surrounding circumstances is to create this licence which is not coming under the Rent Acts and is binding as written." It also stated that there had been no oral agreements or different representations or explanations given. The couple signed identical agreements with the same date, executed on the same day.[12] The sharing term was never operated. The Court of Appeal, giving undue weight to the express statement of intention, held that they were licensees. The House of Lords held unanimously that they

**Contemp-
oraneous
agreements**

---

[8] *ibid.* at 454 (*per* Lord Bridge).
[9] [1989] 2 E.G.L.R. 35. See also *Mikeover Ltd v. Brady* [1989] 3 All E.R. 618.
[10] [1990] 1 A.C. 417; *Nicolaou v. Pitt* [1989] 1 E.G.L.R. 84; *cf. Mikeover Ltd v. Brady*, above.
[11] [1978] 1 W.L.R. 1014, above, p. 19.
[12] This fact alone is not conclusive: *Stribling v. Wickham* [1989] 2 E.G.L.R. 35, above.

were joint tenants. Bingham L.J. in the Court of Appeal had
said:

> "The written agreements cannot possibly be construed
> as giving the occupants, jointly or severally, exclusive
> possession of the flat or any part of it. They stipulate
> with reiterated emphasis that the occupants shall not
> have exclusive possession."[13]

To this, Lord Templeman replied:

**Express
intentions not
decisive**

> "My Lords, in *Street v. Mountford* this House stipulated
> with reiterated emphasis that an express statement of
> intention is not decisive and that the court must pay
> attention to the facts and surrounding circumstances
> and to what people do as well as to what people say."[14]

Unlike *A.G. Securities v. Vaughan*,[15] the agreements were
not independent but interdependent. Both would have been
signed or neither. Therefore they had to be read together.
The couple were joint tenants because they applied to rent
jointly, and sought and enjoyed exclusive possession[16] of the
whole flat. The artificiality of the arrangement lay in the
pretence that the two contemporaneous and identical

**Sharing term a
pretence**

agreements created obligations which were several rather
than joint. The sharing term was repugnant to the true
purpose, and no-one could suppose that was ever intended
to be acted on.[17] The flat was too small,[18] and the terms of
the agreement (for example the obligation to pay for *all* gas
and electricity consumed) were reasonable only on the basis
that the couple would occupy alone. The sharing term had
been introduced for no other purpose than to disguise the
true character of the agreement, to deceive the court, and to
prevent the protection of the Rent Act.

In construing the documents, the court must consider the

**Admissibility of
surrounding
circumstances**

surrounding circumstances, including the relationship
between the occupiers, the course of negotiations, the nature
of the accommodation and the intended and actual mode of
occupation. The subsequent conduct of the parties was
irrelevant as an aid to construction, but was admissible as
evidence on the question whether the documents were

---

[13] [1990] 1 A.C. 417 at 446.
[14] *ibid.* at 463.
[15] Above.
[16] Lord Templeman in fact referred throughout to exclusive *occupation*.
[17] The Court of Appeal had considered it to be practicable, thereby
distinguishing *Somma v. Hazelhurst*, above. See also *Jackson v. Tyshoe
Ltd*, *Legal Action*, March 1988, p. 21. The occupiers were tenants despite
a sharing term in *Duke v. Wynne* [1990] 1 W.L.R. 766, where the owner
never suggested that sharing was a serious possibility.
[18] As in *Aslan v. Murphy* [1990] 1 W.L.R. 766 (room 4'3" by 12'6").

genuine. In the present case, the substance and reality was that the couple had exclusive possession.

Lord Templeman, in holding that the sharing term was inconsistent with the Rent Act, emphasised that the parties cannot contract out of the Act. It was clear that landlords disliked the Rent Act while tenants considered it a necessary protection. His Lordship's view was that the court lacks the knowledge and power to form any judgment on these arguments, which fall to be determined by Parliament. The court's duty is to observe the principle that there can be no contracting out.

No contracting out

A final point is that the parties in *Antoniades v. Villiers* were contractually bound to pay only half of the total rent each. Joint tenants, of course, are jointly and severally liable to pay the whole rent. Lord Templeman considered that the landlord, if he so chose, could require each of the joint tenants to pay half the rent. This factor would not prevent the finding of a tenancy. Lord Oliver, on the other hand, considered that, by reading the two documents together, the parties would be jointly and severally liable for the whole rent. It has since been held by the Court of Appeal in *Mikeover Ltd v. Brady*[19] that there could be no joint tenancy where each occupier was liable to pay only his own share of the rent. There two occupiers of a two room flat (apparently cohabiting) signed identical agreements on the same day whereby each was granted exclusive occupation subject to the rights of the other and each was liable to pay half only of the rent. The woman later moved out and the defendant remained in occupation. The owner, who had no right to put in a substitute sharer, refused the defendant's offer to pay the whole rent. When the owner later sought possession on the ground of rent arrears, the defendant's contention that he had been granted a joint tenancy (and hence was protected by the Rent Act) was rejected. The agreements were not interdependent and the occupiers were not joint tenants because the absence of joint obligations meant that there was no unity of interest.[20] *Antoniades v. Villiers* was distinguished on the basis that the separate rent obligation there had to be considered in the context of an agreement containing a sham sharing obligation. It was further considered that the weight of authority[21] was against Lord Templeman's view that there could be a joint tenancy without joint and several liability. In the present case the conduct of the parties showed that the rent term was not a sham. Thus the occupiers were licensees. The effect of this decision is that an owner who is willing to forego the

Joint and several liability to pay rent

---

[19] [1989] 3 All E.R. 618; (1990) 106 L.Q.R. 215 (J. Barton).
[20] For the possibility of a tenancy in common, see [1989] 36 E.G. 101; (1992) 142 N.L.J. 575 (S. Bright).
[21] It was also held in *Stribling v. Wickham* [1989] 2 E.G.L.R. 35 that separate rent liability was inconsistent with a joint tenancy.

advantage of joint and several rent liability has an easy
means of avoiding the creation of a tenancy.

Shams

Meaning of "sham"

A submission frequently made by occupiers wishing to
establish a tenancy is that terms apparently having the effect
of preventing exclusive possession may be disregarded as
shams. The word "sham" is used in various senses. The
most well known definition is that of Diplock L.J. in *Snook
v. London & West Riding Investments Ltd*:[22]

> "It means acts done or documents executed by the
> parties to the 'sham' which are intended by them to give
> to third parties or to the court the appearance of
> creating between the parties legal rights and obligations
> different from the actual legal rights and obligations (if
> any) which the parties intend to create. But one thing, I
> think, is clear in legal principle, morality and the
> authorities . . . that for acts or documents to be a 'sham'
> . . . all the parties thereto must have a common
> intention that the acts or documents are not to create
> the legal rights and obligations which they give the
> appearance of creating."

In other words, it does not suffice that one party intends to
deceive the other. This definition is too narrow to be of
much assistance in landlord and tenant cases.

Another aspect of "sham" was mentioned by Dillon L.J.
in *Gisborne v. Burton*,[23] referring to *Somma v. Hazelhurst*[24] as
an example, namely where the parties do intend the
documents to create the legal rights and obligations which
they appear to create, but the documents were nevertheless
a sham because they did not reflect what was actually
happening; in essence the parties "were trying to do what in
law cannot be done." Further guidance was offered in
Hadjiloucas v. Crean.[25] Mustill L.J., after setting out the
Snook definition of "sham," went on to consider the case
where the document does reflect the true agreement
between the parties, but where the language of the
document (in particular its title or description) superficially
indicates that it falls into one legal category whereas when
properly analysed in the light of the circumstances it can be
seen to fall into another. Although not a sham, such an
agreement (of which *Street v. Mountford* was an example)

---

[22] [1967] 2 Q.B. 786 at 802.
[23] [1989] Q.B. 390 at 398.
[24] [1978] 1 W.L.R. 1014; above, p. 19.
[25] [1988] 1 W.L.R. 1006.

would fail to achieve the kind of legal relationship the parties overtly set out to create. It might be added that the construction of an agreement should not be influenced by Rent Act or Housing Act considerations, but that it has often been stated that the court will be astute to detect sham devices whose only object is to disguise the grant of a tenancy and to evade the legislation.[26] The most recent judicial statement, however, favours the "evenhanded" (*i.e.* neutral) approach.[27]

Application of tax doctrine

Another principle recently formulated by the Court of Appeal in *Gisborne v. Burton*[28] is that even if there is no "sham" as described above, an "artificial transaction"[29] may be struck down by the court by invoking the tax doctrine illustrated by such cases as *Furniss v. Dawson*[30] and *W.T. Ramsay Ltd v. I.R.C.*[31] The principle of these cases is that where there is a pre-ordained series of transactions, the individual stages of which have no commercial purpose other than tax avoidance, the court may disregard the individual stages and ascertain the consequences by considering the result of the series as a whole. Adapted to the landlord and tenant context, the principle was held to apply whenever there was a pre-ordained series of transactions intended to avoid some mandatory statutory provision.[32] There seems, however, to be little scope for this doctrine in the context of the lease/licence debate because there is normally only one transaction rather than a pre-ordained series, although it might have some application in the sharer cases. In *Hilton v. Plustitle Ltd*,[33] on the other hand, the Court of Appeal (in a case concerning the company let device) considered that if the facts were consistent with the purported transaction, there was no reason why public policy should override a transaction which was intended to avoid, but not evade, the Rent Acts. *Gisborne v. Burton* was there regarded as a case of agency.

[26] *Street v. Mountford* [1985] A.C. 809 at 825; *Hadjiloucas v. Crean*, above, at 1014; *Buchmann v. May* [1978] 2 All E.R. 993 at 998–999; *O'Malley v. Seymour* (1978) 250 E.G. 1083 at 1088; *cf. Somma v. Hazelhurst* [1978] 1 W.L.R. 1014 at 1024–1025; *Aldrington Garages v. Fielder* (1978) 274 E.G. 557 at 559.

[27] *Stribling v. Wickham* [1989] 2 E.G.L.R. 35.

[28] Above; (1988) 138 N.L.J. 792 (J. Martin); All E.R. Rev. 1988 p. 186 (P. Pettit); [1989] Conv. 196 (C. Rodgers); below, p. 96.

[29] See however *Hadjiloucas v. Crean* [1988] 1 W.L.R. 1006 at 1023, where Mustill L.J. (discussing Lord Templeman's reference to "sham devices *and artificial transactions*" in *Street v. Mountford* [1985] A.C. 809 at 825) regarded "sham" and "artificial transaction" as meaning the same, *cf.* Purchas L.J. at 1017. See, further, *Antoniades v. Villiers*, below.

[30] [1984] A.C. 474.

[31] [1982] A.C. 300.

[32] See also the 1986 Blundell Memorial Lecture, summarised at (1986) 83 L.S. Gaz. 3736 (K. Lewison) and (1987) 84 L.S. Gaz. 403 (P. Freedman).

[33] [1989] 1 W.L.R. 149, below, p. 97. See also *Estavest Investments Ltd v. Commercial Express Travel Ltd* [1988] 2 E.G.L.R. 91.

Review by House of Lords

As we have seen, the House of Lords in *Antoniades v. Villiers*[34] had cause to re-examine the meaning of "sham." This case involved a cohabiting couple who separately signed "licences" which obliged them to share with the owner or other licensees permitted by the owner. This term, which was never operated, would prevent exclusive possession if valid, whereas the couple would be joint tenants if it was a sham. It was held that they did enjoy exclusive possession and were therefore joint tenants, because the landlord did not genuinely intend to exercise the sharing term, save possibly in order to bring pressure to bear to obtain possession. The subsequent conduct of the parties, while not relevant to the construction of the documents, was admissible as evidence on the question whether the documents were genuine.

Subsequent conduct relevant

Lord Templeman explained that if there was an intention, bogus or genuine, to create a licence, it would nevertheless be a tenancy if the rights and obligations satisfied the legal requirements of a tenancy. The grant of a joint tenancy could not be concealed, accidentally or by design, by two documents in the form of "licences."

Referring to *Street v. Mountford*, his Lordship continued

"Pretence" preferred to "sham"

"It would have been more accurate and less liable to give rise to misunderstandings if I had substituted the word 'pretence' for the references to 'sham devices' and 'artificial transactions'."[35]

Street v. Mountford had reasserted that if the language of licence contradicted the reality of lease, the facts must prevail. Facts must prevail over language to avoid the possibility of contracting out of the Rent Acts. In the present case the sharing term was a pretence because the flat was too small. If it had been genuine, the parties would have discussed how the clause would be operated and in whose favour. It was significant that the owner had never attempted to exercise it.

Summary

In the cases disapproved in *Street v. Mountford*,[36] and in *Antoniades v. Villiers* itself, there was a joint tenancy because:

(a) the applicants applied to rent jointly and to enjoy exclusive possession[37];

---

[34] [1990] 1 A.C. 417, above, p. 22. The decision was applied in *Nicolaou v. Pitt* [1989] 1 E.G.L.R. 84, [1989] Conv. 192 (J. Martin), where a married couple signed "licence" agreements. Although there was a spare bedroom and the flat had previously been occupied by three persons, it was held that the owner had no genuine intention to nominate a further occupier.

[35] *ibid.* at 462.

[36] *Somma v. Hazelhurst* [1978] 1 W.L.R. 1014; *Aldrington Garages Ltd v. Fielder* (1978) 37 P.&C.R. 461; *Sturolson & Co. v. Weniz* (1984) 272 E.G. 326.

[37] Lord Templeman in fact referred to exclusive *occupation* throughout his judgment.

(b) the landlord allowed the applicants jointly to enjoy exclusive possession[38] and accepted rent;
(c) the power to deprive them of exclusive possession was inconsistent with the Rent Act;
(d) in the circumstances the power which the landlord insisted upon to deprive them of exclusive possession[39] was a pretence intended only to deprive them of Rent Act protection.

Illustrations of sham terms

A useful illustration of the meaning of sham is provided by *Markou v. Da Silvaesa*,[40] where the owner sought to take advantage of the "lodger" exception of *Street v. Mountford*. The occupant of a one-room flat signed a "lodging agreement" for 26 weeks, under which he was entitled to use the flat from midnight to 10.30 a.m. and noon to midnight each day. "Possession, management and control"[41] were reserved to the owner, who kept the keys. The owner was obliged to do repairs and provide attendance in the form of a housekeeper, cleaning, laundry and rubbish disposal. The owner also reserved the right to move the occupier to a comparable flat in the same building and to remove or replace the furniture. These terms, if not shams, would indicate a licence.

Looking at the individual terms of the agreement, the clause restricting the hours of occupation (which was never enforced) was arguably a sham, and was so extraordinary in a residential agreement as to call for an explanation.[42] The clause giving the owner the right to remove (as opposed to replace) the furniture was a sham, but the right to move the occupier to another room was not, because the owner might reasonably wish to do this in certain circumstances.[43] The Court of Appeal held that where an agreement contained some sham terms, this did not make the whole agreement a sham. The court must strike out the offending terms and look at the remainder, although the presence of sham terms would require the remainder to be examined with "particular circumspection." In the present case the agreement would still be a licence, in spite of the sham terms, if the attendance term was not a sham. However, the owner's case was not sufficiently clear for the summary procedure of Order 113 (available against persons other

Sham terms may not invalidate whole agreement

Summary procedure not available

---

[38] See n. 37 above.
[39] See n. 37 above.
[40] (1986) 52 P.&C.R. 204 (reported *sub nom. Crancour Ltd v. Da Silvaesa* in [1986] 1 E.G.L.R. 80); (1987) 50 M.L.R. 226 (A. Waite).
[41] Similar words were used in the agreement in *Skipton Building Society v. Clayton* (1993) 66 P.&C.R. 223 (tenancy upheld).
[42] A similar clause was held to be a sham in *Aslan v. Murphy* [1990] 1 W.L.R. 766.
[43] See also *Dresden Estates Ltd v. Collinson* (1988) 55 P.&C.R. 47, below, p. 31, where a clause entitling the owner to move a business occupier to other premises was held to indicate a licence, although it was suggested that the clause would have this effect only in a limited class of cases and was not a way around *Street v. Mountford*. This decision is criticised at (1987) 50 M.L.R. 655 (S. Bridge) and [1987] Conv. 220 (P.F. Smith).

than tenants or former tenants). A proper trial was necessary
if any fundamental term was an obvious sham. Purchas L.J.
added that the failure to exercise rights under the agreement
was not conclusive of the question whether there was a
sham.[44] The case was remitted to the county court, where
the attendance term in particular would be examined to see
if access to the room was actually required.

Non-residential licences

Although something of a digression, the application of the
Street v. Mountford[45] principles outside the residential
context will be examined for the sake of completeness.
Street v. Mountford does not expressly deal with the question
whether the principles there laid down are confined to the
residential field, but subsequent cases have treated them as
applicable to business occupation. The issue is less pressing
in the agricultural context because licensees as well as
tenants are protected by the agricultural holdings
legislation.[46]

**Business
occupiers**
Of course, there will be differences in the application of
the principles to business occupation. So, for example, the
inquiry whether the occupier is a tenant or a lodger,
regarded as fundamental in *Street v. Mountford*, will rarely be
appropriate in a business setting.[47] Another distinction lies
in the application of the principle that, once exclusive
possession (for a term and at a rent) is established, the
strong presumption of tenancy is rebuttable by certain
special factors.[48] These special factors, set out in *Street v.
Mountford* (although the list there is not suggested to be
exhaustive), are less likely to arise in the case of business
occupation. While "exclusive possession referable to a legal
relationship other than landlord and tenant"[49] has possible
scope, the "service occupier" exception is inapplicable and
the "no intention to create legal relations" exception is less
likely to apply.

The first business case to arise after *Street v. Mountford*
was *University of Reading v. Johnson-Houghton*,[50] where Lord
Templeman's principles were applied to a "licence"
agreement under which the occupier was entitled to train
and exercise racehorses over gallops on the University's

---

[44] See, further, *Antoniades v. Villiers*, above.
[45] See above, p. 9.
[46] Agricultural Holdings Act 1986, s. 2. See *McCarthy v. Bence* [1990] 1
E.G.L.R. 1; [1991] Conv. 58 (C. Rodgers); *Colchester B.C. v. Smith*
[1991] Ch. 448 (not discussed on appeal at [1992] Ch. 421); *Ashdale
Land & Property Co. Ltd v. Manners* [1992] 2 E.G.L.R. 5.
[47] See *Dresden Estates Ltd v. Collinson* (1988) 55 P.&C.R. 47.
[48] See above, p. 14.
[49] See *Essex Plan Ltd v. Broadminster Ltd* (1988) 56 P.&C.R. 353
(possession referable to equitable interest under option to take lease).
[50] [1985] 2 E.G.L.R. 113; [1986] Conv. 275 (C.P. Rodgers); [1986] Conv.
344 at 350 (S. Bridge).

land. As the agreement conferred exclusive possession it was held to create a tenancy. Hence the tenant was protected by the Landlord and Tenant Act 1954. Similarly in *London & Associated Investment Trust plc v. Calow*,[51] where, contrary to the usual position, the occupiers were claiming to have merely a licence determinable at will, in order to avoid liability to pay rent for business premises after departing without notice. As the occupiers had enjoyed exclusive possession, they were tenants. Consequently they were liable for the rent. It was held that the *Street v. Mountford* principles were fully applicable to business occupiers, although it was pointed out that many common business arrangements such as the use of parts of the floor area in large stores, or stalls, did not involve exclusive possession. In *Ashburn Anstalt v. Arnold*,[52] the Court of Appeal held that business occupiers holding under a "licence" which conferred exclusive possession were tenants even though no rent was payable, but merely the outgoings. The arrangement was that the occupiers would later be granted a lease in a new development. Although a rent-free lease is clearly possible, the decision has been criticised on the ground that the absence of rent (and of any express intention to grant a lease) was strongly indicative of a licence.[53]

Where no rent

In *Dellneed Ltd v. Chin*,[54] the possible loophole of a "management agreement" was stopped. The case concerned a "Mai Toi" agreement, whereby a novice takes over the running of a Chinese restaurant, using the established name, to see if he is successful. Here the tenant of such a restaurant executed a document purporting to create a "management agreement." It was stated to be a licence and not a tenancy. The keys were handed over and the occupant went into possession and spent £33,000 on fittings and equipment. He carried on business on his own account, taking the profits and bearing the losses. He had exclusive possession of the entire premises covered by the head lease. The agreement prohibited alterations and additions, contained a repair obligation, prohibited changing the name of the restaurant, and reserved a right of entry to the grantor to ensure that the restaurant was being properly run. All these terms were inconsistent with the notion that the occupant was a licensee or a mere manager. He was not merely taking over the management of the existing business, but was starting up his own business. The terms of the document were intended to mislead and were an attempt to avoid a breach of the covenant in the head lease against subletting or parting with possession. The occupant was

"Management agreement"

Terms inconsistent with licence

[51] (1987) 53 P.&C.R. 340; [1987] Conv. 137 (S. Bridge).
[52] [1989] Ch. 1. (Since overruled on the finding of a "term"; see above, p. 12).
[53] See [1988] Conv. 201 at 203 (M.P. Thompson).
[54] (1987) 53 P.&C.R. 172; [1987] Conv. 298 (S. Bridge).

accordingly a tenant and entitled to security of tenure. The argument that there was no intent to create legal relations was rejected.

No exclusive possession

Other business occupiers have failed to establish a tenancy for lack of exclusive possession, as in the case of "shop space" in part of the ground floor of a building in Camden Lock Market.[55] A stallholder may, however, have a tenancy.[56] In *Dresden Estates Ltd v. Collinson*,[57] the occupier of a workshop and store held under an agreement, called a licence, whereby exclusive possession was expressly denied, the rights were not assignable, and the grantor reserved the right to move him to other adjoining premises. Some provisions, on the other hand, were more indicative of a tenancy, for example the reservation by the grantor of a limited right to enter and carry out work. The agreement was held to be a licence. The right to move the occupier elsewhere was particularly relied on as denying exclusive possession, although the Court of Appeal warned against reading the decision as a way around *Street v. Mountford*, saying that such a clause would be appropriate only in a limited class of cases.[58] The point was also made that business and residence cases were not the same because there was no such thing as a business lodger. It seems, however, that in appropriate circumstances a business lodger is a possibility.[59]

---

[55] *Smith v. Northside Developments Ltd* (1988) 55 P.&C.R. 164. Initially the occupation was shared with a third party. When the third party left and was not replaced, this did not convert the licence to a tenancy. It may be more difficult to establish that an existing licence has been converted to a tenancy than to establish that an initial arrangement is a tenancy. See also *Mikeover Ltd v. Brady* [1989] 3 All E.R. 618; *Essex Plan Ltd v. Broadminster Ltd* (1988) 56 P.&C.R. 353; [1989] Conv. 55 (J.E.M.); *Esso Petroleum Ltd v. Fumegrange Ltd* [1994] 2 E.G.L.R. 90.

[56] *Graysim Holdings Ltd v. P&O Property Holdings Ltd* [1994] 1 W.L.R. 992.

[57] (1988) 55 P.&C.R. 47; [1987] Conv. 220 (P.F. Smith); (1987) 50 M.L.R. 655 (S. Bridge). The weakness of this decision lies in its reliance on passages from *Halsbury* which pre-date *Street v. Mountford*.

[58] See above, p. 28.

[59] *Vandersteen v. Agius* (1993) 65 P.&C.R. 266.

3 THE PROTECTION FROM EVICTION ACT 1977

This Act affords protection to residential tenants and certain licensees.[1] First, it provides civil and criminal remedies for unlawful eviction and harassment. Secondly, it prohibits forfeiture without a court order while any person is lawfully residing. Thirdly, it prohibits the recovery of possession on termination of a tenancy without a court order where any person is lawfully residing at the end of the tenancy. Fourthly, it imposes requirements beyond those of the common law for the validity of notices to quit in certain cases. For residential occupiers who do not enjoy security of tenure, the Act is their only source of statutory protection.

Derivation
    The provisions were originally contained in Part III of the Rent Act 1965 (which followed the temporary Protection from Eviction Act 1964). These sections, and section 16 of the Rent Act 1957, were consolidated by the Protection from Eviction Act 1977, which was subsequently amended by the Housing Acts of 1980 and 1988.

1988 amendments
    The effect of the Housing Act 1988 was to strengthen the criminal offence of harassment and to provide a civil remedy of damages for unlawful eviction and harassment. As far as possession orders and notices to quit are concerned, the broad effect of the 1988 amendments was that the rights of certain licensees were enhanced while those of certain tenants were diminished. These matters are discussed below.

Unlawful eviction and harassment

Section 1 of the 1977 Act imposes criminal penalties[2] for unlawful eviction and harassment. The Housing Act 1988 provides a further criminal offence of harassment[3] and also introduces a civil action in tort for unlawful eviction.[4] These three matters will be considered in turn.

---

[1] The special provisions in s. 4, relating to agricultural employees, are omitted as being outside the scope of this book.

[2] Fine or imprisonment, or both: s. 1(4), as amended by the Criminal Law Act 1977. See also s. 1(6) (offence by corporate body). An unlawfully evicted tenant is unintentionally homeless. For housing rights, see *R. v. Bristol City Council, ex p. Bradic, The Times*, February 6, 1995.

[3] s. 29.

[4] ss. 27, 28.

Unlawful eviction and harassment: the original offences

Residential occupier

The offences under section 1 of the 1977 Act may be committed against a "residential occupier," which means a person occupying the premises as a residence, whether under a contract or by virtue of any enactment or rule of law giving him the right to remain in occupation or restricting the right of any other person to recover possession of the premises.[5] This definition includes, therefore, contractual licensees,[6] tenants having leasehold interests under the general law (whether or not they have security of tenure), and tenants having statutory rights to occupy, for example statutory tenants under the Rent Act 1977.

Unlawful eviction

By section 1(2), the offence of unlawful eviction occurs where any person (*i.e.* not just the owner) unlawfully deprives the residential occupier of his occupation of the premises or any part thereof, or attempts to do so, unless he proves that he believed, and had reasonable cause to believe, that the residential occupier had ceased to reside in the premises.[7]

Need not be permanent

It was held in *R. v. Yuthiwattana*[8] that the offence under section 1(2) must have the character of eviction. This need not be permanent, but locking the tenant out overnight would not suffice, section 1(3)[9] being more appropriate in such a case. In *Costelloe v. London Borough of Camden*,[10] on the other hand, where the occupier was excluded for an hour, it was held that this could be within section 1(2) if the landlord intended it to be permanent but for some reason (for example after intervention by the police) the occupier was re-admitted.[11]

Harassment

By section 1(3), the offence of harassment is committed if any person with intent to cause the residential occupier of any premises:

(a) to give up the occupation of the premises or any part thereof; or

(b) to refrain from exercising any right or pursuing any remedy in respect of the premises or part thereof;

---

[5] Protection from Eviction Act 1977, s. 1(1).

[6] Unless the licence has been effectively terminated: *R. v. Blankley* [1979] Crim. L.R. 166. Former unprotected tenants (including "rental purchasers", by Housing Act 1980, Sched. 25, para. 6) are within the definition in cases where the landlord's right to possession may not be enforced without a court order under s. 3 (below) or, in cases of forfeiture, under s. 2 (below). See also Criminal Law Act 1977, s. 6, as amended by Criminal Justice and Public Order Act 1994, s. 72 (offence to use or threaten violence to secure entry).

[7] See *R. v. Davidson-Acres* (1980) Crim. L.R. 50.

[8] (1984) 128 S.J. 661.

[9] See below.

[10] [1986] Crim. L.R. 249; [1987] Conv. 265 (J. Hill).

[11] Re-instatement may be ordered by mandatory interlocutory injunction; *Parsons v. Nasar* (1991) 23 H.L.R. 1.

does acts likely to interfere with the peace or comfort of the residential occupier or members of his household, or persistently withdraws or withholds services[12] reasonably required for the occupation of the premises as a residence. The world "likely" was substituted for the word "calculated" by the Housing Act 1988.[13] The offence is now easier to establish, but still requires an intent to cause the occupier to leave or to refrain from exercising his rights.

Although section 1(3)(b) refers to "rights", it has been held that the offence does not require conduct which is actionable as a civil wrong. Thus in *R. v. Burke*[14] the offence was committed where the landlord disconnected the front door bell even though the tenant of the basement had no contractual entitlement to a front door bell. It was clear from the fact that the offence of harassment could be committed by persons other than the landlord that contractual entitlements were not decisive.

Defence   It has been held that a person accused of an offence under section 1(3) has a defence if he honestly believed, with reasonable grounds, that the occupant was not a "residential occupier."[15]

Examples   In *R. v. Yuthiwattana*,[16] it was held that harassment under section 1(3) need not breach the right of occupation. The offence was committed by refusing to supply a key when the tenant's was missing. This may be contrasted with *Schon v. Camden London Borough Council*,[17] holding that an intention to make the occupier give up occupation for two weeks to enable repairs to be done would not be within section 1(3). The landlord and tenant had failed to agree on alternative accommodation while the work was in progress. The landlord had no intention that the tenant should go permanently, nor had he caused the ceiling to fall in with the intent of causing her to go. There was said to be a strong argument that "occupation" had the same meaning as under the Rent Act 1977, that is to say that the tenant could still be regarded as in occupation even though absent if her possessions were there and she intended to return.[18] If, therefore, the tenant moved out for repairs, she was still in residence. Hence there was no intent to make her give up occupation within section 1(3)(a). The landlord's acts could have fallen within section 1(3)(b) as intending to cause the

---

[12] The withdrawal of services voluntarily provided is not included: *McCall v. Abelesz* [1976] Q.B. 285.

[13] s. 29(1).

[14] [1991] 1 A.C. 135 (other acts of harassment were also committed).

[15] *R. v. Phekoo* [1981] 1 W.L.R. 1117. The requirement of reasonable grounds is criticised at [1981] Conv. 377 (M. Wasik). The question could also arise under s. 1(2).

[16] See above. See also (1989) *Legal Action*, June, p. 21.

[17] (1987) 53 P.&C.R. 361. See [1987] Conv. 265 (J. Hill), suggesting that the decision conflicts somewhat with *R. v. Yuthiwattana* and indicates that the courts interpret "occupation" in s. 1(2) and s. 1(3) differently.

[18] This is the test formulated in *Brown v. Brash* [1948] 2 K.B. 247: see below, p. 98.

tenant to refrain from exercising any right (*i.e.* her right to occupy in person for the two-week period), but this had not been pleaded. It was emphasised that section 1(3) creates one offence, not two. The local authority[19] could have framed one charge with alternative intents.

Another example is *R. v. Ahmad*,[20] where the landlord asked the tenant to vacate temporarily while improvements were done. A dispute subsequently arose and the flat became uninhabitable. It was held that the landlord's failure to complete the building works, although a breach of the tenancy agreement, did not fall within section 1(3). The Act did not create a duty to rectify damage already caused by an act which had been done without either of the intentions necessary to constitute an offence under section 1(3).

The further offence of harassment

The original offence[21] under section 1(3), discussed above, requires a specific intent to cause the occupier to give up occupation or to refrain from exercising any rights. The provision has been strictly interpreted and convictions have been correspondingly difficult to secure. To remedy this situation the Housing Act 1988[22] provides for a further offence of harassment, which, it was envisaged, would be easier to prove.

Section 1 of the 1977 Act is amended to include subsection (3A), which provides that the landlord[23] of a residential occupier or an agent[24] of the landlord shall be guilty of an offence if, subject to subsection (3B) below:

(a) he does acts likely[25] to interfere with the peace or comfort of the residential occupier or members of his household; or

(b) he persistently withdraws or withholds services reasonably required for the occupation of the premises in question as a residence;

---

[19] By whom proceedings may be instituted under the Protection from Eviction Act 1977, s. 6. See (1991) *Legal Action*, April, p. 8 (G. Strudwick).

[20] (1987) 84 Cr.App.R. 64.

[21] Both before and after the amendment in Housing Act 1988, s. 29(1).

[22] s. 29(2).

[23] Defined in s. 1(3C) as meaning the person who would be entitled to occupation but for the residential occupier's right to remain in occupation or a restriction on the person's right to recover possession, and any superior landlord under whom that person derives title. S. 1(4) and (6) (penalties and offences by corporate bodies) apply to the further offence as to the original.

[24] "Agent" is not defined. See *R. v. Mitchell* (1994) 26 H.L.R. 394 and its civil counterpart *Sampson v. Wilson, The Times*, April 19, 1995, below, p. 39. Compare "any person" in s. 1(3).

[25] *cf. R. v. Ahmad* (1987) 84 Cr.App.R. above.

Knowledge or constructive knowledge and (in either case) he knows, or has reasonable cause to believe, that the conduct is likely to cause the residential occupier to give up the occupation of the whole or part of the premises or to refrain from exercising any right or pursuing any remedy in respect of the whole or part of the premises.

Defence A defence is provided by section 1(3B), whereby a person does not commit the section 1(3A) offence if he proves that he had reasonable grounds for doing the acts or for withdrawing or withholding the services in question. This defence will presumably be available where, for example, the occupier has failed to pay for the services in the manner required by his contract.[26]

Summary The difference between section 1(3) and section 1(3A) lies in the intention necessary to constitute the offence. In other words, the *actus reus* is the same but the *mens rea* is different. The original offence of harassment requires a specific intention to cause the occupier to give up occupation or refrain from exercising his rights, whereas the new offence merely requires knowledge, or reasonable cause to believe, that this will be the likely result. Clearly this offence is easier to establish than the offence under section 1(3) of the 1977 Act, notwithstanding the substitution of the word "likely" for "calculated" in section 1(3).[27]

The statutory tort

Infringement of the original section 1 of the 1977 Act was held to give rise to no civil cause of action under the statute,[28] although civil remedies were likely to exist under the general law.[29]

This was changed by section 27 of the Housing Act 1988, which provides a remedy in damages for the new tort[30] of unlawful eviction. This section covers the following three classes of act (committed after June 9, 1988)[31]:

(a) a landlord (referred to as "the landlord in default") or any person acting on behalf of the landlord in default

---

[26] The defence established in *R. v. Phekoo* [1981] 1 W.L.R. 1117, above, p. 35, in relation to s. 1(3) presumably applies equally to the further offence.

[27] See above, p. 35. For the view that local authorities are not using their powers sufficiently, see *Forced Out* (Shelter Publications). For statistics, see *Law and Order in Private Rented Housing* (Campaign for Bedsit Rights).

[28] *McCall v. Abelesz* [1976] Q.B. 585.

[29] See below, p. 45.

[30] s. 27(4)(a). This does not bind the Crown: s. 44(2)(a).

[31] See *Jones v. Miah* (1992) 24 H.L.R. 578 (retrospective element is not a breach of the European Convention for the Protection of Human Rights and Fundamental Freedoms).

**Unlawful
eviction**

unlawfully deprives the residential occupier[32] of any premises of his occupation of the whole or part of the premises;

(b) a landlord (referred to as "the landlord in the default") or any person acting on behalf of the landlord in default

Attempts

attempts unlawfully to deprive the residential occupier of any premises of his occupation of the whole or part of the premises, as a result of which the residential occupier gives up his occupation of the premises as a residence;

(c) a landlord (referred to as "the landlord in default") or any person acting on behalf of the landlord in default

Harassment

does acts likely to interfere with the peace or comfort of the residential occupier or members of his household, or persistently withdraws or withholds services reasonably required for the occupation of the premises as a residence, knowing or having reasonable cause to believe that the conduct is likely to cause the residential occupier:

   (i) to give up his occupation of the premises or any part thereof; or

   (ii) to refrain from exercising any right or pursuing any remedy in respect of the premises or any part thereof, as a result of which the residential occupier gives up his occupation of the premises as a residence.

It will be noted that this civil action does not apply to harassment or attempted unlawful eviction which do not result in the occupier's departure, although other civil remedies may be available in these cases.[33] Section 27 follows the wording of the offence in section 1(3A) of the Protection from Eviction Act 1977. A criminal conviction is not, however, necessary to establish the tort. It has been held that section 27 requires a "positive act" by the landlord, so that no tort was committed where the landlord merely put up a notice advising the tenant to leave because the landlord's mortgagee was about to take possession.[34]

Persons liable

"Landlord" for the purposes of section 27 is defined in section 27(9) as "the person who, but for the occupier's right to occupy, would be entitled to occupation of the premises and any superior landlord under whom that person derives title." A superior landlord may, therefore, commit the tort if he does the acts complained of. One question which arose in *Jones v. Miah*[35] was whether a purchaser in possession before completion could be "the landlord" within section 27. The owner of premises consisting of a

---

[32] By s. 27(9) this bears the same meaning as in s. 1 of the 1977 Act. It includes tenants (protected and unprotected) and licensees: see above, p. 34.

[33] Below, p. 45. See *Murray v. Aslam* [1994] E.G.C.S. 160.

[34] *Shafer v. Yagambrun*, noted (1994) *Legal Action*, December, p. 16.

[35] (1992) 24 H.L.R. 578; [1993] Conv. 84 (S. Bridge); below, p. 43.

restaurant and four bed-sitting rooms contracted to sell them to the defendants with vacant possession. The conditions of sale incorporated into the contract envisaged that the purchaser might be let into occupation before completion as a licensee. The owner (who had since disappeared) supplied the defendants with keys to the residential floors. With the owner's concurrence they changed the locks and evicted the plaintiff tenants before completion of the contract. The Court of Appeal held that the defendants fell within the definition of "landlord" and were liable under the Act. They were the owners in equity after entering into the contract for sale. At the time of the eviction the defendants were persons who "would be entitled to occupation" but for the occupiers' rights because the contract so provided. The use of the word "occupation" rather than "possession" indicated that occupation as a licensee sufficed. On any other view a purchaser could avoid liability by evicting before completion.

Section 27 imposes liability where the acts in question are done by the "landlord in default" or by "any person acting on behalf of the landlord in default" who does the acts in question. In *Sampson v. Wilson*[36] the freeholder of flats, A, had given the management of the property to B before going abroad. A owed money to B and agreed that B should collect the rents until the debt was paid off. B was in poor health and so gave the management of the property to C. Without B's authority C harassed the plaintiff tenants, causing them to leave. The plaintiffs sued A, B and C for damages for the statutory tort. The Court of Appeal held that A alone was liable. A was the landlord within section 27 and B acted as his agent. In the High Court it had been held that the meaning of the phrase "any person acting on behalf of the landlord" was intended to be as broad as possible and was wide enough to include, for example, independent contractors and persons such as C. The main issue on appeal was whether the landlord and his agent

Joint liability could be jointly liable. The general rule at common law is that, where a principal is liable for the torts of his agent, they are regarded as joint tortfeasors. Section 27(3), however, provides that the liability is that of the "landlord in default." Rejecting the tentative view of the majority in *Jones v. Miah*,[37] it was held that only the landlord could be liable for what he did or what was done on his behalf, agents being liable only for their own personal torts. This was clear from the wording of section 27(3), which contrasted with that of subsections (1) and (2), and from the damages formula of section 28, which was designed to expropriate the gains which a landlord could make from an eviction. The question whether A was entitled to be indemnified by B against the liabilities to which he became exposed by B's failure to

[36] *The Times*, April 19, 1995.
[37] (1992) 24 H.L.R. 578, above.

discharge his duties as agent competently was remitted to the High Court.

Defence   There is a defence if the defendant proves that he believed, with reasonable grounds, that the residential occupier had ceased to reside in the premises at the time when he was deprived of occupation or when the attempt was made or the acts were done as a result of which he gave up occupation.[38] Similarly, if liability would arise by virtue only of the doing of acts or the withdrawal or withholding of services, if the defendant had reasonable grounds for doing the acts or withdrawing or withholding the services.

Further, no liability arises if, before proceedings to enforce the liability are finally disposed of, the former
Reinstatement   residential occupier is reinstated in the premises so that he becomes again the residential occupier,[39] or where this occurs as a result of a court order made at the request of the former residential occupier.[40]

Where the tort has been committed, the court may in two cases reduce the amount of damages to such amount as it thinks appropriate. This may be done if it appears to the court:

(a) that, prior to the event which gave rise to the liability, the conduct of the former residential occupier or any person living with him in the premises concerned was
Mitigation   such that it is reasonable to mitigate the damages for which the landlord in default would otherwise be liable[41]; or

(b) that, before the proceedings were begun, the landlord in default offered to reinstate the former residential occupier in the premises in question and either it was unreasonable of the former residential occupier to refuse the offer or, if he had obtained alternative accommodation before the offer was made, it would have been unreasonable of him to refuse that offer if he had not obtained that accommodation.[42]

The issues of reinstatement and mitigation arose in *Tagro v. Cafane*,[43] where the landlord had changed the locks of a bed-sitting room in order to evict the tenant. The following day the tenant obtained an *ex parte* injunction to be readmitted. A few days later the landlord offered her the new key, but the door was broken and the room had been

[38] s. 27(8). The defence seems inappropriate to cases of atttempted unlawful eviction.
[39] See *Murray v. Aslam* [1994] E.G.C.S. 160 (no claim where re-admitted after two hours). It is not expressly stated that the occupier should have the same status as before, although this may be implicit in the word "reinstated".
[40] s. 27(6). Civil remedies under the general law may still be available in such cases: see below, p. 45.
[41] See *Sullman v. Little* [1993] 11 C.L. 210 (damages reduced where tenant in breach of covenant against keeping animals).
[42] s. 27(7).
[43] [1991] 1 W.L.R. 378.

ransacked and possessions stolen. The tenant found other accommodation and sought damages for the statutory tort. The landlord claimed that by giving the tenant a new key he had reinstated her and therefore under section 27(6)(b) no liability arose because the court had made an order (the injunction) as a result of which she had been reinstated. On this point it was held that the tenant had not been reinstated: the provision of a key to a broken door of a wrecked room was not reinstatement, which in any event required the consent of the tenant.[44] The defence under section 27(6)(b) was not, therefore, available. The landlord also invoked section 27(7)(b), arguing that damages should be reduced because he had offered to reinstate the tenant before the proceedings were begun and it was unreasonable to refuse the offer. Section 27(7)(b) was held inapplicable because, for reasons mentioned above, there had been no offer to reinstate the tenant. The view was expressed that the words "before the proceedings were begun" in section 27(7)(b) referred to the proceedings to recover damages under the Act and not to any earlier proceedings relating to the eviction, such as the injunction in the present case. Thus if the landlord's conduct had amounted to an offer to reinstate, section 27(7)(b) could have applied even though the offer was made after the injunction proceedings.

Measure of damages

The remedy for the statutory tort is damages in respect of the former occupier's loss of the right to occupy the premises as his residence.[45] The measure of damages is governed by section 28 of the Housing Act 1988. Interest may not be awarded.[46] Section 28 provides that the basis for the assessment of damages is the difference in value, determined as at the time immediately before the residential occupier ceased to occupy the premises as his residence, between:

(a) the value of the interest of the landlord in default determined on the assumption that the residential occupier continues to have the same right to occupy the premises as before that time; and

(b) the value of that interest determined on the assumption that the residential occupier has ceased to have that right.

The "interest of the landlord in default" means his interest in the building in which the premises in question are comprised (whether or not that building contains any other

---

[44] If a tenant unreasonably refuses to be reinstated, the defence under s. 27(6)(b) will not be available but damages may be reduced under s. 27(7)(b).

[45] s. 27(3).

[46] *Jones v. Miah* (1992) 24 H.L.R. 578.

premises) together with its curtilage.[47] One does not look just at the value of a flat, for example, but at the value of the block if owned by the landlord, when making the comparison in values set out above.

Valuation assumptions   For the purpose of the valuations referred to above, it is assumed[48]:

(a) that the landlord in the default is selling his interest on the open market to a willing buyer[49]; and
(b) that neither the residential occupier nor any member of his family[50] wishes to buy; and
(c) that it is unlawful to carry out any substantial development of any of the land in which the landlord's interest subsists or to demolish the whole or part of any building on that land.

Development value   The reference in assumption (c) to "substantial development" is a reference to development other than:

(a) development for which planning permission is granted by a general development order for the time being in force and which is carried out so as to comply with any condition or limitation subject to which planning permission is so granted; or
(b) a change of use resulting in the building in which the premises in question are comprised or any part of it being used as, or as part of, one or more dwelling-houses.[51]

The Housing Bill contained an assumption which would have eliminated any development value, but this was subsequently modified by assumption (c) above, thereby enhancing the amount of damages in cases where the landlord's interest has development value of a kind contemplated by section 28(6).

Mitigation   As we have seen, the court may in certain cases reduce the amount of damages payable in the light of mitigating circumstances.[52]

Effect of section 28   The broad effect of section 28 is that the landlord must pay the difference between the vacant possession value and the value subject to the occupier's rights. The greater the security of the occupier, the larger this sum will be. The object of these provisions, of course, is to prevent the landlord from making a profit from his act of unlawful eviction or harassment. In cases where the occupier has substantial security, for example where he is a protected tenant under the Rent Act 1977 with potential successors and paying less than the market rent under the "fair rent"

[47] s. 28(2).
[48] s. 28(3).
[49] See *Tagro v. Cafane* [1991] 1 W.L.R. 378, below.
[50] As defined by Housing Act 1985, s. 113 (succession to secure tenancies).
[51] s. 28(6). Development value by virtue of planning permission for a non-residential use will not, therefore, be reflected in the damages.
[52] s. 27(7), above, p. 40.

Assessment of damages

system, the damages will be considerable. In this regard it should be noted that county courts have jurisdiction although the damages claimed exceed the normal county court limits.[53] At the other end of the scale, where the occupier is a licensee having no security of tenure, the damages under section 28 will not be substantial. Plaintiffs have been awarded very considerable amounts in numerous county court actions.[54] An award of £31,000 was upheld by the Court of Appeal in *Tagro v. Cafane*,[55] where the tenant of a bed-sitting room in a three storey building was unlawfully evicted. Her landlord held a monthly business tenancy of the whole building from the freeholder and had security of tenure under the Landlord and Tenant Act 1954, Pt. II. The landlord argued that the value of his interest was nil because his tenancy was not assignable. This was rejected on the ground that section 28(3)[56] required the assumption of a sale to a willing buyer. The effect of this provision was held, somewhat questionably, to be that the court must assume a willing buyer who would take a lease from the freeholder with the same covenant against assignment. As the landlord had put in no valuation evidence, the court was entitled to accept the evidence of the tenant's surveyor that the value of the landlord's interest was increased by £31,000 as a result of the eviction, although it was accepted that this was on the high side.

The assessment of damages may be particularly difficult where the property has a mixed use. In *Jones v. Miah*[57] there was a three storey property of which the ground floor was a restaurant and the other floors contained four bed-sitting rooms. The landlord had a leasehold interest in the whole property and agreed to sell it with vacant possession to the defendants for £85,000. This sum was apportioned as to £50,000 for the property and £35,000 for the goodwill of the business and trade fittings. The defendants (with the landlord's concurrence) unlawfully evicted the Rent Act protected tenants of three bed-sitting rooms, two of whom were the plaintiffs, before completing the purchase. The decision of the majority of the Court of Appeal was that each plaintiff should be awarded £8,000 for the statutory tort. This was based on the likelihood (the valuation evidence being unsatisfactory) that the defendants would have paid £25,000 less for the property without vacant possession. This figure represented the difference in value between the landlord's interest subject to the rights of the three evicted tenants and not subject to them. Thus the two plaintiffs were entitled to one third of this sum each,

---

[53] Housing Act 1988, s. 40.
[54] Reports of these decisions are regularly included in *Legal Action*. See also (1993) 143 N.L.J. 844 and 880 (N. Madge).
[55] [1991] 1 W.L.R. 378; [1991] Conv. 297 (C. Rodgers). See also *Haniff v. Robinson* [1993] Q.B. 419 (£26,000 for Rent Act tenant).
[56] Above, p. 42.
[57] (1992) 24 H.L.R. 578.

rounded down to £8,000. Dillon L.J., however, would have awarded a smaller sum on the basis that the £50,000 valuation of the building included £25,000 for the restaurant floor. Thus no bed-sitting room could be worth more than £6,250 and the damages to each plaintiff could not exceed that sum; £5,750 was considered to be the appropriate figure. This reasoning, however, fails to give effect to section 28(2).

Exemplary damages   It does not seem that exemplary damages can be awarded for the statutory tort.[58] The assessment of damages under section 28 in any event achieves the same purpose as exemplary damages, namely the elimination of the wrongdoer's profit. Where exemplary damages are awarded at common law for a tort committed during the unlawful eviction, it seems that they will be set off against any damages awarded for the statutory tort, as explained below.

General law remedies preserved

By section 27(5) of the Housing Act 1988, the introduction of the new civil action does not affect the right of a residential occupier to enforce any liability under the general law in respect of his loss of the right to occupy premises as his residence. However, damages shall not be awarded both **No double damages** in respect of the statutory tort and any other civil liability on account of the same loss.

These other civil actions under the general law, which are discussed below, will continue to be useful in cases outside the scope of the statutory tort, for example where the occupier did not give up occupation, or where he has been reinstated. Similarly where the occupier has no security of tenure, so that even if damages are available for the statutory tort, they will not be great.

The purpose of section 27(5) is to prevent double recovery for loss of occupation rights. Where a plaintiff sues at common law and under the Act, there is no reason why an award for such matters as damage to possessions[59] or personal injury should not be made in addition to damages **Aggravated and exemplary damages** for the statutory tort. It is less clear whether aggravated or exemplary damages which a plaintiff has been awarded for infringement of his common law rights are to be set off against the sum awarded under the Act. In *Jones v. Miah*[60] aggravated damages of £3,000 had been awarded in the county court in addition to damages for the statutory tort. There was no appeal against the award of this additional sum, and thus no decision by the Court of Appeal on the

---

[58] *AB v. South Western Water Services Ltd* [1993] Q.B. 507; (1993) 143 N.L.J. 929 (A. Reed); (1993) 109 L.Q.R. 358 (A. Burrows); Law Com. C.P. No. 132 (1993).
[59] See *Tagro v. Cafane* [1991] 1 W.L.R. 378 (£15,538 for loss of possessions).
[60] (1992) 24 H.L.R. 578.

point of set-off. In *Nwokorie v. Mason*[61] the county court
judge had awarded £500 general damages, £4,500 under
the Housing Act and £1,000 aggravated damages. The
Court of Appeal held that the two smaller sums must be set
off against the Housing Act damages, as they were awarded
for loss of the right to occupy and so section 27(5)
prevented their recovery in addition to the sum awarded for
the statutory tort. No exemplary damages had been
awarded, but it is clear that any such damages would also
have been set off.[62] It was held that, while the plaintiff does
not have to elect between the common law and the statutory
tort, the smaller award must be deducted from the larger.

There seems no reason why exemplary damages should
not be set off in this way, otherwise the defendant would be
in effect deprived of his profit twice over. Aggravated
damages, on the other hand, are awarded in respect of the
manner of the eviction rather than for the "loss of the right
to occupy" within section 27(5). It is strongly arguable that
in cases where aggravated damages are appropriate, they
should be awarded in addition to damages for the statutory
tort.[63]

The general law remedies will now be considered.

Other civil remedies

The acts which amount to the commission of a criminal
offence within section 1 of the 1977 Act are likely to found a
civil cause of action under the general law either in contract
or tort. The appropriate remedy would be an injunction or
damages, or both.[64] In the case of a tenant[65] the lease is

Contract subject to implied (and often express) obligations to give
quiet enjoyment and not to derogate from the grant.
Illustrations which pre-date the enactment of the criminal
offence include *Lavender v. Betts*[66] (removal of doors and
windows), *Perera v. Vandiyar*[67] (cutting off gas and
electricity) and *Kenny v. Preen*[68] (persistent knocking on the
door and uttering threats). All these activities, which would
now amount to the criminal offence of harassment, were
held to be breaches of the implied covenant for quiet
enjoyment.[69] Damages for mental distress are not, however,
available for breach of this covenant.[69]

---

[61] (1994) 26 H.L.R. 60.
[62] *ibid.* at 69.
[63] [1994] Conv. 411 (S. Bridge).
[64] There is also the possibility of criminal compensation; *R. v. Bokhari*
(1974) 59 Cr.App.R. 303.
[65] Licences are possibly also subject to an implied term to give quiet
enjoyment: *Smith v. Nottinghamshire C.C., The Times*, November 13,
1981.
[66] [1942] 2 All E.R. 72.
[67] [1953] 1 W.L.R. 672.
[68] [1963] 1 Q.B. 499.
[69] *Branchett v. Beaney* [1992] 3 All E.R. 910.

Tort

From the point of view of damages, however, the occupier, whether tenant or licensee, may be in a better position if he can establish a tort. He may then be entitled to exemplary damages,[70] which are not available in the case of a contract claim. In *Drane v. Evangelou*,[71] the landlord wanted to recover possession from the tenant in order to house his relatives. While the tenant was out, three men entered (on the landlord's instructions), put out the tenant's belongings and prevented him from re-entering. The landlord's relatives moved in, and the tenant was forced to

Exemplary damages

live elsewhere and to store his goods. The tenant obtained injunctions, which the landlord disobeyed. After 10 weeks the tenant got back into possession. He claimed damages for

Trespass

the unlawful eviction. It was held that the landlord's acts constituted not only a breach of the covenant for quiet enjoyment but also the tort of trespass. As the landlord had behaved outrageously, exemplary damages of £1,000 were awarded. Similarly in *Guppys (Bridport) Ltd v. Brookling*,[72] where the landlord wished to convert and sell off some premises which were occupied by several tenants. During the conversion works he disconnected the electricity, interfered with the water supply and demolished some rooms. The tenants, who were left with no working sanitary facilities, were eventually forced out. The landlord was also in breach of undertakings given to the court in an injunction application. It was held that the landlord was in breach of the covenant for quiet enjoyment and had also committed

Nuisance

the tort of nuisance,[73] for which exemplary damages of £1,000 to each tenant were awarded.

Where defendants are jointly liable, the court may award exemplary damages against one but not the other, to reflect their different roles in the eviction.[74]

Forfeiture

Section 2 of the 1977 Act provides that where any premises are let as a dwelling on a lease which is subject to a right of re-entry or forfeiture, it shall not be lawful to enforce that right otherwise than by proceedings in court while any

Court order required

person is lawfully residing in the premises or part of them.[75] This provision is significant for those tenants who do not have security of tenure, although it is not confined to such tenants. Forfeiture of a protected tenancy under the Rent

---

[70] These must be pleaded; R.S.C. Ord. 18, r. 8(3); C.C.R. Ord. 6, r. 1B.
[71] [1978] 1 W.L.R. 455. See also *Warder v. Cooper* [1970] 1 Ch. 495; *Branchett v. Beaney* [1992] 3 All E.R. 910.
[72] (1984) 269 E.G. 846.
[73] A landlord may commit nuisance against a tenant in respect of the use of his adjoining property: *Sampson v. Hodson-Pressinger* [1981] 3 All E.R. 710.
[74] *Ramdath v. Daley* (1993) 25 H.L.R. 273.
[75] By s. 10, this provision binds the Crown.

Act 1977 may not necessarily entitle the landlord to possession, and a court order based on a ground for possession must be obtained.[76] As will be explained in Chapter 11, assured tenancies may not be terminated by forfeiture.[77]

Questions may arise as to what is meant by "lawfully residing." This is discussed below in the context of section 3, where the same expression is used.

No eviction without possession order

Section 3 of the 1977 Act prohibits eviction without a court order where premises have been let as a dwelling and the occupier continues to reside in the premises after the tenancy has come to an end (*e.g.* by expiry or notice to quit, but not by forfeiture, to which section 2 applies). Breach of this section has been held to give rise to a civil cause of action.[78]

Lawfully residing   By section 3(2), "the occupier" means any person lawfully residing at the termination of the former tenancy. Questions may arise, both here and under section 2, as to what is meant by "lawfully residing." It is not clear whether a sub-tenant whose sub-lease was granted in breach of a covenant against subletting in the lease is within the section, where the breach has not been waived.[79] Clearly such a sub-tenant should be protected as against the tenant.[80] There is no direct authority, but it was held in *Bolton Building Society v. Cobb*[81] that the provision did not protect a tenant against the landlord's mortgagee in cases where the tenancy was not binding on the mortgagee. Where a possession order has been duly obtained, section 3 does not require the landlord to bring separate proceedings against members of the departed former tenant's family who remain in occupation.[82] However, where the tenant remains in occupation after a possession order has been obtained, the protection of section 3 continues until the order is properly executed by a bailiff. A landlord who resorts to self-help to evict the tenant commits the offence of unlawful eviction.[83]

---

[76] Rent Act 1977, ss. 2, 98: see below, p. 11; Housing Act 1988, ss. 5, 7: below, p. 209.

[77] See Housing Act 1988, ss. 5, 7(6).

[78] *Warder v. Cooper* [1970] 1 Ch. 495.

[79] For the view that such a sub-tenant is not within the section see Farrand and Arden, *Rent Acts and Regulations* (2nd ed., 1981) p. 299.

[80] *ibid.*, p. 300.

[81] [1966] 1 W.L.R. 1.

[82] *Thompson v. Elmbridge B.C.* [1987] 1 W.L.R. 1425; [1987] Conv. 450 (J.E.M.); (1988) 51 M.L.R. 371 (J. Driscoll). See also *R. v. Wandsworth County Court, ex p. Wandsworth L.B.C.* [1975] 1 W.L.R. 1314 at 1318.

[83] *Haniff v. Robinson* [1993] Q.B. 419.

The section, which binds the Crown,[84] applies to tenancies which are not "statutorily protected"[85] and provides, therefore, a minimum protection for residential tenants who do not have security of tenure. It applies also to tenancies which are restricted contracts within the Rent Act, and where the right to recover possession arises on the death of a statutory tenant within the Rent Act, there being no statutory tenant by succession.[86] It also protects "rental purchasers."[87]

Housing Act 1988

Section 3 was substantially amended by section 30 of the Housing Act 1988 in relation to the categories of tenancy and licence to which the section applies. Section 3 was primarily concerned with tenancies, but extended to two kinds of licensee even before the 1988 amendments. These were a service occupier with exclusive possession[88] and a licensee having a restricted contract within the meaning of the Rent Act 1977.[89] The reason for the inclusion of the latter was that the scheme of the Housing Act 1980 for the protection of restricted contracts was that the court should have a discretion to suspend a possession order for up to three months. It was essential, therefore, the working of this scheme that restricted contracts, whether tenancies or licences, could not be terminated without a court order.

Licences

Now, by section 3(2B) of the 1977 Act, inserted by the Housing Act 1988, the section is extended to any premises occupied as a dwelling under a licence, other than an excluded licence.[89a] This provision applies whether or not the licensee has exclusive occupation.

Excluded tenancies and licences

Section 3A[90] of the 1977 Act contains a list of excluded tenancies and licences which are not protected by the court order requirement of section 3. A tenancy within these categories will be excluded only if entered into after the

---

[84] s. 10.

[85] Defined in s. 8(1) as a protected tenancy under Rent Act 1977, or a tenancy within Landlord and Tenant Act 1954 (Part I or Part II), Agricultural Holdings Act 1986, Agricultural Tenancies Act 1995 or the Rent (Agriculture) Act 1976, an assured tenancy or an assured agricultural occupancy under Housing Act 1988 or a long tenancy within Schedule 10 of the Local Government and Housing Act 1989.

[86] s. 3(3).

[87] Housing Act 1980, s. 152(1) and Sched. 25, para. 61; see below, p. 58.

[88] s. 8(2).

[89] s. 3(2A). Restricted contracts can no longer be entered into.

[89a] See *Mohamed v. Manek, The Times*, April 28, 1995 (s.3 inapplicable to homeless person occupying bed and breakfast accommodation pending inquiries).

[90] Inserted by Housing Act 1988, s. 31. It is an offence to use or threaten violence to secure entry if there is someone present: Criminal Law Act 1977, s. 6, as amended by Criminal Justice and Public Order Act 1994, s. 72.

commencement date of the Housing Act 1988 (and not pursuant to a contract made before that date).[91] A licence, on the other hand, will be excluded if it falls within section 3A whether granted before or after the 1988 Act. There are five exceptions which apply equally to tenancies and licences, and one applicable to licences only. They are as follows:

1 Accommodation shared with owner

Conditions A tenancy or licence is excluded if the following two conditions are satisfied:

(a) under its terms the occupier shares any accommodation[92] with the landlord or licensor (whether or not in common with other persons); and

(b) immediately before the tenancy or licence was granted and also when it ends, the landlord or licensor occupied as his only or principal home premises of which the whole or part of the shared accommodation formed part.

Joint owners In the case of joint landlords or licensors, occupation by any one of them suffices to bring the exception into operation.

2 Accommodation shared with member of owner's family

Conditions A tenancy or licence is excluded if the following three conditions are satisfied:

(a) under its terms the occupier shares accommodation with a member of the family of the landlord or licensor (whether or not in common with other persons);

(b) immediately before the tenancy or licence was granted and when it ends, the member of the family occupied as his only or principal home premises of which the whole or part of the shared accommodation formed part; and

(c) immediately before the tenancy or licence was granted and when it ends, the landlord or licensor occupied as his only or principal home premises in the same building as the shared accommodation and that building is not a purpose-built block of flats.[93]

The meaning of "accommodation" is the same as under

---

[91] Hence existing tenants were not deprived of protection already enjoyed. See also section 8(5) of the 1977 Act, dealing with the question whether a variation in the terms of a tenancy will have the effect of treating the tenancy as granted at the date of the variation (and hence subject to s. 3A).

[92] This does not include any storage area nor any means of access, but is not confined to "living accommodation" within the meaning of Rent Act 1977, s. 22 and Housing Act 1988, s. 3: see below, pp. 63 and 199.

[93] As defined by Housing Act 1988, Sched. 1, para. 22 (resident landlords). This is the same definition as under Rent Act 1977, Sched. 2, para. 4: see below, p. 84.

Meaning of "member of the family"

Resident landlord rules distinguished

exception (1) above. The position as to joint landlords or licensors is also as set out in relation to exception (1). "Member of the family" has the same meaning as under the Housing Act 1985 in relation to succession to a secure tenancy.[94]

It will be appreciated that exceptions (1) and (2) above are narrower than the "resident landlord" exclusions from the protected tenancy code under the Rent Act 1977[95] and the assured tenancy code under the Housing Act 1988.[96] The main difference is that, for the purpose of the resident landlord rule, there need be no actual sharing of any accommodation. To summarise, where a tenancy granted before the commencement date of the Housing Act 1988 falls within the resident landlord provisions of the Rent Act 1977, the tenant will continue to enjoy a restricted contract, which requires a court order for possession under section 3 of the Protection from Eviction Act 1977. Where a tenancy (or licence) is granted after the commencement of the 1988 Act, no court order is required where the conditions of section 3A are satisfied. Where a tenancy is granted by a resident landlord after the commencement of the 1988 Act, the tenant can have neither a restricted contract nor an assured tenancy.[97] But a tenancy within the resident landlord exception of the 1988 Act does not necessarily satisfy the conditions of section 3A. If it does not, a possession order must still be obtained under section 3.

Assured tenancy

If, however, the tenant shares accommodation with a member of the landlord's family, but the landlord himself does not reside at the premises, the tenant may have an assured tenancy, as the resident landlord rules would not be satisfied. In such a case neither section 3 nor 3A would apply, recovery of possession being governed by the assured tenancy rules, which require a possession order (and a ground for possession).[98]

3 Trespassers

A tenancy or licence is excluded if it was granted as a temporary expedient to a person who entered the premises in question or any other premises as a trespasser (whether or not, before the beginning of that tenancy or licence, another tenancy or licence to occupy the premises had been granted to him).[99] This provision will be significant mainly to local authorities.

[94] Housing Act 1985, s. 113.
[95] Rent Act 1977, s. 12, below, p. 83.
[96] Housing Act 1988, Sched. 1, para. 10.
[97] *ibid.* A restricted contract cannot be granted after the Housing Act 1988: s. 36.
[98] Housing Act 1988, s. 5.
[99] The definition, so far as licences are concerned, closely resembles Housing Act 1985, s. 79(4), whereby licences of this type are excluded from the secure tenancy code (which otherwise applies to licences: s. 79(3)).

4 Holiday occupation

A tenancy or licence is excluded if it confers on the tenant or licensee the right to occupy the premises for a holiday only. As we will see, holiday lettings are excluded from the definition of protected tenancies under the Rent Act 1977[1] and assured tenancies under the Housing Act 1988.[2] In neither case is there any definition of "holiday," and the exception has led to widespread attempts at evasion of the Rent Act 1977.[3] Prior to the enactment of section 3A of the Protection from Eviction Act 1977, tenants with holiday lettings had the protection of the court order requirement. The difficulty now is that such tenants (and licensees)[4] will **Evasion** be denied the opportunity of arguing that the exception has been used as an evasion device unless they are willing themselves to initiate the proceedings.

5 Rent free occupation

A tenancy or licence is excluded if it is granted otherwise than for money or money's worth.

6 Hostel occupation

A licence (but not a tenancy) is excluded if it confers rights of occupation in a hostel, within the meaning of the Housing Act 1985, provided by various specified public bodies such as local authorities, the Housing Corporation, and housing trusts which are either charities or registered housing associations.[4a]

Notice to quit

Common law rules At common law a notice to quit, which is required to terminate a periodic tenancy, may be oral.[5] Subject to any agreement to the contrary, its length must correspond to the period of the tenancy, so that, for example, a monthly tenancy requires a month's notice and a weekly tenancy requires a week's notice, expiring in each case at the end of a completed period of the tenancy.[6] The exception is the yearly tenancy, which requires six months' notice, expiring at the end of a completed year of the tenancy.[7]

---

[1] s. 9.
[2] Sched. 1, para. 9.
[3] See below, p. 74.
[4] Holiday occupation by licensees, however, never fell within the court order requirement of s. 3.
[4a] See *Mohamed v. Manek, The Times*, April 28. 1995.
[5] *Timmins v. Rowlinson* (1765) 3 Burr. 1603.
[6] *Lemon v. Lardeur* [1946] K.B. 613.
[7] *Sidebotham v. Holland* [1895] 1 Q.B. 378. By Agricultural Holdings Act 1986, s. 25, a tenancy of an agricultural holding requires a year's notice. Special rules for business tenancies are found in Landlord and Tenant Act 1954, Part II.

Statutory rules

In the case of a dwelling, however, section 5(1) of the 1977 Act provides that a notice to quit given by either landlord or tenant is invalid unless it is in writing and is given not less than four weeks before the date on which it is to take effect.[8] Further, in the case of a landlord's notice, it must contain certain prescribed information.[9] There is no prescribed form as such for the notice, but it must contain the following information (which has been adapted to include licences, as explained below):

Prescribed information

(a) If the tenant or licensee does not leave the dwelling, the landlord or licensor must get a possession order from the court before the tenant or licensee can be lawfully evicted. The landlord or licensor cannot apply for such an order before the notice to quit or notice to determine has run out.

(b) A tenant or licensee who does not know if he has any right to remain in possession after a notice to quit or a notice to determine runs out can obtain advice from a solicitor. Help with all or part of the cost of legal advice and assistance may be available under the Legal Aid Scheme. He should also be able to obtain information from a Citizen's Advice Bureau, a Housing Aid Centre or a Rent Officer.

Joint tenants

Although a notice to quit given by one of the joint tenants (or landlords) is valid at common law,[10] such a notice cannot deprive the other tenant of the benefit of section 5. In *Hounslow L.B.C. v. Pilling*[11] the tenancy agreement provided that the tenants were required to give four weeks' notice "or such lesser period as the council may accept." One of the joint tenants purported to give notice "with immediate effect." This was accepted by the council, which then sought possession from the other tenant. It was held that although the parties to a tenancy cannot contract out of section 5, it is open to a landlord or tenant to accept a notice of less than four weeks. However, this cannot be done to the detriment of a joint landlord or tenant who has not joined in the notice. Thus the notice was invalid.

Section 5 was substantially amended by the Housing Act 1988,[12] first by extending it to certain licensees, and secondly by excepting certain tenancies from its scope.

---

[8] The notice must also satisfy the common law rule concerning expiry at the end of a completed period of the tenancy: *Schnabel v. Allard* [1967] 1 Q.B. 627.

[9] Notices to Quit (Prescribed Information) Regulations 1988 (S.I. 1988 No. 2201).

[10] *Hammersmith and Fulham L.B.C. v. Monk* [1992] 1 A.C. 478.

[11] [1993] 1 W.L.R. 1242; (1994) 53 C.L.J. 227 (L. Tee). The notice was in any event treated as a notice to exercise a break clause, which cannot be given by one of joint tenants.

[12] s. 32.

Extension to
licences   By section 5(1A), no notice by a licensor or a licensee to
determine a periodic licence[13] of premises occupied as a
dwelling (whether granted before or after the passing of the
1988 Act) shall be valid unless it is in writing, contains such
information as is prescribed, and is given not less than four
weeks before the date on which it is to take effect. The
prescribed information has been set out above. By section
5(1B), this rule does not apply to an excluded licence within
the meaning of section 3A of the 1977 Act, for example one
conferring on the licensee the right to occupy the premises
for a holiday.[14]

Excluded   Section 5(1B) also operates to exclude certain tenancies
tenancies   which were previously protected by section 5. These are
excluded tenancies within the meaning of section 3A of the
1977 Act, for example where the tenant shares
accommodation with the landlord who was occupying the
premises as his only or principal home immediately before
the grant of the tenancy and at its end.[15] Such a tenancy is
only excluded if entered into on or after the date on which
the Housing Act 1988 came into force (unless pursuant to a
contract made before that date).[16] This may be contrasted
with excluded licences, which may have been granted before
the Housing Act 1988. This does not involve any
retrospective deprivation of rights in the case of licences, but
would do if applied to tenancies granted before the 1988
Act.

In the case of these excluded tenancies and licences, only
the requirements of the general law as to termination need
be satisfied.[17] It will be appreciated that these exclusions are
the same as those which apply to possession orders under
section 3.

[13] See *Norris v. Checksfield* [1991] 1 W.L.R. 1241 (licence coterminous with
employment not a periodic licence); *Burgoyne v. Griffiths* (1991) 23
H.L.R. 303.
[14] See above, p. 51.
[15] See above, p. 49.
[16] See also s. 8(5) and (6) of the 1977 Act, dealing with the question
whether a variation in the terms of a tenancy granted before the 1988 Act
will cause it to be treated as a new tenancy entered into at the time of the
variation.
[17] See *Smith v. Northside Developments Ltd* (1988) 55 P.&C.R. 164. (Where
the contract makes no express provision, reasonable notice must be
given. This does not necessarily correspond with the period for
payment.)

II The Rent Act 1977

This Part deals with protected tenancies under the Rent Act 1977. Although these cannot as a general rule be granted after the commencement of the Housing Act 1988, existing tenancies are unaffected by the 1988 Act, save in respect of certain modifications to the succession rules.

Even though tenancies under the 1977 Act are being phased out, much of the material examined in this Part remains relevant under the Housing Act 1988. This is particularly so in relation to such matters as the conditions for protected status, the exceptions to protection and the grounds for possession. In these areas the new rules are substantially modelled on the old.

Transitional provisions

There are certain narrow exceptions to the rule that protected tenancies cannot be entered into[1] after the commencement of the 1988 Act.[2] So, for example, a protected tenancy may be granted after the commencement of the 1988 Act in pursuance of a contract made before the commencement, or to a person who was a protected or statutory tenant of the landlord immediately before the grant.[3] It is clear that this exception applies whether the new tenancy is of the same premises or other premises.[4] Doubt has been expressed[5] as to whether the tenancy *must* be protected or whether the landlord is merely *enabled* to grant a new protected tenancy, but this seems unfounded.[6] Where a possession order has been made on the basis of suitable alternative accommodation,[7] a protected tenancy may be granted in respect of the alternative premises where the court so directs.

---

[1] The words "entered into" do not cover the conversion of a protected tenancy into a statutory tenancy. Clearly a statutory tenancy can arise after the 1988 Act; *Ridehalgh v. Horsefield* (1992) 24 H.L.R. 453; [1993] Conv. 238 (S. Bridge).

[2] Housing Act 1988, s. 34.

[3] This exception does not apply to protected shorthold tenancies: s. 34(2). A new grant to such a tenant creates an assured shorthold tenancy: s. 34(3). For the meaning of "immediately before", see *Dibbs v. Campbell* (1988) 20 H.L.R. 374, [1989] Conv. 98 (S. Bridge). See Appendix, p. 283.

[4] (1994) 29 E.G. 114 (K. Walden-Smith); *Goringe v. Twinsectra Ltd* (April 20, 1994, County Court), noted (1994) *Legal Action*, June, p. 11.

[5] (1989) 139 N.L.J. 71 (D. Carter).

[6] See *Kotecha v. Rimington* (January 16, 1991, County Court), noted (1991) *Legal Action*, March, p. 15; *Milnbank Housing Association v. Murdoch* (Sheriff Court), noted (1994) *Legal Action*, December, p. 14 (secure tenancy); *Giddy v. Murray* (December 6, 1994, County Court), noted (1995) *Legal Action*, March, p. 12.

[7] See below, p. 112.

4 THE PROTECTED TENANCY

A protected tenancy is one which, on termination, will become a statutory tenancy, provided the tenant then satisfies the requirements of section 2 of the Rent Act 1977.[1] In other words, it is a tenancy existing under the general law either as a legal estate or an equitable interest. It is sometimes referred to as a contractual tenancy. Such a tenancy cannot be an assured tenancy.[2]

Conditions   There are two basic conditions to be satisfied if a tenancy is to qualify as a protected tenancy. First, by section 1 of the Act of 1977, it must be "a tenancy under which a dwelling-house (which may be a house or part of a house) is let as a separate dwelling." Secondly, it must not fall within any of the express exclusions from protection contained in Part I of the Act.[3] These matters will be considered in turn. It should be added that, although the Rent Act contains no express **No contracting** prohibition on contracting out,[4] it has long been accepted by **out** the courts that it is not possible for the parties to contract out of the statutory protection.[5]

Definition in section 1

Almost every word of this section has been the subject of litigation. It will be convenient to consider in order the main ingredients of the definition.

"Tenancy"

The only statutory definition of "tenancy" in the Act is **Meaning of** simply to the effect that a sub-tenancy is included.[6] It **tenancy** appears, however, that any kind of tenancy is included, whether fixed or periodic, expressly granted or arising by implication or even at will.[7] Even a tenancy by estoppel is within the Act, as far as the parties to the estoppel are

---

[1] See below, p. 91.
[2] Housing Act 1988, Sched. 1, para. 1.
[3] The exceptions are found primarily in ss. 4–16A.
[4] *cf.* Agricultural Holdings Act 1986, ss. 5, 25; Landlord and Tenant Act 1954, s. 38(1); Leasehold Reform Act 1967, s. 23(1).
[5] *Baxter v. Eckersley* [1950] 1 K.B. 480 at 485; *Brown v. Draper* [1944] K.B. 309 at 313. See also *Street v. Mountford* [1985] A.C. 809, where a term reciting that the occupier had no Rent Act tenancy was ineffective. The inability to contract out was also emphasised in *A.G. Securities v. Vaughan* [1990] 1 A.C. 417.
[6] Rent Act 1977, s. 152(1). For the position as between sub-tenant and head landlord, see s. 137; below, Chap. 9.
[7] *Chamberlain v. Farr* [1942] 2 All E.R. 567; *Dunthorne and Shore v. Wiggins* [1943] 1 All E.R. 577; [1987] Conv. 278 at 285 (P. Sparkes).

concerned.[8] No distinction is drawn between properly granted legal tenancies and others. A mere contract for a lease, assuming it to be specifically enforceable, would confer the benefit of the Act on the tenant under the *Walsh v. Lonsdale*[9] principle.

Licences excluded

More significant is the point that a licence cannot come within section 1, although it can in certain circumstances qualify for the more limited protection of the restricted contract code.[10] The question whether an agreement creates a tenancy or a licence was discussed in Chapter 2.

Rental purchase schemes

Another possibility is that the owner may attempt to avoid the Rent Act by entering into a "rental purchase" agreement with the prospective occupier. The purpose of these schemes is that the occupier will be denied the status of tenant. Under such a scheme the occupier agrees to purchase the property by instalments, completion of the purchase being deferred until the purchase price has been paid.[11] It may be that the parties never intend a conveyance, in which case the arrangement is merely a disguised letting and will be treated as such by the courts.[12] In any event, relief is provided in two ways by the Housing Act 1980. First, the Protection from Eviction Act 1977 is extended to cover a rental purchase agreement, so that a court order for possession is required.[13] Secondly, the court is given power in possession proceedings to adjourn the proceedings, stay execution or postpone the date of possession, imposing such conditions as it thinks fit.[14]

"House"

Section 1 requires a tenancy of a dwelling-house, which may be a house or part of a house. There is no statutory definition of "house", [15] but it clearly includes a flat or even a single room.[16]

Impermanent structures

Questions may arise as to impermanent structures, such as caravans[17] or houseboats.[18] This was discussed in *R. v.*

---

[8] *Stratford v. Syrett* [1958] 1 Q.B. 107.
[9] (1882) 21 Ch.D. 9.
[10] See below, p. 80.
[11] See (1972) 36 Conv. (N.S.) 325 (B.M. Hoggett); Yates and Hawkins, *Landlord and Tenant Law* (2nd ed., 1986) p. 471.
[12] *Martin v. Davies* (1952) 7 H.L.R. 120.
[13] Housing Act 1980, Sched. 25, para. 61.
[14] *ibid.* s. 88. A rental purchase agreement is defined in s. 88(4) as one where the purchase price is to be paid in two or more instalments, completion being deferred until the whole or a specified part of the price has been paid.
[15] *cf.* Leasehold Reform Act 1967, s. 2, giving a narrow (and much litigated) definition because there the property must be such that, on enfranchisement, it can exist as a separate freehold.
[16] See *Curl v. Angelo* [1948] 2 All E.R. 189; *cf. Metropolitan Properties Co. v. Barder* [1968] 1 W.L.R. 286.
[17] See also Caravan Sites Act 1968; Mobile Homes Act 1983 (substantially repealing the Act of 1975).
[18] For further examples, see Megarry, *The Rent Acts* (11th ed., 1988) p. 85; Halsbury (4th ed.), Vol. 27, para. 583.

Rent Officer of Nottingham Registration Area, ex p. Allen.[19] Whether a caravan can be a "house" depends on the circumstances of the letting. It would not be a "house" if let as a moveable chattel, but would be more likely to qualify if completely immobile. There would be difficult borderline cases, but the rent officer should be on guard where the landlord rented out caravans long term, but made superficial arrangements to show some mobility in order to avoid the Act. In the present case, movement from time to time and the ease of disconnection of services (*e.g.* water, electricity, sewage) meant that the caravan was not a "house". It was added that the landlord should act before registration of the rent (on the basis of a protected tenancy) rather than seek judicial review later in the High Court.[20]

Two properties let together A different point on the meaning of "house" is that two distinct properties, let together as one home, can qualify as a "house," for example two flats.[21] This is relevant also to the meaning of the words "a separate dwelling," and is discussed below.

"Let"

The meaning of "tenancy" has already been discussed, and nothing further need be added here.

"As"

Purpose of letting The dwelling-house must be let *as* a separate dwelling; in other words, residence must be contemplated by the lease. If the lease is silent on the matter, then the nature of the premises must be considered. If that also fails to reveal the purpose of the letting, then the *de facto* user is looked at as a last resort.

Terms of lease In *Ponder v. Hillman*[22] the lease described the property as "all that shop and premises." The fact that the property was being used as dwelling accommodation at the date of the proceedings did not bring it within the Rent Act, as residence was not contemplated by the lease. *A fortiori* if the lease actually prohibits residential user.[23] However, even though not initially let as a dwelling, the property may subsequently be so treated if the landlord has affirmatively

---

[19] (1986) 52 P.&C.R. 41; [1985] Conv. 353 (J.E.M.).

[20] The county court can declare the status of the tenancy, but cannot expunge the registration.

[21] *Langford Property Co. v. Goldrich* [1949] 1 K.B. 511.

[22] [1969] 1 W.L.R. 1261.

[23] See *Cooper v. Henderson* (1982) 263 E.G. 592, where the prohibition had been openly broken for some years. As the breach was continuing, waiver was not established. The prohibition, it was said, was not a sham to evade the Rent Act.

assented to a change of user. Mere knowledge does not
suffice.[24]

Difficult questions can arise where property is initially let
for more than one purpose.[25] In *Pulleng v. Curran*[26]property
was let for both business and residential purposes, but the
Mixed lettings   tenant claimed that the business user had ceased. It was held
that it had not, but even if it had, it did not follow that the
Rent Act now applied. The property was not let as a
dwelling, but as a mixed entity. Similarly in *Russell v.
Booker*,[27] where a mixed residential and agricultural letting
was initially protected as an agricultural holding. The
agricultural use declined, so that the tenancy ceased to be an
agricultural holding, but this did not bring it within the Rent
Act. A unilateral change of user by the tenant would not
suffice. Here the tenant could only succeed if there was a
subsequent contract, or if the landlord had accepted rent for
many years with full actual knowledge of the change of user.

It may be helpful to summarise briefly the various possible
permutations. First, the question may arise as to the initial
status of the letting. If it is let for a single purpose, then, as
we have seen, the Rent Act can only apply if that purpose is
residential.[28] If it is initially let for a dual purpose, then the
Rent Act is unlikely to apply. In the case of a mixed business
and residential letting, the Landlord and Tenant Act 1954,
Part II, will apply unless the business element is minimal.[29]
If the letting is part residential and part agricultural, then the
Agricultural Holdings Act 1986 will apply if the tenancy is
substantially agricultural.[30]

Change of user   Secondly, the question may arise on a subsequent change
of user. If the letting changes from solely business (or
agricultural) to solely residential, then the Rent Act cannot
apply unless a new contract can be inferred.[31] Similarly, if
the letting is initially for mixed business (or agricultural) and
residential purposes, and the business (or agricultural) user

---

[24] *Wolfe v. Hogan* [1949] 2 K.B. 194.
[25] See generally [1983] Conv. 390 (J. Martin).
[26] (1982) 44 P.&C.R. 58. The initial letting could not be within the Rent
    Act. See Landlord and Tenant Act 1954, s. 23(1); Rent Act 1977,
    s. 24(3). See also *Henry Smith's Charity Trustees v. Wagle* [1990] 1 Q.B.
    42 (letting of artist's residential studio not brought within Rent Act when
    business user ceased); *Webb v. Barnet L.B.C.* [1989] 1 E.G.L.R. 49;
    [1989] Conv. 125 (J.E.M.) (mixed business and residential letting not
    "let as a separate dwelling"); *Kent Coast Property Investments Ltd v. Ward*
    [1990] 2 E.G.L.R. 86 (shop with flat above not within Rent Act).
[27] (1982) 263 E.G. 513. Nor would the Rent Act apply if the residential
    part was separately assigned: *Lester v. Ridd* [1990] 2. Q.B. 430.
[28] *cf.* the business and agricultural codes, where there is no requirement that
    the property be initially let for those specific purposes. See Landlord and
    Tenant Act 1954, s. 23(1); Agricultural Holdings Act 1986, s. 1.
[29] See below, p. 78.
[30] *Russell v. Booker*, above; Agricultural Holdings Act 1986, s. 1; Rent Act
    1977, s. 26. For lettings on or after September 1, 1995 see Agricultural
    Tenancies Act 1995, s. 1.
[31] *Wolfe v. Hogan*, above.

ceases.[32] Finally, the letting may change from an initial sole use to a mixed use. If a residential letting acquires a business element, the 1954 Act will apply unless the business element is minimal.[33] The 1954 Act will also apply where a business letting takes on a residential element.[34] If a residential letting takes on an agricultural element, the Rent Act will continue to apply until the tenancy becomes substantially agricultural and thereby moves into the Agricultural Holdings Act.[35] In the converse case, where an agricultural holding takes on a residential element, the Agricultural Holdings Act continues to apply unless the residential aspect substantially affects the agricultural character of the tenancy, in which case there is no protection at all.[36]

"A"

The house must be let as *a* separate dwelling, meaning one dwelling and not two or more. So in *Horford Investments v. Lambert*[37] the letting of a house already converted to multiple dwelling units was not a protected tenancy. Perhaps a more borderline case is *St Catherine's College v. Dorling*,[38] where a house was let to the college for sub-letting to students. The house contained rooms suitable for use as study/bedsitting rooms by five students who would share the kitchen and bathroom, but it had not been converted to multiple units. The college sought a rent reduction on the basis that the tenancy was protected, but it was held that the Rent Act did not apply. The property was not let as *a* dwelling, but as several. In such cases the sub-tenancies may be protected as against the tenant, even though the tenancy is not itself protected.[39]

Letting of property containing multiple units

The point discussed above involves the situation where one property has been let as several dwellings. The converse case is where two or more properties have been let together as one dwelling. In such a case the tenancy may be protected. In *Langford Property Co. Ltd v. Goldrich*[40] two self-

Two or more properties let together

---

[32] *Pulleng v. Curran*, above; *Russell v. Booker*, above; *Henry Smith's Charity Trustees v. Wagle*, above. See also *Gurton v. Parrott* [1991] 1 E.G.L.R. 98.

[33] *Lewis v. Weldcrest Ltd* [1978] 1 W.L.R. 1107, below p. 78.

[34] *Ponder v. Hillman*, above.

[35] Rent Act 1977, s. 10; Agricultural Holdings Act 1986, s. 1.

[36] By analogy with *Russell v. Booker*, above.

[37] [1976] Ch. 39. Such a tenancy could be within Landlord and Tenant Act 1954, Part II, if there is a sufficient degree of occupation by the tenant: *Lee-Verhulst (Investments) Ltd v. Harwood Trust* [1972] 1 Q.B. 204; *cf. Bagettes Ltd v. G.P. Estates Co. Ltd* [1956] Ch. 290. A subsequent conversion would not cause the tenancy to be outside s. 1; *Carter v. S.U. Carburettor Co.* [1942] 2 K.B. 288. See also *Grosvenor Estates Belgravia v. Cochran* (1992) 24 H.L.R. 98.

[38] [1980] 1 W.L.R. 66. For the possible application of Landlord and Tenant Act 1954, Pt. II, in such a case, see *Groveside Properties Ltd v. Westminster Medical School* (1983) 47 P.&C.R. 507, below p. 73.

[39] Unless the sub-tenancy is a student letting or otherwise excluded. For the position against the head landlord, see Rent Act s. 137(3), below p. 163.

[40] [1949] 1 K.B. 511. For similar problems arising under s. 2, see *Kavanagh v. Lyroudias* [1985] 1 All E.R. 560.

contained flats, which were separately rated and not adjoining, but which were used as one home, were held to constitute one dwelling. This may be contrasted with *Metropolitan Properties Co. Ltd v. Barder*[41] where a protected tenant of a flat was later granted a tenancy of a room across the corridor. The rent was paid by the same cheque. When the landlord gave notice to quit the room, the tenant claimed protection for the room and the flat together. He failed, as the Act could only apply if the room was let with the flat as a single unit, whereas here it was let by a different contract and on different terms. Nor, on the facts, was the room a separate dwelling on its own.

Finally, in *Grosvenor (Mayfair) Estates v. Amberton*[42] two flats were let by the same demise. At that time one was occupied by licensees, with only a remote possibility that the two could be occupied together. There was, however, a covenant to use them as a "strictly private residence." It was held that the covenant did not displace the evidence that they were not let as a separate dwelling. It might have been otherwise if the parties had contemplated the early removal of the licensees and the idea that the tenant would then live in both. In other words, it was not fatal to the argument that the tenant could not get immediate possession of both flats. Here, however, they were let as two flats, subject to the future possibility of their use as one dwelling at an unspecified date. This did not suffice.

"Separate"

Shared accommodation

The question whether a dwelling is "separate" depends primarily on the extent to which any accommodation is shared, and with whom. The occupant must enjoy exclusive possession of some accommodation before there can be a tenancy at all. In addition to the demised premises, however, the tenant may be entitled to share certain rooms, such as a kitchen or bathroom, either with his landlord or with other tenants. These two situations will be considered in turn. It should be noted that the question of sharing under discussion here is sharing under the terms of the tenancy.[43]

Sharing with landlord

As far as sharing with the landlord is concerned, a distinction grew up between "living accommodation" and other accommodation. If the tenant shared "living accommodation" with his landlord, then he was not fully protected, but had the benefit of what is now a restricted contract. If, however, the shared accommodation was not "living accommodation," then the tenant was fully protected. What, then, is meant by "living

---

[41] [1968] 1 W.L.R. 286. See also *Dunnell (R.J.) Property Investments Ltd v. Thorpe* [1989] 2 E.G.L.R. 94; *Tyler v. Royal Borough of Kensington and Chelsea* (1991) 23 H.L.R. 380.

[42] (1983) 265 E.G. 693.

[43] Rent Act 1977, ss. 21–23.

Living accommodation

accommodation"? The basic test is that rooms where simultaneous use is likely are "living" rooms. Thus kitchens[44] and sitting rooms are within the description, whilst, generally speaking, bathrooms[45] and halls are not. Much depends, however, on the extent of the shared user in the particular case.[46] The rationale of this rule is clear: it would be undesirable to confer security of tenure in such cases of sharing, which involve "the right of simultaneous use of a living room in such a manner that the privacy of the landlord or tenant, as the case may be, is invaded."[47] The present rules are contained in section 21 of the 1977 Act, providing that the tenant has a restricted contract in cases where the sharing precludes a protected tenancy.

Resident landlords

Much of the old learning on shared accommodation was made redundant by the introduction of the resident landlord rules by the 1974 Act. These rules, as we will see,[48] operate to give the tenant a restricted contract instead of a protected tenancy, and no security at all in the case of tenancies granted after the Housing Act 1988. The resident landlord rules do not require any element of sharing, but merely that the landlord should be resident in the same building. In the case of sharing, discussed above, there is likely to be a resident landlord.[49] But the old sharing rules remain significant in the context of tenancies granted before the Act of 1974. In such cases the resident landlord rules do not apply retrospectively, provided the tenancy is unfurnished.[50] So in the case of a pre-1974 unfurnished tenancy granted by a resident landlord, the sharing rules must still be considered. It might be added that in the case of tenancies granted after the commencement of the Housing Act 1988, the sharing of accommodation with the landlord or his family may exclude the tenancy from the benefit of the court order and four-week notice to quit rules under the Protection from Eviction Act 1977.[51]

Sharing with other tenants

It remains to consider the position where the tenant, in addition to his separate accommodation, shares other accommodation with persons other than the landlord, for example with other tenants. This situation is dealt with by section 22 of the 1977 Act, providing that the tenant has a protected tenancy of his "separate accommodation" in spite of the sharing element. No distinction is drawn between "living" and other accommodation. Thus a tenancy can be protected even though the tenant has the right to share a

---

[44] *Neale v. Del Soto* [1945] K.B. 144.
[45] *Goodrich v. Paisner* [1957] A.C. 65.
[46] *ibid.*; *Marsh Ltd v. Cooper* [1969] 1 W.L.R. 803.
[47] *Goodrich v. Paisner*, above, at 76.
[48] See below, Chap. 5.
[49] *cf. Marsh Ltd v. Cooper* [1969] 1 W.L.R. 803. It was said in *Gray v. Brown* (1993) 25 H.L.R. 144 that a non-resident landlord can reserve the right to share, which can be genuine even if not exercised. Such a reservation must be unambiguous.
[50] Rent Act 1977, Sched. 24, para. 6.
[51] See above, p. 49.

kitchen or bathroom with other tenants.[52] In addition to protection for his "separate accommodation," section 22 also protects the tenant in the use of the shared accommodation. Any term in his tenancy providing for the

Termination or modification of rights

termination or modification of his right to use any of the shared accommodation which is "living accommodation" is of no effect,[53] save to the extent that it permits a variation in the persons in common with whom the tenant can use the shared accommodation, or an increase in their number.[54] No order for possession of the shared accommodation can be made unless a similar order is being (or has been) made as to the separate accommodation.[55] However, that is without prejudice to the power of the county court, on the landlord's application, to make such order as the court thinks just to terminate the tenant's right to use any of the shared accommodation other than "living accommodation," or to modify his right to use any of the shared accommodation, whether by varying or increasing the number of persons entitled to use it, or otherwise.[56]

"Dwelling"

There is no requirement that the property should be the tenant's own dwelling[57] (although, if it is not, he will not acquire a statutory tenancy[58]). Nor need it to be his sole dwelling.[59]

Meaning of dwelling

The test is whether the major activities of daily living, such as sleeping, eating and cooking, are to take place on the premises. Thus a bedsitting-room with cooking facilities can be a dwelling even though the occupier shares bathroom facilities elsewhere in the building.[60] A room without a cooker can be a "dwelling" if a cooker could easily be installed but the occupier does not wish to have one, preferring to eat cold food or takeaways.[61] In *Wright v. Howell*[62] there was a letting of an unfurnished room with no cooker or water supply. The tenant later installed a cooker. The room was originally a bedroom for the tenant, whose relatives had a flat upstairs, but he later began to sleep

---

[52] See *Gray v. Brown* (1993) 25 H.L.R. 144.
[53] *ibid.* s. 22(3).
[54] *ibid.* s. 22(4).
[55] *ibid.* s. 22(5).
[56] *ibid.* s. 22(6). Such an order can be made only where the terms of the tenancy would permit the termination or modification of the tenant's rights; s. 22(7).
[57] *Feather Supplies Ltd v. Ingham* [1971] 2 Q.B. 348 (where a father took a tenancy for the occupation of his son). See also the cases on company and institutional tenants, below, p. 95.
[58] See below, p. 91.
[59] *Langford Property Co. Ltd v. Tureman* [1949] 1 K.B. 29.
[60] *Westminster City Council v. Clarke* [1992] 2 A.C. 288.
[61] *Palmer v. McNamara* (1991) 23 H.L.R. 168 (holding also that the room was a "dwelling" even though the occupier preferred, because of ill health, to sleep at a friend's house).
[62] (1948) 92 S.J. 26.

upstairs. The tenancy was unprotected, the court emphasising the fact that the tenant no longer slept there.

But the mere fact of sleeping on the premises is insufficient. In *Curl v. Angelo*[63] an hotel-keeper rented two rooms of a house as sleeping accommodation for guests and employees. This was not protected, as a "dwelling" requires more than one residential activity. Thus a bedroom with an en-suite bathroom but with no cooking facilities and where cooking is forbidden is neither a "dwelling-house" nor "let as a separate dwelling",[64] although, as noted above[65] section 22 of the 1977 Act modifies this principle in cases where the tenant shares kitchen facilities with other tenants.

Before leaving the definition of a protected tenancy, the contents of section 26 of the 1977 Act should be noted.

Land or premises let together with a dwelling-house Section 26 provides that any land or premises let together with a dwelling-house shall, unless it consists of agricultural land exceeding two acres, be treated as part of the dwelling-house. The circumstances here envisaged are that the dwelling is the main part of the letting, the other land or premises being ancillary.[66] The effect of this provision is basically threefold. First, if the tenant has security as to his house, his security extends to property let with it, such as garages, gardens or outhouses.[67] Secondly, when considering the rateable value limits,[68] the entire property must be brought into account and not just the house. Thirdly, neglect of the ancillary property can be the basis of a ground for possession in the same manner as neglect of the house.[69] The relevant time for considering whether the property is ancillary to the house (or vice versa) is the date of the application to court (or, possibly, the hearing) as opposed to the date of the letting.[70]

Tenancies excluded from protection

Assuming that the tenancy qualifies under section 1 as the letting of a house as a separate dwelling, it may nevertheless be excluded from protection by the express exceptions primarily contained in sections 4 to 16A of the 1977 Act.

---

[63] [1948] 2 All E.R. 189. See also *Lyons v. Caffery* (1983) 266 E.G. 213, below, p. 85.

[64] *Central YMCA Housing Association v. Saunders* (1991) 23 H.L.R. 212; *Central YMCA Housing Association Ltd and St Giles Hotel Ltd v. Goodman* (1992) 24 H.L.R. 109. (These decisions concern the secure tenancy regime of the Housing Act 1985, which has no equivalent to R.A. 1977, s. 22.)

[65] p. 63.

[66] Contrast s. 6, below, p. 69, as to dwelling-houses let together with other land.

[67] *Langford Property Co. Ltd v. Batten* [1951] A.C. 233; *Bradshaw v. Smith* (1980) 255 E.G. 699.

[68] See below.

[69] *Holloway v. Povey* (1984) 271 E.G. 195 (neglect of the garden). See Case 3, below, p. 119.

[70] *Russell v. Booker* (1982) 263 E.G. 513.

Many of the exclusions operate also in the context of assured tenancies under the Housing Act 1988, as discussed in Part III. Some of the exceptions (such as business lettings) are based on the use of the property. Others (such as lettings with board or at a low rent) depend on the terms of the tenancy. Or the exclusion may depend on the status of the landlord (for example Crown or local authority lettings) or of the tenant (as with student lettings). Some of the excluded tenancies will be protected by other statutory codes. It is proposed to deal with them in the order of the Act.

Tenancies above the rent or rateable value limits

The tenancy is excluded if the demised property exceeded the rateable value limits on the "appropriate day." By section 25(3), the "appropriate day" is March 23, 1965 if the property was then rated, or in any other case (*i.e.* where the property was built after that date) the date it first appeared in the valuation list. Where the demised property is only part of a house, the rateable value of that part alone is considered. In such a case the rateable value of the house must be apportioned.[71]

Rateable value limits   In the following statement of the rateable value limits, the higher figure in each pair relates to Greater London.[72] The limits are set out in section 4, and are as follows:

(a)   if the appropriate day is on or after April 1, 1973[73] the limit is £1,500 or £750;

(b)   if the appropriate day is on or after March 22, 1973[74] but before April 1, 1973, the tenancy is excluded if the rateable value exceeded £600 or £300 on the appropriate day *and* exceeded £1,500 or £750 on April 1, 1973;

(c)   if the appropriate day is before March 22, 1973, the tenancy is excluded if the rateable value exceeded £400 or £200 on the appropriate day *and* exceeded £600 or £300 on March 22, 1973 *and* exceeded £1,500 or £750 on April 1, 1973.

The complexity of these rules results primarily from the rating revaluation which took place in 1973. A dwelling-house is deemed to be within the rateable value limits unless **Alteration in valuation list**   the contrary is shown.[75] Where the valuation list is altered after the appropriate day with effect from a date not later than the appropriate day, then the value as altered is taken.[76]

[71] Rent Act 1977, s. 25(1).

[72] *ibid.* s. 4(2).

[73] The date the revised rating assessments under s. 68 of the General Rate Act 1967 took effect.

[74] The date the Counter-Inflation Act 1973 was passed.

[75] Rent Act 1977, s. 4(3); *R. v. Westminster (City) London Borough Rent Officer, ex p. Rendall* [1973] 1 Q.B. 859. Disputes go to the county court: Rent Act 1977, s. 25(2).

[76] *ibid.* s. 25(4). See *Rodwell v. Gwynne Trusts* [1970] 1 W.L.R. 327; *Guestheath Ltd v. Mirza* (1990) 22 H.L.R. 399.

Abolition of domestic rates   Domestic rating was abolished on April 1, 1990 and replaced by the community charge, itself since replaced by council tax. The rules discussed above continue to apply to tenancies granted before the abolition of rating. In the rare cases where protected tenancies can be granted on or after the date of abolition[77] the high rateable value exclusion is replaced by the rule that a tenancy cannot be protected if **High rent**   the current rent exceeds £25,000 a year.[78]

These rent and rateable value limits are fairly high. It is unusual for a tenancy to be excluded on this ground. The rationale of the exception is clear: tenants of expensive properties do not need the protection of the Rent Act.

Tenancies at a low rent

By section 5, a tenancy is not protected if it is either rent-free,[79] or if the rent is less than two-thirds of the rateable value on the appropriate day (as defined above).

Exclusion of long leases at ground rents   The main purpose of this provision is to exclude long leases from the Rent Act. Long-leaseholders normally pay a premium and, thereafter, a ground rent, which will usually be less than two-thirds of the rateable value on the appropriate day. Such tenancies do not need the protection of the Rent Act, because they are protected by the similar provisions of Part I of the Landlord and Tenant Act 1954 (and sometimes by the Leasehold Reform Act 1967 or the Leasehold Reform, Housing and Urban Development Act 1993). However, there is no exclusion of long leases as such from the Rent Act. If the rent exceeds the two-thirds figure, the tenancy will, therefore, be protected.

Current rent relevant   While the rateable value is fixed at the appropriate day, the rent level is determined when the matter arises. In other words it is the current rent which must be at least two-thirds of the fixed rateable value figure. Thus a tenancy can fall out of protection if a rent reduction takes it below the two-thirds figure.[80] Similarly, a rent increase can bring the tenancy into protection.

Abolition of domestic rates   The above rules apply to tenancies granted before the abolition of domestic rating on April 1, 1990. In the rare cases where protected tenancies can be granted on or after that date[81] the exclusion applies to tenancies where there is

---

[77] See Housing Act 1988, s. 34; above, p. 55.
[78] R.A. 1977, s. 4, as amended by S.I. 1990/434, pursuant to Local Government and Housing Act 1989, s. 149. See also s. 4(5) ("rent" does not include service charges, insurance and so forth) and s. 4(6) (tenancy deemed protected unless contrary shown).
[79] Such a tenancy, if granted after the commencement of the Housing Act 1988, is an "excluded tenancy" for the purposes of the Protection from Eviction Act 1977, see above, p. 51.
[80] See *Williams v. Khan* (1982) 43 P.&C.R. 1, noted at [1980] Conv. 389–392 and [1981] Conv. 325–326, where the view is taken that rent "payable" under s. 5 means the contractual rent, so that a reduction in the registered rent by the Rent Officer would not cause the protection to cease.
[81] See Housing Act 1988, s. 34; above, p. 55.

either no rent or the current rent does not exceed £1,000 a year in Greater London or £250 elsewhere.[82]

Meaning of rent   What is meant by "rent" for the purpose of section 5? If no monetary rent is paid, services can constitute rent at common law, but can only be rent for Rent Act purposes if quantifiable. So if a tenant who is an employee of the landlord pays no rent but is paid a smaller wage on that account, his tenancy can be protected, the rent being the amount by which his wages have been reduced.[83] Where money payments are described as "rent", this label is not conclusive, although the court will normally accept it. If the payments in fact represent a contribution towards shared outgoings, they will not be rent.[84]

Another point is that "rent," for the purpose of section 5, means the total money payment payable by the tenant to the landlord.[85] In the case of long tenancies (exceeding 21 years), however, section 5(4) provides that "rent" does not include any sums payable by the tenant which are expressed to be payable in respect of services, repairs, insurance and so forth. The purpose of this provision is to prevent a long tenancy being brought into the Rent Act by an increase in the service charge.[86]

A premium, if genuine, is not "rent," but a sum described as a premium may be treated as rent if it is a sham device to evade the Rent Act, as is likely to be the case where a premium is payable on the grant of a short lease. In *Samrose Properties v. Gibbard*[87] a short lease was granted at a "premium" and a nominal rent. It was held that the "premium" was in fact rent, so that the tenancy was protected.

Shared ownership leases

Under section 5A[88] qualifying shared ownership leases are excluded from the operation of the Rent Act. These are leases granted under Part V of the Housing Act 1985[89] or

---

[82] R.A. 1977, s. 5, as amended by S.I. 1990/434, pursuant to Local Government and Housing Act 1989, s. 149.
[83] *Montagu v. Browning* [1954] 1 W.L.R. 1039; *cf. Barnes v. Barratt* [1970] 2 Q.B. 657, where the services were unquantifiable.
[84] *Bostock v. Bryant* (1991) 61 P.&C.R. 23 (no "rent" where occupiers sharing with owner paid gas and electricity bills while owner paid rates and water rates); [1991] Conv. 270 (R. Lee).
[85] *Sidney Trading Co. Ltd v. Finsbury B.C.* [1952] 1 All E.R. 460 at 461.
[86] This would result in the tenant being unable to charge a premium on assignment, subject to Rent Act 1977, s. 127, below, p. 189. See *Investment & Freehold English Estates Ltd v. Casement* [1988] 1 E.G.L.R. 100.
[87] [1958] 1 W.L.R. 235.
[88] Introduced by Housing and Planning Act 1986, s. 18 and Sched. 4.
[89] Such leases can no longer be granted under the 1985 Act; Leasehold Reform, Housing and Urban Development Act 1993, s. 107.

Meaning of shared ownership leases granted by a housing association and complying with certain conditions set out in section 5A(2). Broadly speaking, these are long tenancies (99 years or more) where the tenant has paid a premium representing a proportion of the value of the dwelling-house, and under the terms of which the tenant may acquire additional shares in it. Effectively the tenant has purchased a share, and is renting the remainder pending acquisition of further shares. Hence ownership is shared between the landlord and tenant. The purpose of the exclusion is to prevent the system of rent control under the Rent Act from applying, and to ensure that the tenant cannot rely on the provisions of the Rent Act instead of the terms of the lease, for example on default.

Tenancy of a dwelling-house let together with other land

Section 6 provides that, subject to section 26, a tenancy is not protected if the dwelling-house is let together with land other than the site of the dwelling-house. Section 26, as we have seen,[90] provides that land or premises let together with the dwelling-house shall be treated as part of it save in the case of agricultural land exceeding two acres. The distinction between these two provisions lies in the meaning of "let together with." Section 26 refers to other property which is ancillary to the dwelling. Section 6 deals with the **Dwelling ancillary to other property** converse case, where the dwelling is ancillary to some other property which is the main subject of the letting.[91] Thus in *Feyereisal v. Turnidge*[92] the Rent Act did not apply to a letting of a campsite which included a bungalow, because the bungalow was an adjunct to the campsite. The relevant time for deciding what is the dominant purpose of the letting is the date of the application to court (or, possibly, the hearing), and not the start of the tenancy.[93]

A dwelling-house can be "let together with" other property (or vice versa) even though the lettings are not in the same document.[94] Nor need the properties be contiguous.[95] The tenant's position is not changed by the fact that there is a subsequent severance of the reversion, so that there are different landlords of the dwelling and the other property.[96]

It should be added, however, that most of the case law on section 6 deals with mixed lettings of business and residential property. Such lettings could formerly exist as

[90] See above, p. 65.
[91] *cf.* Housing Act 1988, s. 2; below, p. 198.
[92] [1952] 2 Q.B. 29.
[93] *Russell v. Booker* (1982) 263 E.G. 513.
[94] *Wimbush v. Cibulia* [1949] 2 K.B. 564.
[95] *Langford Property Co. v. Batten* [1951] A.C. 223 (flat and garage).
[96] *Jelley v. Buckman* [1974] Q.B. 488.

Effect of business user controlled tenancies, but cannot be regulated tenancies. Any element of business user (which is more than *de minimis*) brings the tenancy within Part II of the Landlord and Tenant Act 1954. Such a tenancy cannot, therefore, be protected, irrespective of section 6.

Subtenants Finally, although the tenancy of a dwelling let together with other property cannot be protected, any sub-tenancy of the dwelling-house alone can be protected as against the tenant and possibly as against the head landlord.[97]

Tenancies with board or attendance

A tenancy is not protected if the dwelling-house is bona fide let at a rent which includes payments in respect of board or attendance.[98] While any payments (which are not *de minimis*) in respect of board exclude the tenancy from protection, payments in respect of attendance do not have this result unless the amount of rent fairly attributable to attendance, having regard to the value of the attendance to the tenant, forms a substantial part of the rent.[99]

Restricted contracts A tenancy excluded from protection by section 7 can be a restricted contract unless, in the case of board, the payments form a substantial proportion of the rent.[1] Thus no tenancy with board can be regulated. If the payments for board are less than substantial, it can be a restricted contract. If they are substantial, the tenancy is outside the Act altogether. In the case of attendance, however, the tenancy is regulated if the payments for it are less than substantial, otherwise it is a restricted contract. It is never outside the Act altogether. These matters are decided as at the date of the grant of the tenancy.

The rationale of the rule is that it would be unduly onerous if a landlord who was obliged by the terms of the tenancy[2] to provide these services should have to provide them indefinitely to a tenant with security of tenure. However, the lack of definition of "board" and "attendance" gave rise to the possibility of evasion.

As the dwelling must be a bona fide let at a rent including payments for board and attendance, clearly these services must be genuinely provided, otherwise the term is **Meaning of** disregarded as a sham.[3] Apart from that, the section **board** contains little guidance. Clearly there is no requirement of full board, but it must be more than *de minimis* (for example,

---

[97] Rent Act 1977, s. 137(3), below, p. 163.
[98] *ibid.* s. 7(1). See also s. 23. Of course, the provision of board and attendance can indicate a licence only, but there is no reason why a tenancy cannot be created with such terms.
[99] *ibid.* s. 7(2).
[1] *ibid.* s. 19(5).
[2] s. 7 does not apply if the board or attendance are voluntarily provided.
[3] *Palser v. Grinling* [1948] A.C. 291; *Wilkes v. Goodwin* [1923] 2 K.B. 86.

an early morning cup of tea.[4]) The matter was examined by the House of Lords in *Otter v. Norman*,[5] where the property had a communal basement dining room with a kitchen staffed by the landlord's employees. The tenants were provided with a "continental breakfast" consisting of rolls with butter and jam, tea or coffee, milk for cereals provided by the tenants, and a glass of milk to take up to their rooms. No question was raised as to the bona fides of the arrangement, which was not regarded as an artificial device. It was held that this meal came within the meaning of "board,"[6] so as to exclude the tenants from protection. In reaching this conclusion their Lordships adopted the views of the majority in *Wilkes v. Goodwin*,[7] which Parliament had not interfered with in the ensuing 65 years. "Board" was subject to an implicit requirement that ancillary services involved in preparing the meal and providing crockery and cutlery were included.[8] Their Lordships did not consider that the exception would appeal to unscrupulous landlords as a "soft option" in view of the cost of the food and the housekeeping chores involved in preparing, serving and clearing up after the admittedly modest meal.

Ancillary services

Meaning of attendance

"Attendance" means the provision of services which are personal to the tenant, such as cleaning his room, supplying clean linen, delivering his mail, or taking away his refuse.[9] It does not embrace services performed for lessees in common, such as cleaning the common parts or providing central heating.[10] In *Marchant v. Charters*[11] the occupier of a room in a residential hotel could get a meal from the housekeeper, and was entitled to the provision of clean linen and the cleaning of his room. He was held, in fact, to be a licensee, but even if there had been a tenancy, it would not have been protected because these services constituted substantial attendance.

Meaning of substantial

Many of the authorities on the meaning of "substantial" were decided before the Rent Act 1974, at a time when substantial payments for furniture also took the tenancy out of protection. While this is no longer the case, the decisions on furnished lettings remain useful guides as to the meaning

---

[4] *Wilkes v. Goodwin*, above; *cf. R. v. Battersea, Wandsworth, Mitcham and Wimbledon Rent Tribunal, ex p. Parikh* [1957] 1 W.L.R. 410, suggesting that a sandwich is "board."

[5] [1989] A.C. 129; (1988) 51 M.L.R. 645 (C.P. Rodgers). Similarly in Scotland: *Holiday Flat Co. v. Kuczera*, 1978, S.L.T. (Sh. Ct.) 47; *cf.* the county court decision in *Dale (Rita) v. Adrahill and Ali Khan* [1982] C.L.Y. 1787 (held no board where breakfast was available in a different building 250 yards away, and not everyone took breakfast).

[6] The definition was taken from the *Shorter Oxford English Dictionary* (3rd ed.).

[7] Above.

[8] Hence the provision of groceries or vending machines would not suffice.

[9] See *Nelson Developments Ltd v. Taboada* (1992) 24 H.L.R. 462.

[10] *Palser v. Grinling*, above.

[11] [1977] 1 W.L.R. 1181.

of "substantial" in the context of attendance. A broad, non-arithmetical approach is the correct one.[12]

Housing Act 1988

The "board and attendance" exception is not preserved by the Housing Act 1988. New lettings of this kind will, therefore, fall within the assured tenancy code if all the other conditions are satisfied, while lettings in existence before the 1988 Act continue to be excluded from the protected tenancy code.

Student lettings

Section 8, re-enacting a provision introduced by the 1974 Act, excludes from protection a tenancy granted to a person "who is pursuing, or intends to pursue, a course of study[13]

Institutional lettings only

provided by a specified[14] educational institution." The tenancy must be granted by that institution or by another specified institution or body of persons. The time for determining the applicability of section 8 is the grant of the tenancy.

The purpose of the exception is to prevent security of tenure of college accommodation arising in favour of former students, to the detriment of the current student population. Such lettings may, if granted before the Housing Act 1988, fall within the restricted contract code, from which they are not expressly excluded.

Another result of section 8 is that where the property is subject to such student lettings during part of the year, the institution can let the property at other times, *i.e.* during the

Vacation lettings

vacation, with the benefit of a mandatory ground to recover possession on termination of the vacation letting.[15] This is also the position under the Housing Act 1988.[16]

The specified institutions include universities, colleges and certain institutions for higher education. Private landlords are not within this section, as they are not within the policy of the exception, although it might be argued that the student accommodation shortage would be eased if

Scheme for private landlords

private lettings were similarly treated. However, a private landlord can indirectly obtain the benefit of the section by letting to the educational institution with a covenant against sub-letting except on excluded student lettings. The letting to the institution may be a protected tenancy, and therefore subject to rent control, but cannot become a statutory tenancy on termination, because an institution cannot "reside."[17] On termination of the head lease, the student

---

[12] *Palser v. Grinling*, above; *Woodward v. Docherty* [1974] 1 W.L.R. 966; *Nelson Developments Ltd v. Taboada*, above.

[13] It is not clear whether taking a sabbatical year, for example to carry out Students' Union activities, would be included.

[14] By statutory instrument: s. 8(2). See the Assured and Protected Tenancies (Lettings to Students) Regulations 1988 (S.I. 1988 No. 2236) and annual amendments, most recently S.I. 1993 No. 2390.

[15] Rent Act 1977, Sched. 15, Case 14; see below, p. 133.

[16] Housing Act 1988, Sched. 1, para. 8; Sched. 2, Ground 4.

[17] See below, p. 95.

sub-tenants will have no security against the head landlord.[18] Such a scheme is illustrated by *St Catherine's College v. Dorling*,[19] where, however, even the head tenancy was unprotected because, on the facts, the house was not let "as a separate dwelling." Such schemes are not frowned upon as evasion devices, but rather encouraged as easing the student accommodation shortage.[20]

The implications in the decision in *Groveside Properties Ltd v. Westminster Medical School*[21] for these private landlord schemes should, however, be noted. In that case a furnished flat was let to the school to house its students. The school paid the outgoings and kept keys, and the School Secretary

Possibility of business tenancy made frequent visits. The school's tenancy was held to be a business tenancy within Part II of the Landlord and Tenant Act 1954. The school had a sufficient degree of occupation, and the running of the medical school was within the statutory definition of "business" which, by section 23(2), includes any "activity" by a body of persons. While, of course, the medical school was not run on the demised premises, the fostering of a collegiate spirit was carried on there, and this was part of the education process. So the landlord avoided the Rent Act, but found itself subject to the 1954 Act, under which the tenant, while having to pay the market rent, has security of tenure. Of course it is not argued that all such student lettings will qualify as business tenancies as a result of this case, but the landlord should be aware of the possible application of the 1954 Act.

Halls of residence Finally, it might be added that the occupation of a college hall of residence is not likely to be a protected tenancy even apart from section 8. First, it is more likely to be a licence than a tenancy, and secondly, even if a tenancy, it is likely to be excluded by section 7 (board and attendance).

Holiday lettings

Like student lettings, this exception was first introduced by the 1974 Act. The current provision is section 9 of the 1977 Act, whereby a tenancy is not protected "if the purpose of the tenancy is to confer on the tenant the right to occupy the dwelling-house for a holiday." Such lettings are also excluded from the restricted contract code.[22]

Out of season lettings As in the case of student lettings, where the property is subject to a holiday letting for part of the year, the landlord can let the property at other times, *i.e.* out of season, with the benefit of a mandatory ground to recover possession on

---

[18] See Rent Act 1977, s. 137, below, p. 156. Sub-tenants who are not protected as against the tenant are not within s. 137.
[19] [1980] 1 W.L.R. 66; see above, p. 61.
[20] *ibid.*
[21] (1983) 47 P.&C.R. 507; [1984] Conv. 57 (J.E.M.).
[22] Rent Act 1977, s. 19(7).

termination of the out of season letting.[23] This continues to be the case under the Housing Act 1988.[24]

Meaning of holiday

The lack of a statutory definition of "holiday" has encouraged attempts at evasion by landlords. Of course, most cases of holiday occupation do not involve tenancies. Even if they do, it might be argued that the property is not let as a *dwelling*. However that may be, the problem is to know what is meant by a holiday letting. The leading case is *Buchmann v. May*,[25] involving a three-month letting to an Australian national with a temporary visitor's permit. She had already occupied for about two years under a series of short lettings. The document, signed by the tenant, stated that the letting was "solely for the purpose of the tenant's holiday in the London area." The Court of Appeal took the dictionary meaning of "holiday" as "a period of cessation from work or a period of recreation" as a workable

Onus on tenant to establish sham

definition, if not too narrowly construed. It was held that where the tenancy is stated to be for a holiday, the onus is upon the tenant to establish that the document is a sham, or the result of a mistake or misrepresentation, adding that the court would be astute to detect a sham where it appeared that the term had been inserted to deprive the tenant of Rent Act protection. On the facts, the tenant failed to discharge this onus, so the tenancy was not protected.

The tenants succeeded in *R. v. Rent Officer for the London Borough of Camden, ex p. Plant*,[26] involving a letting for six months, where it was held that the landlord could not have genuinely intended a holiday letting when he knew that the tenants would occupy for the purpose of their work as student nurses. The tenant might also succeed if, being a foreigner with language difficulties, he can show that he did not understand the terms of the lease.[27]

It has been held in the county court that the common concept of a "working holiday" is included in the meaning of "holiday."[28] It should be added that disputes as to the status of the tenancy frequently arise upon an attempt to register a "fair rent." The jurisdiction of the rent officer in such a case is discussed in Chapter 10.[29]

It should be added that holiday lettings entered into on or after the commencement of the Housing Act 1988 are

---

[23] *ibid.* Sched. 15, Case 13.
[24] Housing Act 1988, Sched. 1, para. 9; Sched. 2, Ground 3.
[25] [1978] 2 All E.R. 993.
[26] (1980) 257 E.G. 713. See also *R. v. Rent Officer for Camden, ex p. Ebiri* [1981] 1 W.L.R. 881.
[27] See *Francke v. Hakmi* (unreported), discussed in [1984] Conv. 286 (T.J. Lyons).
[28] *McHale v. Daneham* (1979) 249 E.G. 969 (six months' letting, extended to nine months, of property in Maida Vale, to foreign tenants); *cf. R. v. Croydon and South West London Rent Tribunal, ex p. Ryzewska* [1977] Q.B. 876. For an examination of various county court and unreported cases, see [1984] Conv. 286 (T.J. Lyons).
[29] See below, p. 185. See particularly *R. v. Rent Officer for Camden, ex p. Ebiri*, above.

"excluded tenancies" for the purposes of the Protection from Eviction Act 1977, which means that (in addition to exclusion from assured status) they do not get the benefit of the court order and four-week notice to quit rules.[30]

Agricultural tenancies

A tenancy is not protected if the dwelling is comprised in an agricultural holding or farm business tenancy[31] and is occupied by the person responsible for the control of the farming of the holding.[32] Such tenancies are protected by the agricultural legislation. The applicability of this exception is judged as at the date of the application to court.[33] Unlike the Rent Act, the Agricultural Holdings Act does not require that the letting be initially for agricultural purposes. Hence it is possible for a tenancy to move out of Rent Act protection on a subsequent change to agricultural user, but the converse is not possible.[34]

Sub-tenants   If a dwelling which is part of an agricultural holding or farm business tenancy sublet, the sub-tenant may be protected against the tenant, and against the head landlord.[35]

Tenancies granted by resident landlords

Resident landlords   Such tenancies are excluded from protection by section 12, but are within the restricted contract code if granted before the Housing Act 1988. They are fully discussed in Chapter 5.

Crown lettings

Such lettings were formerly excluded by section 13 of the 1977 Act, but this was amended by section 73 of the Housing Act 1980. The present position is that a tenancy is excluded where the interest of the immediate landlord belongs to the Crown or to a government department, but can be protected where the interest of the immediate **Exceptions to** landlord belongs to the Duchies of Lancaster or Cornwall, **rule** or is under the management of the Crown Estate Commissioners. The 1980 amendment applies retrospectively, provided the tenancy was still in existence when it came into effect.[36]

[30] See above, pp. 47 and 51.
[31] Agricultural Holdings Act 1986, s. 1; Agricultural Tenancies Act 1995, s. 1.
[32] Rent Act 1977, s. 10, as amended by the 1995 Act. A farm business tenancy cannot be created before September 1, 1995, thus the exclusion is of minimal application.
[33] *Russell v. Booker* (1982) 263 E.G. 513; [1983] Conv. 390 (J. Martin).
[34] *Russell v. Booker*, above, discussed above, at p. 60.
[35] Rent Act 1977, s. 137(3), reversing *Maunsell v. Olins* [1975] A.C. 373; Agricultural Tenancies Act 1995, Sched., para. 28.
[36] *Crown Estate Commissioners v. Wordsworth* (1982) 44 P.&C.R. 302. As to tenancies of health service property, see National Health Service and Community Care Act 1990, s. 60 and Sched. 8, para. 19.

Sub-tenants

The fact that the head landlord is the Crown does not preclude a protected tenancy in favour of a sub-tenant, as against the tenant.

As the application of section 13 depends on the current ownership of the landlord's interest, as opposed to the circumstances at the grant of the tenancy, a tenancy can become, or cease to be, protected on an assignment of the landlord's interest by or to the Crown, as the case may be.

Transfer of reversion

Local authority lettings

Transfer of reversion

Section 14 excludes a tenancy from protection when the interest of the immediate landlord belongs at any time to a local authority (or to various other bodies, such as the Commission for the New Towns). As with Crown lettings, the matter is not judged as at the grant of the tenancy, but depends upon the current ownership of the reversion. Hence the tenant's status can be changed by a transfer of the reversion.[37] Thus a subtenant who had a protected tenancy as against the tenant became a secure tenant on surrender of the head lease to the local authority landlord.[38]

Since the Housing Act 1980 (now Part IV of the 1985 Act) it is possible for local authority tenants to have security of tenure under the concept of the "secure tenancy." Such tenancies are outside the scope of this book.

Housing association tenancies

Tenancies are excluded by section 15 at any time when the interest of the immediate landlord belongs to certain housing associations, housing trusts, the Housing Corporation or Housing for Wales.[39] "Housing association" and "housing trust" are defined by the section.[40]

Housing association tenancies formerly came within the secure tenancy code. The special regime for housing association tenancies has been removed by the Housing Act 1988 with respect to lettings after its commencement.[41] Such tenancies are not excluded from the assured tenancy code.

Housing co-operative tenancies

Similarly excluded, by section 16, are tenancies in respect of which the immediate landlord's interest at any time belongs to a housing co-operative, as defined by the Housing Act 1985.

---

[37] See Housing Act 1985, s. 109A, providing that if a local authority becomes landlord of a statutory tenant, the tenancy is treated as a contractual tenancy on the same terms, so that Part IV of the 1985 Act (secure tenancies) applies. See also Housing Act 1988, s. 35(5).
[38] *Basingstoke and Deane Borough Council v. Paice, The Times,* April 3, 1995.
[39] Housing Act 1988, Sched. 17, para. 99.
[40] As amended by Housing (Consequential Provisions) Act 1985, Sched. 2.
[41] Housing Act 1988, s. 35.

Such tenancies may qualify as "secure tenancies" under section 28 of the 1985 Act.

Assured tenancies

Old assured tenancies

The "old style"[42] assured tenancies were introduced by the Housing Act 1980, with a view to encouraging investment in new housing for letting in the private sector. They were residential tenancies which were excluded from the Rent Act,[43] but which had a system of security of tenure modelled on the business tenancy code. The incentive to the landlord was that a market rent was payable.

An assured tenancy was one which would otherwise qualify as a protected (or housing association) tenancy but for its exclusion from those codes, and which satisfied certain conditions, broadly that the property was newly built or improved and that the landlord was a body such as a housing association, pension fund or financial institution.

Conversion to new assured tenancies

These "old-style" assured tenancies cannot be granted after the commencement of the Housing Act 1988. Those existing at that time were converted to "new-style" assured tenancies under the 1988 Act.[44]

Tenancies of premises with a business use

Section 24 of the 1977 Act provides that a tenancy cannot be regulated if it is a tenancy to which Part II of the Landlord and Tenant Act 1954 applies.[45]

Mixed lettings

Prior to the Housing Act 1980, a tenancy of a dwelling with a partial business use could be within the Rent Act as a controlled (but not a regulated) tenancy. Upon the abolition of controlled tenancies by the 1980 Act, these mixed user tenancies became business tenancies within the 1954 Act, which does not require the tenancy to be solely for business purposes.[46]

In order to qualify as a business tenancy (and thereby be excluded from the Rent Act), the tenancy need not have been initially let for business purposes. All that is required is that the tenancy includes premises which are occupied by the tenant for the purposes of a business carried on by him,

[42] To distinguish them from assured tenancies under the Housing Act 1988; see below, Chap. 11.
[43] s. 16A, now repealed by Housing Act 1988, Sched. 18.
[44] Housing Act 1988, ss. 1(3), 37. There is no conversion if the landlord is the Crown or a local authority; s. 1(4).
[45] On-licensed premises have been brought within the 1954 Act by the Landlord and Tenant (Licensed Premises) Act 1990. Such tenancies are now excluded from the Rent Act by s. 24 of the 1977 Act, leaving s. 11 (exclusion of on-licensed premises) with no scope for operation.
[46] Landlord and Tenant Act 1954, s. 23(1).

Meaning of business

or for those and other purposes.[47] "Business" is defined as including "a trade, profession or employment," and including "any activity carried on by a body of persons whether corporate or unincorporate."[48]

Clearly a tenancy cannot be within the Rent Act unless, by section 1, it is a tenancy of a house let as a dwelling. So, as we have seen, a letting for business purposes cannot be a protected tenancy even though the tenant uses it for residence.[49] Nor can such a tenancy become protected if the business use is abandoned.[50]

Degree of business use

Where a tenancy is initially within the Rent Act, it will cease to be a protected tenancy if a business use develops, unless the business element can be regarded as insignificant. In *Lewis v. Weldcrest*[51] the tenant, an elderly woman, took in five lodgers at little or no profit, primarily for company. Whether such an activity was a "business" was a question of degree, to which decisions on user covenants were not relevant. No single factor was decisive, but the number of lodgers, the money charged and the size of the house were relevant. It was held that the tenant remained within the Rent Act, it being significant that she derived no commercial advantage from the arrangement. Of course, the tenant would continue to have security of tenure even if the tenancy had moved into the business code, but would have had to pay a higher rent, the market rent payable under business tenancies being higher than the Rent Act "fair rent." The result was similar in *Royal Life Saving Society v. Page*,[52] where the tenant was a doctor. He used the demised property as his home and had consulting rooms nearby. The landlord agreed that he could see patients at home occasionally. In fact he only saw one or two patients a year there, in emergency. It was held that the business activity was incidental and insignificant, hence it was a protected tenancy. Decided with this case was another, which fell on the other side of the line. In *Cheryl Investments Ltd v. Saldanha*,[53] a flat was let to a tenant who was a partner in a business with no trade premises. The tenant worked at home, installing office equipment and receiving frequent business visitors. Although initially within the Rent Acts, as soon as the tenant equipped the premises for business the 1954 Act applied, thereby excluding the Rent Act.

---

[47] *ibid.* The business user must not be unlawful: s. 23(4).
[48] Landlord and Tenant Act 1954, s. 23(2).
[49] *Ponder v. Hillman* [1969] 1 W.L.R. 1261; above, p. 59.
[50] *Pulleng v. Curran* (1982) 44 P.&C.R. 58; above, p. 60.
[51] [1978] 1 W.L.R. 1107. See also *Gurton v. Parrott* [1991] 1 E.G.L.R. 98 (dog breeding and kennelling incidental to residence); *Wright v. Mortimer,* July 28, 1994 (county court), noted (1994) *Legal Action,* December, p. 15 (work at home by art historian, amounting to 30% of professional time, was incidental to residence).
[52] [1978] 1 W.L.R. 1329.
[53] *ibid.* The business user was apparently not in breach of covenant. See also *Groveside Properties Ltd v. Westminster Medical School* (1983) 47 P.&C.R. 507, above, p. 73; *Durman v. Bell* (1988) 20 H.L.R. 340.

Presumably, if the business user had ceased, the tenancy would have become protected again, as it was initially let as a dwelling.

Sub-tenants

Finally, where the head tenancy is a business tenancy but the property includes residential accommodation, a sub-tenant of the residential part can have a protected tenancy as against the tenant.[54] The question whether he has rights against the head landlord on termination of the tenancy is discussed below.[55]

Parsonage houses

Church of England

Church of England parsonage houses are excluded from the Rent Act, not by express provision in the latter, but by virtue of the Pluralities Act 1838.[56] There is no such exception in respect of other denominations, although the 1977 Act provides a ground for possession of a regulated tenancy where the dwelling is held for the purpose of being available for occupation by a minister of religion, and is required for such occupation.[57]

Other denominations

Exemption by ministerial order

Finally, section 143(1) of the 1977 Act provides that the Secretary of State may, by order, provide that dwelling-houses in a particular area shall not be the subject of a regulated tenancy if he is satisfied that the number of persons seeking to become tenants is not substantially greater than the number of dwelling-houses available.[58] Any such order may contain transitional provisions to avoid or mitigate hardship. No such order has yet been made.

Protected shorthold tenancies

A special type of protected tenancy is the protected shorthold tenancy, which was introduced by the Housing Act 1980 in order to encourage residential lettings in the private sector. It must be distinguished from the assured shorthold tenancy, introduced by the Housing Act 1988, which is discussed in Chapter 12. The "old-style" protected shorthold tenancy cannot be created after the commencement of the 1988 Act,[59] but those previously granted continue in their original form. Because protected

[54] Rent Act 1977, s. 24(3).
[55] *ibid.* s. 137(3); see below, p. 163.
[56] See *Bishop of Gloucester v. Cunningham* [1943] 1 K.B. 101. The general provisions of the 1977 Act do not detract from the specific provisions of the 1838 Act.
[57] Rent Act 1977, Sched. 15, para. 15.
[58] For the effect on rent of reduced scarcity, see below, p. 176.
[59] Housing Act 1988, Sched. 18, repealing Housing Act 1980, s. 52, except in relation to tenancies entered into before the commencement of Part I of the 1988 Act (*i.e.* January 15, 1989).

shorthold tenancies enjoy less security than ordinary
protected tenancies, they are unlikely to survive as long as
the latter and for that reason are dealt with only briefly here.

Definition   A protected shorthold is a tenancy which satisfies the
requirements of an ordinary protected tenancy plus three
further conditions:[60]

(i)   the grant is for a term certain of one to five years;
(ii) it is not terminable by the landlord[61] during the
      contractual term save by forfeiture;
(iii) before the grant the landlord gave the tenant a notice in
      prescribed form stating that the tenancy was to be a
      protected shorthold.

There are special restrictions on assignment.[62] As an anti-
avoidance measure, a protected shorthold tenancy cannot be
granted to a person who, immediately before the grant, was
a protected or statutory tenant of the dwelling-house.[63]

Rent control   The protected shorthold tenancy is subject to rent control
in the same way as a protected tenancy. As far as security is
concerned, the feature of the protected shorthold is that the

Ground for   landlord can invoke a special mandatory ground for
possession   possession on termination of the contractual term or
subsequently.[64] This is why the tenant must be given a
contractual term of at least a year. Other grounds for
possession may be available, although they are unlikely to be
relied on. When the contractual term ends an occupying
tenant will acquire a statutory tenancy in the ordinary way
until possession is recovered. The succession rules will also
apply, although in modified form.[65]

Restricted contracts

Although not within the regulated tenancy regime, it is
convenient here to mention the lesser protection afforded by
Definition   the restricted contract. A restricted contract is a contract
"whereby one person grants to another person, in
consideration of a rent which includes payment for the use
of furniture or services, the right to occupy a dwelling as a
residence."[66] This was the main protection for furnished
tenancies before they were brought within the regulated
tenancy regime by the Rent Act 1974. Since that date the
main effect of the restricted contract has been to protect

---

[60] Housing Act 1980, s. 52.
[61] The tenant may terminate by written notice notwithstanding the terms of
the tenancy; *ibid.* s. 53.
[62] *ibid.* s. 54.
[63] *ibid.* s. 52(2); *cf. Dibbs v. Campbell* [1988] 2 E.G.L.R. 122; see below, p.
140.
[64] Case 19; see Chap. 7.
[65] Housing Act 1988, s. 39(7); see below, p. 147.
[66] R.A. 1977, s. 19(2). "Services" are defined by s. 19(8). There is no
requirement that a substantial part of the rent be attributable to furniture
or services.

tenants of resident landlords, who do not have a regulated tenancy.[67] With respect to such tenancies the requirement of furniture or services is not applicable.[68] Certain other tenancies excluded from the regulated tenancy provisions also have the benefit of a restricted contract, as do certain contractual licensees.[69]

No security of tenure

The protection conferred by the restricted contract consists primarily of rent control. Restricted contracts entered into since the Housing Act 1980 have no security of tenure, but merely the benefit of the requirement of a court order for possession, which may be suspended for a maximum of three months.[70] Restricted contracts cannot be created after the commencement of the Housing Act 1988.[71] For that reason they are dealt with only in outline, as, owing to their lack of security, they have been phased out far more quickly than regulated tenancies.

Exclusions

Exclusions from the restricted contract code include cases where the landlord's (or licensor's) interest belongs to a local authority, housing association or the Crown. Similarly, where a substantial proportion of the rent is attributable to board, or in the case of holiday occupation.[72]

Rent control

Either party to a restricted contract may refer the rent to a rent tribunal, which must approve, reduce or increase the rent to such sum as it thinks reasonable in all the circumstances, or dismiss the reference.[73] The rent as approved, reduced or increased is then registered and, subject to exceptions, cannot be reviewed for two years.[74] It is unlawful to require or receive a rent which exceeds the registered rent.[75]

---

[67] above, p. 48.

[68] R.A. 1977, s. 20.

[69] See *Luganda v. Service Hotels Ltd* [1969] 2 Ch. 209; *Marchant v. Charters* [1977] 1 W.L.R. 1181.

[70] R.A. 1977, s. 106A.

[71] H.A. 1988, s. 36(1). See also s. 36(2) (variation in terms may result in loss of protection).

[72] R.A. 1977, s. 19(5), (7).

[73] *ibid.* ss. 77, 78.

[74] *ibid.* ss. 79, 80.

[75] *ibid.* s. 81.

5 RESIDENT LANDLORDS

Prior to the Rent Act 1974 the general position was that tenants of unfurnished premises were protected whilst tenants of furnished premises were not. One justification for this was that the Act should always provide for a class of unprotected tenants in order to encourage letting. In any event the classification was not entirely arbitrary, as the tenant who had furnished the premises himself would be more greatly disadvantaged by lack of security than the more mobile tenant of furnished premises. However, the ease with which landlords could furnish premises and thus avoid the Act[1] led to a need for a more rational distinction between protected and unprotected tenants. The result was the Rent Act 1974, bringing furnished tenants into protection and introducing the distinction between tenants of resident and non-resident landlords.[2] This, it was hoped, would encourage owners to let any rooms in their homes which they did not require, in the knowledge that the tenants would not have full security of tenure. This policy must be borne in mind when construing the legislation.[3] That full security would be inappropriate in such circumstances is self-evident. As it was said in *Bardrick v. Haycock*,[4] "the mischief at which the section was aimed was the mischief of that sort of social embarrassment arising out of close proximity."

The present provisions are contained in section 12 and Schedule 2 of the 1977 Act, as amended by section 65 of the Housing Act 1980.

Relevance of sharing   It should be noted that the concept of sharing accommodation[5] is not relevant to the resident landlord rules, which may be satisfied even if no rooms are shared. However, in the case of lettings after the commencement of the Housing Act 1988, tenants who share accommodation with the landlord (or his family) are excluded from the benefit of the court order and four-week notice to quit rules of the Protection from Eviction Act 1977.[6]

[1] Prior to the decision in *Woodward v. Docherty* [1974] 1 W.L.R. 966, which made it more difficult to satisfy the "furnished" test.
[2] For transitional provisions, see Rent Act 1977, Sched. 24, para. 6.
[3] *O'Sullivan v. Barnett* [1994] 1 W.L.R. 1667.
[4] (1976) 31 P.&C.R. 420 at 424.
[5] See above, p. 62.
[6] See above, p. 49. Tenants of resident landlords do not have assured tenancies under the 1988 Act.

Statutory conditions[7]

Tenancies granted on or after August 14, 1974 are not protected if the following conditions are all satisfied:

Definitions (1) *The dwelling-house forms part only of a building and, except in a case where the dwelling-house also forms part of a flat, the building is not a purpose-built block of flats.* A "flat" is a dwelling which forms part only of a building and is separated horizontally from another dwelling forming part of the same building; a "purpose-built block of flats" is one which as constructed contained (and contains) two or more flats.[8]

The rationale of this requirement is that if a landlord owns several flats in a block, living in one and letting the others, he is not within the policy of the resident landlord exception, as he is not sharing his house in any real sense. The original provision was modified by section 65 of the Housing Act 1980 (as to tenancies granted on or after November 28, 1980), so that the condition may be satisfied in the case of an individual flat in a purpose-built block which the landlord lives in and which he has let off in part to a tenant: such a case is within the policy of the resident landlord exception.

Meaning of purpose-built The meaning of "purpose-built" arose in *Barnes v. Gorsuch*,[9] where a Victorian House, later converted to flats, did not satisfy the definition. "As constructed" means as originally constructed. The conversion did not start the construction anew. On the facts, there was no ground for saying that the identity of the building had changed, although the possibility of such an argument was admitted, for example in a case where the property was completely gutted and rebuilt inside. As to the "close proximity" principle,[10] it was agreed that people cannot always lead separate lives without "social embarrassment" even in a purpose-built block, and that sometimes in conversions they can. But the conditions exclude purpose-built blocks because they are likely to be places where the occupiers lead separate lives.

Meaning of building (2) *At the grant of the tenancy the landlord occupied as his residence another dwelling forming part of the building.*[11] "Building" is not defined in the Act. No doubt it does not include adjoining terraced houses or a pair of semi-detached

---

[7] Rent Act 1977, s. 12(1), as amended by Housing Act 1980, s. 65. It seems that the landlord need own no interest in the building: Farrand and Arden, *Rent Acts and Regulations* (2nd ed., 1981) p. 49.
[8] *ibid.* Sched. 2, para. 4.
[9] (1982) 43 P.&C.R. 294.
[10] *Bardrick v. Haycock,* above.
[11] Or, in the case of a flat in a purpose-built block, forming part of the flat.

houses, which would not be within the policy of the rule. In
any case a statutory definition is unlikely to have resolved
the borderline cases which follow.[12]

In *Bardrick v. Haycock*[13] a house was converted to flats.
The landlord pulled down an adjoining garage and built an
extension (having its own front door) where he resided. This
was held not to be "part of the building," hence the tenants
were protected. This decision was applied in principle by the
Court of Appeal in *Griffiths v. English*,[14] but a different
conclusion was reached on basically similar facts. The main
house was divided into flats. There was a single storey
extension at either side, with no communicating door. The
landlord, who lived in one extension, was held to be a
resident landlord. This is a question of fact for the judge at
first instance to decide. The appellate court will interfere
only if he has erred in law, and not if, as here, it is a
borderline case where different views can reasonably be
held.

The two dwellings must be in the same building both at
the grant of the tenancy and at the end of it. Thus if one
house is converted into two during the tenancy, the resident
landlord rules may not be satisfied.[15]

Occupation as a residence

Even where there is no dispute as to the "building,"
questions can arise as to whether the landlord occupies
another dwelling-house in that building as his residence. In
Lyons v. Caffery[16] a basement contained a bed-sitter,
kitchen, bathroom and sunroom. The bedsitter was let to a
tenant, who shared the kitchen[17] and bathroom with the
landlord, who occupied the remainder. It was held that the
resident landlord condition was not satisfied. The essential
living and sleeping room was let and the remainder was not
a dwelling-house. This emphasis on sleeping facilities is
clearly consistent with decisions on "dwelling-house" and
"residence" in sections 1 and 2 of the Act.[18] A landlord who
does not sleep on the premises may, however, be a resident
landlord in special circumstances. In *Palmer v. McNamara*[19]
the landlord reserved a room in the building where he kept
his possessions and spent his days. He did not have a cooker
but took his meals (cold meals and takeaways) in the room.

---

[12] See the volume of litigation on the statutory definition of "house" in the
Leasehold Reform Act 1967.
[13] (1976) 31 P.&C.R. 420 (C.A.).
[14] (1982) 261 E.G. 257; [1983] Conv. 147 (J.E.M.). See also *Wolff v.
Waddington* (1990) 22 H.L.R. 72.
[15] *Lewis-Graham v. Conacher* (1992) 24 H.L.R. 132 (but still one building
on facts as separation incomplete).
[16] (1983) 266 E.G. 213 (C.A.).
[17] Why, then, was the tenant not excluded from protection on the ground
that he shared "living accommodation" with the landlord? (See above, p.
62.)
[18] See *Regalian Securities Ltd v. Scheuer* (1982) 263 E.G. 973 (s. 2); *Curl v.
Angelo* [1948] 2 All E.R. 189 (s. 1).
[19] (1991) 23 H.L.R. 168; [1991] Conv. 289 (J. Martin); see above, p. 64.

Owing to ill-health he preferred to sleep at a friend's house. The Court of Appeal held that he was a resident landlord. He had no other residence.

A novel point arose in *O'Sullivan v. Barnett*,[20] where the resident landlord and tenant decided to move both households to another house, where a new tenancy was granted. In fact the tenant moved a few weeks before the landlord, who was completing works on the new house while still sleeping at the old house. It was held that the landlord satisfied the requirement of residing in the same building at the grant of the tenancy. The question did not depend on fine matters of timing.

(3) *At all times since the grant of the tenancy the landlord (or his successor) has occupied as his residence another dwelling forming part of the building.*[21] The landlord is treated as occupying as a residence if he fulfills the same conditions as a statutory tenant must fulfill under section 2 of the Act.[22] Hence the case law on the statutory tenancy[23] applies here also. One perhaps unforeseen consequence of this is that liberal decisions favouring the tenant, for example the "two homes" cases,[24] can here be utilised by the landlord. It cannot have been the intention of Parliament that the resident landlord exception could be relied on in respect of more than one property or in cases involving lengthy absence from the premises. The provisions may be contrasted with those relating to resident landlords under the Housing Act 1988, where the "only or principal home" requirement prevents the exception from applying to more than one property.[25]

Two homes cases

Joint landlords

The question of joint landlords was resolved in *Cooper v. Tait*[26] where the Court of Appeal held that residence by one of joint landlords satisfied the condition. This is clearly satisfactory, as absurd and unjust results would flow from any other view, for example if a married couple let the property and then separated.

If this condition ceases to be satisfied, the tenancy becomes protected. Although a protected tenancy cannot normally be granted after the Housing Act 1988, that Act does not seem to prevent a protected tenancy arising in this way.

---

[20] [1994] 1 W.L.R. 1667.
[21] Or, in the case of a flat in a purpose-built block, forming part of the flat. The condition is satisfied where the landlord's interest is held on trust and the beneficiary resides: Sched. 2, para. 2.
[22] Sched. 2, para. 5. Thus a company cannot be a resident landlord.
[23] See below, p. 93. See *Jackson v. Pekic* (1990) 22 H.L.R. 9.
[24] See below, p. 103. See *Wolff v. Waddington* (1990) 22 H.L.R. 72.
[25] Housing Act 1988, Sched. 1, para. 10.
[26] (1984) 271 E.G. 105. See also (on Case 11) *Tilling v. Whiteman* [1980] A.C. 1 and (on joint tenants) *Lloyd v. Sadler* [1978] Q.B. 774.

"Period of disregard"

Clearly continuous residence cannot be expected, as the landlord will ultimately die or sell the property, and his successor cannot always practicably take up occupation immediately. Hence the thread of occupation by the landlord is preserved by the provision of "periods of disregard." Basically a period of 28 days (extendable to six months by giving notice) may be disregarded in the case of a lifetime transfer, while the period is two years where the landlord's interest becomes vested in personal representatives, "trustees as such" or the President of the Family Division of the High Court[27] (*i.e.* prior to the appointment of administrators on intestacy).[28] The provisions are complex and badly drafted, and have troubled the Court of Appeal and House of Lords on several occasions.

Length of period of disregard

Personal representatives

Here the provisions have been amended by the Housing Act 1980, but the position prior to the amendment must be considered, as the interpretation of the original provisions continues to have relevance in the cases of purchasers and trustees, discussed below.

Position prior to the Housing Act 1980   In determining whether condition (3) was fulfilled, the 1977 Act provided that a period not exceeding 12 months while the landlord's interest was vested in personal representatives could be disregarded. Clearly the tenant would become protected if no notice was served during this period, and no successor took up residence by the end of it. But what if (assuming a periodic tenancy) notice was served during this period? The matter arose in *Landau v. Sloane*.[29] A majority of the House of Lords, reversing the Court of Appeal, held that the personal representatives could recover possession after the 12-month period even though no successor had gone into residence. The purpose of the rule was to give them the same rights as the landlord. Otherwise there would be no inducement to let, as it would be unjust to the estate if the tenant became protected. The house would often be the most valuable asset in the estate, and the successor would not normally wish to reside. What of the tenant's status during this period? Not surprisingly, he was not a trespasser. He was a person holding over, against whom no order for possession could be made save on grounds that

Effect of notice to quit during period of disregard

---

[27] After the commencement of the Law of Property (Miscellaneous Provisions) Act 1994 such property vests in the Public Trustee; *ibid.*, s. 14.

[28] Sched. 2, para. 1, as amended by Housing Act 1980, s. 65.

[29] [1982] A.C. 490, criticised [1981] Conv. 225 (A. Sydenham).

would terminate a regulated tenancy.[30] Thus the personal representatives had the same rights as a resident landlord, save that they could not recover possession until the end of the period of disregard. Lord Roskill dissented, considering that the resident landlord status was a privilege that was lost if the conditions were not satisfied, the conditions requiring residence at all times save in the period of disregard.

It was agreed that a contractual tenancy would become protected (in the absence of residence by the landlord's successor) if not terminated during the period of disregard.[31] A statutory tenancy can arise on subsequent termination.[32]

Effect of Housing Act 1980, section 65   The rule discussed above was amended in two respects. First, the 12-month period was extended to two years. Secondly, and presumably in response to the Court of Appeal decision in *Landau v. Sloane*, it is now provided that condition (3) (the continuous residence rule) is deemed satisfied during this two-year period. The result of this is that the personal representatives can actually recover possession after serving notice to quit (assuming a periodic tenancy) without waiting until the end of the two-year period, and without establishing grounds to terminate a regulated tenancy.[33] This aspect of the amendment applies only to deaths after November 28, 1980, but difficult questions have arisen as to the retrospective operation of the provision extending the period from 12 months to two years.

This was the issue before the Court of Appeal in *Caldwell v. McAteer*.[34] It had already been suggested in *Williams v. Mate*[35] that section 65 was retrospective in the sense that personal representatives could take advantage of the extended period even where the 12-month period had expired before section 65 came into operation, provided the tenancy had not already become statutory.[36] In *Caldwell v. McAteer* the landlord died on October 31, 1979. After the (then) 12-month period of disregard, the tenant became protected, no beneficiary having gone into residence. If notice to quit had been given subsequently but prior to the coming into operation of section 65, the tenancy would have become statutory. However, section 65 came into operation on November 28, 1980, and extended the 12-month period to two years. Within the two-year period, the personal representatives gave notice to quit (expiring October 17, 1981). It was held that section 65 applied retrospectively,

Recovery of possession within the two-year period

Retrospective operation of section 65

---

[30] Sched. 2, para. 3 (this restriction no longer applies to personal representatives after the 1980 amendment: see below).

[31] See also *Williams v. Mate* (1983) 46 P.&C.R. 43.

[32] Sched. 2, para. 7 (described as obscurely drafted in *Williams v. Mate* above).

[33] See *Bevan v. Johnston* [1990] 2 E.G.L.R. 33.

[34] (1984) 269 E.G. 1039; [1985] Conv. 127 (J.E.M.).

[35] See above.

[36] The tenancy would have become statutory if no notice was served until after the 12-month period (no beneficiary having gone into residence).

thus enabling the personal representatives to recover possession at the end of the two-year period. It was admitted that the result was anomalous and the Act ill-drafted, but denied that this construction deprived the tenant of a vested right, as no statutory tenancy had yet arisen. This, it is submitted, is unconvincing. It is difficult to think of other examples where protected tenants have been retrospectively deprived of that status. The basic characteristic of a protected tenancy is the right to a statutory tenancy. Some retrospective effect could have been given to section 65 by applying it to cases where the "period of disregard" was already running, but the tenant had not yet acquired a protected tenancy because the period had not expired when section 65 came into effect.

Purchasers[37]

Extension by written notice

No recovery of possession within the period of disregard

The 1977 Act provided for a period of disregard of 14 days, increased to 28 days by the Act of 1980. If, during this period, the purchaser gives written notice to the tenant of his intention to reside in the building, the period may be extended to six months. Thus if the contractual tenancy does not terminate during this period, the tenant becomes protected if the purchaser has not moved in by the end of the period of disregard. If a notice to quit has been served during this period, then presumably the reasoning of *Landau v. Sloane*[38] continues to apply, as the 1980 Act only enables personal representatives to recover possession during the period.[39] Hence the purchaser can recover possession at the end of the period even if he has not moved in.[40]

It should be noted that the period of disregard starts running only on completion of the purchase. The purchaser cannot give his "extension notice" until the property is legally vested in him. Thus difficulties may arise if the vendor has moved out before completion.[41]

"Trustees as such"[42]

The 12-month period originally provided was increased by the 1980 Act to two years, but that Act made no further amendment here. Thus the position is in principle similar

---

[37] The category in fact comprises any lifetime transfer.
[38] See above.
[39] Although, by Sched. 2, para. 3, the purchaser may do so by establishing a ground which would terminate a regulated tenancy.
[40] What if his intention to reside was not genuine?
[41] See [1978] Conv. 255 (J.T.F.), discussing whether such an interval of non-occupation before completion could, if short, be disregarded as *de minimis*, or whether the express periods of disregard preclude this. By analogy with *Department of the Environment v. Royal Insurance plc* (1987) 54 P.&C.R. 26 (on Landlord and Tenant Act 1954, s. 37), it is unlikely that the *de minimis* principle would allow departure from the strict time limits.
[42] Or the President of the Family Division or the Public Trustee (on intestacy); above, p. 87.

No recovery of possession within the period of disregard to that of the purchaser, discussed above. Possession can be recovered after the period of disregard if notice to quit has been served within it, even though no successor has gone into occupation. If the contractual tenancy has not terminated within the period the tenant becomes protected in the absence of occupation by a successor by the end of the period.

Meaning of trustees as such The difficulty is as to the precise scope of the phrase "trustees as such." There is, as yet, no direct authority, but it was suggested in *Williams v. Mate*[43] that it is not confined to an *inter vivos* trust, but applies to trustees under a will or intestacy. Where the property vests first in a personal representative and then in trustees, the two periods of disregard are not mutually exclusive but can be added.[44]

Anti-avoidance Finally, even if conditions (1), (2) and (3) are all satisfied, it should be noted that the resident landlord rules do not apply to a tenancy granted to a person who, immediately before the grant, was a protected or statutory tenant of that dwelling or another dwelling in the building.[45] Thus a tenant, once protected, cannot lose his status by the grant of a new tenancy by a resident landlord.

Status of a tenant of a resident landlord

Finally, it remains to consider the position of a tenant deprived of full protection by the resident landlord rules. While he cannot have a regulated tenancy, the tenant does **Restricted contract** have the protection of a restricted contract.[46] Briefly, this means that rent control applies, but not security of tenure, although the tenant cannot be evicted without a court order, which may be suspended for up to three months.[47] As will be seen in Chapter 11, a tenancy granted on or after January 15, 1989, by a resident landlord does not have the protection of a restricted contract.[48]

---

[43] (1983) 46 P.&C.R. 43. See also [1991] 11 E.G. 78 and 12 E.G. 52 (M. Pawlowski).

[44] See, further, Farrand and Arden, *Rent Acts and Regulations* (2nd ed., 1981) p. 48, and Pettit, *Private Sector Tenancies* (2nd ed., 1981) pp. 58–59, canvassing further difficulties in the interpretation of "trustees as such".

[45] Rent Act 1977, s. 12(2), as amended. See *Dibbs v. Campbell* [1988] 2 E.G.L.R. 122 (meaning of "immediately before").

[46] See above, p. 80.

[47] Housing Act 1980, s. 69. The court has no discretion to extend the three-month period, for example by suspending the possession order so long as rent and arrears are paid: *Bryant v. Best* [1987] 2 E.G.L.R. 113.

[48] Housing Act 1988, s. 36.

6 THE STATUTORY TENANCY

Section 2 of the 1977 Act provides that:

> "after the termination of a protected tenancy of a dwelling-house the person who, immediately before that termination, was the protected tenant of the dwelling-house shall, if and so long as he occupies the dwelling-house as his residence, be the statutory tenant of it."

The matters to be considered in this Chapter include the juridical nature of the statutory tenancy, the meaning of the words "if and so long as he occupies the dwelling-house as his residence," and the terms of the statutory tenancy.

It might be added that, although a protected tenancy cannot normally be granted after the Housing Act 1988, a statutory tenancy may still arise on termination of a protected tenancy after that Act. A statutory tenancy may also continue to arise on termination of a long tenancy under the Landlord and Tenant Act 1954, Part I. In the case of a long tenancy terminating on or after January 15, 1999, however, the tenant will instead be entitled to an assured periodic tenancy.[1]

Nature of the statutory tenancy[2]

The statutory tenancy, unlike the protected tenancy which preceded it, is neither a legal estate nor an equitable interest in the land. It does, however, have some of the attributes of a proprietary interest. It might best be described as a hybrid interest created by statute, in some respects personal to the tenant, in others proprietary in nature.

Binding on purchaser from landlord

Although not an interest in land in the accepted sense, the statutory tenancy is clearly binding on third parties, including purchasers, who acquire the landlord's interest. In describing the status of the statutory tenant, Scrutton L.J. said "I take it that he has a right as against all the world to remain in possession until he is turned out by an order of the Court . . . "[3] The binding effect of the tenancy stems not from the characteristics of any legal or equitable interest

[1] Local Government and Housing Act 1989, s. 186 and Sched. 10. The new regime will apply also to long tenancies granted on or after April 1, 1990, whenever they terminate.
[2] See, generally, [1980] Conv. 351 (C. Hand); *White v. Barnet L.B.C.* [1990] 2 Q.B. 328 at 336.
[3] *Keeves v. Dean* [1924] 1 K.B. 685 at 694. See also *Jessamine Investment Co. v. Schwartz* [1978] Q.B. 264, below, p. 167.

(which, as stated above, it is not), but from the provisions of
the Act. There is, however, an exception to the rule that the
tenancy binds "all the world." A mortgagor may grant a
tenancy although his mortgage excludes the power of
leasing. Any such tenancy will, of course, bind the
mortgagor, but will not bind the mortgagee (unless he
accepts the tenant), whose title is paramount.[4]

Right to
possession
The statutory tenant, then, is entitled to enjoy possession
of the property until he decides to terminate the tenancy or
the landlord successfully asserts a ground for possession
against him. As with any other tenancy, his right to
possession gives him the right to maintain an action in
trespass against third parties. Unlike other tenancies,
however, he must satisfy the residence requirements
(discussed below) in order to keep his tenancy alive. The
statutory tenancy clearly has a monetary value. Although the
tenant cannot assign it for a premium[5] (or, generally, at all),
he may receive payment from the landlord as a condition of
giving up possession.[6] If a protected tenant is deprived of the
opportunity to acquire a statutory tenancy by reason of the
negligence of his solicitors, substantial damages based on
the cost of acquiring similar rights of occupation are
available.[7]

Not assignable
The reason why the statutory tenancy is often described as
merely a personal right to occupy is primarily because it is
not assignable. An ordinary tenancy is assignable, but may
be subject to a prohibition in the terms of the tenancy. A
statutory tenancy, on the other hand, is not capable of
assignment. To this rule there are two exceptions: the court
may order a transfer of the tenancy in matrimonial
proceedings,[8] and the landlord may agree to a transfer of the
statutory tenancy to a third party.[9] One result of the limited
transmissibility of the statutory tenancy is that, if a statutory
tenant goes bankrupt, there is no transfer of his tenancy to
his trustee in bankruptcy, and hence no loss of Rent Act
rights.[10]

Succession
Nor can the statutory tenancy be left by will, although, as
we will see, up to two statutory transmissions may take place
in favour of members of the family of the deceased tenant.[11]

---

[4] *Dudley and District Benefit Building Society v. Emerson* [1949] Ch. 707;
   Britannia Building Society v. Earl [1990] 1 W.L.R. 422, below, p. 141.
[5] See below, p. 185.
[6] Rent Act 1977, Sched. 1, para. 12. The tenant commits an offence if he
   receives payment from any person other than the landlord.
[7] *Murray v. Lloyd* [1989] 1 W.L.R. 1060; [1990] Conv. 446 (J.E.M.). For
   tax reasons the lease was taken in the name of a company, which, as
   explained below, cannot acquire a statutory tenancy. Damages of
   £115,000 were awarded.
[8] Below, p. 108. The jurisdiction is to be extended to cohabitants.
[9] Rent Act 1977, Sched. 1, para. 13, below, p. 108.
[10] *Reeves v. Davies* [1921] 2 K.B. 486. As to the bankruptcy of a protected
   tenant, see below, p. 94.
[11] See below, Chap. 8. In the case of deaths after the Housing Act 1988,
   successors other than the original tenant's spouse take assured tenancies.

Subletting

A statutory tenant may, however, sublet part of the premises, even though he has no "estate" out of which to sublet.[12] If, on the other hand, he sublets the whole of the premises, then although a valid sub-tenancy is created,[13] the act of subletting causes the statutory tenancy to cease, as the tenant can no longer satisfy the residence requirement of section 2.[14]

Disclaimer of headlease

It has been held that a statutory subtenant has *locus standi* to apply for a vesting order where the liquidator has disclaimed the headlease. Such a vesting order may be sought under section 181 of the Insolvency Act 1986, which applies to a person who claims "an interest" in the disclaimed property. This "interest" does not have to be proprietary, but means any financial interest adversely affected by the disclaimer.[15] If an applicant declines to accept a vesting order, section 182(4) provides that he shall be "excluded from all interest in the property." If, however, a statutory subtenant declines to accept a vesting order he is not deprived of his status because "interest" in this subsection is confined to proprietary interests such as underleases and mortgages and does not include a statutory subtenancy.[16]

Closing order

Finally, a statutory tenancy is neither a "lease" within section 317 of the Housing Act 1985 nor a "tenancy" within section 621 of that Act, with the result that a statutory tenant cannot apply to court for a variation of the tenancy when a closing order is in force. Such a variation, had it been possible, could have imposed repair obligations on the landlord, resulting in the removal of the closing order and of the landlord's right to possession.[17]

The requirement of occupation as a residence

As stated above, a statutory tenancy arises on termination of a protected tenancy, so long as the tenant continues to occupy the dwelling-house as his residence. This is so

---

[12] But even if the contractual tenancy did not prohibit sub-letting, a sub-letting of the whole gives rise to a ground for possession under Case 6, below, p. 211.

[13] So that the sub-tenant, though subject to Case 6, may have rights under Rent Act 1977, s. 137: see below, p. 160.

[14] See *Trustees of Henry Smith's Charity v. Willson* [1983] Q.B. 316, below, p. 160. It may be otherwise in the case of a short subletting, where the tenant intends to return; *Leslie & Co. Ltd v. Cumming* [1926] 2 K.B. 417.

[15] *In re Vedmay Ltd* (1995) 69 P. & C.R. 247.

[16] *ibid.*

[17] *Johnson v. Felton* [1994] E.G.C.S. 135. For the effect of a closing order, see below, p. 139.

whether the former protected tenancy terminated by expiry, notice to quit,[18]forfeiture,[19] or any other method.[20] As the tenant is entitled by statute to remain in possession, acceptance of rent by the landlord after termination of the protected tenancy will not normally give rise to the inference of a new contractual tenancy.[21]

The occupation must be that of the person who was the protected tenant on termination of the tenancy. Since the amendment to the insolvency legislation by the Housing Act 1988 a protected tenancy is excluded from the bankrupt's estate[22] (provided that no premium can lawfully be required on assignment[23]) and thus does not vest in the trustee in

Bankruptcy   bankruptcy. The effect of this is that a bankrupt tenant who continues to reside can acquire a statutory tenancy on termination of the protected tenancy. The tenancy will, however, vest in the trustee in bankruptcy if the trustee serves notice in writing on the bankrupt,[24] but he may not disclaim the tenancy without leave of the court.[25] In such a case the bankrupt former tenant cannot acquire a statutory tenancy because he was not the protected tenant on termination of the tenancy.[26]

The main issue is to define the meaning of the phrase "if and so long as he occupies the dwelling-house as his residence," which is fundamental to the statutory tenancy. The numerous case-law illustrations might best be understood by dividing them into the following categories.

---

[18] But see Case 5, below, p. 120. giving a discretionary ground for possession where the *tenant* gives notice to quit and then stays on.

[19] The reason for the forfeiture will normally give rise to a discretionary ground for possession under Case 1 (breach), below, p. 117.

[20] cf. *Dibbs v. Campbell* (1988) 20 H.L.R. 384; below, p. 140 (surrender). No statutory tenancy arises on rescission of a protected tenancy; *Killick v. Roberts* [1991] 1 W.L.R. 1146; below, p. 141.

[21] *Murray, Bull & Co. Ltd v. Murray* [1953] 1 Q.B. 211.

[22] Housing Act 1988, s. 117, amending Insolvency Act 1986, s. 283. (Similarly in the case of assured and secure tenancies).

[23] Premiums are lawful in certain cases (see below, p. 188). If the tenancy can be assigned for value, then clearly it should be available to the creditors.

[24] Insolvency Act 1986, s. 308A, inserted by Housing Act 1988, s. 117. This would be necessary if disclaimer is intended, as where the tenancy is onerous (*cf. City of London Corporation v. Bown* (1990) 22 H.L.R. 33), or if the trustee wishes to acquire the benefit of a profitable subletting. The trustee's title relates back to the commencement of the bankruptcy except against a purchaser in good faith, for value and without notice of the bankruptcy.

[25] *ibid.*, s. 315, as amended by Housing Act 1988, s. 117.

[26] This was the general rule before the 1988 amendments where the trustee in bankruptcy of a protected tenant disclaimed: *Smalley v. Quarrier* [1975] 1 W.L.R. 938; *Eyre v. Hall* [1986] 2 E.G.L.R. 95. For the position of a statutory subtenant on disclaimer by the head tenant's liquidator, see *In re Vedmay Ltd* (1995) 69 P. & C.R. 247.

Company and institutional tenants

Such tenants can qualify as protected tenants, and hence enjoy the benefit of rent control.[27] They cannot, however, acquire statutory tenancies, because neither a company nor any other institution is capable of residence.[28] Occupation by servants or agents does not suffice.

Company lets   Hence the attraction of the common "company let" scheme as a device to avoid security of tenure. To regard such a letting as inevitably a sham would be to rewrite the company law doctrine of corporate personality. If the actual occupant is a licensee, he will have no rights against the landlord. If, on the other hand, he is a lawful sub-tenant, he may have rights not only against the company but also against the head landlord on determination of the company's tenancy.[29] One effect of *Street v. Mountford*[30] may be that it will be more difficult to establish that the occupier is in fact the licensee of the company, as opposed to its sub-tenant. It is likely, however, that the letting to the company will prohibit subletting, so that any sub-tenancy will be unlawful unless the breach is waived.

Real and nominal tenants   There are, however, certain dicta, although not very persuasive, to the effect that a non-occupying "nominal" tenant might not be recognised if the "real" tenant is known to be someone else. In *Cove v. Flick*,[31] where a tenant who rented a home for his family's occupation failed to establish a statutory tenancy, Denning L.J. (as he then was) said:

> "I can well see that the court would not allow a landlord to evade the Act by taking an absent member of the family as nominal tenant when the real occupier and real tenant was to be a present member."[32]

Similarly in *S.L. Dando Ltd v. Hitchcock*,[33] where the manager of the tenant company resided. Residence by an agent was held insufficient, otherwise a tenant could get security as to several dwellings. This would be contrary to the purpose of the Rent Act, which is to protect the tenant's enjoyment of his home. But Denning L.J. again said:

[27] *cf. St Catherine's College v. Dorling* [1980] 1 W.L.R. 66, above, p. 61, where the tenancy was not even protected, as the house was not let as "a" separate dwelling.

[28] *St Catherine's College v. Dorling*, above; *Hiller v. United Dairies (London) Ltd* [1934] 1 K.B. 57. See also *Murray v. Lloyd* [1989] 1 W.L.R. 1060. Similarly an individual non-occupying tenant can be protected, but not statutory: *Feather Supplies v. Ingham* [1971] 2 Q.B. 348 (father took tenancy for occupation of student son). Compare assured tenancies under the Housing Act 1988, which must be granted to an "individual": see below, p. 196.

[29] Rent Act 1977, s. 137: below, p. 156.

[30] [1985] A.C. 809: above, p. 9.

[31] [1954] 2 Q.B. 326n.

[32] *ibid*. at 328.

[33] [1954] 2 Q.B. 317.

"Let me add a word of caution. I can well see that the
court would not allow the landlord to avoid the Acts by
taking someone as a nominal tenant, well knowing that
the real tenant was someone else. The court would then
look to the realities of the situation."[34]

There seem to have been no cases where the argument
has succeeded. What must be shown is that the agreement
is a sham, which traditionally means that the parties must
have had a common intention that their acts or documents
are not to create the legal rights and obligations which they
give the appearance of creating.[35] This is clearly not the case
where the tenant company is responsible for the payment of
the rent and the performance of the covenants. So in
Firstcross Ltd v. East West (Export/Import) Ltd,[36] where a flat
was let to a company for its director's occupation, no
statutory tenancy could arise. In the absence of any
allegation that the agreement was a sham, it could not be
claimed that the director was the "real" tenant. Similarly in
Metropolitan Properties Co. Ltd v. Cronan,[37] where May L.J.
said that this:

"apparent exception, if indeed it can ever be made good
in law, applies only where the landlord grants the
tenancy to the nominal tenant as a sham and for the
purpose of being free of the burdens of the Rent Acts to
which he would otherwise be subject in respect of the
'real' tenant. Where by a genuine transaction, albeit
that the true facts are known to the landlord, the latter
lets a dwelling-house to one person ... for the purpose
of its occupation by another ... then when the
contractual tenancy expires I do not think that the
[occupier] is entitled to the protection of the Rent
Acts."[38]

This admittedly gave the landlord the best of both worlds,
but he was entitled to make what use he wished of the
premises.

Even if it cannot be established that the agreement is a
sham, another line of argument appears from the decision of
a majority of the Court of Appeal in *Gisborne v. Burton*,[39] a
Application of   case on agricultural holdings. It was there held that the
tax doctrines   doctrine of the tax case *Ramsay v. I.R.C.*[40] applied to a

---

[34] *ibid.* at 322.
[35] *Snook v. London & West Riding Investments Ltd* [1967] 2 Q.B. 786 at 802.
     "Sham" may now have a wider meaning, as discussed at p. 25 above.
[36] (1981) 41 P.&C.R. 145; [1982] Conv. 151 (J. Martin).
[37] (1982) 44 P.&C.R. 1; [1982] Conv. 384 (J. Martin).
[38] (1982) 44 P.&C.R. 1 at 9.
[39] [1989] Q.B. 390; (1988) 138 N.L.J. 792 (J. Martin).
[40] [1982] A.C. 300; *Furniss v. Dawson* [1984] A.C. 474. See also 1986
     Blundell Memorial Lectures, summarised at (1986) 83 L.S. Gaz. 3736
     (K. Lewison) and (1987) 84 L.S. Gaz. 403 (P. Freedman).

scheme to avoid security of tenure. Under that doctrine, the court will disregard the individual stages in a pre-ordained series of transactions having no purpose other than the avoidance of some mandatory statutory provision and will look at the effect of the scheme as a whole. This is so even though no part of the transaction can be regarded as a sham. In this case a sub-tenant was held in law to be the tenant where a tenancy to the landlord's wife and a sub-tenancy by her were created contemporaneously in order to avoid security under the agricultural holdings legislation. In substance the landlord had granted a tenancy to the "sub-tenant" by two steps instead of one. Ralph Gibson L.J. dissented, holding that the court has no power to treat a transaction between private individuals as something other than it really was merely because the social purpose of some legislation would be served by so treating it.

This principle, if correct, would not apply to a genuine letting to a company for the occupation of its directors or employees, but could apply where a landlord insists on letting via a company (or other institution) purely to avoid security of tenure.[41]

In *Hilton v. Plustitle Ltd*,[42] however, the company let device was upheld even though the company was set up solely for the purpose of avoiding the Act. The company had no bank account, rent being paid by the occupier's cheque. *Gisborne v. Burton*[43] was regarded as a case of agency (*i.e.* the landlord's wife acted as his agent in granting the sublease) and was therefore distinguishable. The Court of Appeal expressed the view that there was no reason why public policy should override the transaction which was deliberately intended to avoid, but not evade, the Rent Acts. Otherwise public policy would be contradicting section 2 of the 1977 Act and the decisions which had been founded on it.

The matter arose again before the Court of Appeal in *Kaye v. Massbetter*,[44] where the landlord insisted that the tenant must be a company in order to avoid the Rent Act. Because the plaintiff, the intending occupier, was an undischarged bankrupt, two friends purchased a company on his behalf. The tenancy agreement provided that the plaintiff was the guarantor and the "permitted occupier." The arrangement was held not to be a sham. It was not a case of attempting to contract out of the Rent Act as the Act did not apply. The fact that matters were so arranged to

---

[41] *cf. St Catherine's College v. Dorling* [1980] 1 W.L.R. 66, above, p. 61.
[42] [1989] 1 W.L.R. 149. See also *Estavest Investments Ltd v. Commercial Express Travel Ltd* [1988] 2 E.G.L.R. 91 (decided 1987), holding that a company let scheme was not a sham because the company tenant, rather than the occupier, performed all the obligations under the tenancy. This suggests that, without these factors, the result might have been different.
[43] See above.
[44] (1991) 62 P.&C.R. 558; *cf. Navinter v. Pastoll* (March 21, 1990, C.A.), (1990) *Legal Action*, June, p. 13 (considered arguable in summary proceedings under R.S.C. Ord. 113 that occupier was the tenant where he personally signed the acceptance of an offer to renew a company let).

avoid the Rent Act did not mean that the arrangement was
not genuine. Whether it was genuine was a question of fact.
Here the rent was paid by the plaintiff. The landlord always
dealt with the plaintiff until the latter consulted a rent
officer. Thereafter the landlord addressed communications,
including the notice to quit, to the company. These factors
were not enough to constitute a sham, which would require
the plaintiff to show that it was not the intention of the
parties that the company should be subject to the tenancy
obligations. It seems, therefore, that the courts are much
more reluctant to find that a company let is a sham than
they are to find that a "licence" is a sham.[45]

Absentee tenants

"To retain possession or occupation for the purpose of
retaining protection the tenant cannot be compelled to
spend twenty-four hours in all weathers under his own
roof for three hundred and sixty-five days in the year."[46]

While trivial absences clearly do not break the thread of
occupation, the question is to what extent may a more
prolonged absence be overlooked. This, as will be seen, is a
question of degree, relevant considerations being the length
of and reason for the absence, the tenant's intention, and
the occupation of the premises during his absence.

The classic case is *Brown v. Brash and Ambrose*,[47]where
the tenant was absent through imprisonment for two years,
leaving his mistress and children in occupation. She
subsequently left, taking the children and most of the
Requirements of furniture. Thereafter the tenant's relatives sometimes came
residence in to clean. It was held that the tenant was no longer
residing. The fact that his absence was involuntary did not
assist him. Clearly, temporary absences, for example for
holidays, are irrelevant. Nevertheless, as Asquith L.J.
explained,

"absence may be sufficiently prolonged or
uninterrupted to compel the inference, prima facie, of a
cesser of possession or occupation. The question is one
of fact and degree. Assume an absence sufficiently
prolonged to have this effect: The legal result seems to
us to be as follows: (1) The onus is then on the tenant
to repel the presumption that his possession has

[45] See above, p. 25. See further (1989) 105 L.Q.R. 167 (P. Baker); (1989)
Legal Action, February, p. 21 (N. Madge); [1989] Conv. 196 (C.
Rodgers); (1989) 52 M.L.R. 557 (P. Sparkes); (1990) 140 N.L.J. 620
and 1399 (T. Radevsky) and 1205 (G. Webber); [1992] Conv. 58 (P.
Luther).
[46] *Brown v. Brash and Ambrose* [1948] 2 K.B. 247 at 254.
[47] See above. See also *Poland v. Earl Cadogan* [1980] 3 All E.R. 544,
holding that the test for residence under the Rent Act is less stringent
than that which applies in the context of enfranchisement under the
Leasehold Reform Act 1967.

ceased.[48] (2) In order to repel it he must at all events establish a de facto intention on his part to return after his absence. (3) But we are of opinion that neither in principle nor on the authorities can this be enough. To suppose that he can absent himself for five or ten years or more and retain possession and his protected status simply by proving an inward intention to return after so protracted an absence would be to frustrate the spirit and policy of the Acts. . . . (4) Notwithstanding an absence so protracted the authorities suggest that its effect may be averted if he couples and clothes his inward intention with some formal, outward, and visible sign of it; that is, installs in the premises some caretaker or representative, be it a relative or not, with the status of a licensee and with the function of preserving the premises for his own ultimate homecoming. There will then, at all events, be someone to profit by the housing accommodation involved, which will not stand empty. It may be that the same result can be secured by leaving on the premises, as a deliberate symbol of continued occupation, furniture, though we are not clear that this was necessary to the decision in *Brown v. Draper*.[49] Apart from authority, in principle, possession in fact (for it is with possession in fact and not with possession in law that we are here concerned) requires not merely an '*animus possidendi*' but a '*corpus possessionis*,' namely, some visible state of affairs in which the *animus possidendi* finds expression. (5) If the caretaker (to use that term for short) leaves or the furniture is removed from the premises, otherwise than quite temporarily, we are of opinion that the protection, artificially prolonged by their presence, ceases, whether the tenant wills or desires such removal or not."[50]

The animus possidendi and corpus possessionis

The tenant failed, therefore, because although he had the necessary "*animus possidendi*," there was no sufficient "*corpus possessionis*."[51] The converse was the case in *Colin Smith Music v. Ridge*,[52] where a statutory tenant lived with his mistress and children. The tenant left, intending never to return, and surrendered the tenancy to the landlord, who

[48] The burden of proving that the tenant has gone out of residence is on the landlord. See, further, *Roland House Gardens Ltd v. Cravitz* (1974) 29 P.&C.R. 432.

[49] [1944] K.B. 309. Furniture was regarded as sufficient in *Hoggett v. Hoggett* (1980) 39 P.&C.R. 121 and *Gofor Investments Ltd v. Roberts* (1975) 29 P.&C.R. 366, but not in *Jackson v. Pekic* (1990) 22 H.L.R. 9 (suggesting, however, that personal possessions might suffice). See also *Brickfield Properties Ltd v. Hughes* [1988] 1 E.G.L.R. 106.

[50] [1948] 2 K.B. 247 at 254–255.

[51] This has been criticised in [1991] Conv. 345 and 432 (A. Brierley) on the ground that the "*corpus possessionis*" is merely evidence of the "*animus possidendi*," so that its absence should not automatically defeat the tenant.

[52] [1975] 1 W.L.R. 463. See Family Homes and Domestic Violence Bill 1995, below, p. 100.

claimed possession. The mistress claimed that the statutory
tenancy continued. Her claim failed, the court indicating,
however, that the position would have been otherwise if they
had married, as a wife can occupy on her husband's behalf.[53]
It seems that the tenant must have an intention to return
(except where the spouse occupies) at the time of leaving
rather than at any later date.[54] If he does have this intention
initially but later abandons it, his claim will fail.[55] A
conditional intention to return does not suffice if there is
little prospect of the conditions being satisfied.[56]

Illustrations   The statutory tenancy has survived prolonged absences
due to ill health,[57] even, it seems, where death terminates the
intention to return.[58] Nor was there any loss of the statutory
tenancy in *Richards v. Green*,[59] where the tenant left to look
after his parents, and, after their death, remained in their
house in order to sell it. He left his possessions in his flat, to
which he intended to return. He was away for two and a half
years, and was still away at the trial. The fact that he had
inherited the house, worth £90,000, and consequently did
not need protection, was irrelevant. In *Atyeo v. Fardoe*[60] the
statutory tenant wished to move out of his bungalow for the
winter because of its poor condition and his wife's
pregnancy. He arranged for his son to move in, and
purported to transfer the tenancy to him, to be retransferred
in the spring. The tenant left his possessions in the
bungalow. It was held that his statutory tenancy continued.
As the purported assignment was a nullity,[61] it could have no
effect in law. A case which perhaps goes too far is *Gofor
Investments Ltd v. Roberts*.[62] The tenant went abroad,
intending to return in eight to ten years, after her children
had been educated. Her furniture remained at the property,
where family members sometimes stayed. It was held that
such a prolonged absence would not cause the loss of the

---

[53] See below.
[54] See (1986) 83 L.S. Gaz. 2073 (M.P. Thompson), discussing the
differing views in *Gofor Investments Ltd v. Roberts* (1975) 29 P.&C.R. 366.
[55] *Duke v. Porter* [1986] 2 E.G.L.R. 101; [1987] Conv. 205 (J.E.M.).
[56] *Robert Thackray's Estates Ltd v. Kaye* (1989) 21 H.L.R. 160 (conditional
upon landlord doing works, which he had no intention of doing); [1989]
Conv. 450 (S. Bridge); *cf. Wigley v. Leigh* below (sufficient where
conditional upon health improving). See also *Cove v. Flick* [1954] 2 Q.B.
326 at 328; *Brickfield Properties Ltd v. Hughes* [1988] 1 E.G.L.R. 106.
[57] *Wigley v. Leigh* [1950] 2 K.B. 305; *Tickner v. Hearn* [1960] 1 W.L.R.
1406 (mental hospital); *cf. McLoughlin's Curator Bonis v. Motherwell D.C.*
(1994) S.L.T. 31 (loss of security under Scottish secure tenancy
provisions when in hospital for 5 months and incapable of forming intent
to return home).
[58] This may be inferred from *Foreman v. Beagley* [1969] 1 W.L.R. 1387,
below, p. 151, where the statutory tenant died in hospital. Her son's
claim to succeed to the statutory tenancy failed on the facts.
[59] (1983) 268 E.G. 443.
[60] (1978) 37 P.&C.R. 494.
[61] See below, p. 108.
[62] (1975) 29 P.&C.R. 366.

statutory tenancy. This decision was applied in *Brickfield Properties Ltd v. Hughes*,[63] where the statutory tenant and his wife had left the London flat in question in 1978 in order to move to a Lancashire cottage which the wife had inherited. Since that time their adult children had lived in the flat. The tenant's wife had returned on three occasions, and the tenant had not returned at all prior to the trial in 1987. They intended to return permanently when they could no longer cope with living at the cottage due to advancing years. The Court of Appeal held that the tenant must show a practical or real possibility of fulfilling his intention to return within a reasonable time.[64] Applying that test the tenant succeeded, although it was a borderline case. Ralph Gibson L.J. sympathised with the view that some cases went too far in discerning an intention to return. It was added that some absences (for example for reasons of education, employment, government service or illness) might be regarded as more meritorious than others.[65]

Finally, it is not clear whether the statutory tenancy would survive where the tenant intends to return but is debarred from doing so by an injunction under the Domestic Violence and Matrimonial Proceedings Act 1976.[66]

Where the tenant's spouse resides

Common law rule

The general rule, as we have seen, requires an intention to return on the part of the absent tenant in order to keep the statutory tenancy alive. To this rule there is an important exception, which is now statutory. The common law principle was that if the wife of the absent tenant continued in occupation, her occupation was that of her husband, so that the statutory tenancy survived even if he did not intend to return.[67] This was a special case, deriving perhaps from the old doctrine that the husband and wife were one. It may also have been attributable to the husband's duty to maintain his wife, which explains why the common law principle did not apply where the wife was the absentee tenant and the husband remained: she had no duty to maintain him. Nor did the principle apply to any other relationships, such as cohabitation outside marriage.[68] The principle has been extended by statute. The current provision is section 1(6) of the Matrimonial Homes Act 1983, providing that a spouse's occupation under section 1

Statutory rule

---

[63] [1988] 1 E.G.L.R. 106, criticised [1988] Conv. 300 (S. Bridge).
[64] Applying *Tickner v. Hearn* [1960] 1 W.L.R. 1406.
[65] [1988] 1 E.G.L.R 106 at 109; *Gofor Investments Ltd v. Roberts*, above, at 373.
[66] The problem appears solved by cl.9 of the Family Homes and Domestic Violence Bill. See (1978) 128 N.L.J. 154 (J. Martin).
[67] See *Wabe v. Taylor* [1952] 2 Q.B. 735.
[68] To be changed by Family Homes and Domestic Violency Bill, cl.9.

of the 1983 Act[69] shall, for the purpose of the Rent Act 1977, be treated as possession by the other spouse. This may be relied on by husbands also, unlike the common law principle. The tenant spouse remains liable under the tenancy,[70] but, by section 1(5), payments by the occupying spouse are as good as if made by the tenant spouse.

Illustrations   In *Hoggett v. Hoggett*[71] the husband was a protected tenant. He purported to surrender the tenancy to the landlord.[72] The wife at that time was temporarily at a women's refuge, but intended to return, and had the right to do so under section 1 of the Matrimonial Homes Act (now the Act of 1983). It was held that no surrender by operation of law was possible where the tenant's wife was still occupying. The wife was regarded as occupying, as she satisfied the *Brown v. Brash*[73]test. Thus the tenancy continued, and a purported re-letting of the property by the landlord to the husband's mistress gave the latter no rights against the wife.

The position was somewhat different in *Hulme v. Langford*,[74] where a protected tenant left his wife and went to live elsewhere. The wife remained, paying rent, until her death in 1982. In 1977 the tenant had requested the landlord to change the rent book so as to make his wife the tenant, but this was never done. In 1978 the tenancy became statutory after service of a notice to quit. Subsequently a fair rent was registered, the wife being named as the tenant. Upon her death the husband resumed possession "with commendable speed."[75] The Court of Appeal upheld his claim that he was still the statutory tenant, rejecting the landlord's argument that there had

---

[69] Section 1 gives occupation rights to the spouse of a person who is entitled to occupy a dwelling-house by virtue of a beneficial estate or interest or contract or by virtue of any enactment. The 1983 Act is to be repealed and re-enacted. Defects in the drafting of s. 1(6) are cured by cl. 4(3)(a) of the Family Homes and Domestic Violence Bill. The new provisions apply with modifications to cohabitants and former spouses.

[70] *Griffiths v. Renfree* [1989] 2 E.G.L.R. 46 (rent arrears). The liability could be terminated by an order under s. 1(3) of the 1983 Act. See, however, [1990] Conv. 58 (J.E.M.).

[71] (1980) 39 P.&C.R. 121.

[72] This was not done by deed or writing, so could only be effective in any event as a surrender by operation of law. Presumably a surrender by deed would have ended the protected tenancy, but would not have prejudiced the wife's right to claim that the statutory tenancy survived, relying on Matrimonial Homes Act 1983, s. 1(6); *cf. Friendship Housing Association v. Buchanon* (county court), noted (1994) *Legal Action*, December, p. 13 (implied surrender by tenant ended rights of occupying spouse).

[73] See above.

[74] (1985) 50 P.&C.R. 199; [1986] Conv. 272 (J.E.M.). It was left open whether s. 1(5) of the Matrimonial Homes Act 1967 (now the Act of 1983), whereby occupation by the spouse is deemed to be possession by the tenant, would prejudice the establishment of a re-letting to the spouse.

[75] (1985) 50 P.&C.R. 199 at 205.

been a surrender and a re-letting to the wife. While such a surrender could occur on a tripartite agreement to re-let to the wife, there was insufficient evidence to support a re-letting here, hence the husband continued as statutory tenant while his wife occupied.

However, a spouse can only rely on this principle in relation to a matrimonial home,[76] and during the subsistence of the marriage. In *Metropolitan Properties Ltd v. Cronan*[77] the tenant left the property, where his wife and child remained, with no intent to return. The parties were subsequently divorced. The landlord was held entitled to possession, as **Effect of divorce** the wife's protection ceased on the divorce. The wife should have taken steps to secure a transfer of the tenancy upon her divorce.[78] (Under the present law, a transfer order may be made after the decree absolute, but only where the statutory tenancy still exists[79]). The court also rejected the novel proposition that there was a similar exception in favour of the tenant's "abandoned child," who could, it was argued, assert that the statutory tenancy continued where the child occupied, even though the tenant did not intend to return. Finally, the Family Homes and Domestic Violence Bill will enable cohabitants, former cohabitants and former spouses to seek occupation orders where the tenancy still exists. Such orders can preserve a statutory tenancy in the way described above.

The "two homes" cases[80]

We have already seen that, in appropriate circumstances, two properties can be regarded as a single home.[81] In such cases a statutory tenancy can clearly arise. The case to be considered here, however, is where the two properties are not let as a single home. The tenant may own one home and rent another, as to which he asserts a statutory tenancy. Or he may rent two homes, and assert a statutory tenancy as to either or both. As will be seen, such claims may succeed, although the court takes a strict approach in order to avoid "the proposition that a sailor could have a statutory tenancy at every port."[82] The first issue is to decide whether it is properly a case of "two homes." In most cases of absence, the tenant will be living elsewhere, but it is not always appropriate to describe the tenant as having two homes.

---

[76] *Hall v. King* (1988) 55 P.&C.R. 307.
[77] (1982) 44 P.&C.R. 1; [1982] Conv. 384 (J.E.M.). See also *Crago v. Julian* [1992] 1 W.L.R. 372.
[78] See below, p. 108.
[79] *Lewis v. Lewis* [1985] A.C. 828, below, p. 109.
[80] See generally (1986) 83 L.S. Gaz. 2073 (M.P. Thompson). A similar question can arise in the context of succession. See *Swanbrae Ltd v. Elliott* [1987] 1 E.G.L.R. 99, below, p. 151.
[81] See above, p. 61.
[82] *Hallwood Estates Ltd v. Flack* (1950) 66 T.L.R. (Pt. 2) 368 at 370, *per* Sir Raymond Evershed, M.R.

**Not all dwellings
are homes**

Thus in *Richards v. Green*[83] the court declined to regard the tenant as a "two homes man." The rented flat was his sole home, which he continued sufficiently to occupy, hence his statutory tenancy survived. Another example is *Regalian Securities Ltd v. Scheuer*.[84] The statutory tenant of a flat moved into a house bought by his future wife and established a home there. He still used the flat to work in, and kept his clothes and furniture there, and his mail was also sent there. He ate and slept at the house for most of the year. In the winter the house was let and the family stayed elsewhere, "camping" at the flat for about two months a year. It was held that the tenant was no longer entitled to the statutory tenancy of the flat. It was not a "two homes" case, as the house was his only real home. His continuing occupation of the flat did not have the character of residence that is within the contemplation of the Rent Act.

**Protection for
either or both
homes**

Where, however, the circumstances are such that the tenant can properly be regarded as having two homes, it is established that Rent Act protection may be retained as to either or both.[85] So in *Langford Property Co. Ltd v. Tureman*,[86] where the tenant rented a town flat and owned a country home, he was held entitled to a statutory tenancy of the flat. Similarly in *Brickfield Properties Ltd v. Hughes*,[87] where the tenant was held to have retained his statutory tenancy of a flat, in spite of a prolonged and continuing absence by reasons of his moving to a cottage inherited by his wife. A "pied-à-terre," however, will not suffice,[88] nor will a "holiday home."[89]

A difficult case is *Kavanagh v. Lyroudias*,[90] where a tenant of two adjoining properties was held not to be entitled to a statutory tenancy of one, as he did not occupy it separately from the adjoining premises as a complete home. He was tenant of No. 21, which he shared with a friend, but later took a tenancy of No. 23 as well, from the same landlord, to get an extra bedroom. He slept at No. 23, but ate and used the bathroom at No. 21. He was held to have no statutory tenancy of No. 23, as his occupation of it did not have the character of residence, which requires all the essential

---

[83] (1983) 268 E.G. 443, above; *Heglibiston Establishment v. Heyman* (1978) 36 P.&C.R. 351. (Statutory tenancy continued although the tenant spent only two or three nights a week at the property, and was often abroad. It was his sole home.) See also *Hampstead Way Investments Ltd v. Lewis-Weare*, below.

[84] (1984) 47 P.&C.R. 367; [1983] Conv. 146 (J.E.M.). See also *Crocker (D.J.) Securities (Portsmouth) Ltd v. Johal* [1989] 2 E.G.L.R. 102 (no statutory tenancy of flat where only real home was in Malaysia).

[85] *Hallwood Estates Ltd v. Flack* [1950] W.N. 268; *Haskins v. Lewis* [1931] 2 K.B. 1; *Skinner v. Geary* [1931] 2 K.B. 546.

[86] [1949] 1 K.B. 29.

[87] [1988] 1 E.G.L.R. 106, above, p. 101.

[88] *Beck v. Scholz* [1953] 1 Q.B. 570; *cf. Blanway Investments Ltd v. Lynch* (1993) 25 H.L.R. 379.

[89] *Walker v. Ogilvy* (1974) 28 P.&C.R. 288.

[90] [1985] 1 All E.R. 560.

activities of living. It seems, however, that his tenancy of No. 23 was initially protected.[91] The House of Lords has subsequently commented[92] that the reasoning of the Court of Appeal in this case was marred by a failure to consider whether the two properties together constituted the tenant's residence.

Restatement of principles

The House of Lords reviewed the "two homes" principle in *Hampstead Way Investments Ltd v. Lewis-Weare*.[93] A statutory tenant married and moved to a nearby house, retaining his flat, where he slept five times a week after night work. His clothes were kept in the flat, and his mail was sent there; however, he did not eat there. The tenant's stepson lived in the flat, but the tenant paid the outgoings of both properties. The House of Lords held that while it was possible to have two homes within section 2,[94] if one is occupied occasionally or for a limited purpose, it is a question of fact and degree whether the tenant is "residing" there. If the tenant occupied two different parts of the same house under different lettings by the same landlord, carrying on some activities in one part and the rest in the other, he would not be protected as to either part, unless it could be regarded as a single combined letting.[95] If he owns a dwelling-house which he occupies as his home for most of the time, and is tenant of another, which he occupies rarely

Question of fact and degree

or for a limited purpose, it is a question of fact and degree whether the second is a home. In the present case the tenant's limited use of the flat was insufficient. It was not his home, but the stepson's.[96] Nor could the house and flat be regarded as one living unit. Hence the tenant is unlikely to succeed if the property which is used only to a limited extent is used for convenience rather than necessity, which is likely to be the case if the two properties are geographically close.[97]

This "fact and degree" test has been criticised on the basis that the House of Lords should have taken the opportunity to declare that the policy of the Act is that the tenant should not be protected if the property is not his main residence.[98]

Comparison with secure and assured tenancies

It is interesting to compare the requirements of public sector secure tenancies and assured tenancies. By section 81 of the Housing Act 1985 and section 1 of the Housing Act 1988 respectively, the tenant can only obtain protection as to his only or principal home. No doubt the possibility of the "two homes man" was not present to the minds of the drafters of the original Rent Act legislation, which was

---

[91] Contrast the cases on "dwelling" for the purpose of Rent Act 1977, s. 1: above, p. 64.
[92] In *Hampstead Way Investments Ltd v. Lewis-Weare*, below.
[93] [1985] 1 W.L.R. 164.
[94] Confirming *Langford Property Co. Ltd v. Tureman*, above.
[95] *Wimbush v. Cibulia* [1949] 2 K.B. 564, above, p. 69.
[96] *cf. Brickfield Properties Ltd v. Hughes* [1988] 1 E.G.L.R. 106, above, p. 101.
[97] See (1986) 83 L.S. Gaz. 2073 (M.P. Thompson).
[98] [1985] Conv. 224 (P.F. Smith).

designed for the poorer classes. Subsequent experience has
indicated the need for a specific provision in the Housing
Acts.[99]

Finally, it might be added that a lenient interpretation of
section 2, in particular the "two homes" cases and those
involving lengthy absences, has repercussions on the

**Resident
landlords**

resident landlord rule, discussed in Chapter 5. In order to
satisfy that rule, and thereby deprive the tenant of full
protection, the landlord must occupy part of the same
building as his residence.[1] This requires him to fulfil the
same conditions as a statutory tenant must fulfil under
section 2.[2] Hence the *Brown v. Brash*[3] test is imported here,
with the result that landlords can presumably rely on the
cases which were decided on the basis of furthering the
policy of the Rent Act to protect the tenant. Perhaps a
stricter approach might be expected in the context of
resident landlords.[4]

Joint tenants

The Rent Act makes no express provision for joint
tenancies.[5] On a literal reading of section 2 in the case of a
joint protected tenancy, the statutory tenancy can only arise
if both tenants continue to reside, as they together constitute

**One of joint
tenants can be
statutory tenant**

the tenant. The matter arose in *Lloyd v. Sadler*,[6] where one
joint tenant left while the tenancy was still protected. The
other remained, and subsequently claimed a statutory
tenancy. The Court of Appeal, rejecting the literal
approach, upheld the tenant's claim. As the policy of the Act
was to protect the tenant, the Act should be construed in his
favour. The strict law of joint tenancy did not apply. It was
argued that this result would prejudice the landlord, who,
during the protected tenancy, had been able to look to both
tenants for the rent. However, if the rent was not paid, there
would be a ground for possession.[7] In any case, if one joint
tenant had died during the protected tenancy, the other
would have become sole tenant (and subsequently sole
statutory tenant) by survivorship. No doubt if both had
remained, they would have become joint statutory tenants.

Problems relating to the application of the succession
rules to joint tenancies are discussed in Chapter 8.

[99] But see the lax interpretation of the Housing Act 1985 provision in
Crawley B.C. v. Sawyer (1988) 20 H.L.R. 98, below, p. 197, which adds
little to the basic concept of occupation as a residence. See [1988] Conv.
300 at 303 (S. Bridge).
[1] Rent Act 1977, s. 12.
[2] *ibid.* Sched. 2, para. 5.
[3] See above.
[4] See *Jackson v. Pekic* (1990) 22 H.L.R. 9. *cf.* Housing Act 1988, Sched. 1,
para. 10, stipulating the "only or principal home" test for resident
landlords under the 1988 Act.
[5] See generally [1978] Conv. 436 (J. Martin), comparing other statutory
codes. See, in particular, Housing Act 1988, s. 45(3).
[6] [1978] Q.B. 774.
[7] Under Case 1, below, p. 117.

Terms of the statutory tenancy

Terms of protected tenancy continue so far as consistent with the Act

Section 3(1) of the 1977 Act provides that the statutory tenant, so long as he retains possession, "shall observe and be entitled to the benefit of all the terms and conditions of the original contract of tenancy, so far as they are consistent with the provisions of this Act." As a general rule, therefore, the type of covenants which are regarded as "touching and concerning" the land at common law, such as the covenant to repair or the covenant for quiet enjoyment, will continue into the statutory tenancy. Section 3(2) expressly provides that the statutory tenant shall afford the landlord access and reasonable facilities for executing repairs which the landlord is entitled to execute.[8]

Terms which have been regarded as inconsistent include, obviously, the covenant to yield up possession at the end of the tenancy,[9] and also an option to purchase the reversion "at any time" at a fixed price.[10]

The Act makes express provision as to the terms of the statutory tenancy in three further respects.

Rent

The rent payable under the statutory tenancy is not necessarily the same as that payable under the previous protected tenancy. This is discussed in Chapter 10.

Notice

Length of notice

By section 3(3), a statutory tenant shall be entitled to give up possession only if he gives such notice as would have been required under the protected tenancy (*i.e.* if periodic), or, if no notice would have been required (*i.e.* if fixed term), on giving not less than three months' notice. By the Protection from Eviction Act 1977, section 5,[11] a minimum of four weeks' notice is required for a periodic tenancy. A landlord who obtains a possession order against a statutory tenant is not required to give notice to quit, even though such a notice would have been required during the protected tenancy.[12]

Payment

The statutory tenant may ask or receive payment from the

---

[8] See also s. 148, implying a similar term into protected tenancies. As to improvements, see Housing Act 1980, s. 81(1).

[9] *Barton v. Fincham* [1921] 2 K.B. 291.

[10] *Longmuir v. Kew* [1960] 1 W.L.R. 862. The option was exercisable only during the contractual tenancy. *cf. William McIlroy Ltd v. Clements* [1923] W.N. 81 (option to renew).

[11] See above, p. 52. Housing Act 1988 provides exceptions which are not relevant here.

[12] Rent Act 1977, s. 3(4).

landlord as a condition of giving up possession, but commits an offence if he asks or receives payment from any other person.[13]

We have seen that, according to the case-law discussed in this Chapter, the statutory tenancy ceases if the tenant goes out of residence. What, then, is the position if he loses his statutory tenancy but has not given the notice to quit required by section 3? It seems that while such a tenant loses his rights to a statutory tenancy, he continues to be liable to pay the rent until such a notice is served, unless there is surrender and acceptance.[14] It was left open by the House of Lords in *Lewis v. Lewis*[15] whether in such a case the tenancy would be regarded as subsisting for the purpose of a transfer order to the tenant's divorced wife.

Cesser of residence without notice

Assignment

The prior protected tenancy will have been assignable unless it contained a covenant to the contrary. The statutory tenancy, on the other hand, is not capable of assignment. Any purported assignment of it is a nullity, although if the statutory tenant ceases to reside, the statutory tenancy will normally terminate.[16] If the protected tenancy contained no prohibition against sub-letting, the statutory tenant may sublet. If, however, he sublets the whole, the statutory tenancy will cease, as the tenant will have ceased to reside.[17]

Incapable of assignment

Subletting

There are two exceptions to the rule that the statutory tenancy may not be assigned.

Exceptions to the rule

Where the landlord is a party Where there is a written agreement, to which the landlord is a party, the statutory tenant may give up possession in favour of a third party, who is thereafter deemed to be the statutory tenant.[18]

By court order in matrimonial proceedings [19] By section 7 of the Matrimonial Homes Act 1967, the court was empowered to order the transfer of a statutory (or

[13] *ibid.* Sched. 1, para. 12. Note that a purchaser does not become landlord until completion.
[14] See *Boyer v. Warbey* [1953] 1 Q.B. 234; *King's College, Cambridge v. Kershman* (1948) 64 T.L.R. 547. It seems that the personal representative of a deceased statutory tenant must, in cases where there is no successor, give notice to quit to the landlord. Presumably one of joint statutory tenants who is leaving could serve such a notice, in order to avoid continuing joint and several liability.
[15] [1985] A.C. 828: below.
[16] See *Atyeo v. Fardoe* (1978) 37 P.&C.R. 494: above, p. 100. Contrast the position at common law, where a tenancy may be effectively assigned, although in breach of covenant.
[17] See below, p. 160. See also Case 6: below, p. 121.
[18] Rent Act 1977, Sched. 1, para. 13. See *Daejan Properties Ltd v. Mahoney* [1995] E.G.C.S. 4 (landlord estopped from denying that para. 13 complied with).
[19] See [1982] Conv. 334 (A. Arden).

protected) tenancy on divorce or annulment.[20] Such an order could not be made after decree absolute. This power was extended by the Matrimonial Homes and Property Act 1981, so that a transfer order could be made on the granting of a decree of divorce, nullity or judicial separation, "or at any time thereafter." Thus the power continues exercisable after decree absolute. This provision is now contained in Schedule 1, paragraph 1, of the consolidating Matrimonial Homes Act 1983. It has since been enacted that the transfer order may be made without any decree of divorce, nullity, etc., where an application is made by a party to a marriage for an order for financial relief.[21]

Transfer after decree absolute

The question which arose in *Lewis v. Lewis*[22] was whether the provision in the 1981 Act, giving the court jurisdiction after decree absolute, was retrospective. the parties were divorced before the provision was in operation. The House of Lords held that it was not retrospective. Even if it had been, it would not have availed the wife, as the statutory tenancy came to an end on decree absolute.[23] Where the statutory tenant no longer resides, his spouse's occupation will only keep the statutory tenancy alive until decree absolute.[24] The statutory provisions relating to transfer orders use the present tense: "Where one spouse is entitled ... to occupy a dwelling-house by virtue of a protected tenancy or statutory tenancy. . . ."[25] Hence the court has no jurisdiction where the statutory tenancy has already terminated. This result is not only clearly correct but also, it is submitted, desirable. It would be unfair to the landlord to resurrect a statutory tenancy which has ceased to exist.

It remains to consider the circumstances in which a transfer order can be made after decree absolute. This can clearly be done if the tenancy is still protected, as occupation by the tenant is not there required. Where the tenancy is statutory, it will only continue after decree absolute if the tenant himself remains in occupation. In such a case the spouse may apply for a transfer order, whether occupying with the tenant spouse or non-occupying. If the tenant is not in occupation, the spouse must apply before decree absolute. The decision in *Crago v. Julian*[26] serves as a warning to the tenant's spouse. In that case the husband had a weekly protected tenancy. In divorce proceedings he

---

[20] Until the enactment of the Family Homes and Domestic Violence Bill 1995, there is no such jurisdiction in the case of unmarried couples. See, generally, *Wiseman v. Simpson* [1988] 1 W.L.R. 35 (secure tenancy).

[21] Matrimonial and Family Proceedings Act 1984, s. 22.

[22] [1985] A.C. 828; [1985] Conv. 128 (J.E.M.).

[23] See *Metropolitan Properties Ltd v. Cronan* (1982) 44 P.&C.R. 1, p. 103.

[24] Matrimonial Homes Act 1983, s. 1(6). Former spouses will have greater rights under cl.9 of the Family Homes and Domestic Violence Bill.

[25] Matrimonial Homes Act 1983, Sched. 1, para. 1.

[26] [1992] 1 W.L.R. 372; [1992] Conv. 268 (J. Martin) and 375 (P. Sparkes); (1993) 23 Fam. Law 8 (G. Posner); *cf. City of Westminster v. Peart* (1992) 24 H.L.R. 389.

undertook to transfer the tenancy to his wife. Both parties assumed that nothing further needed to be done, but in fact a deed should have been executed to assign the weekly tenancy.[27] The wife remained in occupation until a notice to quit was served. She had no defence to the possession action because the protected tenancy had never been assigned to her and thus no statutory tenancy could arise on its termination at a time when the tenant was no longer occupying and the marriage had already ended.

The Matrimonial Homes Act, of course, applies only to married couples. Following recommendations of the Law Commission,[28] the Family Homes and Domestic Violence Bill[29] makes similar provisions with respect to cohabitants and former cohabitants. The order may be made "at any time after" they cease to live together as husband and wife. Clearly the tenancy must still exist, although a statutory tenancy may survive the tenant's absence where the cohabitant has obtained an occupation order. The jurisdiction is confined to dwelling-houses where the cohabitants lived together as husband and wife. Various matters must be taken into account, including the respective suitability of the parties as tenants, and the landlord will have an opportunity to be heard. Compensation may be ordered to be paid to the transferor.

Children Act 1989   At present there is a jurisdiction under the Children Act 1989 to order the transfer of a tenancy which is wider than the Matrimonial Homes Act in that it extends to unmarried couples. It provides that the court can order either or both parents to transfer to the applicant, for the benefit of the child, or to the child himself, "such property to which the parent is, or the parents are, entitled (either in possession or in reversion)" as is specified in the order.[30] This could be invoked in relation to a protected tenancy,[31] but it would not seem applicable to a statutory tenancy, which is not "property" within the meaning of the provision.[32]

---

[27] Law of Property Act 1925, s. 52(1). It is otherwise where the court makes a transfer order under the Matrimonial Homes Act 1983, Sched. 1, para. 2(1). This takes effect without further documentation.

[28] Law Com. No. 207 (1992); *Family Law: Domestic Violence and Occupation of the Family Home.*

[29] Sched. 4.

[30] s. 15 and Sched. 1, para. 1(2)(e). This replaces Family Law Reform Act 1987, s. 12, which amended the Guardianship of Minors Act 1971.

[31] See *K. v. K.* [1992] 1 W.L.R. 530 (secure tenancy); *Pearson v. Franklin* [1994] 1 W.L.R. 370 (housing association tenancy); *B. v. B. (Transfer of Tenancy)* (1994) 24 Fam. Law 250 (secure tenancy).

[32] There is no definition.

7 RECOVERY OF POSSESSION

A statutory tenancy terminates if one of the following four events occurs[1]:

(a) the tenant yields up possession after giving proper notice (as discussed in Chapter 6);

(b) the tenant dies without leaving a successor to the statutory tenancy (to be discussed in Chapter 8);

(c) the landlord obtains a court order based on one of the grounds for possession in the Rent Act 1977; or

(d) some other event occurs such as a change of user or transfer of the reversion to a person not bound by the Act, whereupon the tenant ceases to be entitled to retain possession as statutory (or protected) tenant.

No contracting out
It does not suffice that the tenant has merely agreed to give up his rights. In *Appleton v. Aspin*[2] the landlord agreed to sell to a purchaser with vacant possession. Before exchange of contracts the purchaser required the protected tenant to make an undertaking not to enforce her rights, in consideration of the purchaser entering into the contract with the vendor landlord. The tenant signed the contract of sale. The purchase was completed but the tenant refused to vacate. The purchaser's action against the tenant failed, as he had no ground for possession under the Rent Act. The hardship to the purchaser was irrelevant to the construction of the Act. The desired result could have been achieved by an assignment of the tenancy to the purchaser before completion.[3]

Discretionary and mandatory grounds
Two things should be noted about the statutory grounds for possession. First, some are discretionary, so that the court will only grant possession if it considers it reasonable to do so, while others are mandatory. Secondly, if the tenancy is still protected (as opposed to statutory), the landlord must be able to terminate it under the general law, for example, by forfeiture or notice to quit, in addition to establishing a statutory ground for possession. If the tenancy is already statutory, the landlord can go straight to the

---

[1] If wrongfully evicted, the statutory tenant may obtain damages under the Protection from Eviction Act 1977 (as amended) or at common law, see above, Chap. 3. If unable to obtain an injunction in time to restrain unlawful eviction, he may obtain a mandatory injunction to restore him to possession.

[2] [1988] 1 W.L.R. 410; [1988] Conv. 212 (S. Bridge); *Barton v. Fincham* [1921] 2 K.B. 291.

[3] A protected tenancy is assignable if there is no prohibition in the lease. A statutory tenancy may be assigned with the landlord's consent; see above, p. 108.

grounds for possession, as the common law methods of termination no longer apply. Although no notice to quit is required in such a case, a failure to warn the tenant or send a letter before action may affect the issue of reasonableness if the ground is discretionary.[4] Many of the grounds appear also in the assured tenancy regime under the Housing Act 1988.

Overcrowding

Before examining the grounds for possession, the effect of overcrowding should be mentioned. Section 101 of the Rent Act 1977 provides that at any time when a dwelling-house is overcrowded, within the meaning of the Housing Act 1985, in such circumstances as to render the occupier guilty of an offence, nothing in Part VII of the Act (dealing with recovery of possession from protected or statutory tenants) shall prevent the immediate landlord of the occupier from obtaining possession. A former restriction whereby the section's application was confined to premises used "by members of the working classes or of a type suitable for such use" was finally repealed in 1985.[5]

The effect of section 101 is to deprive the tenant of his security while the overcrowding lasts, but rent control still applies prior to the making of a possession order. Of course, section 101 does not enable the landlord to recover possession against a protected tenant unless he is in a position to terminate the contractual tenancy.

If the overcrowding has ceased before the hearing, the landlord will be unable to recover possession.[6] Nor may he do so if the local authority has licensed the overcrowding, as the occupier then commits no offence.[7]

Although not specifically dealt with in the 1977 Act, a similar principle applies to unfit houses.[8]

Suitable alternative accommodation

This is dealt with under a separate heading because, although in effect a ground for possession, it does not appear in the statutory list of grounds for possession, discussed below.

[4] *White v. Wareing* [1992] 1 E.G.L.R. 271 (holding also that it is reasonable to assume that a periodic tenancy which has lasted a long time has been converted to a statutory tenancy.)
[5] Housing (Consequential Provisions) Act 1985, Sched. 2. Overcrowding is not dealt with in the Housing Act 1988 in relation to assured tenancies.
[6] *Zbytniewski v. Broughton* [1956] 2 Q.B. 673; *Henry Smith's Charity Trustees v. Bartosiak-Jentys* (1992) 24 H.L.R. 627 (holding also that there is no power to suspend the order under Rent Act 1977, s. 100).
[7] Housing Act 1985, s. 327. Nor is the offence committed where the overcrowding occurs solely by reason of a child attaining a specified age, if the tenant has applied to the local authority for alternative accommodation: *ibid.* s. 328.
[8] See *Buswell v. Goodwin* [1971] 1 W.L.R. 92, below, p. 139.

By section 98 of the 1977 Act, the court may make an order for possession if it is satisfied that suitable alternative accommodation is available for the tenant (or will be available for him when the order takes effect[9]). Such an order will not be made unless the court considers it reasonable to make it. Whether the alternative accommodation is suitable depends on the extent to which the statutory criteria are fulfilled.[10] The alternative accommodation need not be offered by the landlord himself. A local authority certificate to the effect that the authority will provide suitable alternative accommodation for the tenant in the district by a specified date is conclusive evidence as to the availability of suitable alternative accommodation, although this does not determine the question of whether it is reasonable to make the order.[11] Failing such a certificate, accommodation is deemed suitable if it satisfies two broad requirements: first as to security of tenure, and secondly as to its suitability to the particular circumstances of the tenant. As far as security is concerned, the alternative accommodation must be premises let as a separate dwelling in such manner that there will be either a protected tenancy (other than one to which any of the mandatory grounds for possession, discussed below, will apply[12]) or on terms which will afford security reasonably equivalent to such a protected tenancy. "Reasonably equivalent" security will be provided by a local authority secure tenancy, or by a long fixed term letting.[13] Even after the commencement of the Housing Act 1988, the court may order that the new tenancy be a protected tenancy, if it considers that an assured tenancy would not afford adequate security.[14]

Statutory criteria for suitability

As far as the particular tenant's requirements are concerned, the alternative accommodation must be reasonably suitable to the needs of the tenant and his family with regard to proximity to work,[15] to the means of the tenant, and to the needs of the tenant and his family as regards extent and character. If the current tenancy is furnished, so must the proposed tenancy of the alternative accommodation be. One way of establishing that the alternative accommodation is reasonably suitable to the tenant's needs with regard to rental and extent is for the landlord to show that it is similar in those respects to dwelling-houses provided in the neighbourhood by the local

Local authority certificate

[9] Earlier availability does not suffice if no longer available at the hearing. See *Fennbend v. Millar* (1988) 20 H.L.R. 19.
[10] Set out in Rent Act 1977, Sched. 15, paras. 3–8.
[11] *Dame Margaret Hungerford Charity Trustees v. Beazeley* [1993] 2 E.G.L.R. 143.
[12] Housing Act 1980, Sched. 25, para. 58.
[13] See county court cases discussed in Pettit, *Private Sector Tenancies* (2nd ed., 1981) p. 193.
[14] Housing Act 1988, s. 34(1).
[15] See *Yewbright Properties Ltd v Stone* (1980) 40 P.&C.R. 402.

authority for persons whose needs as regards extent are
similar (in the opinion of the court) to those of the tenant.
For this purpose a local authority certificate stating the
extent and rental of accommodation it provides to meet the
needs of tenants with families of a specified size is conclusive
evidence of those facts.[16] While such a certificate is
conclusive as to the rental and extent of such local authority
accommodation, it is for the court, not the authority, to
decide if the alternative accommodation proposed by the
landlord is similar to that provided by the authority.[17]

Naturally the statutory criteria outlined above cannot deal
with every circumstance, hence there is much case-law on
the meaning of suitable alternative accommodation. The
question whether the alternative accommodation is suitable
must be kept distinct from the question whether, even
though suitable, it is reasonable to make the possession
order. In *Battlespring v. Gates*,[18] an elderly widow was
offered a similar, but more pleasant and comfortable flat.
This was suitable alternative accommodation, but it was not

**Must be suitable
and reasonable**

reasonable to make the order, because the widow had lived
there for 35 years and was attached to her flat and its
memories. The question of reasonableness is for the judge in
the first instance, whose finding will not be upset on appeal
unless he has misdirected himself.[19] It involves a
consideration of both landlord and tenant (and even of the
community[20]). Here the landlord's interest in recovering
possession was purely financial. There was nothing wrong in
that, but the position was different from that of a landlord
who wished to recover possession because he had nowhere
to live himself.

Needs of family

As we have seen, the needs not only of the tenant but also
of his "family" must be taken into account. It was held in
Kavanagh v. Lyroudias[21] that the word bears the same
meaning as it does in the context of succession to the
statutory tenancy.[22] In that case the tenant shared his home
with a sick friend. The friend was held not to be "family,"
hence his needs were not relevant to the suitability of any

---

[16] Rent Act 1977, Sched. 15, para. 5(2).
[17] *Jones v. Cook* (1990) 22 H.L.R. 319; [1991] Conv. 152 (S. Bridge).
[18] (1983) 268 E.G. 355. See also *Gladyric Ltd v. Collinson* (1983) 267 E.G.
761 (understanding that property to be let for a short time only held
relevant to reasonableness); *Michburn Ltd v. Fernandez* [1986] 2
E.G.L.R. 103.
[19] It should be added that an appeal from a finding of fact is possible;
County Courts Act 1984, s. 77(6); *Law Land plc v. Sinclair* (1992) 24
H.L.R. 57.
[20] *Dame Margaret Hungerford Charity Trustees v. Beazeley* [1993] 2.
E.G.L.R. 143 (possession required to repair and reconstruct listed
building: benefit to community outweighed detriment to tenant).
[21] [1985] 1 All E.R. 560. See also *Standingford v. Probert* [1950] 1 K.B.
377; *Roberts v. Macilwraith-Christie* [1987] 1 E.G.L.R. 224 (lodger not
included).
[22] See below, Chap. 8. For the meaning of "family" in a tenant's covenant,
see *Wrotham Park S.E. v. Naylor* (1991) 62 P.&C.R. 233 (servants
included).

alternative accommodation. However, it would not be reasonable to make a possession order where the alternative accommodation would be such that the tenant would have to share a cramped flat with the friend or eject him. In the context of the similar provisions applicable to secure tenancies under the Housing Act 1985, a possession order was set aside as having been made without jurisdiction where the tenant's wife was not joined as a party.[23] It was held that every member of the tenant's family living on the premises had an interest in the suitability of the alternative accommodation. The provisions, it was said, could only work if such persons with an interest in the proceedings were allowed to be joined as defendants.

The question whether the alternative accommodation is suitable to the tenant's "needs" as regards extent and **Housing needs** character requires a consideration of his *housing* needs. In **only** *Hill v. Rochard*[24] the tenants occupied a large period country house with grounds and a paddock for their pony. The landlord offered a modern detached house with no paddock on an estate outside a village. This was held to be suitable alternative accommodation. The present tenancy allowed the tenants to enjoy amenities far beyond their housing needs, but the Rent Act was not concerned with matters such as proximity to entertainment, recreation and sport. Similarly in *Lohan v. Hilton*[25] where a terraced house with no garage, situated on a council estate, was held suitable for a tenant of a bungalow with gardens and a double garage on a private estate.

Environment Environmental matters, however, are relevant. In *Redspring v. Francis*,[26] the tenant had lived for 30 years in a small flat in a quiet residential road. The tenant had the use of a garden, but the bathroom was shared. The landlord offered a flat with larger rooms and an exclusive bathroom, but no garden. This flat was in a busy road, next door to a fried fish shop, and near to a hospital, cinema and public house. In addition, the local authority planned to use a yard at the back as a transport depot. The Court of Appeal, finding that this was not suitable alternative accommodation, held that the environment could be considered, as well as the physical character of the property. Here the difference was in kind and not merely of degree. In

---

[23] *Wandsworth L.B.C. v. Fadayomi* [1987] 1 W.L.R. 1473; [1987] Conv. 450 (J.E.M.). The couple were separated although still living under the same roof.

[24] [1983] 1 W.L.R. 478; [1983[Conv. 320 (P.F. Smith). See also, in the context of public sector secure tenancies, *Enfield L.B.C. v. French* (1985) 49 P.&C.R. 223, where the need for a garden as a hobby was a "need" within the statute, although on the facts it was outweighed by other considerations.

[25] [1994] E.G.C.S. 83.

[26] [1973] 1 W.L.R. 134. See also *Roberts v. Macilwraith-Christie* [1987] 1 E.G.L.R. 224 (reasonable to make order where tenant in Kensington Square offered flat in Shepherd's Bush).

Dawncar Investments Ltd v. Plews[27] the tenant, who had a
young child, had a flat in a quiet road in Hampstead. The
landlord failed to establish that a flat in Kilburn was suitable
alternative accommodation. Although the flat itself was
better, it was in a busy commercial road used by heavy
lorries and was near a timber yard, railway and two public
houses.

Cultural and religious needs

Redspring v. Francis was distinguished by the Court of
Appeal in *Siddiqui v. Rashid*,[28] where the tenant, a Muslim,
had a flat in London and worked in Luton. His friends were
all in London, where he attended a mosque and a cultural
centre. The offer of a flat in Luton was held suitable. While
the court could consider the environment, it need not
consider the society of friends, nor the tenant's cultural or
spiritual interests.

Part of same dwelling

It is established that a part of the property which is the
subject-matter of the current letting can constitute
alternative accommodation. In *Mykolyshyn v. Noah*,[29] the
letting comprised a bedroom, kitchen and sitting-room. The
sitting-room was used only to store furniture. The landlord,
wishing to take it over as a bedroom for his children, offered
the same flat minus the sitting-room. This was held to be
suitable alternative accommodation.

Sublet parts

This principle is useful where the tenant has sublet part of
the property. The landlord can effectively take over the
sublet part[30] by offering the tenant the remainder. The
policy of the Rent Act is to protect the tenant in his home,
and not to let him profit from his security by subletting.
However, there is no hard and fast rule. So in *Yoland Ltd v.
Reddington*,[31] where the tenant had sublet part to friends
(who shared the bathroom and garden), an offer of the
remainder was held suitable, but nevertheless it was not
reasonable to make the order. The tenant would no longer
be surrounded by sub-tenants of his own choosing and the
landlord (an investment company which had purchased the
reversion) might leave the other part empty and uncared for.

Discretionary grounds for possession

The various "Cases" giving rise to a ground for possession
are set out in Schedule 15 of the 1977 Act. Part I of that
Schedule contains 10 "Cases" which are discretionary. The
court must consider it reasonable to make such an order.[32]

---

[27] (1993) 25 H.L.R. 639.
[28] [1980] 1 W.L.R. 1018.
[29] [1970] 1 W.L.R. 1271. See also *McDonnell v. Daly* [1969] 1 W.L.R.
1482, holding (at a time when dwellings with a partial business use could
be within the Rent Act) that an offer of a part of the same dwelling could
not be suitable alternative accommodation when the "subtracted" part
(an artist's studio) was necessary to the tenant's professional needs.
[30] For the sub-tenant's position, see Rent Act 1977, s. 137, below, p. 156.
[31] (1982) 263 E.G. 157.
[32] Rent Act 1977, s. 98(1).

We have already seen, in the context of suitable alternative accommodation, some of the factors which have been relevant to the exercise of the discretion. It does not follow from the fact the landlord is being reasonable in requiring possession that it is reasonable to order possession: "because a wish is reasonable, it does not follow that it is reasonable in a court to grant it."[33] The general principle has been stated by Lord Greene M.R. in *Cumming v. Danson*.[34] The judge must consider:

Issue of reasonableness

"all relevant circumstances as they exist at the date of the hearing. That he must do in what I venture to call a broad, common-sense way as a man of the world, and come to the conclusion giving such weight as he thinks right to the various factors in the situation. Some factors may have little or no weight, others may be decisive, but it is quite wrong for him to exclude from his consideration matters which he ought to take into account."

The issue of reasonableness is for the county court judge to decide. The Court of Appeal will not interfere with the exercise of his discretion unless he has erred in law.

It is now proposed to consider in turn the various discretionary grounds for possession.

Case 1

Rent arrears or other breach

"Where any rent lawfully due from the tenant has not been paid or any obligation of the protected or statutory tenancy ... has been broken or not performed."

Defences   The first question to consider is whether the tenant is in breach. In the case of rent arrears, the tenant will have a defence if he has a valid set-off or counterclaim for a sum at least as great as the arrears,[35] or if the landlord has not

---

[33] *Shrimpton v. Rabbits* (1924) 131 L.T. 478 at 479, in the context of Case 9, below.
[34] [1942] 2 All E.R. 653 at 655. See also *Cresswell v. Hodgson* [1951] 2 K.B. 92, where Denning L.J. said (at 97) that the possession order must be "reasonable having regard to the interests of the parties concerned and also reasonable having regard to the interests of the public." In *Chiverton v. Ede* [1921] 2 K.B. 30 at 44–45, McCardie J. said that the discretion must be exercised "in a judicial manner having regard on the one hand to the general scheme and purpose of the Act, and on the other to the special conditions, including to a large extent matters of a domestic and social character."
[35] *Crompton v. Broomfield* [1990] E.G.C.S. 137; *Televantos v. McCulloch* (1991) 23 H.L.R. 412; [1992] Conv. 270 (J. Martin). See also *Mountain v. Hastings* (1993) 25 H.L.R. 427 at 438.

complied with his obligation under section 48 of the
Landlord and Tenant Act 1987 to provide information to
the tenant.[36]

Assuming a breach is established, Case 1 is primarily
concerned with a tenant who has a "bad record."[37] The
landlord is unlikely to recover possession in the case of an
isolated breach. The commencement of proceedings is the
date at which the breach must exist, but possession is
unlikely to be ordered where the tenant has paid arrears
before judgment, unless there is a long history of arrears.[38]

Likelihood of suspension In any event, the court has a discretion to suspend the
operation of a possession order on conditions, for example
as to the payment of arrears.[39] Indeed, this is the common
practice.

As far as breaches other than non-payment of rent are
concerned, Case 1 applies to express and implied
obligations, whether or not continuing.[40] If the breach has
been remedied, however, this will be significant to the issue
of reasonableness.[41]

Waiver The common law doctrine of waiver is not fully applicable
to statutory tenancies, hence acceptance of rent in the
knowledge of a breach will not inevitably preclude the
landlord from invoking Case 1,[42] even if the acceptance is
unqualified.[43] This is because waiver relates strictly to
forfeiture, which is not applicable to a statutory tenancy.[44]

Case 2

Nuisance, annoyance, illegal or immoral user "Where the tenant or any person residing or lodging
with him or any sub-tenant of his has been guilty of
conduct which is a nuisance or annoyance to adjoining
occupiers, or has been convicted of using the dwelling--

---

[36] *Hussain v. Singh* [1993] 2. E.G.L.R. 70; *Dallhold Estates (U.K.) Pty Ltd
v. Lindsey Trading Properties Inc.* [1994] 1 E.G.L.R. 93. (Unpaid rent
becomes due as soon as the 1987 Act is complied with); *Rogan v.
Woodfield Building Services Ltd* (1995) 27 H.L.R. 78; [1995] Conv. 154
(M. Haley).

[37] *Dellenty v. Pellow* [1951] 2 K.B. 858.

[38] Common Law Procedure Act 1852, s. 212 (entitling the tenant to a stay
of proceedings if he pays arrears and costs before trial) does not,
however, apply to a statutory tenant: *Dellenty v. Pellow*, above. See,
generally, *Bird v. Hildage* [1948] 1 K.B. 91; *Hayman v. Rowlands* [1957]
1 W.L.R. 317.

[39] Rent Act 1977, s. 100, below, p. 137. Distress is restricted by s. 147.

[40] See *Florent v. Horez* (1984) 48 P.&C.R. 166 (breach of covenant against
business user); *Empson v. Forde* [1990] 1 E.G.L.R. 131 (access for
repairs).

[41] *Brown v. Davies* [1958] 1 Q.B. 117.

[42] *Oak Property Co. Ltd v. Chapman* [1947] K.B. 886 (where the acceptance
was qualified). See also *Chrisdell Ltd v. Johnson* (1987) 54 P.&C.R. 257.

[43] *Trustees of Henry Smith's Charity v. Willson* [1983] Q.B. 316; *cf. Carter v.
Green* [1950] 2 K.B. 76.

[44] Although it will, of course, apply if the tenancy is still protected.

house or allowing the dwelling-house to be used for immoral or illegal purposes."

Meaning of annoyance

"Annoyance" is wider than "nuisance," and has been described as something which reasonably troubles the mind and pleasure, not of a fanciful person, but of the ordinary sensible inhabitant of a house.[45] Possession may be ordered in respect of a nuisance which has abated, if there is a likelihood that it will arise again.[46]

Occupiers may be "adjoining" even though their premises are not physically adjacent, provided they are near enough to be affected.[47]

Type of conviction

Where possession is sought on the basis of a conviction for immoral or illegal user, the conviction must relate to the premises. As Scrutton L.J. has said:

> "it is enough if there is a conviction of a crime which has been committed on the premises and for the purpose of committing which the premises have been used; but it is not enough that the tenant has been convicted of a crime with which the premises have nothing to do beyond merely being the scene of its commission."[48]

In *Abrahams v. Wilson*[49] the tenant had been convicted of possession of drugs. It was said that if the drugs were merely found in the tenant's pocket or handbag, this would not amount to using the premises, in contrast to the case where the premises were used for storage or as a hiding-place. Even if the tenant had used the premises, possession was not ordered. Although in most such cases it will be considered reasonable to grant possession, here the discretion was exercised in favour of the tenant, because she was unable to work and had a child to support, hence she would suffer hardship if evicted.

Case 3

Deterioration in condition of dwelling

"Where the condition of the dwelling-house has, in the opinion of the court, deteriorated owing to acts of waste by, or the neglect or default of, the tenant or any person residing or lodging with him or any sub-tenant of his . . . where the court is satisfied that the tenant has not, before the making of the order in question, taken such

---

[45] *Tod-Heatley v. Benham* (1888) 40 Ch.D. 80 at 98. As to racial harassment as nuisance, see (1990) *Legal Action*, March, p. 13. Abusive language may suffice; *Woking Borough Council v. Bistram* (1995) 27 H.L.R. 1 (secure tenancy; order made but suspended).

[46] *Florent v. Horez* (1984) 48 P.&C.R. 166 (activities of Turkish Cypriot organisation on the premises).

[47] *Cobstone Investments Ltd v. Maxim* [1985] Q.B. 140; [1985] Conv. 168 (T.J. Lyons).

[48] *S. Schneider & Sons v. Abrahams* [1925] 1 K.B. 301 at 310.

[49] [1971] 2 Q.B. 88.

steps as he ought reasonably to have taken for the removal of the lodger or sub-tenant, as the case may be."

Case 3 can apply even if there is no breach of any obligation of the tenancy.[50] A modern example is *Holloway v. Povey*,[51] where the garden of a cottage was seriously neglected. The "dwelling-house," as is apparent from section 26,[52] includes the garden. The possession order was suspended for a year, on condition that the tenant tidied the garden and kept it tidy for that time. A further point was that the tenant, who had succeeded to the statutory tenancy on his mother's death, could not be held responsible for any neglect prior to his mother's death.

Case 4

Deterioration in condition of furniture

"Where the condition of any furniture provided for use under the tenancy has, in the opinion of the court, deteriorated owing to ill-treatment by the tenant or any person residing or lodging with him or any sub-tenant of his . . . where the court is satisfied that the tenant has not, before the making of the order in question, taken such steps as he ought reasonably to have taken for the removal of the lodger or sub-tenant, as the case may be."

This ground was introduced by the Rent Act 1974, which brought furnished tenancies into full protection.

Case 5

Notice to quit by tenant

"Where the tenant has given notice to quit and, in consequence of that notice, the landlord has contracted to sell or let the dwelling-house or has taken any other steps as the result of which he would, in the opinion of the court, be seriously prejudiced if he could not obtain possession."

This deals with the situation where the tenant changes his mind after giving notice. The notice to quit must be valid[53]; a mere agreement to surrender will not suffice.[54]
The landlord cannot invoke Case 5 if he merely intends to sell.[55]

[50] *Lowe v. Lendrum* (1950) 159 E.G. 423.
[51] (1984) 271 E.G. 195.
[52] See above, p. 65.
[53] *De Vries v. Sparks* (1927) 137 L.T. 441.
[54] *Standingford v. Bruce* [1926] 1 K.B. 466.
[55] *Barton v. Fincham* [1921] 2 K.B. 291.

Case 6

Assignment or subletting without consent

"Where, without the consent of the landlord, the tenant has[56] ... assigned or sublet the whole of the dwelling-house or sublet part of the dwelling-house, the remainder being already sublet."

The purpose of this ground, it has been said, is "to give some protection to a landlord against the risk of finding some person wholly unknown to him irrevocably installed in his property."[57]

A statutory tenancy, as we have seen,[58] is incapable of assignment. It has been suggested that this ground originated at a time when it had not been established that a statutory tenancy could not be assigned and when the rules as to the requirement of residence for statutory tenants had not been fully developed.[59] Even though a statutory tenant may sublet, a subletting of the whole will normally terminate the statutory tenancy in any event, as the tenant will have ceased to reside. In such circumstances the main reason for invoking Case 6 will be to recover possession against the sub-tenant, as explained below.[60]

Breach not required

Case 6 applies even if the subletting is not in breach of any obligation in the tenancy,[61] although the absence of any breach will be relevant to the exercise of the discretion.[62]

Meaning of consent

"Consent" need not be written, and may be implied. It suffices that it was given at any time before commencement of the proceedings.[63] It is doubtful whether mere waiver constitutes consent.[64]

Effect on sub-tenant

The significance of Case 6 cannot be fully appreciated without a consideration of the rights of the sub-tenant. This will be fully discussed in Chapter 9. For present purposes, it must suffice to explain that a lawful sub-tenant may have rights against the head landlord under section 137 of the 1977 Act. In the case of a subletting in breach of covenant, therefore, there will be a discretionary ground for possession against the tenant, and the sub-tenant will have no rights under section 137. Where the subletting is not unlawful, we

[56] Since certain dates specified in paragraphs (b) to (d).
[57] *Hyde v. Pimley* [1952] 2 Q.B. 506 at 512.
[58] See above, p. 108. It is not clear whether Case 6 applies to a purported assignment.
[59] Yates and Hawkins, *Landlord and Tenant Law* (2nd ed., 1986) p. 454.
[60] See *Chrisdell Ltd v. Johnson* (1987) 54 P.&C.R. 257.
[61] If it is in breach, Case 1 will also apply.
[62] See *Leith Properties Ltd v. Byrne* [1983] Q.B. 433; [1983] Conv. 155 (J. Martin); *Trustees of Henry Smith's Charity v. Willson* [1983] Q.B. 316; [1983] Conv. 248 (J. Martin); *Pazgate Ltd v. McGrath* (1984) 272 E.G. 1069.
[63] *Hyde v. Pimley* [1952] 2 Q.B. 506. See also *Regional Properties Co. Ltd v. Frankenschwerth* [1951] 1 K.B. 631.
[64] Otherwise a tenant who had sublet in breach of covenant would be better off than a tenant whose subletting was not a breach. See [1983] Conv. 248 at 252 (J. Martin); *cf.* Pettit, *Private Sector Tenancies* (2nd ed., 1981) p. 204.

have seen that Case 6 nevertheless applies to terminate the tenancy. In such a case the sub-tenant may invoke the protection of section 137, but it has been held that Case 6 is also available against him in these circumstances.[65] The issue of reasonableness must, however, be decided as between the landlord and the sub-tenant.

Case 7

This Case, relating to controlled tenancies, was repealed by the Housing Act, 1980.

Case 8

Required for employee

"Where the dwelling-house is reasonably required by the landlord for occupation[66] as a residence for some person engaged in his wholetime employment . . . and the tenant[67]was in the employment of the landlord or a former landlord, and the dwelling-house was let to him in consequence of that employment and he has ceased to be in that employment."

Misrepresentation or concealment

If a possession order is granted, but it subsequently appears that it was obtained by misrepresentation or concealment of material facts, section 102 gives the court power to order the landlord to compensate the tenant.

Joint landlords

In the case of joint landlords, it presumably suffices that only one of them was the employer of the original tenant and of the proposed new occupier.[68]

Case 9

Required for occupation by landlord or family

"Where the dwelling-house is reasonably required by the landlord for occupation as a residence[69] for–
(a) himself,[70] or
(b) any son or daughter or his over 18 years of age, or
(c) his father or mother, or
(d) the father or mother of his wife or husband,

---

[65] *Leith Properties Ltd v. Byrne*, above; *Trustees of Henry Smith's Charity v. Willson*, above.
[66] Not necessarily under a tenancy. See generally *R.F. Fuggle v. Gadsden* [1948] 2 K.B. 236.
[67] This means the original tenant. Case 8 is, therefore, available against any statutory tenant by succession on his death: *Bolsover Colliery Co. Ltd v. Abbott* [1946] K.B. 8.
[68] By analogy with *Tilling v. Whiteman* [1980] A.C. 1, below, p. 130. It has, however, been held that the Case does not apply where the landlord is not the sole employer: *Grimond v. Duncan* [1949] S.C. 195 (employment by partnership including the landlord). *cf.* Case 9, below.
[69] Occupation with a view to sale does not suffice: *Rowe v. Truelove* (1976) 241 E.G. 533; *cf. Lipton v. Whitworth* (1994) 26 H.L.R. 293 (Case 11, below).
[70] This includes all "normal emanations" of himself, such as his wife or children under 18: *Ritcher v. Wilson* [1963] 2 Q.B. 426.

and the landlord did not become landlord by purchasing the dwelling-house or any interest therein."[71]

It is further provided that the court shall not make a possession order if satisfied that, having regard to all the circumstances, including the question whether other accommodation is available for the landlord or the tenant,

Greater hardship greater hardship would be caused by granting the order than by refusing to grant it.[72]

Compensation As with Case 8, the court may order compensation under section 102 in cases of misrepresentation or concealment.[73]

Whether the house is "reasonably" required is a separate issue from the question whether it is "reasonable" to make the order.[74]

Onus of proof Although the onus of proving that the dwelling is "reasonably required" is on the landlord, the onus of proving greater hardship is on the tenant.[75]

Landlord by purchase The "landlord by purchase" restriction is to prevent a sitting tenant from being evicted by a purchaser who has bought the property subject to his tenancy. Clearly the original landlord is not a landlord by purchase; nor is a person who acquired the reversion by will. "Purchase" bears its common meaning of commercial acquisition for money or money's worth. In *Thomas v. Fryer*[76] the landlord left the property by will to his four children. One daughter bought out the shares of the others. She was held not to have become landlord by purchase, but by a domestic arrangement. In *Mansukhani v. Sharkey*[77] the landlords transferred the property to their son in consideration of "natural love and affection." The property was subject to a mortgage of £14,000 and the son covenanted in the transfer to discharge the mortgage liabilities. It was held that this was a gift of mortgaged property and so the son was not a landlord by purchase. It was a family matter, not a commercial bargain. In *Amaddio v. Dalton*[78], on the other hand, the landlord could not invoke Case 9 where he had purchased the property from the deceased original landlord's son, using a gift of money from her estate to do so. The original landlord wished her employee to have the

---

[71] After certain dates specified in paragraphs (i) to (iv).
[72] Rent Act 1977, Sched. 15, Part III, para. 1. See, generally, (1986) 136 N.L.J. 447 (H.W. Wilkinson).
[73] See *Neil v. Kingsnorth* (1987), noted (1988) *Legal Action*, March, p. 21 (exemplary damages awarded where landlord sold the property for conversion into flats). For the valuation of a statutory tenancy see *Murray v. Lloyd* [1989] 1 W.L.R. 1060; above, p. 92.
[74] *Shrimpton v. Rabbits* (1924) 131 L.T. 478; above, p. 117.
[75] *Sims v. Wilson* [1946] 2 All E.R. 261; *Manaton v. Edwards* [1985] 2 E.G.L.R. 159.
[76] [1970] 1 W.L.R. 845. See also *Littlechild v. Holt* [1950] 1 K.B. 1 (person acquiring reversion from a person who became landlord by purchase cannot be in any better position).
[77] (1992) 24 H.L.R. 600.
[78] (1991) 23 H.L.R. 332; [1991] Conv. 291 (J. Martin).

tenanted property but could not devise it to him as she had only a life interest, remainder to her son. In her will she expressed the hope that her son would offer to sell the property to the employee and provided a legacy of the purchase price conditional on the offer being made and accepted. It was held that this did not constitute a gift of the property and that the employee became landlord by purchase.

Landlord's personal representatives

Normally personal representatives, although clearly "landlords," cannot invoke Case 9, either for their own benefit (because their occupation would be a breach of trust if they have no beneficial interest), or for the benefit of a beneficiary.[79] In exceptional cases, however, they may succeed, as in *Patel v. Patel*,[80] where the personal representatives were trustees for the deceased landlord's children. As they had adopted the children and planned to live in the house with them, there was no breach of trust.

Time for establishing need

Another question is whether the landlord must have an immediate need for the property. The relevant time for establishing that he reasonably requires the property is the date of the hearing.[81] A prior need which no longer exists is insufficient, but what of a future need? In *Kidder v. Birch*[82] the plaintiff and her elderly mother owned a small cottage which had been let to the tenants since 1948, and lived themselves in a rented house, which would be too large and expensive to run after the mother's death, which had not yet occurred. A possession order was granted, but suspended until the mother's death. On appeal, it was held that the landlord must show a need in the ascertainable and not too distant future. The possession order was varied so that it could be executed if the mother's death should occur within 12 months. If it did not occur within that period, the order should not be executed at all. No doubt this principle is equally applicable to other grounds where the landlord must show that he requires the property for some purpose.

Change of circumstances

A related problem is where the circumstances have changed between the hearing in the lower court and on appeal. If the lower court refused the possession order, the Court of Appeal is entitled to consider any change of circumstances. Where, however, the lower court made a possession order, the role of the Court of Appeal is to consider whether the order was rightly made, with regard to the circumstances at the date of the order.[83]

---

[79] *Parker v. Rosenberg* [1947] K.B. 371.
[80] [1981] 1 W.L.R. 1342; [1982] Conv. 443 (J.E.M.).
[81] *Alexander v. Mohamadzadeh* (1986) 51 P.&C.R. 41; [1986] Conv. 274 (J.E.M.). The date of the proceedings, however, is the relevant date for Case 1: *Bird v. Hildage* [1948] 1 K.B. 91.
[82] (1983) 265 E.G. 773; [1982] Conv. 444 (J.E.M.). The decision answers some of the questions raised in *Alexander v. Mohamadzadeh*, above.
[83] *King v. Taylor* [1955] 1 Q.B. 150; *Alexander v. Mohamadzadeh* (1986) 51 P.&C.R. 41; *Manaton v. Edwards* [1985] 2 E.G.L.R. 159; *Coombs v. Parry* (1987) 19 H.L.R. 384.

Greater hardship   As far as the question of greater hardship is concerned, the court should consider all who may be affected — "relatives, dependants, lodgers, guests, and the stranger within the gates — but should weigh such hardship with due regard to the status of the persons affected, and their 'proximity' to the tenant or landlord, and the extent to which, consequently, hardship to them would be hardship to him".[84] In *Thomas v. Fryer*[85] the landlord succeeded when evidence established that her mental health would deteriorate if she did not recover possession. The landlord was also successful in *Manaton v. Edwards*,[86] where he was living in a caravan, which was an unsuitable matrimonial home for his newly arrived Russian wife. The tenant, whose family included a baby, would be rehoused by the local authority under the homeless persons legislation. While this might initially involve bed and breakfast accommodation, the long term prospects would be better. Similarly in *Hodges v. Blee*,[87] where the tenant of a maisonette was in poor financial circumstances, had two dogs to accommodate, and would not be entitled to local authority accommodation. The landlord succeeded where he needed the accommodation for his sons who, although earning, had very unsatisfactory accommodation, one living in a warehouse. In *Baker v. MacIver*,[88] on the other hand, the tenant established greater hardship where the landlord, himself a protected tenant of other property, had been offered a large sum and alternative accommodation by his own landlord, but preferred to obtain possession of his own property. The tenant, however, who had no savings, had poor prospects of finding other suitable accommodation in the private or public sector. These cases illustrate the difficulties where there is hardship on both sides. The decision on the balance of hardship is for the judge at first instance, whose ruling will not be overturned on appeal unless it was wrong in law.

Joint landlords   It has been held that Case 9 cannot be invoked by joint landlords unless both wish to occupy.[89] The matter was left open in the House of Lords in *Tilling v. Whiteman*,[90]where a

---

[84] *Harte v. Frampton* [1948] 1 K.B. 73 at 79.
[85] See above. See also *Bostock v. Tacher de la Pagerie* [1987] 1 E.G.L.R. 104 (landlord's anorexic daughter needed accommodation); *Lohan v. Hilton* [1994] E.G.C.S. 83 (tenanted bungalow more suitable for landlord's sick wife than landlord's present accommodation, provided by his employer).
[86] [1985] 2 E.G.L.R. 159; [1986] Conv. 273 (J.E.M.). *cf. Fernandes v. Parvardin* (1982) 264 E.G. 49. (Landlord wanted property for son. Tenants, Iranian students with a child, established greater hardship by showing that they had tried unsuccessfully to get alternative accommodation and were not eligible for council housing. The best they could hope for would be local authority temporary accommodation.)
[87] [1987] 2 E.G.L.R. 119; [1987] Conv. 449 (J.E.M.). See also *Coombs v. Parry*, above.
[88] (1990) 22 H.L.R. 328; [1991] Conv. 152 (S. Bridge).
[89] *Baker v. Lewis* [1947] K.B. 186; *McIntyre v. Hardcastle* [1948] 2 K.B. 82.
[90] [1980] A.C. 1: below, p. 130.

contrary view was taken of Case 11 (discussed below). If it is
correct that one of joint landlords cannot invoke Case 9,
then it follows that joint landlords cannot seek possession of
the property as a residence for a son or daughter over 18
unless they are both the child's parents; they cannot seek
possession of the property as a residence for a parent unless
they are siblings; and they cannot seek possession of the
property as a residence for a parent-in-law at all.[91] The
difficulties inherent in the narrow construction of
"landlord" perhaps indicate that a wider construction might
be appropriate, but the narrow construction was assumed to
be correct by the Court of Appeal in *Bostock v. Tacher de la
Pagerie*.[92] There, however, the problem was avoided on the
ground that the joint owner (the landlord's daughter) who
alone wished to occupy was merely an equitable tenant in
common having no legal title. Thus the case could be
treated as one where the landlord required the dwelling-
house as a residence for his daughter. The Court of Appeal
has since confirmed, applying a purposive construction, that
the wider view is correct. In *Potsos v. Theodotou*[93] the joint
landlords, a married couple, were able to use Case 9 to
recover possession for residence by the wife's son, who was
the husband's stepson. It was held that because paragraph
(d) (required for parent-in-law) must be construed as
meaning the parent-in-law of either landlord, the other
paragraphs must be similarly construed. Previous views to
the contrary were in any event *obiter*. Thus paragraph (b),
which means "any son or daughter of theirs, or of either of
them, over 18 years of age," was satisfied.

Case 10

**Tenant
overcharging
subtenant**

"Where the court is satisfied that the rent charged by
the tenant—

(a) for any sublet part of the dwelling-house which is a
     dwelling-house let on a protected tenancy or
     subject to a statutory tenancy is or was in excess of
     the maximum rent for the time being recoverable
     for that part, having regard to Part III of this Act,
     or

(b) for any sublet part of the dwelling-house which is
     subject to a restricted contract is or was in excess
     of the maximum (if any) which it is lawful for the
     lessor, within the meaning of Part V of this Act to
     require or receive having regard to the provisions of
     that part."

As will be seen in Chapter 10, the rent control provisions
of the 1977 Act make it unlawful for the landlord to receive

---

[91] This limb of Case 9 was added after *Baker v. Lewis* above, where the
      foregoing propositions were accepted by Asquith L.J. (*obiter*).
[92] See above; [1987] Conv. 206 (J.E.M.).
[93] (1991) 23 H.L.R. 356; [1991] Conv. 292 (J. Martin).

rent in excess of the statutory limits. Case 10 gives the head landlord a ground for possession where the tenant who has sublet part infringes these rules. It clearly has no application where the sub-tenancy is not within the Rent Act.

Mandatory grounds for possession

These are the grounds where, by section 98(2), the court *shall* make a possession order. There is no discretion to refuse if the ground is established. The mandatory grounds are set out in Part II of Schedule 15 of the 1977 Act as amended by the Housing Act 1980, and will now be considered in turn. Some of them are available, in addition to the assured tenancy grounds, against a successor to a protected or statutory tenant who succeeds to an assured tenancy.[94]

Case 11

The owner-occupier ground

Conditions

"Where a person (in this Case referred to as 'the owner-occupier') who let the dwelling-house on a regulated tenancy had, at any time before the letting, occupied it as his residence and —

(a) not later than the relevant date[95] the landlord gave notice in writing to the tenant that possession might be recovered under this Case,[96] and

(b) the dwelling-house has not [since certain dates specified in paragraphs (i) to (iii)] been let by the owner-occupier on a protected tenancy with respect to which the condition mentioned in paragraph (a) above was not satisfied, and

(c) the court is of the opinion that of the conditions set out in Part V of this Schedule one of those in paragraphs (a) and (c) to (f) is satisfied."

The conditions in Part V of the Schedule referred to above are:

[94] See below, p. 147. Those available are Cases 11, 12, 16, 17, 18 and 20. Any notices given to the predecessor under Cases 13, 14 or 15 of the Rent Act are treated as given for the purposes of the corresponding grounds in Housing Act 1988. See Housing Act 1988, Sched. 4, para. 13.

[95] Defined by Rent Act 1977, Sched. 15, Pt. III, para. 2, as being the date of the commencement of the regulated tenancy, subject to various exceptions.

[96] By analogy with *Fowler v. Minchin* [1987] 1 E.G.L.R. 108 and *Springfield Investments Ltd v. Bell* (1990) 22 H.L.R. 440, on Case 16 (below, p. 134), the notice must state specifically that possession might be recovered under the provisions of the Act. Although it need not follow any particular form, it must make it clear that the ground is compulsory. For the dispensing power, see below, p. 130.

(a) that the dwelling-house is required as a residence for the owner or any member of his family who resided with him when he last occupied it as a residence; or

(c) that the owner has died and the dwelling-house is required as a residence for a member of his family who was residing with him at the time of his death; or

(d) that the owner has died and the dwelling-house is required by a successor in title as his residence or for the purpose of sale with vacant possession; or

(e) that a mortgagee requires the dwelling-house for the purpose of exercising the power of sale, where the mortgage was granted before the tenancy; or

(f) the owner requires the dwelling-house for the purpose of sale, so that the proceeds may be used to acquire a dwelling-house more suited to his needs with regard to his place of work.[97]

It is further provided that if the main conditions (a) or (b) above are not complied with, the court may dispense with either or both of them, if of the opinion that it is just and **Dispensing** equitable to order possession. The scope of this dispensing **power** power will be considered below.

The purpose of Case 11 was to enable an owner-occupier who was going away for some period, for example to work abroad, to let the property during his absence, secure in the knowledge that he could recover possession on his return. In some ways Case 11 overlaps with Case 9, but the requirements are different in many respects.[98]

Some consternation was caused by the decision of the Court of Appeal in *Pocock v. Steel*[99] in which it was held that **No requirement** Case 11 did not apply unless the landlord had resided in the **of occupation** property immediately prior to the current letting. The **immediately** difficulty in this can be seen in the example of a landlord **before current** working abroad: if the tenant left while the landlord was still **letting** away, he would have to resume occupation before re-letting. This decision was quickly reversed by the Rent (Amendment) Act 1985, making it clear that the landlord's occupation need not have immediately preceded the current letting. Case 11 applies to each of a series of lettings, provided that condition (b) (which may in any event be dispensed with by the court) is satisfied, without any necessity for residence by the landlord before each of them.

It was held in *Naish v. Curzon*[1] that a landlord can satisfy

---

[97] Conditions (c) to (f) were added by the Housing Act 1980, which is retrospective on this point, save that conditions (c) and (d) do not apply if the owner-occupier died before November 28, 1980.
[98] As to lettings after the commencement of Housing Act 1988, see Sched. 2, Ground 1, below, p. 229.
[99] [1985] 1 W.L.R. 229.
[1] (1986) 51 P.&C.R. 229; followed in *Davies v. Peterson* [1989] 1 E.G.L.R. 121, where the landlord had visited England for a few weeks a year and wished to live at the property when in London. *cf. Ibie v. Trubshaw* (1990) 22 H.L.R. 191 (Case 11 not satisfied where landlord's girlfriend occupied and landlord stayed on visits from Nigeria).

Quality of residence Case 11 even though his prior residence was temporary or intermittent. Here the landlord lived mainly in South Africa for a period of years prior to the letting, but resided from time to time in the property, when visiting the country on business and for holidays. His future proposed use of the property would be similar. Likewise in *Mistry v. Isidore* [2] where Case 11 was satisfied by a landlord whose prior occupation consisted of use on weekdays for a period of eight or nine weeks before the letting, during which time he had no home elsewhere. The requirement relating to prior residence and intended future residence is less strict than that which applies to resident landlords,[3] and the question is one of fact and degree.

No doubt occupation of a very temporary nature, however, would not qualify as "residence" at all, save in the

Intention to sell case of a genuine change of mind. In *Lipton v. Whitworth*[4] the landlords, a married couple, went to America to work and let the house (in Essex) subject to Case 11. The wife later returned with one child, intending to look for work in the north but to live in the house until she could sell. Possession was ordered in the county court but the tenant sought leave to appeal out of time 20 weeks later, having found that the property was up for sale. It appeared that the wife had occupied for about three weeks only but could not settle because of marriage problems. The possession order was upheld. The selling of the property did not establish that the wife did not intend to reside at the time of the hearing and could be explained by a change of mind. An ultimate intention to sell is not inconsistent with an intention to reside.[5]

Another question which has arisen is whether the landlord must be reasonable in requiring the property as a residence. In contrast with Case 9, the word does not appear in the

Need not be reasonable conditions of Case 11. It was held in *Kennealy v. Dunne*[6] that there is no requirement of reasonableness. It is sufficient that the landlord can show a genuine intention to occupy within a reasonable time. The fact that he does not need to do so is irrelevant.

Joint landlords It has already been noted that the Rent Act fails to deal expressly with the question of joint landlords or tenants. This has arisen in the context of Case 9, discussed above, and also in relation to the statutory tenancy[7] and to the

---

[2] [1990] 2 E.G.L.R. 97. See also *Jones v. White* (1994) 26 H.L.R. 477 (future use as *'pied-à-terre''* sufficed but failed on other grounds).

[3] Above, p.86.

[4] (1994) 26 H.L.R. 293. The property was sold before the appeal hearing, and the issue was one of costs.

[5] Distinguishing *Rowe v. Truelove* (1976) 241 E.G. 533, above, p. 122, where the sole intention was to sell. That was a decision on Case 9, where there is a further requirement of reasonableness.

[6] [1977] 1 Q.B. 837; (1977) 41 Conv. (N.S.) 287 (D. MacIntyre).

[7] See above, p. 106.

resident landlord rules.[8] The issue arose in the present
context in *Tilling v. Whiteman*,[9] where only one of joint
landlords wished to resume occupation. A majority of the
House of Lords, reversing the Court of Appeal, held that
Case 11 was satisfied. Although the general policy of the Act
was to protect the tenant, the policy of Case 11 was to
encourage letting, and it should, therefore, be construed in
the landlord's favour. The authorities to the contrary on
Case 9, discussed above, were distinguished on the basis
that the wording of that Case was different. This is a
satisfactory result, as hardship would otherwise arise where,
for example, a married couple let the property and
subsequently separated, so that only one wished to resume
occupation.[10] It would be unfortunate if he was thereby
precluded from relying on Case 11, a result which would
fortuitously improve the tenant's position.

Illustrations of dispensing power   As stated above, conditions (a) and (b) may be dispensed
with by the court if just and equitable to do so. In *Minay v.
Sentongo*[11] the dispensing power was exercised where the
landlord had sent a condition (a) notice, but it did not
arrive. The condition was not complied with, because a
notice had to be received in order to be "given" under Case
11. Similarly in *Fernandes v. Parvardin*,[12] where the landlord
had given the tenant an oral notice, which accordingly did
not satisfy condition (a). It was just and equitable to order
possession, as the tenant had appreciated the position
throughout. While all members of the Court of Appeal
agreed that the dispensing power should be exercised, there
was disagreement as to its scope. Stephenson L.J. thought
the court should consider all the circumstances, including
the balance of hardship. The majority view, however, was
narrower, requiring the court to consider only whether any
injustice or inequity flowed from the failure to comply
precisely with Case 11. Where there was no
misunderstanding by the tenant, there would be no such
injustice or inequity, and general questions of hardship were
Differing views on scope of power   not relevant. The matter was reviewed in *Bradshaw v.
Baldwin-Wiseman*,[13] where property was let on an ordinary
regulated tenancy which was never intended to be
temporary. No condition (a) notice had been served, nor
was there any suggestion at the grant that the landlord might
wish to recover possession for his own use. It was held that
the dispensing power was not to be exercised in such a case.
The tenant must appreciate the position when he takes the

[8] See above, p. 86.
[9] [1980] A.C. 1; (1980) 39 C.L.J. 37 (K.J. Gray).
[10] As in *Lipton v. Whitworth*, above.
[11] (1983) 45 P.&C.R. 190.
[12] (1982) 264 E.G. 49. Similarly in *Davies v. Peterson* [1989] 1 E.G.L.R.
    121; [1989] Conv. 287 (J.E.M.); but distinguished in *Jones v. White*
    (1994) 26 H.L.R. 477.
[13] (1985) 49 P.&C.R. 382; [1985] Conv. 354 (J.E.M.).

property.[14] The Court of Appeal considered the views expressed in *Fernandes v. Parvardin*,[15] and preferred that of the minority, to the effect that all the circumstances should be examined. Here the landlord would clearly have failed on either view. So in the case of an oral condition (a) notice, the *Bradshaw* view effectively gives the court a general discretion, whereas according to the majority in *Fernandes*, the landlord is likely to succeed because no injustice flows from the failure to give written notice. If no notice at all has been given, the landlord is likely to fail on either view.[16]

Subsequent decisions have followed the *Bradshaw* view, whereby the court has a general discretion. In *Jones v. White*[17] an oral notice of the landlords' intention to return was given at a time when neither side believed there was any security of tenure. In due course the landlords gave a written advance warning of the date of their return. The dispensing power was not exercised because the above factors were outweighed by the hardship the tenants would suffer. They had lived there for 20 years, the husband was in poor health, they would get only local authority bed and breakfast accommodation and would have to get rid of their furniture and dogs. The landlords, on the other hand, planned to use the house only as a *"pied-à-terre"* for up to three months a year. The wide view has also been adopted in the context of the Case 19 dispensing power.[18]

Expedited procedure

Finally, when possession is sought under Case 11 (or under the other mandatory grounds discussed below), an expedited procedure is available.[19] Proceedings may be commenced by originating application, with a supporting affidavit. The period of notice between service of the application and the hearing is shorter than usual, and may be as little as seven days.[20] The matter can be heard by a registrar and is often in chambers. However, the expedited procedure is not available where the landlord wishes to invoke the court's dispensing power, discussed above.[21]

---

[14] cf. *Minay v. Sentongo*, above.
[15] Above. The wide view of the scope of the dispensing power is impliedly supported by *Davies v. Peterson*, above, where the court took rent arrears into account in considering the exercise of the power. For the view that the similar provision in Ground 1 of the Housing Act 1988 favours the narrow view of the scope of the power, see (1989) 139 N.L.J. 252 (F. Webb).
[16] Save in the rare case where the notice has been sent but not received: *Minay v. Sentongo*, above.
[17] (1994) 26 H.L.R. 477; *Ibie v. Trubshaw* (1990) 22 H.L.R. 191 (dispensing power not exercised where no prior notice although tenants knew their occupation was intended to be temporary).
[18] *Dunnell (R.J.) Property Investments Ltd v. Thorpe* [1989] 2 E.G.L.R. 36 (prior notice condition dispensed with on considering all the circumstances); below, p. 135.
[19] Rent Act (County Court Proceedings for Possession) Rules 1981 (S.I. 1981 No. 139).
[20] Seven days for Cases 11, 12 and 20; 14 days for Cases 13–19.
[21] See *Minay v. Sentongo*, above.

Case 12

**Retirement
homes**

Conditions

"Where the landlord (in this Case referred to as 'the
owner' intends to occupy the dwelling-house as his
residence at such time as he might retire from regular
employment and has let it on a regulated tenancy before
he has so retired and–

(a) not later than the relevant date[22] the landlord gave
notice in writing to the tenant that possession
might be recovered under this Case; and

(b) the dwelling-house has not, since 14th August
1974,[23] been let by the owner on a protected
tenancy to which the condition mentioned in
paragraph (a) above was not satisfied; and

(c) the court is of the opinion that of the conditions set
out in Part V of this Schedule one of those in
paragraphs (b) to (e) is satisfied."

Paragraph (b) of Part V of the Schedule, referred to in main
condition (c), is to the effect that the owner has retired from
regular employment and requires the dwelling-house as a
residence. Paragraphs (c) to (e)[24] are as set out in respect of
Case 11, above.

**Dispensing
power**

As with Case 11, the court may dispense with either or
both of main conditions (a) or (b) if it is considered just and
equitable to order possession. The authorities on Case 11,
discussed above, will presumably apply here also.

There is, as yet, no authority on Case 12. Presumably one
of joint landlords may invoke it, by analogy with *Tilling v.
Whiteman*.[25] Difficulties could arise as to the meaning of
"regular employment." For example, does it cover the self-
employed?[26] Unlike Case 11, there is no requirement that
the landlord should have previously resided at the property.
Like Case 11, it is not necessary that the landlord's
requirement of the property as a residence should be
reasonable.

Case 13

**Out of season
letting**

"Where the dwelling-house is let under a tenancy for a
term of years certain not exceeding 8 months and–

(a) not later than the relevant date[27] the landlord gave
notice in writing to the tenant that possession
might be recovered under this Case; and

---

[22] See n. 95, above.

[23] Case 12 was introduced by the Rent Act 1974.

[24] Paragraphs (d) and (e) were added by the Housing Act 1980.

[25] [1980] A.C. 1, above. Otherwise there would be hardship in the case of a
married couple, if the wife did not work or retired earlier than the
husband.

[26] For further problems, see Farrand and Arden, *Rent Acts and Regulations*
(2nd ed., 1981) p. 208.

[27] See n. 95, above.

(b) the dwelling-house was, at some time within the period of 12 months ending on the relevant date, occupied under a right to occupy it for a holiday."

This ground, therefore, permits recovery in the case of out of season lettings of holiday accommodation, and is designed to encourage such lettings,[28] so that accommodation with a seasonal use may be more fully utilised. We have seen that the holiday lettings themselves are not within the Rent Act.[29] It is not necessary, however, that the holiday occupation should take the form of a letting.[30] Establishing whether the "holiday occupation" was indeed of that character could give rise to problems similar to those arising under section 9 in the case of holiday lettings.[31]

Case 14

Vacation lettings of student accommodation

"Where the dwelling-house is let under a tenancy for a term of years certain not exceeding 12 months and–
(a) not later than the relevant date[32] the landlord gave notice in writing to the tenant that possession might be recovered under this Case; and
(b) at some time within the period of 12 months ending on the relevant date, the dwelling-house was subject to such a tenancy as is referred to in section 8(1) of this Act."

Section 8 excludes institutional student lettings from protection.[33] The purpose of Case 14, therefore, is to facilitate vacation lettings of student accommodation.[34] It is based on the same policy as Case 13.

It is not necessary that the vacation letting should be by an institutional landlord. The Case could be relied on by a private landlord who lets the property during the vacation, where during term he lets to an institution for subletting to students within section 8.

Case 15

Occupation by minister of religion

"Where the dwelling-house is held for the purpose of being available for occupation by a minister of religion as a residence from which to perform the duties of his office and —

---

[28] The position is similar under Housing Act 1988, below, p. 233.
[29] See above, p. 73.
[30] It has been suggested that the landlord's own holiday occupation would suffice: Farrand and Arden, above, p. 209; Yates and Hawkins, *Landlord and Tenant Law* (2nd ed., 1986) p. 461; *cf.* Pettit, *Private Sector Tenancies* (2nd ed., 1981) p. 219, considering that such occupation would be based on the landlord's rights as owner, and not a "right to occupy it as a holiday." The latter view, it is submitted, is preferable.
[31] See above, p. 74.
[32] See n. 95 above.
[33] See above, p. 72.
[34] Similarly under Housing Act 1988: below, p. 233.

(a) not later than the relevant date[35] the tenant was given notice in writing that possession might be recovered under this Case, and

(b) the court is satisfied that the dwelling-house is required for occupation by a minister of religion as such a residence."

We have seen that lettings of Church of England parsonages are excluded from the Rent Act.[36] There is no such exclusion for other religions, but Case 15 provides a ground for possession in the circumstances set out above.

Cases 16 to 18

Agricultural employees

These Cases deal with the recovery of possession of dwelling-houses formerly (but not currently) occupied by persons in agriculture, which are now required for an agricultural employee. They are outside the scope of this book.

Case 19

Shorthold tenancies

"Where the dwelling-house was let under a protected shorthold tenancy (or is treated under section 55 of the Housing Act 1980 as having been so let) and —

(a) there either has been no grant of a further tenancy of the dwelling-house since the end of the protected shorthold tenancy or, if there was such a grant, it was to a person who immediately before the grant was in possession of the dwelling-house as a protected or statutory tenant[37]; and

(b) the proceedings for possession were commenced after appropriate notice by the landlord to the tenant and not later than 3 months after the expiry of the notice.[38]

Conditions of notice

A notice is appropriate for this Case if —

(i) it is in writing and states that proceedings for possession under this Case may be brought after its expiry; and

(ii) it expires not earlier than 3 months after it is served nor, if, when it is served, the tenancy is a periodic tenancy,[39] before that periodic tenancy could be brought to an end by a notice to quit served by the landlord on the same day;

[35] See n. 95 above.

[36] See above, p. 79.

[37] This refers to the former shorthold tenant (or his successor on death) holding over under a further contractual tenancy or under a statutory tenancy. See *Gent v. de la Mare*, below.

[38] This requirement cannot be waived by the tenant; *Ridehalgh v. Horsefield* (1992) 24 H.L.R. 453; [1993] Conv. 238 (S. Bridge).

[39] The initial shorthold tenancy must be for a fixed term, but Case 19 continues to apply where another tenancy, which might be periodic, was granted to the former shorthold tenant. See below.

(iii) it is served —
    (a) in the period of 3 months immediately preceding the date on which the protected shorthold tenancy comes to an end; or
    (b) if that date has passed, in the period of 3 months immediately preceding any anniversary of that date; and
(iv) in a case where a previous notice has been served by the landlord on the tenant in respect of the dwelling-house, and that notice was an appropriate notice, it is served not earlier than 3 months after the expiry of the previous notice."

Dispensing power

This case concerns recovery of possession from shorthold tenants and was introduced by section 55 of the Housing Act 1980. Under section 55(2) of that Act, the Case can apply to a tenancy which does not strictly satisfy the conditions applicable to a shorthold tenancy if the court considers it just and equitable to make a possession order.[40] The rules as to the timing of the landlord's notice are somewhat complicated.[41]

Continued availability of ground after end of tenancy

The effect of Case 19 is that the landlord is not obliged to seek possession at the earliest opportunity. Failure to do so does not prejudice his right to invoke it at a later stage. The right to possession may be asserted against the original tenant who is holding over after expiry as a statutory tenant, or against a member of his family who succeeded to the tenancy on death.[42] Case 19 continues to apply where a new tenancy, fixed or periodic, was granted to the former shorthold tenant or his successor after the shorthold tenancy ended. The later tenancy is not shorthold,[43] but the landlord's rights are preserved. This can be seen from *Gent v. de la Mare*,[44] where a shorthold tenancy was granted for one year under an agreement which provided for the landlords to give three months' notice if they did not wish to renew the tenancy. After the initial term expired, the tenant held over, the landlords neither having given notice nor having indicated any intention to renew. As the initial term was clearly shorthold, it was held that Case 19 continued to apply even though the tenant no longer had a shorthold tenancy. By paragraph (a), the Case applies not only where the current tenancy is shorthold, but where the tenant continues in possession as statutory tenant or under a further contractual tenancy.

---

[40] *i.e.* if Housing Act 1980, s. 52(1)(b), relating to notice before the grant, is not satisfied; above, p. 80; *Dunnell (R.J.) Property Investments Ltd v. Thorpe* [1989] 2 E.G.L.R 94; [1990] Conv. 449 (J.E.M.).

[41] See [1982] Conv. 29 at 41–42 (P. Smith); *Henry Smith's Charity Trustees v. Kyriakou* (1990) 22 H.L.R. 66.

[42] Where Case 19 was applicable to the predecessor, a successor who would otherwise have taken an assured tenancy takes an assured shorthold tenancy: Housing Act 1988, s. 39(7), below, p. 147.

[43] Housing Act 1980, s. 52(2), (5); Case 19, para. (a).

[44] [1988] 1 E.G.L.R. 104; [1988] Conv. 200 (J.E.M.).

Case 20

Member of armed forces

"Where the dwelling-house was let by a person (in this Case referred to as 'the owner') at any time after the commencement of section 67 of the Housing Act 1980 and —

(a) at the time when the owner acquired the dwelling-house he was a member of the regular armed forces[45] of the Crown;

(b) at the relevant date[46] the owner was a member of the regular armed forces of the Crown;

(c) not later than the relevant date the owner gave notice in writing to the tenant that possession might be recovered under this Case;

(d) the dwelling-house has not, since the commencement of section 67 of the Act of 1980 been let by the owner on a protected tenancy with respect to which the condition mentioned in paragraph (c) above was not satisfied; and

(e) the court is of the opinion that–
  (i) the dwelling-house is required as a residence for the owner; or
  (ii) of the conditions set out in Part V of this Schedule one of those in paragraphs (c) to (f) is satisfied."

The conditions in paragraphs (c) to (f) of Part V of the Schedule referred to above have been set out in the context of Case 11.

Dispensing power

As with Cases 11 and 12, the court may dispense with either or both of main conditions (c) or (d) if it is just and equitable to make a possession order.

Unlike Case 11, the landlord need not have resided in the property prior to the letting.

Possession orders

A preliminary point is that a statutory tenancy does not end on the making of a possession order. This will occur only when the order is properly executed. Where a landlord resorts to self-help after obtaining a possession order, the tenant can obtain damages for unlawful eviction.[47]

Adjournment, suspension etc.

As far as the discretionary grounds under Part I of Schedule 15 are concerned, the court[48] has jurisdiction, under section 100 of the 1977 Act, either to adjourn the

---

[45] Within the meaning of section 1 of the House of Commons Disqualification Act 1975.

[46] See n. 95, above.

[47] *Haniff v. Robinson* [1993] Q.B. 419; above, p. 47.

[48] For the jurisdiction of the county court, see Rent Act 1977, s. 141. In the case of the discretionary grounds, the county court has jurisdiction even if the case is not within the normal financial limits.

possession proceedings for such time as it thinks fit, or, on the making of a possession order or at any time before its execution,[49] stay or suspend execution of the order or postpone the date of possession for such time as it thinks fit.

Conditions
Unless it would cause exceptional hardship to the tenant or would be otherwise unreasonable,[50] the court must impose conditions as to payment of any arrears, rent or mesne profits and such other conditions as it thinks fit on any such adjournment, stay, suspension or postponement. If the conditions are complied with, the court may, if it thinks fit, discharge or rescind the possession order. If the tenant fails to comply with conditions imposed, for example in an adjournment, the landlord may apply for a possession order.[51] These powers of the court are commonly exercised, especially where possession is sought on the basis of rent arrears.

Setting aside
A possession order made in circumstances where the hearing should have been adjourned will be set aside and a new trial ordered.[52] It should be added that a possession order can be set aside even after it has been executed.[53]

Conditional and absolute orders
As mentioned above, a conditional order may be discharged if the conditions are complied with. Under a conditional order, the tenancy continues.[54] An absolute order, on the other hand (although capable of suspension or postponement) terminates the tenancy immediately.[55] An absolute order cannot be discharged, but may be converted to a conditional order and then discharged.[56]

Mandatory grounds
The wide powers exercisable under section 100 do not apply to the mandatory grounds for possession. By section 89 of the Housing Act 1980, the possession order in such cases shall not be postponed (whether by the order or any variation, suspension or stay of execution) to a date later than 14 days after the making of the order, unless

---

[49] The court can set aside a possession order even though it has been executed before the making of the application: *Peabody Donation Fund (Governors) v. Hay* (1987) 19 H.L.R. 145 (secure tenancy); *cf. Scott-James v. Chehab* [1988] 2 E.G.L.R. 61. See further n. 53, below.

[50] For examples, see Farrand & Arden, *Rent Acts and Regulations* (2nd ed., 1981) pp. 130-131.

[51] *Mills v. Allen* [1953] 2 Q.B. 341. The court may make more than one suspension order even if the tenant has broken the terms of the original order; *Vandermolen v. Toma* (1981) 9 H.L.R. 91.

[52] *Verrilli v. Idigoras* [1990] E.G.C.S. 3.

[53] *Tower Hamlets L.B.C. v. Abadie* (1990) 22 H.L.R. 264; R.S.C. Ord. 37, r. 2. See also (1992) *Legal Action*, November, p. 14 and (1995) *Legal Action*, April, p. 20 (C. Johnson).

[54] *Sherrin v. Brand* [1956] 1 Q.B. 403 (successor could acquire tenancy on death of tenant where breach of conditional order but landlord had taken no steps to enforce the order). The position is different with secure tenancies under the Housing Act 1985, where breach of a suspended conditional order terminates the tenancy: *Thompson v. Elmbridge* [1987] 1 W.L.R. 1425; [1987] Conv. 450 (J.E.M.); (1988) 51 M.L.R. 371 (J. Driscoll).

[55] *American Economic Laundry v. Little* [1951] 1 K.B. 400 (where tenant died before execution of order, no successor could acquire the tenancy).

[56] *Payne v. Cooper* [1958] 1 Q.B. 174; *Mills v. Allen*, above.

exceptional hardship would be caused by requiring
possession to be given up by that date. In such
circumstances it shall not be postponed beyond six weeks
from the making of the order.[57]

**Rights of
tenant's spouse**

Another point to consider is the position of the tenant's
spouse. It is provided by section 75 of the Housing Act 1980
that if a tenancy is terminated by possession proceedings at a
time when the tenant's spouse or former spouse, having
rights of occupation under the Matrimonial Homes Act
(now the Act of 1983),[58] is occupying the dwelling-house,
then the spouse or former spouse shall have the same rights
in relation to any adjournment, stay, suspension or
postponement, so long as he or she remains in occupation,
as he or she would have if those rights of occupation were
not affected by the termination of the tenancy. The spouse,
therefore, has *locus standi* to apply to court for the exercise of
its powers of suspension, postponement and so forth.

Consent orders

Finally, the question arises as to the court's jurisdiction to
make a consent order for possession. There is no such
jurisdiction unless the tenant concedes that the facts
necessary to support the order are present.[59] If the parties to
a possession action agree that the premises are outside the
Act or that the defendant's possession is not protected, the
court has no duty to consider these facts before making the
order.[60] The matter arose in the context of Case 9 in *R. v.
Newcastle upon Tyne County Court, ex p. Thompson*,[61] where
the tenant had not conceded that he was not protected, nor
that the landlord reasonably required the flat, nor that the
balance of hardship favoured the landlord, nor that it was
reasonable to make the order. The possession order was
quashed in judicial review proceedings. The court's advice
to practitioners was that there must be a plain admission of
the qualifying condition for a ground for possession if an
agreement is to be embodied in a possession order relating
to premises covered by section 98 of the 1977 Act. The
tenant must concede that the circumstances of the particular
Case exist, and, where relevant, that the balance of hardship
favours the landlord, and that it is reasonable to make the
order. It has recently been held, however, in the context of

---

[57] It was held in *Bain v. Church Commissioners* [1989] 1 W.L.R. 24, that
s. 89 applied only to the powers of the county court and did not affect
those of the High Court.

[58] These rights terminate on divorce. As to transfer on divorce, see above,
p. 108.

[59] *R. v. Bloomsbury and Marylebone County Court, ex p. Blackburne* [1985] 2
E.G.L.R. 157; (1986) 83 L.S. Gaz. 1701 (J. Stocker). See also *Barton v.
Fincham* [1921] 2 K.B. 291; *Thorne v. Smith* [1947] K.B. 307;
Wandsworth L.B.C. v. Fadayomi [1987] 1 W.L.R. 1473.

[60] *Syed Hussain Bin Abdul Rahman Bin Shaikh Alkaff v. A.M. Abdullah
Sahib & Co.* [1985] 1 W.L.R. 1392 (P.C.). There might be special
considerations if in subsequent proceedings the defendant established
that his agreement was pursuant to a compromise involving his being
paid a sum of money.

[61] [1988] 2 E.G.L.R. 119, criticised at [1989] Conv. 98 (S. Bridge).

a secure tenancy, that the tenant's admission need not be express. An admission may be implied from the terms of the order. Whether such an implication can be made depends on the terms of the order construed in the light of the circumstances.[62]

Termination apart from the grounds for possession

In addition to the grounds for possession, there are certain other circumstances in which protected and statutory tenants may cease to enjoy Rent Act security of tenure. As we have seen, a statutory tenancy terminates if the tenant ceases to reside, although his liabilities continue until he gives proper notice under section 3 to the landlord.[63] Other circumstances requiring discussion include the following:

Unfit houses

Closing orders

The Housing Act 1985[64] provides that nothing in the Rent Act shall prevent recovery of possession while a closing order is in force.[65] The policy of public health statutes overrides that of the Rent Act. The tenant cannot resist the possession action even if the disrepair which has given rise to the closing order is the landlord's fault.[66] Where the tenancy is still protected, the landlord cannot seek possession until the contractual tenancy has been terminated, for example by notice to quit.[67] If the tenancy is already statutory, however, he can seek possession immediately.[68]

Change of user

A tenancy which is initially a protected tenancy under the Rent Act will cease to be so protected if a change of user brings it within some other code of statutory protection, for example those relating to business tenancies or agricultural holdings, thereby excluding it from the Rent Act. So in

Business user

Cheryl Investments Ltd v. Saldanha[69] a protected tenant who equipped the dwelling-house for business lost Rent Act protection, as the tenancy now qualified as a business tenancy under the Landlord and Tenant Act 1954, Part II. The landlord in such cases may recover possession (if at all) under that Act.

Change in status of occupier

Change to licensee

A protected or statutory tenancy will cease if the tenant ceases to be a tenant, for example by becoming a licensee, whereupon the tenancy is surrendered by operation of law.[70] Any arrangement whereby it is alleged that a tenant has become a licensee will be closely scrutinised, but there is no

Business user
Cheryl Investments Ltd v. Saldanha[69] a protected tenant who equipped the dwelling-house for business lost Rent Act protection, as the tenancy now qualified as a business tenancy under the Landlord and Tenant Act 1954, Part II. The landlord in such cases may recover possession (if at all) under that Act.

Change in status of occupier

Change to licensee
A protected or statutory tenancy will cease if the tenant ceases to be a tenant, for example by becoming a licensee, whereupon the tenancy is surrendered by operation of law.[70] Any arrangement whereby it is alleged that a tenant has become a licensee will be closely scrutinised, but there is no presumption of undue influence between landlord and tenant.[71]

Surrender of tenancy
In *Dibbs v. Campbell*[72] the parties had intended to create a shorthold tenancy, but upon realising that the tenancy did not qualify as shorthold (and was, therefore, an ordinary protected tenancy), it was agreed that the tenant should surrender the tenancy in order that a new shorthold tenancy might be created. This was done by formal deed of surrender, and the new shorthold tenancy was granted on the following day. The tenant had planned to vacate temporarily in between the surrender and grant, but in the event this was not done. When the landlord later sought possession of the shorthold tenancy under Case 19,[73] the tenant claimed that the surrender had merely ended the protected tenancy so that he then acquired a statutory tenancy (which, not being shorthold, could not be terminated by Case 19). It was held that it was not necessary to hand over the keys or physically vacate the property in order to surrender a protected tenancy. This could be achieved by conduct and intention, and had been done in the present case. It was held to be clear that a protected or statutory tenant could surrender by operation of law by yielding up possession or its equivalent, and *a fortiori* by signing a deed of surrender in clear terms. It might be added, however, that this was a case on rather special facts where there was no doubt as to the bona fides of the arrangement, which reflected the true intentions of both parties.

A statutory tenancy will also cease if the tenant acquires title against the landlord under the Limitation Act 1980 by

---

[69] [1978] 1 W.L.R. 1329, above, p. 78.
[70] *Foster v. Robinson* [1951] 1 K.B. 149. A mere agreement to become a licensee would not suffice.
[71] *Mathew v. Bobbins* (1980) 41 P.&C.R. 1.
[72] [1988] 2 E.G.L.R. 122; *Collins v. Claughton* [1959] 1 W.L.R. 145. See Appendix, p. 283.
[73] See above, p. 134.

Adverse possession

failing to pay rent for the necessary period.[74] It has been held, however, that a statutory sub-tenancy does not terminate as against the head landlord where possessory title is acquired as against the tenant.[75]

Rescission

In *Killick v. Roberts*[76] the tenant had acquired his protected tenancy by fraudulently misrepresenting that he was having a house built, to which he would move. The fraud was not discovered until the protected tenancy had expired and a statutory tenancy had arisen. It was held that the landlord could rescind the contract, thereby terminating the statutory tenancy. Rescission during the protected tenancy would have prevented a statutory tenancy from arising. The policy of the Rent Act was not to protect those who should never have had a contract.

Eviction by a person not bound by the tenancy

Eviction by mortgagee

This involves the situation where the landlord is a mortgagor, whose mortgage prohibits the power of leasing. Any tenancy granted binds the landlord (by estoppel) but does not bind the mortgagee, who can recover possession.[77] This is so whether the tenancy is protected or has become statutory as against the landlord by the time of the possession action.[78] The position is, of course, otherwise if the tenancy was granted before the mortgage,[79] or if the mortgagee has accepted the tenant, or, it has been held, if the mortgagee seeks possession otherwise than in good faith.[80]

Transfer of reversion

This may be contrasted with the position where the immediate reversion is transferred to a body not bound by the Rent Act, for example, the Crown.[81] Here the tenancy will bind the new landlord (to the extent that it can do so under the general law), but the Rent Act will cease to apply. So where a subtenant had a protected tenancy as against the

---

[74] The Act extends to statutory tenants: *Jessamine Investment Co. v. Schwartz* [1978] Q.B. 264.
[75] *Jessamine Investment Co. v. Schwartz*, above.
[76] [1991] 1 W.L.R. 1146; [1992] Conv. 269 (J. Martin); (1992) 51 C.L.J. 21 (L. Tee).
[77] *Dudley and District Benefit Building Society v. Emerson* [1949] Ch. 707.
[78] *Britannia Building Society v. Earl* [1990] 1 W.L.R. 422 (holding also that the tenants could not seek relief under s. 36 of the Administration of Justice Act 1970); [1990] Conv. 450 (S. Bridge); (1991) 54 M.L.R. 142 (C. Douzinas and R. Warrington).
[79] Unless the "landlord" had no title at the grant of the tenancy: *Abbey National Building Society v. Cann* [1991] 1 A.C. 56, overruling *Church of England Building Society v. Piskor* [1954] Ch. 553. See also *Walthamstow Building Society v. Davies* (1990) 60 P.&C.R. 99 (remortgage).
[80] *Quennell v. Maltby* [1979] 1 W.L.R. 318.
[81] See above, p. 76. Where a local authority becomes landlord of a statutory tenant, Housing Act 1985, s. 109A provides that the tenancy is treated as a contractual tenancy on the same terms, so that Part IV of the 1985 Act (secure tenancies) applies. See also Housing Act 1988, s. 35(5).

tenant, he became a secure tenant on surrender of the head tenancy to the local authority landlord.[82]

Destruction of the premises

In the case of a protected tenancy, destruction of the premises will not terminate the tenancy, unless the doctrine of frustration applies.[83] Where the tenancy is statutory, however, it will come to an end on destruction of the premises, as the tenant can no longer occupy the dwelling-house as his residence.[84] If, on the other hand, the premises are merely uninhabitable, the statutory tenancy continues, provided the tenant intends to return.[85]

Other cases

Planning breaches

Low rent

Ministerial order

Another possibility may be where the premises are subject to an enforcement notice following a breach of planning control under the Town and Country Planning Act 1990.[86]

Other cases involve the situation where the tenancy does not terminate, but ceases to be subject to the Rent Act. This would occur if the rent falls below two-thirds of the rateable value on the "appropriate day."[87] Similarly if the Secretary of State should exercise his powers under section 143[88] of the 1977 Act, whereupon dwelling-houses in areas specified in his order would cease to be the subject of a regulated tenancy.

---

[82] *Basingstoke and Deane Borough Council v. Paice, The Times,* April 3, 1995.

[83] This will rarely be the case: *National Carriers Ltd v. Panalpina (Northern) Ltd* [1981] A.C. 675.

[84] *Ellis & Sons Amalgamated Properties Ltd v. Sisman* [1948] 1 K.B. 653.

[85] *Morleys (Birmingham) Ltd v. Slater* [1950] 1 K.B. 506 (war damage).

[86] The Act does not provide a specific ground for possession against a Rent Act tenant, but see s. 102(6) (duty of local planning authority to secure provision of suitable accommodation for residents displaced by the order); *R. v. East Hertfordshire D.C., ex p. Smith, The Times,* January 25, 1990.

[87] See above, pp. 67–68 and n. 80.

[88] See above, p. 79. Any former protected tenancy would continue to exist under the general law. Any statutory tenancy would apparently terminate, but subject to transitional provisions under s. 143(2), which expressly refers to provisions to avoid or mitigate hardship.

8 STATUTORY TENANTS BY SUCCESSION

Although, as we have seen, the statutory tenancy is a personal right which is not assignable,[1] it is nevertheless capable of transmission on death. This can occur on the death of the original tenant, and again on the death of the first successor. Hence the landlord might be unable to recover possession for a very considerable period. The purpose of the succession rules is to further the policy of the Rent Act that the tenant should enjoy security of tenure in his home. His security would be seriously impaired if the landlord could eject his family, for example his elderly widow, on his death. It is questionable, however, whether a second succession is justifiable. It might be noted that the more recent legislation conferring security on public sector tenants permits only one succession to the tenancy.[2] Similarly in the case of assured tenancies under the Housing Act 1988, where succession rights are very limited and operate once only, in favour of the spouse or cohabitant.[3] In another context, succession rights to tenancies of agricultural holdings were withdrawn by the Agricultural Holdings Act 1984 (now the Act of 1986) save in respect of tenancies granted before that Act.

1988 amendments   The policy of the Housing Act 1988 is to phase out protected and statutory tenancies under the Rent Act 1977. However, as existing tenancies are preserved, this will take a long time to achieve in view of the succession rules. These rules are, therefore, restricted somewhat by the 1988 Act in relation to deaths after its commencement.[4] In the account which follows the rules relating to tenants dying before the commencement of the 1988 Act will be outlined as well as the new rules. The old rules are likely to remain relevant for some time. In *Dyson Holdings Ltd. v. Fox*,[5] for example, the tenant died in 1961, but the matter was not litigated until 1973.

The current provisions are contained in Schedule 1 of the 1977 Act, as amended by the Housing Acts 1980 and 1988. They apply on the death of a person ("the original tenant") who, immediately before his death, was a protected tenant

---

[1] See above, Chap. 6.
[2] Housing Act 1985, s. 87.
[3] See below, p. 212.
[4] Housing Act 1988, s. 39 and Sched. 4.
[5] [1976] Q.B. 503.

of the dwelling-house or the statutory tenant of it by virtue of his previous tenancy.

The first successor

Original tenant dying before January 15, 1989

Spouse The first successor is the surviving spouse (if any) of the original tenant, if residing in the dwelling-house[6] immediately before the death of the original tenant. The spouse is the statutory tenant "if and so long as he or she occupies the dwelling-house as his or her residence."[7] If **Member of the** there is no such spouse, the first successor is a person who **family** was "a member of the original tenant's family," residing with him at his death and for the period of six months immediately before his death. Such a person is the statutory **More than one** tenant if and so long as he occupies the dwelling-house as **claimant** his residence. If there is more than one claimant, then the successor may be decided by agreement,[8] or, in default of agreement, by the county court.[9]

"Spouse" is not defined, and presumably means a party to a valid (or voidable) marriage which subsisted until the tenant's death. Claimants other than spouses could be regarded as members of the tenant's "family" if they were cohabiting with the tenant or were relatives in the ordinary **Cohabitants** way. There is considerable authority on the question of whether cohabitants could qualify as members of the tenant's family, but this has little scope for application save in relation to deaths before the commencement of the Housing Act 1988. Broadly, the position was that the fact of cohabitation did not suffice unless there was a sufficient degree of stability and permanence.[10]

The meaning of "family" in cases not involving cohabitation is discussed in the following section.

Original tenant dying on or after January 15, 1989

As under the previous law, the spouse of the deceased tenant is entitled to be the first successor, if residing in the dwelling-house immediately before the death. The rules

---

[6] There is no need to show residence *with* the tenant.
[7] This requirement is identical to that of s. 2, and thus imports the test laid down in *Brown v. Brash* [1948] 2 K.B. 247; above, p. 98.
[8] The agreement is that of the claimants. The landlord has no right to participate.
[9] This may be contrasted with the public sector. If there is more than one claimant, the successor is selected by the landlord in default of agreement.
[10] The leading cases were *Dyson Holdings Ltd v. Fox* [1976] Q.B. 503; *Helby v. Rafferty* [1979] 1 W.L.R 13; *Watson v. Lucas* [1980] 1 W.L.R. 1493.

applicable to the spouse are extended by the Housing Act 1988 to persons living with the original tenant as his or her wife or husband.[11]Thus the question is no longer whether a cohabitant is a member of the deceased tenant's family, but simply whether the parties were living together as husband **Extended** and wife. No minimum period of living together is specified, **meaning of** but no doubt the status of "living together" cannot be **"spouse"** acquired overnight.[12] It appears that the "living together" test is easier to satisfy than the "member of the family" test which, as mentioned above, required a degree of stability and permanence. Factors such as whether there were any children and whether the woman used the man's name, which were emphasised in some of the earlier decisions, will not be relevant. However, the parties must have done more than merely live in the same household.[13] It seems that **Homosexual** homosexual couples will not satisfy the test of living with the **couples** tenant "as his or her wife or husband." In *Harrogate Borough Council v. Simpson*[14] the claim of the surviving member of a lesbian couple failed. This arose in the context of a secure tenancy under the Housing Act 1985, which defines "family" as including persons who "live together as husband and wife."[15] It is likely that the result would be the same if the matter arose under the Rent Act succession rules.

More than one If there is more than one claimant in the above category, **claimant** the county court, in default of agreement, is to decide who shall be treated as the surviving spouse.[16] Such disputes are likely to be rare, as they could arise only where the cohabitation takes place in the dwelling-house in which the spouse is also residing, or where the deceased tenant was cohabiting with two persons, and all were living in the same dwelling-house.

Where the successor is the spouse or a person treated as the spouse, he or she is entitled to a statutory tenancy under the Rent Act 1977 by way of succession. One further succession is possible on the first successor's death, as explained below.

Member of the Where there is no spouse or person treated as a spouse, **family** the first successor is a member of the original tenant's family

---

[11] Rent Act 1977, Sched. 1, para. 2(2) (inserted by Housing Act 1988, Sched. 4, para. 2).

[12] *cf. Tuck v. Nicholls* [1989] 1 F.L.R. 283 (Domestic Violence and Matrimonial Proceedings Act 1976).

[13] *City of Westminster v. Peart* (1992) 24 H.L.R. 389; [1993] Conv. 154 (J. Martin). A divorced couple were not living together "as husband and wife" where they were attempting a reconciliation and the woman spent about half her time in her own flat.

[14] (1985) 17 H.L.R. 205. Leave to appeal was refused; *The Times*, March 1, 1985. The European Commission of Human Rights dismissed the claim: *Application No. 11716/85 v. U.K.*.

[15] Housing Act 1985, s. 113.

[16] Rent Act 1977, Sched. 1, para. 2(3) (inserted by Housing Act 1988, Sched. 4, para. 2).

Examples

who was residing with him in the dwelling-house for the period of two years immediately before his death.[17] In the event of more than one claimant, the successor is decided by agreement or by the county court, as above. "Family" is not defined by the Rent Act 1977 nor by the Housing Act 1988.[18] Clearly such relationships as parents, children,[19] grandchildren,[20] brothers and sisters,[21] are included, but the mere fact of a blood relationship is not necessarily sufficient. In *Langdon v. Horton*[22] it was held that the tenant's two first cousins, who had lived with her for many years, were not members of her "family".

De facto relationships

As far as *de facto* relationships are concerned (*i.e.* where there is no legal relationship by blood or marriage), the leading authority is the decision of the House of Lords in *Carega Properties S.A. (formerly Joram Developments Ltd) v. Sharratt*.[23] The tenant was an elderly widow. The claimant was a young man who had moved in with her and stayed for nearly 20 years, until her death. The parties had a platonic "aunt/nephew" relationship. In rejecting the man's claim, the House of Lords held that the only *de facto* relationships which were recognised for succession purposes were the "common law" spouse and the parent/child relationship where the child was young, for example where the child had not been legally adopted.[24] Two adults having a platonic relationship could not be regarded as "family" by acting, for example, as brother and sister or father and daughter.[25] Such persons were members of the same household, but not

[17] Rent Act 1977, Sched. 1, para. 3, as amended by Housing Act 1988, Sched. 4, para. 3. Where the original tenant dies within 18 months after the commencement of the 1988 Act, the two-year requirement is deemed satisfied by a person who resided with the tenant for six months immediately before the commencement of the 1988 Act and until the tenant's death. The two-year rule is more onerous than the six-month rule relating to successions before the 1988 Act, but the Housing Bill as originally drafted specified five years.

[18] For secure tenancies see Housing Act 1985, s. 113, which includes (in addition to spouses and cohabitants), a parent, grandparent, child, grandchild, brother, sister, uncle, aunt, nephew or niece. Any relationship by marriage is treated as a relationship by blood, and any relationship of the half-blood is treated as a relationship of the whole blood. "Child" includes a stepchild, and an illegitimate person is treated as the legitimate child of his mother and reputed father.

[19] Including illegitimate, adopted (whether legally or *de facto*) and stepchildren: *Brock v. Wollams* [1949] 2 K.B. 388. It seems that a minor can succeed to the tenancy. See *Portman Registrars & Nominees v. Mohammed Latif* (county court) noted at [1988] 18 E.G. 61 (D. Williams), where a 16-year-old daughter succeeded.

[20] *Hedgedale v. Hards* (1991) 23 H.L.R. 158.

[21] *Price v. Gould* (1930) 143 L.T. 333.

[22] [1951] 1 K.B. 66.

[23] [1979] 1 W.L.R. 928; (1980) 39 C.L.J. 31 (P. Tennant); (1980) 96 L.Q.R. 248 at 260–268 (A. Zuckerman). Ironically, the tenant was the widow of Salter J., who had pondered the meaning of "family" in *Salter v. Lask* [1925] 1 K.B. 584.

[24] See *Brock v. Wollams* [1949] 2 K.B. 388; *Jones v. Whitehill* [1950] 2 K.B. 204.

[25] See *Ross v. Collins* [1964] 1 W.L.R. 425.

members of the same family. Step and in-law relations, however, might qualify.[26]

A modern application of this principle is *Sefton Holdings Ltd v. Cairns*,[27] where the property had been let in about 1939. On the tenant's death in 1965 the daughter succeeded to the tenancy. On the daughter's death in 1986 the defendant claimed as second successor. She had moved in with the family in 1941 at the age of 23. She had no family of her own and was treated as a daughter. As far as the parent/child relationship with the original tenant was concerned, no case covered the *de facto* adoption of an adult. This point, however, did not need to be pursued, as the issue was whether she was a member of the daughter's family. It was held that the relationship of *de facto* sisters was insufficient. She was a member of the household, not of the family.

Assured tenancy

A successor other than a spouse or person treated as a spouse acquires not a statutory tenancy but an assured tenancy, from which no further succession is possible.[28] The assured tenancy is a periodic tenancy of the same dwelling-house, under which the periods of the tenancy are the same as those for which rent was last payable under the predecessor's tenancy.[29] The terms are the same as under the predecessor's tenancy, subject to section 13 of the 1988 Act (rent increases)[30] and section 15 (no assignment or subletting without consent).[31] If the original tenant had a shorthold tenancy,[32] the successor has an assured shorthold tenancy.[33]

Where the successor has become entitled to an assured tenancy by succession, the landlord may recover possession on the basis of the grounds relating to assured tenancies or certain of the mandatory grounds relating to statutory tenancies.[34]

---

[26] *Ross v. Collins*, above, approved by the House of Lords in *Carega Properties S.A. v. Sharratt*.

[27] [1988] 2 F.L.R. 109; [1988] Conv. 197 (J.E.M.); (1988) 85 L.S. Gaz. No. 19, p. 13 (G. Howells).

[28] Housing Act 1988, s. 17(2)(c). Thus the successor has less security than the predecessor.

[29] *ibid*, s. 39(6). See also s. 39(9), dealing with the case where the predecessor had a fixed-term tenancy at his death. (Variation of the terms is possible under s. 6.)

[30] See below, p. 250.

[31] See below, p. 206.

[32] See above, p. 79.

[33] Housing Act 1988, s. 39(7) (whether or not the conditions of s. 20 are satisfied: below, p. 221).

[34] *ibid*, Sched. 4, para. 13. The Rent Act grounds applicable are Cases 11, 12, 16, 17, 18 and 20. Any notices given to the predecessor under Cases 13, 14 or 15 of the Rent Act are treated as given for the purposes of the corresponding grounds in the 1988 Act.

The second successor

First successor dying before January 15, 1989

Spouse

Member of the family

If the first successor continued to be the statutory tenant until his death, then on his death any surviving spouse took priority if residing in the dwelling-house at the death of the first successor. In the absence of any such spouse, the second successor was a member of the first successor's family who resided with him for six months immediately prior to his death. In the event of more than one such member, the position is as mentioned above in the case of the first succession.

First successor dying on or after January 15, 1989

No succession from assured tenancy

Where the first successor (not being a spouse or a person treated as a spouse) took an assured tenancy by way of succession, no second succession is possible.[35] Where the first successor took a statutory tenancy by way of succession, one more succession is possible, although the conditions to be satisfied are more stringent than those applicable to deaths before the commencement of the 1988 Act. These rules apply where the first successor (being a member of the family of the original tenant) succeeded before the 1988 Act but died after it, or where the first successor (being the spouse of the original tenant or a person treated as a spouse) succeeded after the 1988 Act.

Member of family

The second successor[36] is a person who:

(a) was a member of the original tenant's family[37] immediately before that tenant's death; and
(b) was a member of the first successor's family immediately before the first successor's death; and
(c) was residing in the dwelling-house with the first successor at the latter's death and for the period of two years[38] immediately before the death.

Assured tenancy

If there is more than one claimant, the successor is decided by the county court in default of agreement, as with the previous cases. The second successor takes an assured periodic tenancy,[39] the terms and grounds for possession being the same as in the case of a first successor taking an assured periodic tenancy, as explained above.[40]

---

[35] Housing Act 1988, s. 17(2)(c). See Sched. 2, Ground 7, giving the right to possession where an assured periodic tenancy devolves under the will or intestacy of the tenant.

[36] Rent Act 1977, Sched. 1, para. 6, as substituted by Housing Act 1988, Sched. 4, para. 6.

[37] See above, p. 145.

[38] Where the first successor dies within 18 months after the commencement of the 1988 Act, the requirement is as set out in note 17 above.

[39] Housing Act 1988, s. 39(5). See *Daejan Properties Ltd v. Mahoney* [1995] E.G.C.S. 4.

[40] See above, p. 147.

The main reason why the new rules are harder to satisfy is that, in addition to the longer period of residence, the claimant must show a familial relationship with the original tenant as well as with the first successor. The new provision is designed to deal with the situation where the claimant is **Examples** the child of the original tenant and first successor. It is unlikely to include the spouse of the first successor, because he or she would not normally be able to satisfy the condition of being a member of the original tenant's family. It is possible that a parent of the original tenant or the first successor (being the parent-in-law of the other party) might succeed,[41] but such cases would be rare. The rules may be easier to satisfy where the first successor inherited before the 1988 Act and was, therefore, not necessarily the spouse of the original tenant.

Effect of new grant Where, after the succession, a new contractual tenancy was granted to the successor, this cannot operate to increase the number of successions. In the case of a new grant to a first successor, there can be one further succession on his death. In the case of a new grant to a second successor, there can be no further succession on his death.[42]

Where no succession rights arise on the death of a statutory tenant (because he was the second successor or because no person qualifies as a successor), then any person who continues to occupy the dwelling-house is protected by section 3 of the Protection from Eviction Act 1977, whereby **Court order** it is unlawful for the landlord to enforce his right to recover possession without a court order. Where a statutory tenant dies in circumstances where there can be no transmission of the tenancy, presumably his personal representatives should give notice to the landlord under section 3(3) of the Rent Act 1977."[43]

Devolution of contractual tenancy

As noted above, the succession rules come into operation whether the original tenancy was statutory or still protected at the tenant's death. If it was a protected tenancy, then it will pass to some beneficiary under the tenant's will or upon his intestacy.[44] This beneficiary may or may not be the same

---

[41] See above, p. 147. "Step" relationships may provide other possibilities.
[42] Rent Act 1977, Sched. 1, para. 10.
[43] By analogy with *Boyer v. Warbey* [1953] 1 Q.B. 234 and *King's College, Cambridge v. Kershman* (1948) 64 T.L.R. 547, above, p. 108.
[44] See *Trustees of the Gift of Thomas Pocklington v. Hill* [1989] 2 E.G.L.R. 87; [1989] Conv. 289 (J.E.M.); where weekly protected tenancy passed to the tenant's daughter on his death, was later assigned to her sister, and subsequently became a statutory tenancy. The result would probably have been the same if the daughter had also qualified as a statutory successor, as explained below.

Suspension

person as the first successor. The somewhat curious result, it has been held, is that the protected, *i.e.* contractual, tenancy "goes into abeyance" for the period during which there is a successor. In *Moodie v. Hosegood*[45] a protected tenant died intestate, whereupon the tenancy vested in the Probate judge under section 9 of the Administration of Estates Act 1925. His widow continued to reside in the house. The landlord, having determined the contractual tenancy by serving notice to quit on the Probate judge, sought to recover possession from the widow. The House of Lords upheld her claim to remain in possession as statutory tenant by succession. Lord Morton explained the position as follows:

> "if a contractual tenancy is still subsisting at her husband's death, and devolves on someone other than the widow, it is not destroyed but the rights and obligations which would ordinarily devolve upon the successor in title of the contractual tenant are suspended, so long as the widow retains possession of the dwelling-house. "[46]

Thus a notice to quit given to or by the contractual tenant in such circumstances will not affect the successor's rights. If the successor remains in residence beyond the termination of the contractual tenancy, then the person entitled to the contractual tenancy under the general law will never enjoy any rights. If, however, the contractual tenancy continues until the end of any tenancy by succession, then the rights and obligations under it will "revive."

Where beneficiary is the successor

A further problem arises where the person entitled under the general law to succeed to the contractual tenancy is the same person as the successor. In what capacity does he continue to occupy? If he takes as successor there can be no more than one further transmission. If he can be regarded as occupying in right of the protected tenancy, then there may be two further transmissions after his death. This was the position in *Whitmore v. Lambert*,[47] where the protected tenant's widow was entitled under his will, and under the statutory succession provisions. She continued to reside, but did not prove the will. It was held that she had taken as contractual tenant, so that on her death a statutory tenant by succession could take as if on the death of an original tenant. The amendments in the Housing Act 1988 do not appear to affect these principles.[48]

---

[45] [1952] A.C. 61.

[46] *ibid.* at 74.

[47] [1955] 1 W.L.R. 495. In fact it was unclear whether she qualified as a statutory successor. At the time of the husband's death the succession rules only applied to a tenant dying intestate. It was left open whether this covered the case of a will which had not been proved.

[48] *cf.* succession to assured periodic tenancies under Housing Act 1988, s. 17, providing that the tenancy does not devolve under the tenant's will or intestacy.

The meaning of "residing with" the tenant

The requirements are different according to whether the claimant is the tenant's spouse[49] or a member of his family. The spouse need only show residence in the dwelling-house immediately before the death, which includes the case of separated spouses living under the same roof but not together. A member of the family, on the other hand, must show residence *with* the tenant for the period of two years[50] immediately prior to the death. "Residing with" bears its ordinary natural meaning, and means more than "living at."[51] In *Foreman v. Beagley*[52] the tenant had been in hospital for the last three years of her life. Her son took up residence during the last year (at a time when the required period was six months). His claim failed. He came in as a "caretaker," and there had never been any community of living with his mother. It might have been otherwise if he had lived with her before her illness and had continued to live there during her absence. This case was distinguished in *Hedgedale v. Hards*,[53] where a grandson moved in with his grandmother, the tenant, in August 1987 in order to help look after her. The following month she broke her arm and went to stay with her daughter. She returned around Christmas and died in May 1988. The relevant period of residence required of a member of the family at that time was six months, but at the start of that period the tenant was absent, although intending to return. As both parties intended the grandson to be a permanent resident, he could be regarded as "residing with" the tenant throughout the six month period, although she was absent for four months. The claim failed in *Swanbrae Ltd. v. Elliott*[54] where the tenant's daughter had her own home two miles away, where she lived with her adult son. When the tenant became ill, the daughter slept at her home three or four nights a week for over six months (then the required period) to look after her. She retained the tenancy of her own home, paid the outgoings there and had her mail sent there. It was held that she was not residing with her mother. The fact that she had a permanent home of her own was not fatal to the claim but successful cases

---

[49] Including, in the case of deaths after the commencement of Housing Act 1988, a person living with the tenant as his or her wife or husband: Sched. 4, para. 2.

[50] Or six months in the case of deaths before the 1988 Act.

[51] *Foreman v. Beagley* [1969] 1 W.L.R. 1387; *Swanbrae Ltd v. Elliott* [1987] 1 E.G.L.R. 99.

[52] Above. See also *Morgan v. Murch* [1970] 1 W.L.R. 778, where the tenant's son deserted his wife and returned to his mother. He was held to be residing with his mother even though he remained the tenant of his former matrimonial home.

[53] (1991) 23 H.L.R. 158; criticised [1991] Conv. 432 (A. Brierley).

[54] See above; [1987] Conv. 207 (J.E.M.) and 349 (J. Hill).

would be rare in such circumstances.[55] It was a question of fact and degree. In the present case the daughter had moved in for a limited time and for a limited purpose. She had not established a "settled home" with her mother. A rare case where a claimant with her own property was successful was *Hildebrand v. Moon*[56] where a daughter with her own flat moved back to her mother's home to nurse her for over six months before her death. She slept at her mother's every night. Although she retained her flat she had been contemplating selling it before her mother's death. Her claim was upheld. She had made her home with the tenant, unlike the daughter in *Swanbrae Ltd v. Elliott*.[57]

Physical absence   Physical absence of the claimant, for example in hospital or on military service, may be disregarded if his intention to reside is continuing.[58]

The mere fact of residence in the same dwelling-house is not sufficient to establish residence with the tenant. Hence the claimant will not succeed if he was a sub-tenant of part of the property, sharing some rooms with the tenant.[59] However, the claimant (the tenant's granddaughter) succeeded in *Collier v. Stoneman*[60] where she had little contact with the tenant, having her own room but sharing the kitchen.

The 1977 Act did not originally deal with the question whether the whole of the six-month (now two-year) period
Must be in the   of residence with the tenant must have taken place in the
dwelling-house   dwelling which is the subject matter of the claim. The point
in question   arose under the similar provisions of the Housing Act 1985 in *Waltham Forest L.B.C. v. Thomas*,[61] where the tenant and his brother lived together in a council house for over two years before moving to another. Shortly after the move the tenant died. The House of Lords upheld the brother's claim to be a successor, holding that the period of residence did not need to be in the same property throughout the relevant period. The position is otherwise under the Rent Act, however, because the 1977 Act was amended by the Housing Act 1988, providing that the period of residence must have been "in the dwelling-house."[62] This is one of several differences between the private and public sector

---

[55] *Morgan v. Murch*, above, was regarded as a case where the claimant in reality had no other home. Also distinguished was *Peabody Donation Fund Governors v. Grant* (1982) 264 E.G. 925, below, p. 198. See also the "two-homes" cases on s. 2, above, p. 103.
[56] (1990) 22 H.L.R. 1.
[57] Above.
[58] *Middleton v. Bull* [1951] W.N. 517; *Tompkins v. Rowley* (1949) 153 E.G. 442.
[59] *Edmunds v. Jones* [1957] 1 W.L.R. 1118n.
[60] [1957] 1 W.L.R. 1108.
[61] [1992] 2 A.C. 198.
[62] Housing Act 1988, Sched. 4. This amendment applied the decision in *South Northamptonshire D.C. v. Power* [1987] 1 W.L.R. 1433 (on the Housing Act 1985) to the Rent Act 1977, but *Power* was overruled in *Waltham Forest L.B.C. v. Thomas*.

succession rules, although it is not obvious why there should be a difference on this point.

More than one claimant

No joint successors

As stated above, the position where more than one claimant is qualified to succeed to the tenancy is that the county court decides who is the successor, in default of agreement between the claimants. There is no question of joint successors. In *Dealex Properties Ltd v. Brooks*,[63] decided at a time when the wording of the statutory provision was less clear than under the 1977 Act, Harman L.J. said that joint successors would lead to "fearful confusion." There would be a "sort of tontine which will last for so long as the survivor of them is in existence. I think that under the Rent Acts a tenant must be a single person because it is a status of irremovability which belongs to him, and I do not think to anyone but him."[64]Diplock L.J. also feared that any other construction would lead to "absurd consequences."[65] In so far as a statutory tenancy may be held jointly,[66] this reasoning is not convincing, but the statute is clear. Similarly in the cases where succession to an assured tenancy is permitted; there cannot be joint successors.[67] In the public sector, there is equally no provision for joint successors, although the position is different in that, in default of agreement, the landlord selects the successor.[68]

Determination by court

The agreement between the claimants as to who is the successor may be inferred.[69] Pending any such agreement, the statutory tenancy exists although the identity of the tenant is not settled. In *Williams v. Williams*[70] the parties failed to agree, whereupon the matter fell to be decided by the county court. The claimants were the tenant's son and her widower (the case being decided at a time when a widower had no priority over other family members). The son had treated the tenant well, while the widower had treated her badly. But the son was not in financial need, whereas the widower was. On appeal, the widower's claim was upheld. His needs outweighed the son's merits, although hardship was not the sole test.

[63] [1966] 1 Q.B. 542. See further *Daejan Properties Ltd. v. Mahoney* [1995] E.G.C.S. 4.
[64] *ibid.* at 551.
[65] *ibid.* at 554.
[66] See *Lloyd v. Sadler* [1978] Q.B. 774, above, p. 106. Likewise an assured tenancy: Housing Act 1988, s. 1.
[67] Housing Act 1988, s. 17(5).
[68] Housing Act 1985, s. 89(2).
[69] *Dealex Properties Ltd v. Brooks*, above; *Trayfoot v. Lock* [1957] 1 W.L.R. 351.
[70] [1970] 1 W.L.R. 1530.

Where the original tenants were joint tenants

The final matter to be considered is a somewhat problematical area which has yet to be fully considered by the courts. It may be that only one of the joint protected tenants becomes the statutory tenant,[71] in which case the successor rules will presumably apply in the ordinary way. More difficult is the situation where both tenants become statutory tenants. If both die together,[72] there seems no reason why the successor rules should not apply, but must the successor be a member of the family of both tenants? Probably this is not required, as a literal construction of the Act has not found favour in other contexts involving joint tenants (or landlords).[73]

More likely is the situation where one joint statutory tenant dies. It seems unlikely that the succession rules apply. Presumably the survivor becomes sole statutory tenant, to the exclusion of the claims of any successor to the deceased statutory tenant.[74] The succession rules will then operate on the death of the survivor.

These matters have been provided for in the case of succession to assured tenancies under the Housing Act 1988. The survivor of joint tenants is there treated as a successor, so that where can be no further succession on his death.[75] Similarly in the case of public sector secure tenancies, where there can be no succession on the death of the survivor of joint tenants.[76]

---

[71] *Lloyd v. Sadler*, above.
[72] *cf.* Law of Property Act 1925, s. 184.
[73] *Lloyd v. Sadler*, above; *Tilling v. Whiteman* [1980] A.C. 1; above, p. 130; *Potsos v. Theodotou* (1991) 23 H.L.R. 356; above, p. 126; *Halford's Executors v. Boden* (1953) 103 L.J. News. 768 (county court).
[74] See *Daejan Properties Ltd v. Mahoney* [1995] E.G.C.S. 4. (Succession rules did not apply where landlord estopped from denying that daughter had become joint statutory tenant with deceased mother, who was the first successor. Thus daughter continued as statutory tenant and not as assured tenant by way of second succession.)
[75] Housing Act 1988, s. 17.
[76] Housing Act 1985, s. 88.

9 SUB-TENANTS

It is clear that the Rent Act applies between tenant and sub-tenant in exactly the same way as between landlord and tenant.[1] The question to be considered here, however, is the extent to which a sub-tenant, who is protected by the Rent Act as against the tenant, has any rights against the head landlord upon the determination of the mesne tenancy.

Sub-tenants have certain rights against the head landlord under the general law. These rights, mentioned below, may be relied on in addition to any Rent Act rights. In the absence of any general law rights, the sub-tenant must look to the Rent Act alone for his protection.

Common law position
The general rule at common law is that a sub-tenancy cannot survive after the termination of the tenancy from which it derives, for "every subordinate interest must perish with the superior interest on which it is dependent."[2] Thus any subtenancy ends where the tenancy terminates by expiry, by notice to quit served by the landlord or the tenant,[3] or, subject to what is said below, by forfeiture. To this rule there are several exceptions. So, for example,where a tenancy ends, by forfeiture, a sub-tenant may become tenant of the head landlord if he is granted relief from forfeiture by the court.[4] If a tenancy ends by merger or surrender, the sub-tenant's rights are preserved by statute.[5] Similarly in the case of disclaimer of the tenancy.[6] Thus the sub-tenant may invoke these rights, where applicable, whether or not he is within the Rent Act. Section 137 of the Rent Act 1977, discussed below, provides a further exception to the common law rule. If, however, the sub-tenant cannot bring himself within the requirements of that section, he will have no rights against the landlord on the determination of the tenancy,[7] save to the extent that the limited exceptions under the general law can be relied on.

Comparison with other codes
Before considering section 137, mention might briefly be made of the extent to which other codes of statutory protection confer rights on sub-tenants beyond those existing under the general law. At one end of the spectrum, full statutory rights against superior landlords exist in the case of business sub-tenancies[8] and long residential sub--

---

[1] See the definitions of "let" and "tenancy" in Rent Act 1977, s. 152(1).
[2] *Bendall v. McWhirter* [1952] 2 Q.B. 466 at 487.
[3] *Pennell v. Payne* [1995] 2 W.L.R. 261.
[4] Law of Property Act 1925, s. 146(4).
[5] *ibid.* s. 139. It seems that a *statutory* sub-tenant cannot rely on s. 139; *Pittalis v. Grant* [1989] Q.B. 605; *Bromley Park Garden Estates v. George* [1991] 2 E.G.L.R. 95.
[6] *Re Thompson & Cottrell's Contract* [1943] Ch. 97.
[7] *cf. Jessamine Investment Co. v. Schwartz* [1978] Q.B. 264, below, p. 167.
[8] Landlord and Tenant Act 1954, s. 44.

tenancies, in the latter case both as to security of tenure[9] and enfranchisement.[10] At the other end, sub-tenants have no rights under the agricultural holdings legislation.[11] In the middle is the Rent Act régime, under which sub-tenants have some rights against the landlord, but certainly not full rights. The position as to assured tenancies is dealt with in Chapter 11.[12] The point is unlikely to arise in the public sector, where a secure tenancy ceases to be secure if the whole is sublet.[13] Thus no uniformity of treatment can be discerned in the various statutory schemes.

Section 137

A distinction is drawn between cases where the tenant (*i.e.* the sub-tenant's immediate landlord) is himself a Rent Act tenant and where he is not. These situations will be considered in turn.

Sub-tenant of a Rent Act tenant

Discretionary ground against mesne tenant

By section 137(1) if a court makes an order for possession of a dwelling-house from a protected or statutory tenant,[14] and the order is made by virtue of section 98(1)[15] (the discretionary grounds), nothing in the order shall affect the right of any sub-tenant to whom the dwelling-house or any part of it has been lawfully sublet before the commencement of the proceedings to retain possession by virtue of the Act, nor shall the order operate to give a right to possession against any such sub-tenant.

This provision, which will be explained in detail below, applies to protect a sub-tenant of a Rent Act tenant when possession is recovered from the latter on the basis of one of the discretionary grounds for possession. It does not spell out what the sub-tenant's position is, nor does it deal with cases where the tenancy terminates for other reasons. These matters fall within section 137(2), where on the termination

[9] *ibid.* s. 21. (Rent Act 1977, s. 137(5) confers certain rights on Rent Act sub-tenants on termination of a superior long tenancy: below, p. 157.)
[10] Leasehold Reform Act 1967, Sched. 1; Leasehold Reform, Housing and Urban Development Act 1993, Sched. 1.
[11] *Sherwood v. Moody* [1952] 1 All E.R. 389. But see Agricultural Holdings Act 1986, s. 63, (compensation rights where sub-tenancy ends by reason of termination of superior tenancy) and Agricultural Tenancies Act 1995, s. 38(1). See also *Gisborne v. Burton* [1989] Q.B. 390; above, p. 96.
[12] Housing Act 1988, s. 18; below, p. 214.
[13] Housing Act 1985, s. 93. A subletting of part is, however, permitted if the landlord gives written consent: *ibid.* However, there are no express provisions protecting the sub-tenant against the landlord. See *Basingstoke and Deane Borough Council v. Paice, The Times*, April 3, 1995 (subtenant of part acquired secure status as against landlord on surrender of head tenancy).
[14] Or a protected occupier or statutory tenant within the Rent (Agriculture) Act 1976. This aspect will not be dealt with.
[15] See above, p. 116.

of a statutorily protected tenancy,[16] either as a result of a possession order or for any other reason, any sub-tenant to whom the dwelling-house or any part of it has been lawfully sublet shall be deemed to become the tenant of the landlord, on the same terms as if the tenant's tenancy had continued. This subsection would apply, for example, where a statutory

Where mesne tenant ceases to reside

tenancy terminates because the tenant ceases to reside.[17] The reason why the sub-tenant is deemed to become tenant of the landlord is so that a relationship of privity should exist between them enabling their rights and obligations to be mutually enforceable.

Before considering in full the implication of these provisions a few preliminary points should be examined.

(a) Lawful sub-tenant Both subsections (1) and (2) of section 137 are confined to the case where the dwelling has been "lawfully sublet." Thus an unlawful subtenant has no rights under the Act as against the head landlord.[18] He can only invoke the exceptions to the common law rule (where relevant) if the tenancy was still protected, as a statutory tenancy cannot end by the methods envisaged by those exceptions, such as forfeiture.[19]

Meaning of lawful subletting

What is meant by a lawful sub-tenant? Where the subletting was in breach of a prohibition in the tenancy, the dwelling will not be "lawfully sublet" unless the breach has been waived.[20] Thus in *Metropolitan Property Co. Ltd v. Cordery*[21] waiver was established where the landlord's agents knew that the sub-tenant was in residence (the sub-tenant having lived openly in the premises for some years). This knowledge was imputed to the landlord, who had accordingly waived the breach by taking rent. Where, however, the subletting in breach has been done by a statutory tenant, it will be more difficult to establish waiver, as the strict common law rules do not apply. A mere demand for rent with knowledge of the breach does not

---

[16] Defined by s. 137(4) as meaning a protected or statutory tenancy (or a protected occupancy or statutory tenancy within the Rent (Agriculture) Act 1976 or, in certain cases, a tenancy of an agricultural holding). By s. 137(5), a long tenancy at a low rent is treated as a statutorily protected tenancy for the purpose of s. 137(2) if it would have been a protected tenancy but for the low rent. Likewise if it would have been an assured tenancy (Local Government and Housing Act 1989, Sched. 11, para. 53), although it is difficult to see how the subtenant of such a tenant could fall within s. 137(2).

[17] See above, p. 91.

[18] Unless by analogy with *Jessamine Investment Co. v. Schwartz* [1978] Q.B. 264, below, p. 167; (1978) 41 Conv. (N.S.) 96 at 104 (J. Martin).

[19] Apparently a statutory tenancy may end by surrender; see *Dibbs v. Campbell* [1988] 2 E.G.L.R. 122, above, p. 140.

[20] See *Chrisdell Ltd v. Johnson* (1987) 54 P.&C.R. 257; *R.C. Glaze Properties Ltd v. Alabdinboni* (1993) 25 H.L.R. 150. It was held in *Muspratt v. Johnston* [963] 2 Q.B. 383 that waiver did not operate retrospectively so as to validate the subletting *ab initio*. This point will rarely be of significance.

[21] (1980) 39 P.&C.R. 10.

inevitably amount to waiver in such circumstances.[22] If the
tenancy permits subletting of a particular type only, then a
subletting outside the terms specified will be unlawful.[23]
Likewise, if the tenancy, while not expressly prohibiting
subletting, contains a covenant to use the property as a
single dwelling-house only.

We have seen that one of the discretionary grounds for
possession, Case 6, involves the situation where, without the
consent of the landlord, the tenant has sublet the whole of
the dwelling-house or sublet part of it, the remainder being
already sublet.[24] If such a subletting was in breach of the
terms of the tenancy, then it will be unlawful, as discussed

Mere lack of
consent without
breach
above. It is established, however, that Case 6 applies also to
sublettings which did not constitute a breach of the terms of
the tenancy. In *Leith Properties Ltd v. Byrne*[25] where there
was no covenant against subletting, the landlord invoked
Case 6 where the tenant had sublet without consent, seeking
possession against the tenant and the sub-tenant. One
argument was that the subletting must be considered
unlawful as it was within the terms of Case 6. This
argument was rejected. The fact that a subletting gives rise
to a ground for possession under Case 6 does not make it
unlawful for the purpose of section 137. The landlord was,
however, entitled to possession, for reasons explained below.

Finally, where a subletting is unlawful and accordingly
outside the protection of section 137, it seems that it is also
Protection from
Eviction Act 1977
outside the protection of section 3 of the Protection from
Eviction Act 1977[26] (requiring a court order for possession)
because that section applies only where the tenancy (*i.e.* the
head tenancy) is *not* "statutorily protected". As indicated
above, section 137(1) and (2) apply only where the tenancy
is so protected.

(b) Must the sub-tenant himself be a protected or
statutory tenant?   It is clear that the head tenancy must
be a protected or statutory tenancy (and not, for example, a
restricted contract) if section 137(1) and (2) are to apply. It
is less clear whether the sub-tenancy itself must be protected
or statutory. The wording of these provisions may be
contrasted with that of section 137(3) (discussed below),
where it is expressly stated that the sub-tenancy must be

---

[22] *Oak Property Co. Ltd v. Chapman* [1947] K.B. 886 (qualified demand);
Trustees of Henry Smith's Charity v. Willson [1983] Q.B. 316 (unqualified
demand).

[23] *Trustees of Henry Smith's Charity v. Willson*, above (covenant against
subletting without consent save in respect of a term not exceeding six
months); *Patoner Ltd v. Lowe* [1985] 2 E.G.L.R. 154 (tenancy permitted
subletting "consistent with the letting of high-class furnished
accommodation." Sub-tenancy unlawful where second-hand furniture,
no table and substandard armchairs.)

[24] See above, p. 121.

[25] [1983] Q.B. 433; *sub nom. Leith Properties Ltd v. Springer* [1982] 3 All
E.R. 731.

[26] See above, p. 48.

protected or statutory. Section 137(1), as we have seen, permits the sub-tenant "to retain possession by virtue of this Act" when the head tenancy is terminated by a possession order. Subsection (2) provides that he shall, "subject to this Act," be deemed to become tenant of the landlord. It is clear that the sub-tenancy must fall within the Rent Act.

Whether restricted contract included

The problem is whether it is sufficient that it be a restricted contract instead of a protected or statutory tenancy. It is submitted that this is not sufficient.[27] As the sub-tenant who falls within the section has, by section 137(2), the same rights against the head landlord as he had against the former tenant, it is difficult to envisage how this provision could operate in the case of a restricted contract. The usual reason why the sub-tenant has a restricted contract is because the tenant (his immediate landlord) is resident. On termination of the tenant's interest, there would be difficulties in applying the restricted contract rules against the head landlord, who is not resident.[28]

Prior to an amendment by the Housing Act 1988 the difficulty had been compounded by a draftsman's error in the consolidating provisions of the 1977 Act.[29] It is clear that under previous legislation the sub-tenant was only within the equivalent provision if he was protected or statutory.[30] Section 137(1) referred, prior to the 1988 amendment, to the sub-tenant's right to retain possession by "this Part of the Act." This referred to Part IX, which contains no provisions on security of tenure, and was, therefore, an error. The identical words in section 18 of the 1968 Act were contained in a Part conferring security of tenure for protected and statutory tenancies, but which did not deal with restricted contracts. The Housing Act 1988[31] has removed this source of confusion by deleting the words "this Part of" from section 137(1), which now provides that the possession order shall not affect the sub-tenant's right "to retain possession by virtue of this Act." The amendment, however, does not completely resolve the problem, as it is still unclear whether a sub-tenant having a restricted contract is included. It is submitted that such a sub-tenant is not included, in view of the legislative history of the provision and the difficulties in applying the restricted contract rules against the head landlord. This view is

[27] See Megarry, *The Rent Acts* (11th ed., 1988) p. 329. A contrary assumption is made in Yates and Hawkins, *Landlord and Tenant Law* (2nd ed., 1986) p. 465.
[28] Under the resident landlord rules (see above, Chap. 5), a tenant becomes fully protected if the landlord ceases to reside. To apply that rule here would infringe the principle of s. 137(2) that the sub-tenant has the same status against the landlord as if the tenancy continued.
[29] See Farrand and Arden, *Rent Acts and Regulations* (2nd ed., 1981) p. 158. See also Pettit, *Private Sector Tenancies* (2nd ed., 1981) p. 277.
[30] See *Stanley v. Compton* [1951] 1 All E.R. 859.
[31] Sched. 17, para. 25. For the view that sub-tenants having restricted contracts may now be included, see Bridge, *Guide to the Housing Act 1988* (1989) p. 60.

supported by the wording of section 138, discussed below.
Upon this assumption, section 137 will only apply to
subletting of part of a dwelling if the tenant did not reside in
the remainder.[32]

**(c) Can a statutory tenant sublet the whole of the
dwelling?**   Clearly a protected tenant can effectively sublet
the whole or part of the property at common law, so as to
confer an estate on the sub-tenant. (Of course, any such
subletting will be unlawful if in breach of a prohibition in
the tenancy.) Although a statutory tenant has no "estate"
out of which to grant a sub-tenancy, it has long been
accepted that he can effectively sublet part.[33] Doubts have
been expressed, however, as to whether a statutory tenant
can effectively sublet the whole.[34] It has even been suggested
that such a subletting would be "unlawful" (and, therefore,
outside the scope of section 137).[35] The problem is that a
statutory tenant, by the act of subletting the whole, goes out
of residence and thereupon ceases to satisfy the
requirements of section 2 of the 1977 Act.[36] His interest,
therefore, terminates,[37] giving rise to conceptual difficulties
in treating a sub-tenant as deriving a valid title from the
statutory tenant who loses his status by the very act of
subletting.

Section 137 and Case 6 of Schedule 15 clearly refer to
subletting of the whole or part by protected or statutory
tenants, but do not conclusively answer the point. They
could, for example, refer to the situation where the statutory
tenant intends to return and, accordingly, does not lose his
interest.[38]

The matter was touched upon in *Leith Properties Ltd v.
Byrne*[39] but left open, as the subletting there occurred while
the tenancy was contractual. It arose also in *Trustees of Henry
Smith's Charity v. Willson*,[40] where a statutory tenant sublet
the whole. In fact the subletting was unlawful, so that
section 137 did not apply for that reason. The Court of
Appeal however, discussed the issue. Slade L.J felt that the
statutory provisions indicated the possibility of a subletting
of the whole by a statutory tenant, but did not attempt to
"grapple further with the conceptual problems." Ormrod

**Subletting of
part**

**Effect of ceasing
to reside**

---

[32] This is assumed in *Deverall v. Wyndham* (1989) 58 P.&C.R. 12 (where,
however, s. 137 was not in issue).
[33] *Roe v. Russell* [1928] 2 K.B. 117.
[34] *White v. Barnet L.B.C.* [1990] 2 Q.B. 328 at 336; Megarry, *The Rent Acts*
(11th ed., 1988) p. 319; Evans & Smith, *The Law of Landlord and Tenant*
(4th ed., 1993) p. 282.
[35] *Roe v. Russell*, above, at 130, 141. The point was left open in *Keeves v.
Dean* [1924] 1 K.B. 685 and *Oak Property Co. Ltd v. Chapman* [1947]
K.B. 886.
[36] See above, p. 91.
[37] Unless the subletting is temporary and he intends to return; Pettit,
Private Sector Tenancies (2nd ed., 1981) p. 76.
[38] See [1983] Conv. 248 at 249–250 (J. Martin).
[39] [1983] Q.B. 433.
[40] [1983] Q.B. 316; [1983] Conv. 248 (J. Martin).

L.J. however, was more firmly of the view that such a subletting was possible. The Act clearly contemplated it, and it was a mistake to try to impress common law concepts on to the legal relationships created by the Rent Act, from which the incidents of the statutory tenancy must be collected.

Summary of position

In conclusion, it appears that a subletting of the whole by a statutory tenant is not without effect. If the act of subletting causes the statutory tenancy to cease,[41] then the tenant loses his rights automatically. (*i.e.* it is not necessary to invoke Case 6, a discretionary ground, against him). In such a case the sub-tenant, provided the subletting was not unlawful, will be within section 137. However, as explained below, the sub-tenant remains vulnerable to any ground for possession, such as Case 6 itself, which may be invoked against him.

Having considered these preliminary matters, let us now examine the precise effect of the provisions of section 137(1) and (2). A first reading of these provisions may give the impression that a sub-tenant is not prejudiced by the termination of the tenancy, and that he continues to enjoy security of tenure against the head landlord. The authorities indicate that the protection of these provisions is extremely limited.

Effect of Case 6

In *Leith Properties Ltd v. Byrne*[42] a protected quarterly tenant sublet the whole property on a weekly tenancy. This was done without the landlord's consent, but the tenancy did not prohibit subletting. After serving notice to quit, the landlord sought to recover possession from both tenant and sub-tenant under Case 6 (the discretionary ground applicable where the tenant has sublet the whole without consent). It might be noted that as the tenant had gone to Australia, not intending to return, it is difficult to see how her statutory tenancy (to which the protected tenancy had been converted) survived until the proceedings, in which case it should not have been necessary to invoke Case 6

Breach not required

against her.[43] However, on the basis that the landlord did need to establish Case 6 as against the tenant, the Court of Appeal confirmed that Case 6 applied even where the subletting involved no breach on the ground that its purpose was that the landlord should be able to recover possession where there is an assignee or sub-tenant "unknown to and not approved by the landlord." As already mentioned, the fact that Case 6 applied did not mean that the subletting was to be regarded as unlawful.[44] Although section 137 applied to the sub-tenant, it was held that the protection was not absolute. The sub-tenant only becomes tenant of the

[41] *i.e.* because the tenant does not intend to return.
[42] [1983] Q.B. 433; [1983] Conv. 155 (J. Martin).
[43] On this view, the sub-tenant's rights would be governed by s. 137(2).
[44] Distinguishing *Roe v. Russell* [1928] 2 K.B. 117, where it was suggested that a subletting of the whole by a statutory tenant would be unlawful; *cf. Trustees of Henry Smith's Charity v. Willson*, above.

landlord "subject to this Act," and under the Act the landlord could recover possession from him under Case 6, where the words "the tenant" referred to the mesne tenant. Hence a subletting by the tenant gave a ground for possession against the sub-tenant also, notwithstanding that the latter had not assigned or sublet without consent. It was said that, on any other construction, Case 6 would be useless and its purpose defeated. The case was remitted to determine whether it was reasonable to order possession against the sub-tenant.

Procedural protection

Thus the protection of section 137 will often be more apparent than real. The sub-tenant is not entitled to stay in possession without regard to anything the tenant has done. His protection is twofold: first, a possession order obtained against the tenant alone does not affect him (in other words, he must be made a party to the proceedings); secondly, the issue of reasonableness (in the context of the discretionary grounds) must be decided as between landlord and sub-tenant and not merely as between landlord and tenant. The substance of the matter, however, is that the ground invoked against the tenant may also be invoked against the sub-tenant: it is not necessary for the landlord to find a new ground against the latter. It might be added that, as far as Case 6 is concerned, the fact that the subletting was not in breach of the tenancy might make the court less inclined to find it reasonable to make the possession order.[45]

Issue of reasonableness

Other grounds for possession

It remains to consider how far this construction of Case 6 applies to other grounds for possession. It was said that in "some contexts" the word "tenant" as it appears in the discretionary grounds means the last immediate tenant of the landlord. A similar view of case 5 (tenant's notice to quit) was taken in *Lord Hylton v. Heal*[46] to the effect that the ground would be available also against the sub-tenant, even though he had given no notice to quit. It was also suggested in that case that Case 1 (unpaid rent or other breach), Case 2 (nuisance or annoyance) and Case 8 (tenant was landlord's employee and employment has ceased) should be similarly construed. This seems hard on the sub-tenant. If these views are correct, there is hardly a ground which will not be available against the sub-tenant as well as the tenant. Case 10 (tenant charging sub-tenant an excessive rent) cannot be distinguished on its wording from the above-mentioned grounds, but it seems harsh that it should operate against the sub-tenant. It is submitted that Case 10 and Cases 1 to 4 should not be available against the sub-tenant if he himself has not done the act complained of. Otherwise there is indeed little substance in the protection of section 137. However, as the issue of reasonableness must

---

[45] *Trustees of Henry Smith's Charity v. Willson*, above, where, however, it was said that the fact of a breach would only make the court marginally more inclined to make the order.
[46] [1921] 2 K.B. 438.

be decided independently as between the landlord and sub-tenant, it may well be that, assuming these grounds are available against the sub-tenant, the court may not consider it reasonable to grant possession against him where the act complained of is that of the tenant.

The position may be contrasted with that under section 137(3), discussed below, where the sub-tenant will fare better. That subsection applies where the mesne tenancy is not a Rent Act tenancy. In such a case the tenancy cannot terminate by a Rent Act ground for possession. Hence the landlord can only recover possession from the sub-tenant by establishing a ground against him personally.

Where mesne tenancy already terminated The position may also differ where the statutory tenancy has already terminated (for example because the tenant has ceased to reside), so that it will not be necessary to invoke a ground for possession against the tenant. In such a case the sub-tenant will have become tenant under section 137(2), and it would seem that the landlord must establish a ground against him directly.[47] It is difficult to see how an act done in the past by a person who is no longer the tenant at the date of the proceedings should be a ground for possession against the present tenant.

Shorthold tenancy Finally, where the tenant is a shorthold tenant,[48] it is expressly provided that where the whole or part of the property has been sublet,[49] section 137 shall not apply if the landlord becomes entitled to possession as against the tenant.[50] Hence he becomes entitled to possession as against the sub-tenant also.

Sub-tenant of a non-Rent Act tenant

The provisions discussed above do not apply unless the mesne tenant is a protected or statutory tenant. If he is not, the relevant provision is section 137(3). Where a dwelling-house forms part of "premises" which have been let as a whole on a superior tenancy which is not a statutorily protected but the sub-tenancy itself is protected or statutory,[51] then:

> "from the coming to an end of the superior tenancy, this Act shall apply in relation to the dwelling-house as if, in lieu of the superior tenancy, there had been separate tenancies of the dwelling-house and of the remainder of the premises, for the like purposes as

[47] See Pettit, *Private Sector Tenancies* (2nd ed., 1981) p. 274.
[48] See above, Chap. 4.
[49] During the "continuous period" specified in Housing Act 1980, s. 54(3).
[50] Housing Act 1980, s. 54(1). It is not clear whether this provision abrogates any common law rights the sub-tenant may have, as where, for example, the shorthold tenancy ends by surrender or tenant's notice to quit.
[51] The subsection does not apply to a sub-tenancy which is not itself protected; *Grosvenor Estate Belgravia v. Cochran* (1992) 24 H.L.R. 98; [1991] Conv. 393 (P. Smith).

under the superior tenancy, and at rents equal to the just proportion of the rent under the superior tenancy."

Application of section 137(3)

The circumstances envisaged here are that there is a subletting of part to a sub-tenant who is within the Rent Act as against the tenant, but the tenant is not a protected or statutory tenant himself, because, for example, the superior tenancy exceeds the rateable value limits, while the sublet part does not. Another example might be where the head letting, being of multiple dwelling units, is not protected because it is not let as "a" separate dwelling, as explained in Chapter 4. The subsection cannot apply where the head landlord is a body (such as a local authority) to which the Rent Act does not apply.[52]

Effect of section 137(3)

Section 137(3) is somewhat obscure. Its effect is not that there is deemed to be a notional lease of the sublet part direct to the sub-tenant, but that there are deemed to be two notional head leases of the sublet part and of the remainder, so that if the notional head lease of the sublet part would have been protected the sub-tenant may rely on section 137(2) on its determination.[53] The subsection is, therefore, subsidiary to section 137(2). It does not apply where the subletting is of the whole of the premises, presumably because in the circumstances envisaged, such a subletting is unlikely itself to be within the Rent Act.

Purpose of head lease

It seems that section 137(3) applies only where the superior letting was residential, or at least had a dual purpose. In *Maunsell v. Olins*[54] the question was whether a protected sub-tenant of a cottage on a farm could invoke the subsection on the termination of the head tenancy, which was an agricultural holding. The House of Lords held, by a majority, that he could not. The word "premises" in subsection (3) was limited to dwelling-houses and did not apply to a farm. [55]Lord Reid, who found the section "unusually difficult,"[56] held that section 137(3) applied only if the head lease was residential or had two purposes, one of which was residential. In the present case it had only one purpose, which was agricultural.

This decision was partly reversed by the Rent (Agriculture) Act 1976. It is now provided that "premises" in section 137(3) includes an agricultural holding[57] within the meaning of the Agricultural Holdings Act

---

[52] *Basingstoke and Deane Borough Council v. Paice, The Times*, April 3, 1995 (protected sub-tenant of part became secure tenant of the landlord on surrender of the head lease).

[53] *Cadogan (Earl) v. Henthorne* [1957] 1 W.L.R. 1 (on the equivalent provisions of previous legislation). A consequence of this is that s. 137(3) is confined to lawful sub-tenants.

[54] [1975] A.C. 373.

[55] *cf. Bracey v. Read* [1963] Ch. 88 ("premises" includes bare land with no buildings in the context of Landlord and Tenant Act 1954, Pt. II).

[56] [1975] A.C. 373 at 382. Lord Wilberforce commented that the provision did not "convey an impression of conspicuous clarity:" *ibid.* at 385.

[57] Or a farm business tenancy within Agricultural Tenancies Act 1995.

1986. Thus residential sub-tenants of agricultural tenants may be protected by section 137(3).[58] The construction adopted in *Maunsell v. Olins*[59] will continue to apply to cases outside the scope of the amendment.

A somewhat narrow interpretation of *Maunsell v. Olins* was upheld by the Court of Appeal in *Pittalis v. Grant*,[60] where there was a head lease of a shop with a flat above. It was held that the sublet flat was not within section 137(3). The property, being held under a lease of business premises within the Landlord and Tenant Act 1954, Part II, was not a "dwelling house" for the purpose of the 1977 Act, and for that reason was not "premises" within section 137(3). This, it is submitted, is too strict an approach to the concept of a "dwelling-house" for the purposes of the Rent Act, even assuming that the "premises" which are the subject of the head letting must be a "dwelling-house". Neither *Maunsell v. Olins* nor the older authorities[61] compel the conclusion that the application of the Landlord and Tenant Act 1954, Part II to the headlease prevents the property from being a "dwelling-house". This is a question of fact and degree. It should suffice that the head letting is for a dual purpose, one of which is residential.

As explained above, section 137(3) deems there to have been a notional letting of the sublet part, separately from the remainder, "for the like purposes as under the superior tenancy." The natural interpretation of this provision in the case of a headlease of a shop and flat would be that the flat is deemed separately let for residence. Nourse L.J. in *Pittalis v. Grant*, however, regarded the subsection as requiring the assumption that the flat is deemed separately let for *business and* residence, those being the purposes of the superior tenancy. This remarkable interpretation prevents section 137(3) from applying to a case where the superior letting was partly for business purposes. The subsection, on this view, has very little scope for operation. There seems to be no good policy reason why residential sub-tenants of part should have no security against the head landlord where the head letting is a business tenancy. A landlord who wished to avoid this result could have prohibited subletting of the residential part. It is notable that a residential sub-tenant of part of business premises does have security under section 18 of the Housing Act 1988, as discussed in Chapter 11, where the sub-tenancy is granted after the commencement

[58] The sub-tenancy must be a protected or statutory tenancy within s. 99 of the Rent Act 1977 (dwellings let to agricultural workers).
[59] See above.
[60] [1989] Q.B. 605; (1989) 139 N.L.J. 1260 (J. Martin); [1990] Conv. 204 (C. Rodgers). *cf.* Megarry, *The Rent Acts* (11th ed., 1988) p. 333, taking the view that a mixed unit of a shop and flat would be included, at least if the letting had a dual purpose; *i.e.* the flat was not wholly ancillary to the shop.
[61] See *Whitely v. Wilson* [1953] 1 Q.B. 77 and cases there cited. See also Rent Act 1977, s. 24(3).

of the 1988 Act and is itself an assured tenancy. So far as section 137(3) is concerned, however, the narrow view is now established as far as the Court of Appeal.[62]

Furnished sub-tenants

Landlord's obligations

The passing of the Rent Act 1974, bringing furnished tenants into protection, gave rise to a need to modify the provisions of section 137 in order to deal with the situation where the tenancy was unfurnished and the sub-tenancy was furnished. Without any new provision, landlords in such circumstances would be subject to additional obligations, as the sub-tenant's rights in respect of the furniture would become directly enforceable against the landlord under section 137(2).

The present provision is section 138 of the 1977 Act. In cases where section 137(2) applies, the terms on which the sub-tenant is deemed to become tenant of the landlord shall not include any terms as to the provision by the landlord of furniture or services if the following three conditions are satisfied:

(a) the head tenancy was neither a protected furnished tenancy nor a statutory furnished tenancy; and
(b) the sub-tenancy was a protected furnished tenancy or a statutory furnished tenancy, and
(c) the landlord, within six weeks beginning with the termination of the head tenancy, serves notice on the sub-tenant that section 138 is to apply.

Problems with section 138

The reference to furnished tenancies in section 138 is to those where a substantial part of the rent is attributable to furniture.[63]

Secton 138 leaves certain questions unanswered. It will be appreciated that the furniture has been provided by the tenant. If the landlord fails to serve the notice, so that the sub-tenant continues entitled to the provision of furniture, presumably the landlord must make new provision (or, if possible, buy the existing furniture from the tenant), as it is difficult to see why he should receive rent in respect of furniture which belongs to the former tenant. If the landlord does serve the notice, so that he need not provide furniture, presumably the tenant is entitled to remove it.

[62] *Pittalis v. Grant* was applied by the Court of Appeal in *Bromley Park Garden Estates Ltd v. George* [1991] 2 E.G.L.R. 95 (no protection for sub-tenant of flat above business premises); [1991] Conv. 393 (P. Smith). It was distinguished by the county court in *McEvedy v. Howard de Walden Estates Ltd.*, noted (1995) *Legal Action*, March, p. 12, on the ground that the building (a gound floor shop and flats on four upper floors) was let for two distinct purposes and the residential part was greater.
[63] Rent Act 1977, s. 152(1).

Information to landlords

Particulars of subletting

To the extent that landlords may become bound by the rights of sub-tenants, they need to know of their existence. To this end, section 139 of the 1977 Act obliges a Rent Act tenant who has sublet any part on a protected tenancy to supply written particulars to the landlord within 14 days of the subletting. The tenant is liable to a fine not exceeding £25 if he fails to supply the statement, or supplies a false statement. This obligation under Section 139 is confined to sublettings before the Housing Act 1988, as sublettings after that Act cannot normally be protected tenancies.

The statement may provide the landlord with information which will enable him to invoke a ground for possession, such as Case 6 (subletting without consent) or Case 10 (tenant charging sub-tenant an excessive rent).

Subletting outside the terms of section 137

It would be reasonable to assume that a sub-tenant who fails to satisfy the conditions of section 137 would have no rights against the head landlord save those existing at common law. It seems that this assumption cannot be made, in the case of a statutory sub-tenancy, in view of the decision of the Court of Appeal in *Jessamine Investment Co. v. Schwartz*.[64] In that case a 99-year lease was granted in 1874. The lease was assigned, and the assignee granted a weekly protected sub-tenancy in 1937, which became statutory in 1939. The assignee disappeared in 1945, with the result that the sub-tenant, having paid no further rent, acquired title to the leasehold as against the assignee in 1957, under the Limitation Act 1939. When the head lease expired in 1973 the freeholder claimed possession from the sub-tenant. Having held that time could run under the Limitation Act in favour of a statutory tenant and that the statutory sub-tenancy remained in existence after 1957 as against the freeholder notwithstanding its transformation into a leasehold title as against the assignee, the Court of Appeal had to decide whether any provision of the Rent Act (then the Act of 1968) protected the sub-tenant on expiry of the lease. Although a long tenancy is deemed a protected tenancy for the purpose of section 137(2),[65] it was held that the sub-tenant could not rely on section 137(2), which contemplated a sub-tenancy binding on the tenant at the termination of the lease. That was not so here, because of its transformation under the Limitation Act into a leasehold title as against the tenant (*i.e.* the assignee). Even though

---

[64] [1978] Q.B. 264; (1977) 41 Conv. (N.S.) 96 (J. Martin). The decision is criticised in Megarry, *The Rent Acts* (11th ed., 1988) p. 329.
[65] s. 137(5).

**Effect of
section 2**

section 137 did not apply, the Court of Appeal found in favour of the sub-tenant, holding that a statutory sub-tenancy was a right "against all the world." This was the result of section 2, under which a statutory tenancy continues so long as the tenant resides. Reliance was placed on *Keeves v. Dean*[66] where Scrutton L.J. said "I take it that he has a right as against all the world to remain in possession until he is turned out by an order of the Court ... " Scrutton L.J., however, was there discussing the status of a statutory tenant, not a statutory sub-tenant. The argument that section 2 could not assist where section 137 was not satisfied was rejected on the basis that there may be a "lacuna" in the latter section. Also rejected was the argument that the lack of any relationship of privity between the freeholder and the sub-tenant was fatal to the claim.[67]

This decision is, it is submitted, doubtful. It is hardly justified by the terms of section 2, which does not expressly deal with sub-tenancies. It is suggested that section 2 is subject to an overriding principle that a sub-tenancy cannot outlast the tenancy from which it derives unless section 137 applies.[68] This is supported by previous decisions of the Court of Appeal and the House of Lords which were not cited.[69] It is difficult to see why Section 137 should have been enacted if a statutory sub-tenant could simply rely on section 2. Section 138, discussed above, clearly contemplates that a sub-tenancy will only become binding on the landlord if section 137 applies. If the *Jessamine* decision is correct, then other categories of statutory sub-tenant who are not within section 137, even perhaps unlawful sub-tenants, could rely on section 2 to achieve the same result.

In conclusion, therefore, it is submitted that a sub-tenant can rely only on section 137 and not on section 2. The contrary view derives no support from the authorities prior to *Jessamine*, and introduces a privity problem. Section 2 is in general terms and does not specifically deal with sub-tenancies. As Lord Reid has said, in the context of the predecessor to section 137, we should construe it by applying "the 'rule' that a court, when in doubt about two constructions of a statutory provision, should lean towards that construction which involves the least alteration of the common law."[70]

---

[66] [1924] 1 K.B. 685 at 694.

[67] The common law exceptions and s. 137 import a relationship of privity necessary to the enforceability of the parties' rights and obligations, by providing that the sub-tenant becomes direct tenant of the landlord.

[68] This is implicit in *Pittalis v. Grant* [1989] Q.B. 605, above, p. 165.

[69] See *Maunsell v. Olins* [1975] A.C. 373; *Hobhouse v. Wall* [1963] 2 Q.B. 425; *Cow v. Casey* [1949] 1 K.B. 474 (reversed by what is now s. 137(3)); *Dudley and District Permanent Benefit Building Society v. Emerson* [1949] Ch. 707; (1977) 41 Conv. (N.S.) 96 at 102–104 (J. Martin).

[70] *Maunsell v. Olins* [1975] A.C. 373 at 383. See also *South Northamptonshire D.C. v. Power* [1987] 1 W.L.R. 1433 at 1440.

Subletting after January 15, 1989

Where a Rent Act tenant sublets after the commencement of the Housing Act 1988, section 137 of the Rent Act will not apply, because the sub-tenancy will not fall within the 1977 Act. If the subletting qualifies as an assured tenancy under the 1988 Act, the sub-tenant will have the protection of section 18 of the 1988 Act against the head landlord. This is explained in Chapter 11.[71]

---

[71] See below, p. 214.

10 Rent Control

Regulated tenancies

Fair rent system

The general principle applicable to regulated tenancies is that the rent should not exceed a "fair rent." This is explained in detail below, but for the purposes of this introduction it suffices to say that the fair rent is usually less than the market rent because of the disregard of the scarcity element. In other words, the rent is fixed on the basis that there is no shortage of rental accommodation.

Summary of rules

In outline, there is no obligation that a regulated tenancy should have a registered fair rent,[1] but either party may apply to the rent officer for its assessment and registration. In examining the rules relating to the recoverable rent limits, it is necessary to distinguish protected and statutory tenancies. On the grant of a protected tenancy the parties may agree on whatever rent they choose if there is no rent registered in relation to the dwelling-house. A fair rent may subsequently be registered, which becomes the rent limit. If the contractual rent exceeds this, the excess is not recoverable from the tenant. If a rent is already registered on the grant of a tenancy, the contractual rent must not exceed the registered rent. If no rent is registered when the tenancy becomes statutory, the previous contractual rent continues until a higher rent is registered. If a rent is registered, it must not be exceeded. The rent under the statutory tenancy, if lower, may be increased to the level of the registered rent. Once registered, a fair rent cannot be cancelled within two years, nor may it be altered within that period unless on the ground of a change of circumstances. We will see, at the end of this chapter, that the rent control rules cannot be evaded by the charging of a capital sum (premium) on the grant or assignment of the tenancy.

Rent book

It might be mentioned that tenants who pay the rent weekly must be provided with a rent book or similar document by their landlords.[2] This will contain information as to the tenant's rights, for example in relation to rent registration and housing benefit. Failure to provide a rent book, where required, is a criminal offence,[3] but does not prevent recovery of rent by the landlord.[4]

---

[1] The Private Renters Survey 1990 found that 55% of regulated tenancies had a registered rent.
[2] Landlord and Tenant Act 1985, ss. 4–7; Rent Book (Forms of Notice) (Amendment) Regulations 1993 (S.I. 1993 No. 656).
[3] *ibid.* s. 7.
[4] *Shaw v. Groom* [1970] 2 Q.B. 504. The remedy of distress is restricted by Rent Act 1977, s. 147.

The meaning of "fair rent"

The fair rent is determined according to section 70 of the
1977 Act, which specifies matters to be taken into account
and those to be disregarded.

(a) **Matters to be taken into account**   By section 70 (1),
regard is to be had to all the circumstances (other than
personal circumstances) and in particular to the age,
character, locality and state of repair of the dwelling-house.
If furniture is provided under the tenancy,[5] its quantity,
quality and condition must be considered. It has since been
added[6] that regard must be had to any premium (or sum in
Where premium   the nature of a premium) which has been or may be lawfully
lawfully   required or received on the grant, renewal, continuance or
chargeable   assignment of the tenancy. This is to cover the case where a
tenancy has been brought into protection by statute (as in
the case of Crown Estate Commissioners under the Housing
Act 1980).[7] If, as in the latter case, a premium may lawfully
be charged by way of exception to the usual rule,[8] this may
reflect in a higher rent.

As will be explained below, a registered fair rent cannot
normally be altered for two years. It is unclear whether the
Inflation   prospects of inflation over the two-year period may be taken
into account when the rent is initially determined.[9]
Personal   The result of excluding "personal circumstances" is that
circumstances   matters such as the financial situation of the particular
landlord or tenant (including entitlement to grants, reliefs
and benefits) are irrelevant. A circumstance may be
"personal" even though it is common to a particular class of
landlord or tenant.[10] In addition, it was held in *Mason v.
Skilling*[11] that the fact that the tenant was a sitting tenant
with security of tenure was a personal circumstance which
could not affect the rent.
Condition of   As far as the condition of the dwelling-house is
dwelling   concerned, it was held in *Williams v. Khan*[12] that the fair

---

[5] This includes the case where the landlord agrees that the tenant may use
his own furniture instead of the landlord's, which will be removed and re-
installed at the end of the tenancy: *R. v. London Rent Assessment Panel, ex
p. Mota* [1988] 1 E.G.L.R. 89.
[6] By Housing and Planning Act 1986, s. 17.
[7] See above, p. 75.
[8] See below, p. 188.
[9] See Farrand and Arden, *Rent Acts and Regulations* (2nd ed., 1981) p. 92.
[10] *Royal British Legion Housing Association Ltd v. East Midland Rent
Assessment Panel* [1989] 1 E.G.L.R. 131 (landlord's charitable status and
entitlement to a government grant in respect of depreciation of certain
equipment held personal, so that fair rent properly included an allowance
for depreciation).
[11] [1974] 1 W.L.R. 1437. See also *Palmer v. Peabody Trust* [1975] Q.B. 604
(absence of security no ground for rent reduction).
[12] (1982) 43 P.&C.R. 1. See [1980] Conv. 389–392 and [1981] Conv.
325–326 (J.T.F.) on the question whether the fixing of a nominal rent
would have taken the tenancy out of protection as being at a rent less
than two-thirds of the rateable value.

Measure of damages against landlord

rent is not automatically nominal because the property is subject to a closing order on the basis that it is unfit for habitation. The closing order is only one factor, although an important one. If the tenant sues the landlord for damages for breach of the landlord's repair covenant, he is entitled to succeed even though a lower rent has been fixed by the Rent Officer under section 70 (1) on account of the disrepair. In fixing the rent, the Rent Officer would have considered the condition of the premises and the value of the covenant, and would not have assumed that it would never be performed.[13]

Disrepair and improvements

(b) Matters to be disregarded   By section 70 (3), there shall be disregarded any disrepair or defect attributable to the failure of the tenant or any predecessor in title to comply with the terms of the regulated tenancy, and any improvement[14] carried out by the tenant or any predecessor in title,[15] other than pursuant to the terms of the tenancy. A similar principle applies to improvements to furniture or deterioration in its condition due to ill-treatment by the tenant or his lodger or sub-tenant.

Thus the fair rent is not to be decreased under section 70 (1), where the state of repair is a relevant consideration, if the disrepair is attributable to the tenant. Nor does he have to pay more where he has enhanced the premises by improvements which he was not obliged to make.

(c) Scarcity   Fundamental to the fair rent is section 70 (2), whereby it is to be assumed that the number of persons seeking to become tenants of suitable dwelling-houses in the locality on the terms of the regulated tenancy is not substantially greater than the number of such dwelling-houses in the locality which are available for letting on such terms.

Disregard of scarcity

If there is an inadequate supply of rented accommodation, the fair rent is less than a market rent because the scarcity element, which would otherwise increase the rent, is disregarded. Unlike the owner of other commodities, the owner cannot take advantage of shortages in order to increase the rent.

The manner in which the scarcity factor is eliminated is explained below. Before turning to the assessment of the rent, it should be emphasised that scarcity value must be distinguished from amenity value. In *Metropolitan Property*

---

[13] *Sturolson & Co. v. Mauroux* [1988] 1 E.G.L.R. 66.
[14] This is defined by s. 70(4) as including the replacement of any fixture or fitting.
[15] See *Trustees of Henry Smith's Charity v. Hemmings* (1983) 265 E.G. 383 (predecessor in title must have had the tenant's interest, therefore improvement not disregarded when done by predecessor before lease granted to him. It may suffice if done after the contract for the lease but before its grant); distinguished in *Steele v. McMahon* [1990] 2 E.G.L.R. 114, below, p. 187.

Holdings Ltd v. Finegold[16] the amenity in question was an
American school in St. John's Wood, which made the area
desirable to American families, resulting in a shortage of
accommodation. The tenant argued that this introduced a
scarcity element, which should be disregarded. This

**Amenity value
distinguished**

argument was rejected: amenity advantages which increase
the rent under Section 70 (1) do not result in a set-off under
subsection (2) merely because the amenity attracts more
people than can live in the area. Thus the rent will be higher
if there are better amenities. The scarcity test should be
applied over a substantial area,[17] ignoring local scarcity
caused by a particular amenity.

**Effect of reduced
scarcity**

Of prime importance at present is the effect of
deregulation by the Housing Act 1988 on the levels of "fair
rents" payable by Rent Act tenants. The combined effect of
the 1988 Act, encouraging lettings to assured and assured
shorthold tenants at market rents, and the depressed
property market, which has caused many owners to let in
recent years because they are unable to sell, is that the
shortage of rented accommodation has been reduced,
although not eliminated.[18]

The question which has inevitably arisen is whether the
absence of scarcity, if established in the locality in question,
must result in increasing registered rents to market levels. A
subsidiary question is whether, even if scarcity remains,
assured and assured shorthold tenancies may be used as
comparables, as explained below. There is evidence, some
anecdotal, that registered rents have increased steeply since
the passing of the 1988 Act, and far beyond the currently
modest rate of inflation.[19] In 1990 fair rents were up to 50
per cent lower than the market rents paid by assured and
assured shorthold tenants nationally.[20] This gap has since
been eroded. The quarterly Rent Officer Statistics bulletins
published by the Department of the Environment showed
that in the first quarter of 1992 the average rent increase on
re-registration was 25 per cent nationally, with an annual
rate of increase of about 11 per cent. These developments
will be further considered in the account which follows.

(d) Methods of assessment of fair rents   There is no
obligation upon the rent officer (or, on appeal, the rent

---

[16] [1975] 1 W.L.R. 349; (1975) 39 Conv. (N.S.) 295 (D. MacIntyre). *cf.*
Rent Act 1977, s. 70(3)(c) and (d), repealed by Housing Act 1980.
[17] Followed in *Crown Estate Commissioners v. Connor* [1986] 2 E.G.L.R. 97
(Regent's Park).
[18] See *"The State of the Private Rented Sector"*, Joseph Rowntree
Foundation, May 10, 1993 and *Financial Times*, May 12, 1993,
suggesting that nationally scarcity has been significantly diminished.
[19] See *The Times*, February 21, 1992.
[20] The Private Renters Survey 1990 found that the average weekly rent
(excluding housing association tenancies) was £61 for assured tenancies,
£66 for assured shortholds and £27 for regulated tenancies with a
registered rent. The Rent Officer Statistics for 1990 found the average
fair rent to be 60% of the average market rent nationally.

assessment committee) to adopt any particular method of
assessing a fair rent. It has been held, however, that the best

Comparables method is the consideration of comparables, *i.e.* the
registered fair rents of comparable[21] Rent Act tenancies in
the locality. (The use of assured tenancies as comparables is
considered below.) Unless recently registered, a higher sum
should be fixed, to allow for inflation. In *Tormes Property Co.
Ltd v. Landau*[22] the rent assessment committee was held
entitled to reject the landlord's figure, based on a return on
the capital value[23] in favour of comparables. Little weight

Other methods should be given to other methods when comparables were
available. The landlord's calculation was a variation of the
"contractor's theory," based on a return on building costs.
This method, it was said, could do no more than set a
ceiling for the rent. The landlord had estimated replacement
costs, allowing reasonable interest and adding management
expenses. This came to £5,000. A fair return of 8 per cent
led to a rent of £400 a year. This was increased to £565 by
the addition of sums for insurance, equipment and so forth.
The rent assessment committee did not criticise these
figures, but declined to adopt this approach. The fair rent
was fixed at £360, based on comparables. This figure, which
gave a four per cent return, was upheld. It has since been
said by the House of Lords[24] that the "contractor's theory"
is notoriously unreliable and is a method of last resort.

Where no In the absence of comparables, a fair rent may be assessed
comparables by calculating a fair return on capital value. In *Mason v.
Skilling*[25] the fair rent was assessed by looking at
comparables and at the capital value with vacant possession.
The tenant claimed that, as he was a sitting tenant, a lower
figure should be taken to reflect the absence of vacant
possession. It was held that the tenant's security was a
"personal circumstance," to be disregarded under section
70 (1). The higher figure was correct, as a fair rent must be
fair to the landlord as well as the tenant: it must give him a
fair return on his capital. Otherwise if there were two
identical houses, one having a tenant with a wife and young
children (potential successors to the tenancy) and the other
being let to an elderly bachelor (with no successors), the
capital values would be different, but it would be absurd if
the rents were different. The rent assessment committee was
entitled to have regard to the capital value as well as the
comparables.

In the absence of Rent Act tenancies as comparables, the
usual approach has been to assess a market rent and then

---

[21] See *Castle Court Investment Co. (Southampton) Ltd v. Southern Rent
Assessment Panel, The Times*, July 9, 1994 (unimproved property not
comparable to improved property).
[22] [1971] 1 Q.B. 261.
[23] See generally (1987) 282 E.G. 319 (J. Doling).
[24] In *Western Heritable Investment Co. Ltd v. Husband* [1983] 2 A.C. 849.
[25] [1974] 1 W.L.R. 1437.

make a deduction for scarcity. Prior to the Housing Act
1988 the market rent was normally hypothetical, due to the
dearth of equivalent dwellings actually let at market rents.

Assured tenancy Since the advent of the 1988 Act, evidence of market rents
comparables may be obtained by considering the rents of similar
dwellings let under assured or assured shorthold tenancies.
It is clear that such tenancies may be used as comparables in
this way, and will be used increasingly in the future.[26]

Where no It has been argued that the increased supply of private
scarcity rented accommodation means that there is now no scarcity,
so that registered fair rents should be no lower than the
market rents payable under assured and assured shorthold
tenancies. It has been accepted in principle that this is so if
on the evidence there is no scarcity.[27] In such a case it is not
for the Rent Assessment Committee to say that the market
rate established by the evidence is not reasonable.[28]
However, the availability of properties to let under assured
or assured shorthold tenancies is not sufficient to establish
that there is no scarcity. Matters such as long waiting lists
for local authority accommodation, severe pressure on
housing associations and the numbers of homeless people
provide evidence of continuing scarcity, although not all the
people in these categories would be seekers of private rented
accommodation.[29] In any event, even if there is no scarcity,
it does not necessarily follow that a "fair" rent must be a
market rent.[30]

Deduction from Assuming that scarcity is established, the question arises
market rent as to how much should be deducted from a market rent to
reflect the scarcity. The deduction may be difficult to
quantify. In the past figures such as 40 per cent have been
upheld.[31] How much to deduct is a question of fact to be
determined on the evidence, but 40 per cent is now too
high.[32] The formula of "market rent less scarcity" will,
however, rarely be used alone, as there may be other aspects
of "fairness" which should be taken into account.[33] Finally,
a Rent Assessment Committee must give adequate reasons
for adopting the method of assessment it has chosen.[34]

---

[26] *B.T.E. Ltd v. Merseyside and Cheshire R.A.C., ex p. Jones* (1992) 24
H.L.R. 514; *Spath Holme Ltd v. Greater Manchester and Lancashire
R.A.C., The Times*, July 13, 1994.
[27] *B.T.E. Ltd v. Merseyside and Cheshire R.A.C., ex p. Jones*, above; [1992]
Conv. 271 (J. Martin); (1992) *Legal Action*, August, p. 18 (D. Roberts).
[28] *ibid.*
[29] (1992) *Legal Action*, November, p. 17 (D. Roberts). See also
correspondence at [1992] 14 E.G. 56, and the different views expressed
in (1995) 145 N.L.J. 210 (A. Prichard) and at pp. 348, 384 (P. Willan).
[30] (1992) 142 N.L.J. 965 (A. Prichard).
[31] *Western Heritable Investment Co. Ltd v. Husband* [1983] 2 A.C. 849;
Mason v. Skilling [1974] 1 W.L.R. 1437.
[32] *Aspley Hall Estate Ltd v. Nottingham Rent Officers* [1992] 2 E.G.L.R. 187.
[33] *ibid.*
[34] *Spath Holme Ltd v. Greater Manchester and Lancashire R.A.C., The Times*,
July 13, 1994.

The registration of a fair rent

The fair rent is determined by application to the rent officer. An appeal lies to the rent assessment committee, and thence to the High Court on a point of law.[35] Once ascertained, the rent will be registered. It then operates *in rem*, binding protected tenancies of the dwelling-house granted after the registration, unless altered or cancelled, as explained below. It will cease to be operative, however, if it can be said that a subsequent letting is not of the same dwelling-house, for example, because there is a material difference in the extent of the property let.[36] The registration is a nullity from the outset if the tenancy never was protected, for example because the rateable value of the dwelling exceeded the limits.[37]

Who may apply   Application to the rent officer may be made by the landlord or the tenant, or by the parties jointly.[38] In the case of joint landlords or joint tenants, it seems that an application by one alone is ineffective,[39] unless he acted with the express or implied authority of the others.[40]

Procedure before the rent officer is informal. The parties may be represented by lawyers or other persons. It is the usual practice to inspect the premises although there is no obligation, nor indeed any right, to do so.[41]

Prescribed form   The application must be in prescribed form, and must specify the rent which the applicant seeks to register.[42] This is a mandatory requirement, so in *Chapman v. Earl*[43] the application was invalid where no figure was specified. Subject to that, the requirements are directory only, so that exact compliance is not essential. In *Druid Development Co. (Bingley) Ltd. v. Kay*[44] the landlord's application failed to give all the prescribed particulars. The existing rent was incorrectly stated, part of the premises (the garage) was

[35] By judicial review rather than under s. 11 of the Tribunals and Inquiries Act 1992; *Ellis & Sons Fourth Amalgamated Properties Ltd v. Southern Rent Assessment Panel* (1984) 270 E.G. 39; *R. v. London Rent Assessment Panel, ex p. Chelmsford Building Co. Ltd* [1986] 1 E.G.L.R. 175.

[36] See *Gluchowska v. Tottenham B.C.* [1954] 1 Q.B. 439; *cf. Solle v. Butcher* [1950] 1 K.B. 671.

[37] *Guestheath Ltd v. Mirza* (1990) 22 H.L.R. 399; [1990] Conv. 447 (J.E.M.). An estoppel claim failed on the facts.

[38] Rent Act 1977, s. 67(1). The local authority may no longer apply: Housing Act 1988, Sched. 17, para. 22.

[39] By analogy with *Turley v. Panton* (1975) 29 P.&C.R. 397 (restricted contract).

[40] *R. v Rent Officer for the London Borough of Camden, ex p. Felix* [1988] 2 E.G.L.R. 132.

[41] For further details, see Pettit, *Private Sector Tenancies* (2nd ed., 1981) p. 133 *et seq.*

[42] Rent Act 1977, s. 67(2); Rent Act 1977 (Forms, etc.) (Amendment) Regulations 1993 (S.I. 1993 No. 656).

[43] [1968] 1 W.L.R. 135; *cf. R. v. London Assessment Panel, ex p. Braq Investments Ltd* [1969] 1 W.L.R. 970 (valid where figure ascertainable, *e.g.* where a sum per square foot specified).

[44] (1982) 44 P.&C.R. 76.

omitted, and the husband was stated to be the tenant while in fact his wife was a joint tenant. The tenants took no objection and a rent was registered. It was held that they could not later claim that it was invalid. The requirements were directory, and nobody was misled. Either there was adequate compliance, or the inadequacy was waived. It was added that as applications are often made by laymen, a technical approach is to be discouraged.

No application to re-register current rent

An application under section 67(1) to re-register an *existing* rent is invalid. In *R. v. Chief Rent Officer for Royal Borough of Kensington and Chelsea, ex p. Moberley*[45] the tenant, mistakenly fearing that the landlord could increase the rent after three years[46] without reference to the rent officer, applied to re-register the existing rent. The rent officer registered a higher rent, but his determination was quashed as having been made on an invalid application. Section 67 (1) allows only an initial registration or an application to register a different rent.

Procedure

Where the landlord or tenant alone applies, notice must be served on the other party, who may make representations. The rent officer may hold a consultation, at which the parties may be represented. After the decision, the parties are notified and can object within 28 days, whereupon the matter is referred to the rent assessment committee. If the application was a joint one, or if there were no representations, the rent officer will simply make his decision and notify the parties, although a consultation may be held.[47]

In the case of a first registration, the rent officer's duty is to determine a fair rent and register it. If there is already a registered rent (which may be reconsidered according to rules explained below), he will either confirm the existing rent or register a different one.[48]

Services

The amount registered includes any sums payable for furniture or services, whether or not separate from the sums payable for occupation and whether or not payable under separate agreements.[49] Thus the landlord cannot evade full rent control by stipulating separate sums for "rent" and other matters.

Where, under the tenancy, the sums payable vary according to the cost of services or works of maintenance or repair, the amount registered as rent may be entered as a

Variable amount for services

variable amount, if the rent officer (or rent assessment committee) is satisfied that the terms as to variation are

---

[45] [1986] 1 E.G.L.R. 168, criticised by the chief rent officer (Kent registration area) in (1986) 278 E.G. 359, where it is suggested that such re-registrations have been done. See also [1986] Conv. 274 (J.E.M.).
[46] Now two years: Rent Act 1977, s. 67(3), below, p. 183.
[47] The procedure is set out in Rent Act 1977, Sched. 11, as amended by Housing Act 1980, Sched. 6.
[48] Rent Act 1977, Sched. 11, para. 5.
[49] Rent Act 1977, s. 71(1).

reasonable.[50]If the rent officer is not so satisfied, he must assess the proper value to be attributed to services and include the amount in the fixed fair rent.[51] Where a variable rent is registered, the recoverable rent may accordingly be increased within the two-year period (during which registered rents cannot normally be increased) without reconsideration by the rent officer. It has therefore been suggested that the rent officer should be cautious in accepting a variable rent, and that there should be a heavy onus upon the landlord to show that it is reasonable. It is not sufficient that the terms have been operated reasonably in the past; the terms themselves must be reasonable.[52]

Council tax

Prior to the abolition of domestic rates, the fair rent scheme allowed any increase in rates borne by the landlord to be passed on to the tenant. Domestic rating was replaced by the community charge (poll tax), which in turn has been replaced by council tax. In the case of a house in multiple occupation, the landlord is liable to pay the council tax.[53] Council tax liability is taken into account in assessing fair rents in the case of applications for registration after April 1, 1993.[54]

Effective date

Finally, the question when the registered rent takes effect must be considered. By section 72[55] of the 1977 Act, it takes effect from the date when registered by the rent officer or, if determined by a rent assessment committee, from the date of the committee's decision. If the current registered rent is confirmed, the confirmation takes effect from the date it is noted in the register by the rent officer, or, if confirmed by a rent assessment committee, from the date of its decision. This latter point is relevant to the question when the two-year period, during which further alterations cannot normally be made, begins to run. This is discussed below. In the case of a first registration, the effect of section 72 is that the tenant can be disadvantaged by any delay in the proceedings. If the rent finally registered is lower than his contractual rent, he cannot recover any excess for the period prior to the registration.[56] On a re-registration, on the other

---

[50] *ibid.* s. 71(4).
[51] *Firstcross Ltd v. Teasdale* (1984) 47 P.&C.R. 228. See also *Wigglesworth v. Property Holding and Investment Trust plc* (1984) 270 E.G. 555; *Betts v. Vivamat Properties Ltd* (1984) 270 E.G. 849.
[52] Farrand and Arden, *Rent Acts and Regulations* (2nd ed., 1981) pp. 98–99; (1983) 265 E.G. 286 (J.T. Farrand), criticising *Firstcross Ltd v. Teasdale*, above. See also [1983] Conv. 90 (J.T.F.), suggesting that where a variable rent is accepted, a rent exclusive of services should be registered, contrary to the usual practice.
[53] Council Tax (Liability of Owners) Regulations 1992 (S.I. 1992 No. 551), as amended by S.I. 1993 No. 151.
[54] Local Government Finance (Housing) (Consequential Amendments) Order 1993 (S.I. 1993 No. 651).
[55] As substituted by Housing Act 1980, s. 61.
[56] Contrast the original s. 72, whereby the registered rent took effect from the date of the application.

hand, the rent is normally increased in which case the section operates to the tenant's advantage.[57]

Appeal to the rent assessment committee[58]

Either party, if dissatisfied with the rent officer's decision, may appeal to the rent assessment committee, from whose decision appeal lies to court on a point of law. The rent assessment committee may require further information from the parties, and must serve notice on the parties specifying a period of not less than seven days from the service of the notice during which representations may be made. If either party requests to make oral representations, he must be given an opportunity to be heard in person or by means of a lawyer or other person representing him. After making such inquiries it thinks fit, the rent assessment committee will confirm the rent registered or confirmed by the rent officer if it appears to be a fair rent, or, if it does not, determine a fair rent. The parties are then notified of the decision and its date.[59]

Withdrawal of reference

Once an appeal has been initiated, the appellant cannot withdraw the reference unilaterally, but the Rent Assessment Committee can sanction the withdrawal if the parties agree and if it would not prejudice the public interest.[60] The public interest is involved because registration affects neighbouring properties as a result of the fixing of fair rents by looking at comparables.

Duty to give reasons

Rent assessment committees are subject to the rules of natural justice, and to the prerogative orders. They must give reasons for their decisions on request.[61] Questions have arisen as to the extent of this duty. Their reasons must be intelligible. They need not deal with every point raised, but must deal with substantial points. In *Waddington v. Surrey and Sussex Rent Assessment Committee*[62] the committee reduced the rent fixed by the rent officer, stating that they relied on what was found on inspection and on their own knowledge and experience. The landlord's appeal was allowed. The committee must deal with the evidence and, if it is rejected, explain why. Here no satisfactory reason was given for rejecting the next-door comparables.

[57] See Farrand and Arden, *loc. cit*, pp. 100–101.
[58] For the constitution of the committee, see Rent Act 1977, Sched. 10.
[59] These provisions are found in Rent Act 1977, Sched. 11, Pt. I. The committee may decide by a majority, although this fact will not be revealed. See *Picea Holdings Ltd v. London Rent Assessment Panel* [1971] 2 Q.B. 216.
[60] *Hanson v. Church Commissioners for England* [1978] Q.B. 823. See also *R. v. Chief Rent Officer for Royal Borough of Kensington and Chelsea, ex p. Moberley* [1986] 1 E.G.L.R. 168; *R. v. Bristol Rent Assessment Committee, ex p. Dunworth* [1987] 1 E.G.L.R. 102.
[61] Tribunals and Inquiries Act 1992, s. 10; [1979] Conv. 205 (P.Q. Watchman); [1983] Conv. 260 (J.T.F.); (1986) 83 L.S. Gaz. 2904 (D.W. Williams).
[62] (1982) 264 E.G. 717.

A similar situation arose in *R. v. London Rent Assessment Committee, ex p. St. George's Court Ltd*,[63] where the committee gave no explanation for rejecting comparables which were similar flats in the same block determined recently by another committee. The matter was remitted, to see if good reasons could be demonstrated. The reasons subsequently stated were that the tenants had not been represented before the other committee, and the evidence was therefore untested. This was taken to the Court of Appeal in *No. 2*,[64] and the decision quashed as showing an error of law. In effect, the committee was saying that the rent fixed by the other committee was not a fair rent, but it must be assumed to be right in law until shown to be wrong, for example, if cogent evidence or a significant argument was not before it.[65] In the case of a purpose-built block, the evidence must be very weighty justify a departure from a recent fair rent.

The question which arose in *Spath Holme Ltd v. Greater Manchester and Lancashire Rent Assessment Committee*[66]was whether the committee could reject as comparables the rents of assured tenancies in the same block in favour of lower registered fair rents relating to a different block nearby. Weighty reasons were needed to depart substantially from market rents recently agreed on similar flats in the same block. The fact that these were rents of assured tenancies and that scarcity still existed could be weighty reasons, but the committee had failed to give any adequate explanation. The decision was quashed and the matter remitted.

Where the case of services is being considered, the committee, as a basic principle, should give reasons if it rejects the landlord's figures. However, the committee is not obliged to use the costs as a basis. and has a discretion to look at the matter in some other way.[67]

Rent limit for protected tenancies

Limit is contractual rent
The basic principle is that the recoverable rent is the contractual rent. Even if a higher rent is registered, this is not recoverable during the protected tenancy. If, however, the landlord could give a notice to quit, a notice to increase the rent (which satisfies certain conditions) operates as a notice to quit, thus turning the tenancy into a statutory tenancy, governed by the rules explained below.[68]

---

[63] (1983) 265 E.G. 984.
[64] (1984) 48 P.&C.R. 230. See also *Collins v. Murray* (1984) 271 E.G. 287.
[65] See also *Tormes Property Co. Ltd v. Landau* [1971] 1 Q.B. 261.
[66] *The Times*, July 13, 1994; (1995) 145 N.L.J. 210 (A. Prichard) and 348, 384 (P. Willan). See also *B.T.E. Ltd v. Merseyside and Cheshire R.A.C., ex p. Jones* (1992) 24 H.L.R. 514.
[67] *R. v. London Rent Assessment Panel, ex p. Cliftvylle Properties Ltd* (1983) 266 E.G. 44; *Perseus Property Co. Ltd v. Burberry* [1985] 1 E.G.L.R. 114 (depreciation a relevant factor).
[68] Rent Act 1977, s. 49(4). See *Trustees of the Gift of Thomas Pocklington v. Hill* [1989] 2 E.G.L.R. 97.

Excess over registered rent The contractual rent cannot exceed any registered rent.[69] A landlord who charges a higher rent commits no offence, but the excess is recoverable by the tenant.[70] A protected tenant who is dissatisfied with his rent should, therefore, apply for the registration of a lower fair rent. Even if a higher figure is in fact registered, this is not recoverable during the protected tenancy, subject to the notice to quit rule.

Applying the principles of the law of contract, the parties should be free to increase the rent payable under the protected tenancy by agreement. In order to protect the tenant, however, a special rule applies, although it seems often to be ignored in practice. Where there is no registered rent, the rent under a protected tenancy may only be **Rent agreements** increased pursuant to a "rent agreement" satisfying the requirements of section 51. The agreement must be in writing, signed by the parties. It must state that the tenant's security is not affected if he does not enter into the agreement, and that the agreement does not prevent the parties from applying at any time for the registration of a fair rent. This statement must be at the head of the document, and must be in characters not less conspicuous than those used in any other part of the agreement.[71] Rent increased other than pursuant to such an agreement is not recoverable.[72] From the tenant's viewpoint, it is probably easier to apply for a registered rent.

Special rules Finally, special rules apply to determine the rent limit where the tenancy was brought into regulation by the Counter Inflation Act 1973,[73] and where the tenancy was converted from a controlled tenancy to a regulated tenancy.[74]

Rent limit for statutory tenancies

If there is no registered rent, only the previous contractual rent is recoverable. If there is a registered rent, this may not **Effect of** be exceeded. If the registered rent is higher than the **registered rent** contractual rent, the rent may be increased up to the registered rent by a notice of increase in prescribed form.[75] Such a notice of increase may take effect in the middle of a rental period, the increase being apportioned.[76]

Where there is no registered rent, the rent limit during the **Services** statutory tenancy may be adjusted to take account of

---

[69] *ibid.* s. 44(1).
[70] *ibid.* ss. 44(2), 57.
[71] See *Middlegate Properties Ltd v. Messimeris* [1973] 1 W.L.R. 168.
[72] Rent Act 1977, s. 54.
[73] *ibid.* Sched. 7.
[74] *ibid.* s. 52, introduced by Housing Act 1980, s. 68. An agreement purporting to increase the rent is void. The previous rent limit remains until a fair rent is registered.
[75] *ibid*, s. 45; Rent Act 1977 (Forms, etc.) (Amendment) Regulations 1993 (S.I. 1993 No. 655).
[76] *Avenue Properties (St. John's Wood) Ltd v. Aisinzon* [1977] Q.B. 628.

increases in the cost of providing furniture or services. The increase may be agreed in writing by the parties or determined by the county court.[77]

Excess rents   Rent demanded in excess of the rent limit is not recoverable from the tenant, and amounts so paid are recoverable by him from the landlord.[78]

Alteration and cancellation of registered rents

Two-year rule   **(a) Alteration**   A registered rent cannot be altered within two years unless the parties apply jointly, or unless there has been such a change in the condition of the dwelling-house, the terms of the tenancy, the quantity, quality or condition of any furniture, or any other circumstances taken into consideration previously, as to make the registered rent no longer a fair rent.[79] It is doubtful whether mere inflation is a change of circumstances within this provision. No doubt it was intended that the possibility of applying to increase the rent after two years without showing any change of circumstances would cater sufficiently for inflation.

Council tax   A landlord of a house in multiple occupation is liable for council tax.[80] For a transitional period it was possible for such a landlord to seek an interim increase in the registered rent within two years of the registration to reflect this liability if there was a contractual term in the tenancy enabling the landlord to pass on the liability to the tenant as part of the rent.[81] This is no longer possible after March 31, 1994. At present an alteration in the registered rent on account of the landlord's council tax liability can be sought after two years in the usual way.

Change of circumstances   If a change of circumstances to justify an application within two years is established, the rent may be reconsidered in the light of all the circumstances, not merely the change.[82] After the two year period, the question has arisen whether the rent should merely be revised to take account of inflation. In *Kovats v. Corporation of Trinity House*,[83] the tenant, appealing from the rent assessment committee on a point of law, claimed that the committee should have taken inflation alone into account, in the absence of a change of

---

[77] Rent Act 1977, s. 47. It might be easier to apply for a registered rent.
[78] Rent Act 1977, ss. 45, 57.
[79] *ibid.* s. 67(3), as amended by Housing Act 1980, s. 60. By s. 67(4), the landlord alone may apply within the last three months of the two-year period, but, by s. 72, no alteration can take effect until the two years have expired. Where application is made within two years, but the registered rent is confirmed, it seems that the two year period starts afresh; s. 67(5), as amended. See *R. v. Chief Rent Officer for Royal Borough of Kensington and Chelsea, ex p. Moberley* [1986] 1 E.G.L.R. 168.
[80] Council Tax (Liability of Owners) Regulations 1992 (S.I. 1992 No. 551), as amended by S.I. 1993 No. 151.
[81] Rent Act 1977 (Forms, etc.) (Amendment) Regulations 1993 (S.I. 1993 No. 655).
[82] *London Housing and Commercial Properties Ltd v. Cowan* [1977] Q.B. 148.
[83] (1982) 262 E.G. 445.

circumstances. It was held that section 70[84]applied to re-
registrations as well as to first registrations. It was legitimate
to consider the circumstances generally and to look at
comparables. This is because rents do not necessarily
increase precisely in step with inflation. But, of course,
inflation must be a factor. So in *Wareing v. White*,[85] the
Court of Appeal held that the rent assessment committee
had not acted improperly in looking at the Retail Price
Index. The committee had not suggested that rents must be
rigorously kept in line with inflation. General inflation,
amongst other things, could be considered, although
increases in rents in the locality were of more assistance.

It was held by the Court of Appeal in *Kent v. Millmead
Properties Ltd*[86] that a landlord who relet on a furnished
tenancy when the previous tenancy was unfurnished could
charge a higher rent without application to the rent officer
on the basis that the registered rent had become inoperative.
This decision has since been held by the Court of Appeal in
Rakhit v. Carty[87] to have been decided *per incuriam* because
the court was not referred to section 67 (3) of the 1977 Act.
A landlord who has furnished or refurbished the property
must seek an increase by application under section 67 (3) on
the basis of a change in circumstances. The registered rent
would cease to be operative without application to the rent
officer only if the property had undergone such a change in
its structure as to render it a different dwelling-house.

(b) Cancellation   The registered rent may be cancelled so
that a higher rent may be recovered, under section 73 of the
Two-year rule   1977 Act. This is permissible on a joint application after the
two-year period, where a "rent agreement"[88] has been
entered into.

Jurisdiction

Clearly situations may arise where it is disputed whether a
tenancy is a regulated tenancy. For example, it may be
alleged that the tenancy is in fact a licence, or that it is a
restricted contract, or a holiday letting. By section 141 of
the 1977 Act, the county court has jurisdiction to determine
whether a tenancy is protected or statutory, and what the
rent limit is. It has no jurisdiction, however, to determine or
County court   alter a registered rent. So in *Tingey v. Sutton*,[89] where the
jurisdiction   tenant applied to the county court to set aside a rent
registered by the rent officer, it was held that the court had

[84] See above, p. 172.
[85] [1985] 1 E.G.L.R. 125; *R. v. London Rent Assessment Panel, ex p.
Chelmsford Building Co. Ltd* [1986] 1 E.G.L.R. 175.
[86] (1982) 44 P.&C.R. 353.
[87] [1990] 2 Q.B. 315; [1990] Conv. 203 (J.E.M.).
[88] See above, p. 182.
[89] [1984] 1 W.L.R. 1154. See also *Druid Development Co. (Bingley) Ltd v.
Kay* (1982) 44 P.&C.R. 76.

no jurisdiction. The jurisdiction was that of the rent assessment committee, or, on appeal, the High Court.

Duty of rent officer

Disputes as to jurisdiction arise not infrequently before the rent officer. Such was the case in *R. v. Rent Officer for Camden, ex p. Ebiri*[90] where the tenant applied for a fair rent, but the landlord claimed that it was a holiday letting (which would be excluded from protection by section 9 of the 1977 Act). The tenant started county court proceedings to determine the question of protection. Meanwhile the rent officer investigated the matter and was satisfied that it was not a holiday letting, but adjourned the matter *sine die*. The tenant succeeded in obtaining an order of mandamus to have the fair rent determined and registered. While the rent officer could not determine conclusively whether it was a protected tenancy, his duty was to consider the matter and inquire into the facts. If satisfied that the tenancy was protected, he was bound to proceed. He only had a discretion not to proceed if doubtful as to jurisdiction, or perhaps if he knew that the county court would decide the matter within 24 hours. If satisfied that it was not a protected tenancy, he should do nothing until the court held that it was. This, it is submitted, is satisfactory, in view of the rules relating to the date from which a registered rent takes effect, explained above. As the registered rent cannot take effect from a date prior to the registration, it would be undesirable if the tenant had to go on paying a high contractual rent until protracted court proceedings resolved the matter.

Illegal premiums

The restrictions discussed above upon the rent recoverable under a regulated tenancy would not serve their purpose if premiums, *i.e.* capital sums, could be required on the grant or assignment of the tenancy. It is accordingly unlawful to require a premium on the grant or assignment of a regulated tenancy.

It will be appreciated that such premiums are illegal only if the tenancy is within the Rent Act.[91] A premium is, of course, perfectly lawful on the grant of a long lease at a ground rent, where the Rent Act does not apply because the rent is too low. Landlords may not, however, take advantage of this principle in the case of a short lease by charging a premium and ground rent if the arrangement is a sham device to evade the Act. In *Samrose Properties Ltd v. Gibbard*[92] property was let for a year for a lump sum of £35 and a rent of £1 quarterly. The object was to prevent the Rent Act from applying because the rent was less than two-

Sham devices

---

[90] [1982] 1 All E.R. 950; [1983] Conv. 403 (J.E.M.).
[91] Premiums are not unlawful in the case of assured tenancies under the Housing Act 1988, where rent control is minimal: see below, Chap. 14.
[92] [1958] 1 W.L.R. 235. See also *Woods v. Wise* [1955] 2 Q.B. 29.

thirds of the rateable value. It was held that the property had in effect been let at a rent of £39 for the year, so that the Act applied.

The meaning of "premium"

The definition of "premium" in section 128 (1) of the 1977 Act includes "any fine or other like sum" and "any other pecuniary consideration in addition to rent." This definition **Deposits** left it unclear whether a returnable deposit, for example to cover breakages or arrears of rent, was included.[93] The matter was resolved by the Housing Act 1980, section 79, providing that the definition includes any sum paid by way of a deposit, other than one which does not exceed one-sixth of the annual rent and is reasonable in relation to the potential liability in respect of which it is paid.

It is possible that a payment by the tenant of the landlord's costs in relation to the grant of the tenancy will **Loans** constitute a premium.[94] The premium rules also cover the case where a loan (secured or unsecured) is required to be made on the grant or assignment of the tenancy.[95]

The grant of a protected tenancy

By section 119 (1) of the 1977 Act, any person who, as a condition of the grant, renewal or continuance of a protected tenancy, requires in addition to the rent the payment of any premium, shall be guilty of an offence. Similarly, any person who, in connection with the grant, renewal or continuance of a protected tenancy, receives any premium in addition to the rent.[96] In addition to imposing a fine, the court may order the repayment of the premium.[97]

The premium need not be paid to the landlord himself. Thus in *Elmdene Estates Ltd v. White*[98] the offence was committed where the landlord required the tenant to sell his **Payments to** house to a third party at £500 below the market price as a **third parties** condition of the grant of a tenancy of a flat. This was in effect a premium of £500.

While section 119 is directed primarily at landlords, the **Section not** offence may be committed by "any person." So in *Farrell v.* **confined to** *Alexander*[99] the section applied where the tenant surrendered **landlords** the tenancy to the landlord on the basis that the landlord would grant a new tenancy to X, the tenant taking a

[93] See *R. v. Ewing* (1977) 65 Cr.App.R. 4.
[94] *Hansard*, H.L., Vol. 411, col. 585. *cf.* Costs of Leases Act 1958.
[95] Rent Act 1977, ss. 119(1), 120(1). Any sum lent is repayable on demand: s. 125(2).
[96] *ibid.* s. 119(2).
[97] *ibid.* s. 119(3), (4).
[98] [1960] A.C. 528.
[99] [1977] A.C. 59; (1977) 41 Conv. (N.S.) 61 (D. MacIntyre). See also *Saleh v. Robinson* (1988) 20 H.L.R. 424, rejecting the argument that such a premium was condition precedent to the grant of the tenancy as opposed to a "condition of the grant" within s. 119(1).

premium from X. A premium paid on a direct assignment to X would be caught by section 120, discussed below, but the argument that section 119 was confined to landlords was rejected.

The assignment of a protected tenancy

Similar conditions to those discussed above apply to the assignment of a protected tenancy. By section 120, it is an offence to require or receive a premium as a condition of, or in connection with the assignment. Although directed primarily at assigning tenants, the offence, as in the case of

Lawful payments section 119, may be committed by "any person." Certain payments may, however, properly be required by the assignor. These are dealt with by section 120 (3), and include payments in respect of outgoings paid by the assignor which are referable to a period after the assignment, and sums not exceeding the amount of any expenditure reasonably incurred by the assignor in carrying out alterations to the dwelling-house or in providing or improving fixtures.[1]

These rules are confined to protected tenancies because

Statutory statutory tenancies are not generally assignable. A statutory
tenancies tenancy may, however, be assigned by an agreement to which the landlord is a party, but no pecuniary consideration may be required in such a case.[2] Where a statutory tenant gives up possession, he commits an offence if he requests or receives payment or other consideration from any person other than the landlord.[3]

Excessive price for furniture

The premium rules could, of course, be flouted if, instead of asking for a capital sum, the landlord or assigning tenant could achieve the same result by asking excessive prices for furniture and fixtures. To avoid such a possibility, section 123 provides that where the purchase of any furniture[4] is required as a condition of the grant, renewal, continuance or assignment of a protected tenancy, then if the price exceeds the reasonable price of the furniture, the excess is a premium. Local authorities have draconian powers in relation to the enforcement of these provisions,[5] but it is thought that the offence is commonly committed.

Illustrations   An example of the operation of this rule is *Farrell v. Alexander*[6] where £4,000 was required for furniture and fittings which were worth much less. Similarly *Ailion v.*

---

[1] See *Steele v. McMahon* [1990] 2 E.G.L.R. 114 (s. 120(3) not confined to expenditure incurred by assignor after grant of tenancy).
[2] Rent Act 1977, Sched. 1, paras. 13, 14.
[3] *ibid*, para. 12.
[4] Defined by s. 128(1) as including fittings and other articles.
[5] s. 124.
[6] See above. See also *Saleh v. Robinson*, above (£12,000 paid for carpets and curtains worth £200).

Spiekermann,[7] where the prospective assignee agreed to pay
£3,750 for certain chattels, which, it was claimed, were
worth only about £600. Specific performance was ordered
of the contract to assign the tenancy and to transfer the
chattels at a reasonable price.[8]

Advance payments

These are prohibited by section 126, providing that where a
protected tenancy is granted, continued or renewed, any
requirement that rent shall be payable before the beginning
of the rental period in respect of which it is payable shall be
void whether imposed as a condition of the grant or under
its terms. Similarly void is any requirement that rent shall be
payable more than six months before the end of the rental
period in respect of which it is payable (if that period is
more than six months). The consequence of such a

Effect of rule   "prohibited requirement" is that the rent for any rental
period to which it relates is irrecoverable from the tenant. A
fine may be imposed, and any rent paid in compliance with
the prohibited requirement may be ordered to be repaid.[9]

In *R. v. Ewing*[10] it was held that a payment by cheque the
day before the start of the first rental period did not fall
within the prohibition, as the cheque had to be cleared. It
might be otherwise, however, in the case of a cash payment.

Allowable premiums

The situation may arise where a tenant lawfully pays a
premium on the grant or assignment of a tenancy which is

Where tenancy   not within the Rent Act. Subsequently the tenancy becomes
becomes   protected, so that the tenant would suffer hardship if he
protected   could not charge a premium on assignment. To alleviate his
position, premiums may lawfully be charged in such cases.
This could arise where the rent, initially less than two-thirds
of the rateable value, has risen above that limit because of an
increase in the service charge element.[11] Or the tenancy
might have been brought into protection after its grant by
legislation such as the Counter Inflation Act 1973, or by
section 73 of the Housing Act 1980, amending in certain
cases the rule that a tenancy cannot be protected if the
landlord's interest belongs to the Crown. The ability to
charge a lawful premium may reflect in a higher rent.[12]

---

[7] [1976] Ch. 158. For an unusual case where £40,000 was held lawful, see
Nock v. Munk (1982) 263 E.G. 1085 (luxury flat done out by
professional interior decorator).
[8] For guidance on the meaning of "reasonable price", see *Eales v. Dale*
[1954] 1 Q.B. 539.
[9] See Rent Act 1977, s. 126(5) to (9), for further details.
[10] (1977) 65 Cr.App.R. 4. *cf. Official Solicitor v. Thomas* [1986] 2 E.G.L.R.
1 (rent for agricultural holding not paid when landlord receives cheque);
Hannaford v. Smallacombe (1995) 69 P.&C.R. 399.
[11] *i.e.* in cases where the service element is not disregarded under Rent Act
1977, s. 5(4).
[12] Rent Act 1977, s. 70(1)(c) above, p. 172.

Space does not permit an examination here of the detailed provisions applicable in such cases,[13] but it should be noted that the Housing Act 1988 has amended and simplified the rules governing allowable premiums in long leases, with respect to premiums received or required to be paid after its commencement.[14] Nearly all long leases will now satisfy the rules permitting premiums on assignment.

Effect of the premium rules

Criminal offence As already stated, infringement of the rules constitutes a criminal offence, and any premium paid is recoverable by the person who paid it.[15]

It remains to consider the civil law position where a contract has been made which includes a term for payment of an illegal premium. In *Ailion v. Spiekermann*[16] a tenant contracted to assign for an illegal premium. It having become apparent that the premium could not be enforced, the assignor sought to avoid performing the contract by claiming that it was void for illegality. It was held that the contract as a whole was not illegal. The bad part could be **Contract severable** severed, and specific performance granted of the contract to assign without the premium. After all, if the issue of illegality had been raised only after performance of the contract, the premium would be recoverable. But specific performance is a discretionary remedy. It might not be awarded where the assignor was ignorant and the assignee "tempted him with a cheque book," or where the assignor changed his mind before the assignee had altered his position in reliance on the contract. In normal circumstances, however the contract will be specifically enforced. The assignee is not precluded from seeking this remedy even though he knew of the illegality, because the statutory provisions were designed for his protection.

[13] See Rent Act 1977, ss. 121, 127 and Sched. 18; Housing Act 1980, Sched. 8.
[14] Housing Act 1988, s. 115, amending Rent Act 1977, s. 127. See Rodgers, *Housing: The New Law* (1988), Chap. 11. There is, of course, no problem if the lease was granted after the Housing Act 1988, as it could not be a protected tenancy.
[15] Rent Act 1977, s. 125(1).
[16] See above; (1976) 50 Conv. (N.S.) 379 (D. MacIntyre). See also *Rees v. Marquis of Bute* [1916] 2 Ch. 64.

III THE HOUSING ACT 1988

This Part deals with assured and assured shorthold tenancies under the Housing Act 1988.[1] After the commencement of the Act, regulated tenancies and restricted contracts under the Rent Act 1977, discussed in Part II, can no longer be granted. However, although the new regime is radically different from the old, certain basic concepts remain. In particular, the conditions to be satisfied for protected status, the exclusions from protection and the grounds for possession have borrowed much from the previous legislation. Similarly, the distinction between leases and licences, discussed in Part I, continues to be significant.

Although the details are outside the scope of this book, it is convenient to mention here the tax incentives offered to investors to encourage the growth of the new assured tenancies.

Business Expansion Scheme
The Business Expansion Scheme,[2] allowing income tax relief to individual investors, was extended to investments in companies specialising in letting residential properties by way of assured (but not assured shorthold) tenancies.[3] The companies could either build new properties or buy existing ones which were not currently let, and there were various restrictions on the values of the lettable units and the amount to be invested. Qualifying shares could be disposed of after five years without incurring capital gains tax. The initial response to the scheme was encouraging.[4] It also facilitated the transfer of repossessed homes to private sector renting when building societies were permitted to sell such properties to BES companies.[5] The falling property market, however, resulted in a reluctance on the part of the companies to buy properties save on terms that the vendor would subsequently buy them back at a guaranteed price.[6] Department of Environment figures in 1992 indicated that the Business Expansion Scheme had put 12,000 dwellings into the private rented sector.[7] The relief was abolished in relation to shares issued on or after January 1, 1994.[8]

---

[1] See generally Rodgers, *Housing: The New Law* (1988); Bridge, *Guide to the Housing Act 1988* (1989).
[2] Introduced by Finance Act 1983.
[3] Finance Act 1988 ss. 50–53 and Sched. 4.
[4] £320 million was invested in 1988/89; see [1989] 19 E.G. 59 (A. Greaves).
[5] *The Times*, March 15, 1993.
[6] *Financial Times*, September 30, 1989.
[7] *The Times*, February 26, 1992. See further [1992] 12 E.G. 114.
[8] Finance (No. 2) Act 1992, s. 38. This was the date on which the relief was originally scheduled to end.

The current income tax incentive ("rent a room relief")
applies to lettings of furnished accommodation in the
landlord's only or main residence. As this is directed to
lettings by resident landlords, it does not apply to assured
tenancies.[9]

[9] *ibid*. s. 59 and Sched. 10 (relief on income up to £3,250 a year).

11 ASSURED TENANCIES

Introduction This Chapter is concerned with the definition and incidents of the assured tenancy. The grounds for possession and rent control are dealt with in Chapters 13 and 14 respectively.

The policy behind the Housing Act 1988 is to encourage letting in the private sector by introducing a regime which is more attractive to landlords, in particular by diminishing security of tenure and rent control. As far as security of

Protected tenancy compared tenure is concerned, the assured tenancy is not radically different from the protected tenancy under the Rent Act 1977 in so far as termination requires a court order based on a ground for possession. In the case of the assured tenancy, however, there is a greater emphasis on mandatory grounds, although not to such an extent as in the preceding Bill, where certain grounds for possession which are discretionary under the Act were mandatory, as in the case of suitable alternative accommodation. Perhaps the most significant differences between protected and assured tenancies as far as security is concerned lie in the greatly reduced opportunities for succession and in the "only or principal home" test, which is stricter than the "occupation as a residence" test of statutory tenancies.

The difference between the 1977 and 1988 Acts is more

Rent control marked in the context of rent control. As we have seen, the "fair rent" system under the 1977 Act operates to reduce the rent below market levels, whereas rent control under the 1988 Act operates merely to keep the rent from exceeding a market rent in certain cases. Thus the 1988 Act departs from the long-established principle of the Rent Acts that security of tenure without rent control is ineffective.

The assured shorthold tenancy, explained in Chapter 12,

Assured shorthold tenancy compared enables the landlord to recover possession more easily than in the case of assured tenancies or protected shorthold tenancies under the 1977 Act. Although there is a greater degree of rent control, it is unlikely that many tenants will be able to avail themselves of it.[1] In view of these attractions to the landlord, it may be asked why landlords will not invariably choose to let by means of assured shorthold tenancies rather than assured tenancies. Tax relief under the Business Expansion Scheme, however, applied only to assured tenancies, as mentioned above. It should be added

---

[1] See below, p. 225.

that housing association lettings are assured rather than
assured shorthold tenancies.[2]

Increase in lettings

How far the Act has succeeded in encouraging private
sector lettings is not yet clear. The Secretary of State
predicted that there would be 190,000 private sector lettings
under the 1988 Act within the first five years.[3] There has
indeed been an increase in the supply of private sector
lettings in recent years, but, as discussed in Chapter 1, the
increase is attributable in part to the depressed property
market, which has compelled many owners to let during
periods when they have been unable to sell. One view is
that legislation such as the Housing Act 1988 will not
achieve its aim while mortgage interest tax relief remains, as
owner-occupation is still a powerful subsidised alternative to
renting at market levels.[4]

Definition of an assured tenancy

The assured tenancy is defined in section 1 of the 1988 Act.
Before looking at that section, mention should be made of
the general provision relating to joint landlords and joint
tenants. As has been seen in Part II, the absence of any such
provision in the Rent Act 1977 has caused difficulties, for
example in the context of joint protected tenants,[5] the
grounds for possession[6]and the joint resident landlords.[7]

Joint landlords or tenants

The Housing Act 1988 deals with the problem by providing
that where two or more persons jointly constitute either the
landlord or the tenant, then except where Part I of the Act
otherwise provides, any reference to the landlord or the
tenant is a reference to all the persons who jointly constitute
the landlord or the tenant.[8] It will be seen that the definition
in section 1 contains such a contrary provision.

Conditions

By section 1, a tenancy[9] under which a dwelling-house[10] is
let as a separate dwelling is an assured tenancy if and so long
as:

(a) the tenant (or each of joint tenants) is an individual;
and

(b) the tenant (or at least one of joint tenants) occupies the
dwelling-house as his only or principal home; and

---

[2] See the Housing Corporation Circular, "The Tenants' Guarantee" —
Guidance on the Management by Registered Housing Associations of
Housing Accommodation Let on Assured Tenancies Under the Housing
Act 1988 (H.C. 43/88).
[3] H.C. Deb., vol. 106, col. 622, November 30, 1987.
[4] (1989) 52 M.L.R. 661 at 682 (M. Davey). See also (1993) 143 N.L.J.
1271 (N. Hickman), reviewing the Act after the first four years.
[5] *Lloyd v. Sadler* [1978] Q.B. 774.
[6] Particularly Case 9 and Case 11.
[7] *Cooper v. Tait* (1984) 271 E.G. 105.
[8] s. 45(3).
[9] Including a sub-tenancy and an agreement for a tenancy or sub-tenancy:
s. 45(1). As to rental purchase schemes, see above, p. 58.
[10] Meaning a house or part of a house: *ibid.*

(c)   the tenancy is neither within the exclusions listed in Schedule 1, nor excluded by section 1(6) (concerning the housing of homeless persons).[11]

Old assured tenancies

Where immediately before the commencement[12] of the 1988 Act a tenancy was an assured tenancy under the Housing Act 1980,[13] it is converted to an assured tenancy under the 1988 Act on commencement day.[14]

Long leases

It might be added that an assured periodic tenancy will arise on termination of a long residential tenancy on or after January 15, 1999.[15]

Let as a separate dwelling

The "let as a separate dwelling" requirement is identical to section 1 of the Rent Act 1977.[16] Authorities on the meaning of the expression under the 1977 Act, discussed in Chapter 4, will continue to be applicable under the 1988 Act.

Licences

It will be noted that the distinction between leases and licences, discussed in Chapter 2, remains significant in the context of the assured tenancy. However, a landlord may be less concerned to find that his "licensee" is an assured tenant than a protected tenant, because of the reduced security and rent control.[17] It should be added that certain licensees before the commencement of the 1988 Act had the benefit of a restricted contract under the 1977 Act, but that restricted contracts can no longer be granted.[18] Hence a licence granted on or after January 15, 1989 confers no security, although the rights of licensees have been somewhat enhanced by the amendments to the Protection from Eviction Act 1977.[19]

Where conditions cease to be satisfied

The expression "if and so long as" in section 1 indicates that a tenancy which is initially assured will lose that status if the conditions subsequently cease to be satisfied, for example on assignment of the tenancy to a company, on transfer of the reversion to an exempt landlord such as the Crown, where the tenancy for any other reason later falls within the exclusions in Schedule 1, or, more particularly,

---

[11] Where a local authority, in pursuance of its duties under Housing Act 1985, ss. 63, 65(3) or 68(1), makes arrangements with another person to provide accommodation, a tenancy granted by that person cannot be assured before the expiry of 12 months from the date the tenant received notification under ss. 64(1) or 68(3) of the 1985 Act, unless the landlord informs the tenant within that period that the tenancy is assured. This is based on the secure tenancy provisions of Housing Act 1985, Sched. 1, para. 4.

[12] January 15, 1989.

[13] See above, p. 77.

[14] s. 1(3). For exceptions, see s. 37. The application of the 1988 Act to old assured tenancies is modified in certain respects by s. 1(4) and (5). In particular, paras. 1–10 of Sched. 1 (exclusions other than Crown and public landlords) do not apply.

[15] Local Government and Housing Act 1989, s. 186 and Sched. 10. Similarly at the end of a long tenancy granted on or after April 1, 1990, whenever it terminates.

[16] See above, p. 59.

[17] See further (1989) L.S. Gaz. No. 28, p. 25 (P. and A. Kenny).

[18] Housing Act 1988, s. 36(1).

[19] See Chap. 3.

where the tenant ceases to occupy as his only or principal home.

Company lets

In the case of the Rent Act 1977, we saw in Chapter 6 that a letting to a company or institution could be a protected tenancy (and thus attract the benefit of rent control) but could not become a statutory tenancy on termination because a company or institution cannot "reside." A company letting is totally excluded from the new regime, in which there is in any event little rent control. Thus the company let remains a simple and effective device for excluding the assured tenancy code, subject to two provisos. First, it may be argued that the letting to the company is a sham, and that the "real" tenant is the individual occupant. This argument has not yet succeeded in the Rent Act cases.[20] Secondly, it may be argued that, even though there is no sham as such, the company letting is an artificial transaction intended to bypass the Act, which the court may look behind. The argument derives from *Gisborne v. Burton*,[21] where a subletting granted in order to bypass the agricultural holdings legislation was held to be an artificial transaction, with the result that the "sub-tenant" was held to be the direct tenant, and hence protected. It will be noted that, in the case of joint tenants, each must be an individual, so a letting to an individual and a company jointly will not be assured.

Only or principal home

The requirement of occupation as the tenant's "only or principal home" will be harder to satisfy than the statutory tenancy requirement of occupation as a residence, discussed in Chapter 6. An express statement in the tenancy that the dwelling is or is not the tenant's only or principal home may assist but will not be conclusive.[22] We saw that under the Rent Act 1977 the "two-homes" tenant could enjoy a statutory tenancy in relation to either or both dwellings.[23] Under the 1988 Act, it is no objection that the tenant has two homes, but he will only qualify for assured tenancy status in respect of his principal home. Similarly, many of the cases under the 1977 Act where tenants have retained their statutory tenancies in spite of lengthy absences would have a different result under the 1988 Act. However, where the tenant's absence is caused by residence somewhere other than in a different "home" (for example, where he is in prison, or where he is the legendary ship's captain), no doubt he may still satisfy section 1. Presumably the *Brown v. Brash*[24] test (intention to return coupled with some physical sign of that intention on the premises) will continue to apply. In the case of joint tenants, only one need occupy as

Absences

---

[20] See above, p. 95.
[21] [1989] Q.B. 390, above, p. 96; *cf. Hilton v. Plustitle* [1989] 1 W.L.R. 149.
[22] See *Precedents for the Conveyancer*, Vol. I, 5–101. This was a particular problem for BES tenancies, which had to qualify as assured.
[23] See above, p. 103.
[24] [1948] 2 K.B. 247; above, p. 108.

Occupation by spouse

his only or principal home. As in the case of statutory tenancies under the Rent Act 1977, occupation by the tenant's spouse is treated as occupation by the tenant.[25] Hence occupation by a deserted spouse preserves assured tenancy status so long as the marriage continues. The wording of section 1(6) of the Matrimonial Homes Act 1983 (as amended by the Housing Act 1988) is not, however, tailored to the requirement of occupation as the tenant's only or principal home. It merely provides that occupation by the tenant's spouse shall be treated as occupation by the tenant. Mere occupation does not suffice for assured status. Presumably occupation by the tenant's spouse will preserve assured status only if the spouse occupies as his or her only or principal home.[26] An amendment has been proposed by the Law Commission to clarify the point.[27] As in the case of regulated and secure tenancies, the court may order the transfer of an assured tenancy on divorce.[28]

Secure tenancy case-law

The "only or principal home" test applies also to secure tenants under the Housing Act 1985. Case-law on that Act may be relied upon under the 1988 Act. The decided cases, however, indicate that the requirement is not greatly different from the "occupation as a residence" test. In *Crawley Borough Council v. Sawyer*,[29] for example, the secure tenant had moved out in order to live with his girlfriend, and was planning to buy a house with her. He visited the demised flat once a month, and the gas and electricity were cut off. When the relationship with the girlfriend ended, the tenant returned to the flat. It was held that the flat remained his "only and principal home," so that he remained a secure tenant. Some sign of occupation and an intention to return sufficed. The question which home was the "principal" home was a question of fact for the judge at first instance. This case illustrates a distinction between the Housing Act 1985 and the 1988 Act. A secure tenancy exists "at any time when" the conditions are satisfied.[30] Therefore, unless evicted at a time when the conditions are not satisfied, the tenant can come back into protection by later satisfying the

---

[25] Matrimonial Homes Act 1983, s. 1(6). See above, p. 101. Occupation orders granted to cohabitants, former cohabitants and former spouses under cl. 9 of the Family Homes and Domestic Violence Bill will have the same effect.

[26] [1990] Conv. 58 at 59 (J.E.M.). See also *Griffiths v. Renfree* [1989] 2 E.G.L.R. 46, dealing with a similar point in relation to Rent Act tenancies.

[27] Law Com. No. 207 (1992); *Domestic Violence and Occupation of the Family Home.* Clause 4(3)(b) of the Family Homes and Domestic Violence Bill provides that the spouse's occupation as only or principal home shall be treated as occupation by the tenant as only or principal home.

[28] Matrimonial Homes Act 1983, Sched. 1. The Family Homes and Domestic Violence Bill extends the transfer provisions to cohabitants, on or after separation; above, p. 110.

[29] (1988) 20 H.L.R. 98; criticised [1988] Conv. 300 (S. Bridge).

[30] Housing Act 1985, s. 79.

conditions again.[31] Under the 1988 Act, on the other hand, the expression "if and so long as" indicates that loss of protection by ceasing to satisfy the conditions is permanent. Other illustrations include *Peabody Donation Fund Governors v. Grant*,[32] where, in the context of the succession rules, a daughter who lived with her mother for three days a week and with her father for four days a week was held to have her "only or principal home" with her father. In *Notting Hill Housing Trust v. Etoria*[33] a tenant serving life imprisonment, but who expected to be released on licence in 1995, was held to retain secure status after a notice to quit in 1987. His brother occupied as a caretaker. It was regarded as a borderline case, but the tenant had a real possibility of realising his intention to return. In *R. v. Worthing Borough Council, ex p. Bruce*[34] a disabled man who owned a specially adapted house and had a tenancy of a council flat, staying occasionally at the house, was held not to be a secure tenant because the house was his principal home. In *Jennings v. Epping Forest District Council*[35] an elderly couple had a joint tenancy of a council flat. The husband moved to a nursing home and the wife took another flat nearby and arranged to sublet the council flat. It was held that they had lost secure status as the council flat was no longer their only or principal home. In the context of a succession claim a son who lived with his mother but moved to lodgings in London to find work was held in *Roxburgh D.C. v. Collins*[36] to be residing with his mother as his only or principal home. His possessions remained at his mother's, and he returned for holidays. The similar concept of the only or main residence appears in the Leasehold Reform Act 1967. In *Dymond v. Arundel Timms*[37] a tenant of a shop and maisonette was held to occupy the maisonette as her main residence where she owned a cottage in Devon which was sometimes let and sometimes occupied by her sons.

Before leaving the definition of an assured tenancy, certain other matters should be mentioned. By section 2 of the 1988 Act, where a dwelling-house is let together with other land, the other land is to be treated as part of the dwelling-house if and so long as the main purpose of the

Dwelling let together with other land

---

[31] See *South Glamorgan County Council v. Griffiths* (1992) 24 H.L.R. 334 at 339; *Elvidge v. Coventry City Council* [1994] Q.B. 241; *Hussey v. London Borough of Camden* (1995) 27 H.L.R. 5.
[32] (1982) 264 E.G. 925; *City of Westminster v. Peart* (1992) 24 H.L.R. 389.
[33] (1989) *Legal Action*, April, p. 22 (county court).
[34] (1992) 24 H.L.R. 261; *cf. Camden L.B.C. v. Coombs* (1987), unreported, noted (1988) *Legal Action*, March, p. 17 (tenant of London flat who was the owner-occupier of a suburban house retained secure status).
[35] [1992] N.P.C. 93. See also *McLoughlin's Curator Bonis v. Motherwell D.C.* (1994) S.L.T. 31 (secure status lost when in hospital for 5 months and incapable of forming intent to return home).
[36] [1991] S.L.T. 49 (on the Scottish secure tenancy legislation).
[37] (1991) 23 H.L.R. 397.

letting is the provision of a home for the tenant (or for at least one of joint tenants). If and so long as this is not the case, the tenancy is to be treated as not being one under which a dwelling-house is let as a separate dwelling. Although the wording is not identical, section 2 reflects the provisions of sections 6 and 26 of the Rent Act 1977.[38] The effect is that the tenancy can be assured where other premises are ancillary to the dwelling, but cannot be assured where the dwelling is ancillary to some other property which is the main subject of the letting. It has been held that, for the purpose of the similar Rent Act provisions, the relevant time for considering whether the land is ancillary to the dwelling or vice versa is the date of the application to court, not the date of the letting.[39]

Section 2 does not affect any question whether a tenancy is excluded from assured tenancy status by Schedule 1.[40] So if agricultural land exceeding two acres is let together with the dwelling-house, the tenancy cannot be assured even if the main purpose of the letting is residential.[41]

Other miscellaneous matters include the effect of sharing and subletting. Section 3 deals with the case where the tenant has exclusive occupation of "separate accommodation," and under the terms of his tenancy he has the use of other accommodation in common with another person or persons (not including the landlord). The separate accommodation is deemed to be a separate dwelling so that the tenant has an assured tenancy if the other conditions are satisfied.

Sharing with other tenants

This section applies, for example, where the tenant, in addition to his own room or rooms, shares a kitchen or bathroom with other tenants. If the tenant shares with his landlord, he will normally be excluded by the resident landlord rule.[42]

Termination and modification of sharing rights

Any term of the tenancy terminating or modifying the tenant's right to use any of the shared accommodation which is "living accommodation"[43] (such as a kitchen) is of no effect,[44] but terms providing that the persons with whom the tenant shares can be varied or their number increased are effective.[45] These provisions are based on section 22 of the Rent Act 1977.[46] The extent to which the landlord may recover possession of the shared accommodation is governed

---

[38] See above pp. 65 and 69.
[39] *Russell v. Booker* (1982) 263 E.G. 513.
[40] Housing Act 1988, s. 2(2).
[41] *ibid.* Sched. 1, para. 6. Likewise if the tenancy is a business tenancy: *ibid.* para. 4. Provided the business user is not minimal, a tenancy can be a business tenancy even though the main purpose of the letting is residential: above, p. 77.
[42] See below, p. 204.
[43] Defined in s. 3(5). The term was explained at p. 63 above.
[44] s. 3(3).
[45] s. 3(4).
[46] See above, p. 63.

by section 10 of the 1988 Act, which is dealt with in
Chapter 13.[47]

As far as subletting is concerned, section 4 provides that
where the tenant has sublet part but not the whole,[48] then no
part of the dwelling-house is to be treated as excluded from
Sharing with   being a dwelling-house let on an assured tenancy by reason
sub-tenant   only that the sub-tenant has the use of accommodation in
common with other persons. In other words, the fact that
the sub-tenant shares part of the accommodation with the
tenant or another person does not prevent the head tenancy
from being regarded as a separate dwelling as far as the head
landlord is concerned. Section 4 is modelled on section 23
of the Rent Act 1977. Such a sub-tenant is unlikely to have
an assured tenancy as against the tenant because of the
resident landlord exception.[49]

Excluded tenancies

The Housing Act 1988, in Schedule 1, lists 13 types of
Similarity to   tenancy which cannot be assured. They are very similar, and
Rent Act   in most cases identical, to the exclusions under the Rent Act
exclusions   1977. There is no exclusion, however, for tenancies with
board or attendance,[50] nor for housing association tenancies
(other than those granted by fully mutual housing
associations). The application of the assured tenancy regime
to housing association tenancies means that the "fair rent"
system under the Rent Act 1977 does not apply to such
tenancies granted after the 1988 Act. Although not
expressly mentioned, Church of England parsonage houses
are presumably excluded for the same reason as under the
Rent Act 1977.[51] It seems that a tenancy which otherwise
satisfies the conditions of section 1 will become assured if an
exclusion ceases to apply to it. The exceptions will be
discussed in the order in which they appear in the Schedule.

Tenancies entered into before
commencement

A tenancy entered into before, or pursuant to a contract
made before, the commencement of the 1988 Act (January
15, 1989) cannot be assured.[52] Such a tenancy is in any

---

[47] See below, p. 245.
[48] In which case he would not satisfy the occupation requirement of s. 1.
[49] See below, p. 204. s. 4 does not affect the rights between tenant and sub-
tenant: s. 4(2). Nor would the sub-tenant have any rights against the
head landlord: Housing Act 1988, s. 18, below, p. 214.
[50] Because the Rent Act exclusion had been abused; (1989) 52 M.L.R. 661
at 666 (M. Davey).
[51] Pluralities Act 1838: above, p. 79. In the case of other denominations,
see Ground 5, below, p. 234.
[52] Sched. 1, para. 1.

event expressly excluded if it is a protected or secure tenancy, a housing association tenancy, or a protected occupancy under the Rent (Agriculture) Act 1976.[53] There are certain exceptions to the rule that a tenancy granted before the 1988 Act cannot be assured. A pre-commencement tenancy which is subsequently transferred from the public to the private sector may be assured.[54] Also, an "old assured tenancy" existing immediately before commencement is converted to an assured tenancy.[55]

Tenancies of dwelling-houses with high rateable values or at a high rent

Rateable value limits A tenancy entered into before April 1, 1990 (the date on which domestic rating was abolished) under which the dwelling-house had a rateable value exceeding £1,500 in Greater London or £750 elsewhere on March 31, 1990 cannot be assured.[56] In the case of tenancies entered into on or after April 1, 1990 the rateable value exclusion is replaced **High rent** by a high rent exclusion. The tenancy cannot be assured if the rent for the time being exceeds £25,000 a year.[57] "Rent" for this purpose does not include any sum expressed to be payable in respect of services, repairs, insurance and so forth.[58] So, for example, a high service charge cannot take the tenancy out of protection if, without it, the rent does not exceed £25,000.

Tenancies at a low rent

Rateable value rule A tenancy cannot be assured if for the time being no rent is payable.[59] In the case of a tenancy entered into before April 1, 1990 (the date on which domestic rating was abolished), it is excluded if the rent for the time being is less than two-thirds of the rateable value of the dwelling on March 31, 1990.[60] For tenancies entered into on or after April 1, 1990 **Rent limits** the exclusion applies if the rent for the time being does not

---

[53] *ibid.* para. 13, above.
[54] Housing Act 1988, s. 38. For examples, see Bridge, *Guide to the Housing Act 1988* (1989) 16–17.
[55] s. 1(3).
[56] Sched. 1, para. 2A. Part II of Sched. 1 deals with apportionment of rateable values and alterations in the valuation list. These provisions are similar to those applying under the Rent Act 1977, above, p. 66.
[57] Sched. 1, para. 2(1); References to Rating (Housing) Regulations 1990 (S.I. 1990 No. 434).
[58] Sched. 1, para. 2(2).
[59] Sched. 1, para. 3.
[60] Sched. 1, para. 3B.

Meaning of rent

exceed £1,000 a year in Greater London or £250 elsewhere.[61] The purpose of these provisions is primarily to exclude long leases at ground rents. The definition of "rent" for this purpose is as mentioned above in connection with the high rent exclusion.[62] This definition prevents a long lease becoming an assured tenancy where service charges, for example, take the rent above the relevant limits. It also prevents a landlord from being able to rely on the exclusion by artificially allocating parts of the rent to matters such as repairs, so that the "rent" appears to be below the relevant limits.

Business tenancies

A tenancy to which Part II of the Landlord and Tenant Act 1954 applies cannot be assured.[63] This exclusion is identical to that applying under the Rent Act 1977, which is fully discussed in Chapter 4.[64] The exclusion is less significant under the 1988 Act as market rents will be payable for both business and assured tenancies.

Tenancies of agricultural land

Where land exceeds two acres

A tenancy under which agricultural land[65] exceeding two acres is let together with the dwelling-house cannot be assured.[66] Such a tenancy may in any event be an agricultural holding or farm business tenancy and thereby excluded. We have already seen that section 2 of the 1988 Act excludes a tenancy under which a dwelling-house is let together with other land where the main purpose of the letting is not the provision of a home for the tenant.[67] Section 6, however, is subject to Schedule 1. Even where the main purpose of the letting is the provision of a home, the tenancy will, therefore, be excluded where the land is agricultural land exceeding two acres.

---

[61] Sched. 1, para. 3A; References to Rating (Housing) Regulations 1990 (S.I. 1990 No. 434). See Appendix, p. 278 (rent reduction clause to remove security).

[62] Sched. 1, para. 3C.

[63] *ibid.* para. 4. On-licensed premises have been brought within the 1954 Act by the Landlord and Tenant (Licensed Premises) Act 1990. Such tenancies are now excluded from assured status by Sched. 1, para. 4 of the Housing Act 1988, leaving para. 5 (exclusion of on-licensed premises) with no scope for operation.

[64] See above, p. 77.

[65] As defined in General Rate Act 1967, s. 26(3)(a).

[66] Housing Act 1988, Sched. 1, para. 6. This is based on Rent Act 1977, s. 26, above, p. 65.

[67] Above, p. 198.

Tenancies of agricultural holdings

A tenancy under which the dwelling-house is comprised in an agricultural holding (within the meaning of the Agricultural Holdings Act 1986) or a farm business tenancy under the Agricultural Tenancies Act 1995 and is occupied by the person responsible for the control (whether as tenant or as servant or agent of the tenant) of the farming of the holding cannot be assured.[68] This is identical to the exclusion in section 10 of the Rent Act 1977.[69] This exclusion, in contrast with the previous one, operates whether or not the land exceeds two acres.

Lettings to students

Institutional lettings

A tenancy which is granted to a person who is pursuing, or intends to pursue, a course of study provided by a specified educational institution and is so granted by that institution or by another specified institution (such as a registered housing association) or body of persons cannot be assured.[70] Such institutions must be specified by statutory instrument.[71] This is identical to section 8 of the Rent Act 1977, discussed in Chapter 4.[72] It will be noted that lettings by private landlords are not covered. Such a landlord may, however, let to an institution for subletting to students, as explained in Chapter 4.

Holiday lettings

A tenancy the purpose of which is to confer upon the tenant the right to occupy the dwelling-house for a holiday cannot be assured.[73] This is identical to section 9 of the Rent Act 1977, the problems of which are discussed in Chapter 4.[74]

Also excluded from Protection from Eviction Act 1977

It should be added that holiday lettings are now also excluded from the court order and notice to quit requirements of the Protection from Eviction Act 1977.[75]

---

[68] Housing Act 1988, Sched. 1, para. 7, as amended by the 1995 Act.
[69] See above, p. 75.
[70] Sched. 1, para. 8. See Appendix, p. 284 (sharing with non-student).
[71] Assured and Protected Tenancies (Lettings to Students) Regulations 1988 (S.I. 1988 No. 2236), as amended by S.I. 1989 No. 1628, S.I. 1990 No. 1825, S.I. 1991 No. 233, S.I. 1992 No. 515 and S.I. 1993 No. 2390.
[72] See above, p. 72.
[73] Sched. 1, para. 9.
[74] See above, p. 73.
[75] s. 3A, inserted by Housing Act 1988, s. 31, above, p. 51.

Resident landlords

Conditions

A tenancy which satisfies the conditions laid down by the Act in relation to lettings by resident landlords cannot be assured.[76] The conditions (broadly that the tenancy was granted by a person who lived in the building at the grant; that the landlord and his successors continued to live in the building at all times subsequently; and that the building is not a purpose-built block of flats) are closely modelled on the resident landlord provisions of the Rent Act 1977, which are fully explained in Chapter 5. In the account which follows, mention will be made of those aspects of the assured tenancy rules which are different from the protected tenancy rules. Income tax relief has already been mentioned.[77] As in the case of the Rent Act 1977, the resident landlord exception cannot be relied on in respect of a tenancy granted to a person who, immediately before[78] it was granted, had an assured tenancy of the same dwelling-house or of another dwelling-house in the same building, the landlord being the same.[79]

Cannot be granted to existing assured tenant

Periods of disregard

The "periods of disregard," dealing with a change in ownership of the landlord's interest, are the same as under the Rent Act 1977,[80] save that there is a specific provision relating to the situation where the interest is acquired by joint landlords, at least one of whom is an individual.[81] During the "period of disregard" no possession order may be made other than one based on an assured tenancy ground.[82] Failure to satisfy the conditions relating to the "period of disregard" will result in the acquisition by the tenant of assured tenancy status, assuming the tenancy otherwise satisfies the conditions of section 1 of the 1988 Act.

Joint landlords

The corresponding sections of the 1977 Act gave rise to difficulties with respect to joint landlords, because of the absence of any express provision. The matter was resolved by the decision in *Cooper v. Tait*,[83] holding that the satisfaction of the residence conditions by one of joint landlords sufficed. This is expressly confirmed by the 1988 Act.[84]

The resident landlord rules under the 1988 Act differ form the resident landlord rules under the 1977 Act in three significant respects. First, the landlord can only satisfy the

---

[76] Housing Act 1988, Sched. 1, para. 10.
[77] See above, p. 192.
[78] See *Dibbs v. Campbell* [1988] 30 E.G. 49, above, p. 140. See Appendix, p. 183.
[79] Sched. 1, para. 10(3).
[80] See above, p. 87. The 1988 provisions are set out in Part III of Sched. 1.
[81] *ibid.* para. 17(2).
[82] *ibid.* para. 21. This does not apply where the landlord's interest is vested in personal representatives.
[83] (1984) 271 E.G. 105.
[84] Sched. 1, para. 10(2).

**Must be
landlord's "only
or principal
home"**

residence requirements (at the grant and subsequently) if he occupies a dwelling in the same building as his "only or principal home."[85] Under the 1977 Act, the landlord merely had to "occupy as a residence," which imported the same requirement as under a statutory tenancy. This enabled a landlord to establish resident landlord status in respect of more than one home, which is not possible under the 1988 Act.

**No restricted
contract**

Secondly, the tenant of a resident landlord under the 1977 Act enjoyed the protection of a restricted contract.[86] As restricted contracts cannot be created after the commencement of the 1988 Act, a tenancy granted by a resident landlord after that date confers no protection at all.

**Protection from
Eviction Act 1977**

Thirdly, in the case of a tenancy granted after the commencement of the 1988 Act, the tenant is also excluded from the court order and notice to quit requirements of the Protection from Eviction Act 1977 if he shares accommodation with the landlord or a member of his family.[87] Of course, not all tenants of resident landlords share accommodation in this way. If they do not, the 1977 Act will apply.

Crown tenancies

A tenancy under which the interest of the landlord belongs to Her Majesty in right of the Crown or to a government department or is held in trust for Her Majesty for the purposes of a government department cannot be assured.[88]

**Crown Estate
Commissioners
and Duchies**

The exclusion does not extend to cases where the landlord's interest is under the management of the Crown Estate Commissioners,[89] nor where the landlord's interest belongs to the Duchies of Lancaster or Cornwall,[90] nor where the land is held by a health service body.[91] This is similar to the position under the Rent Act 1977. A tenancy which is initially assured will lose that status on transfer of the reversion to the Crown, and a tenancy can become assured on a transfer of the reversion by the Crown, even though initially excluded.

Local authority tenancies, etc.

A tenancy under which the interest of the landlord belongs to a local authority or to various other public bodies, such as

[85] *ibid.* para. 10(1)(b) and (c).
[86] See above, p. 80.
[87] Protection from Eviction Act 1977, s. 3A, inserted by Housing Act 1988, s. 31, above, p. 49.
[88] Housing Act 1988, Sched. 1, para. 11(1).
[89] *ibid.* para. 11(2).
[90] This is the effect of Housing Act 1988, s. 44.
[91] National Health Service and Community Care Act 1990, s. 60. For transitional provisions, see Sched. 8, para. 19.

fully mutual housing associations and housing action trusts,
cannot be assured.[92] There is a similar exception under the
Rent Act 1977,[93] although the excluded bodies are not
identical. Tenants of local authorities may enjoy security of
tenure under the secure tenancy code.

Transitional cases

A tenancy cannot be assured if it is a protected tenancy
under the Rent Act 1977, a housing association tenancy
within the meaning of Part VI of that Act, a secure tenancy
or a protected occupancy under the Rent (Agriculture) Act
1976.[94] With the exception of secure tenancies, most
tenancies within these categories will have been granted
before the commencement of the 1988 Act, and will be
accordingly excluded under the first heading of Schedule
1.[95]

Shared
ownership leases
Shared ownership leases[96] were excluded under the
Housing Bill, but the Act contains no such exclusion (save
that such leases granted by local authorities will be excluded
under that heading). Such leases are excluded from the Rent
Act 1977 in order to prevent the Rent Act system of rent
control from applying. As there is no comparable system for
assured tenancies, the reason for the exclusion is
inapplicable.

Finally, although not listed in Schedule 1, a tenancy
granted by a private landlord pursuant to an arrangement
Homeless
persons
with a local authority for the accommodation of a homeless
person cannot be assured.[97]

Implied terms of assured tenancies

Assignment and
subletting
The most significant implied term relates to assignment and
subletting. Section 15 of the 1988 Act applies to assured
periodic tenancies only, and implies a term that the tenant
shall not assign (in whole or in part) or sublet or part with
the possession of the whole or any part of the dwelling-
house without the consent of the landlord. Section 19 of the
Landlord and Tenant Act 1927 (implying that the

---

[92] Sched. 1, para. 12. See, further, Bridge, *Guide to the Housing Act 1988*
      (1989), p. 25.
[93] See above, p. 76.
[94] Sched. 1, para. 13.
[95] See above, p. 200.
[96] See above, p. 68.
[97] s. 1(6).

landlord's consent shall not be unreasonably withheld) does *not* apply to this implied term. One consequence of this is that the duties imposed on landlords by the Landlord and Tenant Act 1988 will not apply either.

Exceptions

Express terms

By way of exception, no such term is implied under section 15 in the case of a periodic tenancy which is not a statutory periodic tenancy[98] or an assured periodic tenancy arising under Schedule 10 of the Local Government and Housing Act 1989[99] if there is a provision (whether contained in the tenancy or not) under which the tenant is either prohibited (absolutely or conditionally) from assigning, subletting or parting with possession or is permitted to do so (absolutely or conditionally).[1] In other words, no term is implied where the acts in question are either expressly permitted or prohibited. In the case of an *express* conditional prohibition, section 19 of the 1927 Act will apply. Nor is there an implied term under section 15 in the case of a periodic tenancy (not being a statutory periodic

Premiums

tenancy) where a premium is required on the grant or renewal of the tenancy.[2] The general rule, therefore, is that the term is implied in the case of all statutory periodic tenancies arising on termination of fixed-term assured tenancies, and in the case of an assured tenancy which is initially periodic, where there is neither an express term nor a premium obligation.

Fixed terms

Section 15 does not apply to a fixed-term tenancy. In such a case the tenant may assign or sublet unless he has covenanted not to do so. In the case of a conditional covenant (*i.e.* against assignment, etc. without consent), section 19 of the 1927 Act will apply. Mention should also be made of the court's power to order a transfer of an assured tenancy on divorce.[3]

Children Act 1989

There is also jurisdiction under the Children Act 1989 to order a parent (whether married or unmarried) to transfer "property", which can include an assured tenancy, to the other parent, for the benefit of the child.[4]

It might be added that the exchange of tenancies between secure and assured tenants is possible where the assured

[98] See below, p. 210.
[99] *i.e.* on termination of a long residential tenancy; s. 15(3) as amended by Sched. 11, para. 102 of the 1989 Act.
[1] s. 15(3)(a).
[2] s. 15(3)(b). "Premium" is defined in s. 15(4) as a fine or like sum, any other pecuniary consideration in addition to rent, and any deposit exceeding one-sixth of the annual rent.
[3] Matrimonial Homes Act 1983, Sched. 1, as amended by Housing Act 1988, Sched. 17, para. 34. The jurisdiction extends to nullity and judicial separation. See also the Family Homes and Domestic Violence Bill 1995 (cohabitants).
[4] s. 15 and Sched. 1, para. 1 of the 1989 Act; above, p. 110. See *K. v. K.* [1992] 1 W.L.R. 530 (secure tenancy); *B. v. B. (Transfer of Tenancy)* (1994) 24 Fam. Law 250 (secure tenancy); *Pearson v. Franklin* [1994] 1 W.L.R. 370 (housing association tenancy).

tenant's landlord is a body such as the Housing Corporation or a registered housing association.[5]

The second implied term arises under section 16, which applies to all assured tenancies. This is to the effect that the tenant shall afford the landlord access to the dwelling-house and all reasonable facilities for executing therein any repair which the landlord is entitled to execute.[6]

Access for repairs

Security of tenure

An assured tenancy (which term includes an assured shorthold tenancy) can only be brought to an end in the manner authorised by the Act. Although there is no express provision, it is clear from the mandatory wording of section 5 that the parties cannot contract out of the security regime. In this respect the provisions are similar to those of the Rent Act 1977.[7]

No contracting out

Section 5 contains the scheme for security of tenure, and draws a distinction between periodic tenancies and fixed term tenancies. In the case of a periodic tenancy, it is provided that "the service by the landlord of a notice to quit shall be of no effect."[8] If a landlord purports to end an assured tenancy by notice to quit the tenancy still exists. An evicted tenant is entitled to be reinstated, although if the property has been re-let he will have to join the new tenant as a party to the proceedings.[9] A periodic assured tenancy can be terminated either by a *tenant*'s notice to quit[10] or by a court order based on a ground for possession. The grounds and the procedure for invoking them are explained in Chapter 13. It will be noted that the Rent Act concept of the statutory tenancy has no application here. The situation bears more resemblance to the business tenancy regime, in that the tenant's legal estate (or equitable interest) is prolonged until the termination procedure is complied with. Although the landlord does not need to serve a notice to quit, he must serve notice of proceedings under section 8. This is explained in Chapter 13.[11] Of course, if the tenancy ceases to be assured (for example where the tenant ceases to occupy as his only or principal home), the landlord may terminate it under the general law by notice to quit.

Periodic tenancies

Fixed terms

Where the assured tenancy is for a fixed term, it may be

[5] Housing Act 1985, s. 92, as amended by Local Government and Housing Act 1989, s. 163.
[6] See also Sched. 2, Ground 6: below, p. 234. The landlord's repair obligations were increased by Housing Act 1988, s. 116, applying to periodic tenancies and fixed terms under seven years.
[7] See *Appleton v. Aspin* [1988] 1 W.L.R. 410, above p. 57.
[8] s. 5(1).
[9] *Love v. Herrity* (1991) 23 H.L.R. 217.
[10] See below, p. 226 (where the anti-avoidance provisions of s. 5(5) are discussed).
[11] See below, p. 227.

ended by "surrender or other action on the part of the tenant."[12] As far as termination by the landlord is concerned, an assured tenancy cannot be brought to an end except by a court order based on a ground for possession or, "in the case of a fixed term tenancy which contains power for the landlord to determine the tenancy in certain circumstances, by exercise of that power."[13] An assured tenancy, may, therefore, be terminated by the exercise of a

Break clause

break clause, but, as is explained below, a statutory periodic tenancy will then arise (unless the break clause has been operated by the tenant). The reference to ending the

Forfeiture

tenancy by exercise of a landlord's power to determine it does not include forfeiture,[14] but a landlord who has grounds for forfeiture may be able to invoke an appropriate ground. Only certain grounds, however, are available during the currency of a fixed term, and the terms of the tenancy must make provision for it to be terminated on the ground in question (whether by forfeiture or otherwise).[15] The drafting of section 7(6) is obscure. It is not clear whether a standard forfeiture clause will suffice to enable reliance on the relevant grounds or whether the clause must refer specifically to the grounds in question. It has been assumed in the county court that a standard clause suffices even in the case of mandatory ground 8.[16] The better view is that while a standard clause may suffice for reliance on the discretionary grounds, the clause should refer specifically to those mandatory grounds (2 and 8) which can operate during a fixed term, and cautious drafting will include specific reference to all available grounds in the forfeiture clause.[17] A stricter view was taken in the county court in *McDonald v. Tipping*,[18] where a landlord was unable to invoke discretionary grounds 10 and 11 where a standard forfeiture clause did not refer to them. Moreover, the interaction of sections 5(1), 7(6), 20(1) (shortholds) and 45(4) is not free from doubt, and amending legislation may be necessary to clarify the matter.[19] It seems, then, that the concept of forfeiture as such does not apply to assured tenancies. Hence a notice under section 146 of the Law of Property Act 1925 would be ineffective, and relief from forfeiture is inapplicable.[20] The contrary view was taken in

---

[12] s. 5(2). Anti-avoidance provisions are contained in s. 5(5): below, p. 226.
[13] s. 5(1).
[14] s. 45(4) provides that any reference (however expressed) to a power for a landlord to determine a tenancy does not include a reference to a power of re-entry or forfeiture for breach of any term or condition of the tenancy.
[15] s. 7(6): below, p. 226. The applicable grounds are 2, 8 and 10 to 15.
[16] *Patel v. Sullivan*, June 8, 1991, noted (1991) *Legal Action*, September, p. 17.
[17] See (1989) 139 N.L.J. 326 and (1991) 135 Sol. Jo. 728 (C. Rodgers).
[18] November 20, 1991, noted (1992) *Legal Action*, March, p. 14.
[19] See correspondence in (1989) 139 N.L.J. 104, 160 and 326.
[20] (1989) 139 N.L.J. 376 (P. Wilde); *cf.* p. 252 (F. Webb).

the county court in *Patel v. Sullivan*,[21] where it was held that the tenant in a rent arrears case was entitled to relief from forfeiture under section 138 of the County Courts Act 1984 even though the requirements of mandatory ground 8 were satisfied. It is submitted that this is incorrect.[22]

Statutory periodic tenancy

Where a fixed term assured tenancy ends other than by court order or by "surrender or other action on the part of the tenant," the tenant is entitled to remain in possession as a statutory periodic tenant.[23] This will occur, for example, where the tenancy ends by effluxion of time or, as mentioned above, by a break clause operated by the landlord. No statutory periodic tenancy will arise, however, where another tenancy of the same or substantially the same dwelling-house is granted to the tenant on the coming to an end of the fixed term.[24]

This statutory periodic tenancy can only be ended by an act of the tenant or by a court order based on a ground for possession. It is not the same concept as the Rent Act statutory tenancy, but bears some resemblance to the secure tenancy regime, under which a periodic tenancy arises on termination of a fixed-term secure tenancy.[25]

Reversionary tenancies

Where the statutory periodic tenancy (or other periodic assured tenancy) continues beyond the commencement of a reversionary tenancy granted so as to begin on or after the expiry of a fixed term assured tenancy or a date when a periodic tenancy could have been ended (apart from the Act) by notice to quit, the reversionary tenancy takes effect as it had been granted subject to the periodic tenancy.[26]

Terms of statutory periodic tenancy

Where a statutory periodic tenancy arises under section 5, it takes effect in possession immediately on the coming to an end of the fixed term. It is deemed to have been granted by the person who was landlord immediately before the end of the fixed term. The premises are the same as under the fixed term, and the periods of the tenancy are the same as those for which rent was last payable under the fixed term. The other terms (for example, rent) are the same as those of the fixed term immediately before it ended, save that any term providing for determination[27] by the landlord or tenant shall not have effect while the tenancy remains assured.[28]

Assignment and subletting

We have already seen that section 15 implies a prohibition against assignment or subletting without consent into a periodic assured tenancy.[29] This term, in the case of a

---

[21] Above.
[22] See [1994] 05 E.G. 144 (R. Smith), contrasting the wording of s. 82(4) of the Housing Act 1985, which expressly provides that Law of Property Act 1925, s. 146, applies to secure tenancies.
[23] s. 5(2).
[24] s. 5(4).
[25] Housing Act 1985, s. 86.
[26] Housing Act 1988, s. 18(3).
[27] By s. 45(4), this does not refer to forfeiture. An example would be a break clause.
[28] s. 5(3).
[29] See above, p. 206.

statutory periodic tenancy, is not subject to section 19 of the Landlord and Tenant Act 1927 (implying that consent shall not be unreasonably withheld). As explained under the next heading, the Act provides a procedure for varying the terms of a statutory periodic tenancy. The position as to rent increases is dealt with in Chapter 14.

Variation of the terms of a statutory periodic tenancy

Variation within first year
Section 6 provides a mechanism for either party to seek a variation of the terms within the first year of the statutory periodic tenancy. As indicated above, the terms of the statutory periodic tenancy are broadly those of the preceding fixed term tenancy. Section 6 applies to these implied terms[30] with the exception of rent, which is dealt with separately under section 13.[31]

Procedure
Not later than the first anniversary of the ending of the prior fixed term tenancy, either party may serve upon the other a notice in prescribed form[32] proposing different terms and, if appropriate, an adjustment of the rent to take account of the proposed terms.[33]

Reference to rent assessment committee
Within three months of the date of service, the recipient may, by an application in prescribed form,[34] refer the notice to the rent assessment committee. If this is not done, the proposed terms (and any proposed rent adjustment) take effect from such date as is specified in the notice (not falling within the period of three months from the date of service).[35]

Determination by committee
Where a notice is referred to the rent assessment committee, it must consider the proposed terms and determine whether those terms or some other terms (dealing with the same subject matter) might reasonably be expected in an assured periodic tenancy of the dwelling-house in question, on the assumption that this tenancy begins on the ending of the former tenancy and is granted by a willing landlord on the terms of the statutory periodic tenancy (except those sought to be varied).[36] The committee may **Rent adjustment** specify a rent adjustment (up or down) to take account of any variation whether or not such an adjustment is proposed in the notice.[37] In making a determination of the terms or

---

[30] Implied by s. 5(3); *i.e.* terms other than those relating to the extent of the dwelling-house and the periods of the tenancy: s. 6(1)(b).
[31] See below, p. 250.
[32] Assured Tenancies and Agricultural Occupancies (Forms) Regulations 1988 (S.I. 1988 No. 2203) (Form No. 1), as amended by Assured Tenancies and Agricultural Occupancies (Forms) (Amendment) Regulations 1993 (S.I. 1993 No. 654).
[33] s. 6(2).
[34] See n. 32, above. The appropriate form is Form No. 2.
[35] s. 6(3).
[36] s. 6(4).
[37] s. 6(5).

specifying a rent adjustment, the committee must disregard any effect on the terms or the amount of rent attributable to the granting of a tenancy to a sitting tenant.[38]

Effective date

Where the terms are varied and where any rent adjustment is specified by the committee, the new provisions take effect (unless the parties otherwise agree) from such date as the committee may direct. As far as any rent adjustment is concerned, the committee must not direct a date earlier than the date specified in the notice referred to them.[39]

Discontinuance

The committee is not obliged to continue with the determination if the tenancy has ended or if the landlord and tenant give written notice that they no longer require such a determination.[40] There is no appeal from the committee's determination, but judicial review would be available in the case of mistake of law.

Where rent increase also referred

As will be seen in Chapter 14, there is a procedure for referring the determination of a rent increase to the rent assessment committee. Where such a reference is being heard at the same time as the section 6 reference, the committee must determine the terms under section 6 before determining the rent.[41]

Section 6 thus provides an additional role for rent assessment committees.[42] If an analogy may be drawn with business tenancies, a party proposing more onerous terms will not necessarily be able to justify them simply by offering a rent reduction.[43]

Succession to assured tenancies

Periodic tenancies

A limited opportunity for succession is provided by section 17 of the 1988 Act, which applies to assured periodic tenancies only. On the death of a sole[44] tenant under such a tenancy, the tenancy vests in the tenant's spouse, provided the spouse was occupying the dwelling-house as his or her only or principal home immediately before the death.

One succession only

There can be only one succession, because no succession can occur if the tenant was himself a successor within the meaning of the section. There are five situations in which the deceased tenant is regarded as a successor for this purpose.[45]

(a) Where the deceased tenant was himself a successor to the tenancy under section 17. In other words, where the

---

[38] s. 6(6).
[39] s. 6(7).
[40] s. 6(8).
[41] s. 14(6), below, p. 254.
[42] See (1988) 138 N.L.J. 75 (M. Partington), doubting whether they are equipped for the role.
[43] See *O'May v. City of London Real Property Co. Ltd* [1983] 2 A.C. 726; [1988] 44 E.G. 28 (R. Smith).
[44] On the death of a joint tenant, the other joint tenant will take by survivorship. As explained below, no further succession will be possible.
[45] s. 17(2), (3).

deceased tenant was the spouse[46] of the original tenant and subsequently remarried.[47] The second spouse cannot claim.

Inherited tenancy

(b) Where the deceased tenant acquired the tenancy under the will or intestacy of a previous tenant. As explained in Chapter 13, the landlord has a mandatory ground for possession on the death of an assured periodic tenant.[48] No such ground is available in the case of a fixed term. If the beneficiary who acquires the fixed term[49] satisfies the assured tenancy requirements (for example as to occupation as his only or principal home), he will qualify as an assured tenant and will normally acquire a statutory periodic tenancy on termination of the fixed term. On his death, however, no succession is possible under section 17.

Joint tenancy

(c) Where the deceased tenant became sole tenant by virtue of being the survivor of joint tenants.[50]

Rent Act successor

(d) Where the deceased tenant acquired the assured periodic tenancy as successor to a Rent Act tenant dying after the commencement of 1988 Act.[51]

New grant to successor

(e) Where the deceased tenant was a successor within any of the above four categories and was subsequently granted (alone or jointly with others) a new tenancy of the same or substantially the same dwelling-house, having been tenant (alone or jointly with others) of the dwelling-house let under the new tenancy (or of a dwelling-house which is substantially the same as that dwelling-house) at all times since he became a successor.

Spouse or cohabitant

As indicated above, the only person who can succeed to the tenancy under section 17 is the tenant's spouse. "Spouse" has an extended meaning here, and includes a person living with the tenant as his or her wife or husband.[52] As suggested in Chapter 8,[53] it would seem that the test of living together as husband and wife is easier to satisfy than the test of being a member of the tenant's family, which had to be satisfied by cohabiting couples in the context of succession to a Rent Act tenancy in the case of a death prior

---

[46] As defined below.

[47] Or cohabited: see below. Where the successor remarries but subsequently divorces, the spouse is deemed to be a successor if the court orders the transfer of the tenancy, thus no further succession is possible; Matrimonial Homes Act 1983, Sched. 1, para. 2. Similarly on transfer to a cohabitant under the Family Homes and Domestic Violence Bill.

[48] Ground 7: below, p. 237.

[49] Similarly in the case of a periodic tenancy where the landlord does not invoke Ground 7.

[50] See *Bassetlaw D.C. v. Renshaw* [1992] 1 All E.R. 925.

[51] s. 39(5): above, p. 147.

[52] s. 17(4).

[53] See above, p. 145. See also *Tuck v. Nicholls* (1989) 19 Fam. Law 103 (whether cohabitation for two nights sufficed for the purposes of the Domestic Violence and Matrimonial Proceedings Act 1976); *City of Westminster v. Peart* (1992) 24 H.L.R. 389.

to the commencement of the 1988 Act. It appears, however, that the survivor of a homosexual couple will not qualify as a successor.[54]

More than one claimant

Where there is more than one "spouse" as defined above (*e.g.* where there is a lawful spouse and a cohabitant, or two cohabitants), only one can be the successor. This may be decided by agreement, failing which the county court will decide the matter.[55] Such cases will be rare, as both claimants must have been occupying the dwelling-house as their only or principal home.[56]

Ground for possession not available

Where there is a successor, the assured tenancy does not devolve under the tenant's will or intestacy.[57] This, therefore, avoids the difficulty of the tenancy "going into abeyance" during the period of the successor's entitlement, as can occur under the Rent Act 1977.[58] It also means that Ground 7[59] is not available. It will, however, be available on the death of the successor.

Where no successor

Where there is no successor, the landlord may seek possession (in the case of a periodic tenancy) under Ground 7. If, on the other hand, there is nobody in occupation, possession may be recovered without recourse to Ground 7, as there is no longer an assured tenancy. In the case of a fixed term, neither Ground 7 nor the succession rule applies. The tenancy will devolve under the tenant's will or intestacy, and will continue to be assured if the beneficiary satisfies the conditions of section 1.[60]

Finally, greater succession rights are available in the case of housing association tenancies.[61]

Sub-tenants

The assured tenancy regime applies between tenant and sub-tenant in the same way as between landlord and tenant.[62] The question considered here, however, is whether an assured tenant who is a sub-tenant has any rights against the head landlord. Sub-tenants have certain rights at common law on termination of the mesne tenancy.[63] In addition, they are given some protection by section 18 of the 1988 Act. The provisions of section 18 are much simpler than the corresponding provisions of the Rent Act 1977.[64]

Rights against head landlord

[54] *Harrogate B.C. v. Simpson* (1985) 17 H.L.R. 205; above, p. 145.
[55] s. 17(5).
[56] There is no requirement that the spouse must have been living *with* the tenant, although clearly this is required in the "living together" category.
[57] s. 17(1).
[58] See above, p. 150.
[59] See below, p. 237.
[60] See below, p. 238.
[61] See the Model Tenancy Agreement issued by the National Federation of Housing Associations.
[62] Housing Act 1988, s. 45(1).
[63] See above, p. 155.
[64] See above, Chap. 9.

Section 18 provides that if a dwelling-house is for the time being lawfully let on an assured tenancy, and the landlord under the assured tenancy is himself a tenant under a superior tenancy, and the superior tenancy comes to an end, then the assured tenancy continues as a tenancy held of the person whose interest would, apart from the continuance of the assured tenancy, entitle him to actual possession of the dwelling-house.[65] In other words, the sub-tenant becomes assured tenant of the superior landlord. This does not occur

No rights in certain cases where the landlord's interest is such that the tenancy could not be assured.[66] This will be the case, for example, where the superior landlord is the Crown, a local authority[67] or a resident landlord. A further exception arises in the case of an assured sub-tenancy derived from a long residential lease extended under the Leasehold Reform, Housing and Urban Development Act 1993. Such a sub-tenant has no security on termination of the head lease.[68]

In order for section 18 to apply, the sub-tenant must be an assured tenant, but the mesne landlord need not be.[69] Indeed, if the whole is sublet, the mesne tenant, being out of occupation, could not be assured. If it was a subletting of part, the mesne tenant remaining in occupation, the sub-tenancy would not be assured because of the resident landlord rule.[70]

Lawful sub-letting As under the Rent Act provisions, the sub-tenancy must be lawful, *i.e.* not granted in breach of a covenant against sub-letting.[71] There is no restriction in the section upon the manner in which the superior tenancy has terminated.

Grounds for possession Although there is no express provision, it would appear that the head landlord can rely upon any notices previously given by the tenant to the sub-tenant in connection with the availability of certain grounds (*e.g.* Ground 1).[72] It is clear that such notices can be relied upon by successor landlords,[73] provided they satisfy the conditions.

The protection of section 18 appears more substantial than that of section 137 of the Rent Act 1977. We saw in Chapter 9 that the sub-tenant's protection was limited

---

[65] s. 18(1).

[66] s. 18(2).

[67] See *Basingstoke and Deane Borough Council v. Paice, The Times*, April 3, 1995, where a Rent Act sub-tenant of part became secure tenant of the landlord on surrender of the head lease. This would appear applicable to assured sublettings.

[68] s. 59(2)(c) of the 1993 Act.

[69] The head tenancy must, of course, include a dwelling-house, otherwise the sub-tenancy could not be assured. For the position where the head tenant was an assured shorthold tenant, see (1989) 139 N.L.J. 228 (F. Webb).

[70] See above, p. 204.

[71] See above, p. 157. Where the mesne tenant is an assured tenant, such a covenant may be implied under s. 15: above, p. 206. For difficulties as to the application of the Protection from Eviction Act 1977 to an unlawful subtenant, see above, p. 158.

[72] See below, p. 229.

[73] See Sched. 2, Ground 1, para. (b).

because grounds available against the tenant were held
available against the sub-tenant also.[74] It does not seem that
this could be the case under section 18, because, as
mentioned above, it is difficult to envisage a case where both
the mesne tenant and the sub-tenant have assured status.
Where the mesne tenant is a Rent Act tenant who sublets on
an assured tenancy after the Housing Act 1988, section 137
of the 1977 Act cannot operate, but section 18 of the 1988
Act presumably applies.[75]

[74] See above, p. 162.
[75] See above, p. 169.

12 ASSURED SHORTHOLD TENANCIES

Introduction As an alternative to the assured tenancy, the Housing Act 1988 introduced the assured shorthold tenancy.[1] The characteristic of such a tenancy is that the landlord may recover possession more easily than is necessarily the case with an assured tenancy, but that there is a greater degree of rent control in comparison with an assured tenancy. This element of increased rent control is not, however, such that a landlord would be deterred from granting an assured shorthold tenancy.

The assured shorthold tenancy is loosely based on the protected shorthold tenancy under the Rent Act 1977 (introduced by the Housing Act 1980), but is different in significant respects. In particular, the procedure for recovery of possession is less complex.

This Chapter will deal with the definition of the assured **Rent control** shorthold tenancy and recovery of possession. Rent control will be dealt with in Chapter 14.

Qualifying conditions

An assured shorthold tenancy is a tenancy granted on or after the commencement of the Housing Act 1988[2] which satisfies the requirements of section 20(1) of the 1988 Act.
Assured tenancy The tenancy must be within the definition of an assured tenancy, as explained in Chapter 11, and must satisfy three additional requirements:

Further   (a)   it is a fixed-term tenancy[3] granted for a term certain of
conditions   not less than six months[4]; and
      (b)   the landlord has no power to determine the tenancy at

---

[1] See generally (1989) 86 L.S. Gaz. No. 12, p. 34 (C.P. Rodgers); [1994] 05 E.G. 144 (R. Smith). For precedents, see Appendix, pp. 262, 266.

[2] Sched. 1, para. 1.

[3] Meaning any tenancy other than a periodic tenancy: *ibid.* s. 45(1). "Tenancy" includes an agreement for a tenancy. It is doubtful whether the word "granted" provides a contrary context here: *cf.* Rodgers, *Housing: The New Law* (1988) p. 42.

[4] Unlike protected shorthold tenancies, there is no maximum duration. See *Bedding v. McCarthy* (1995) 27 H.L.R. 103, below, p. 219, holding that a term a few hours short of six months was a term of six months.

any time earlier than six months from the beginning[5] of the tenancy; and

(c) a notice was served by the prospective landlord[6] on the prospective tenant before the assured tenancy was entered into, in such form as may be prescribed, stating that the tenancy was to be a shorthold tenancy.[7]

Rights of re-entry

As far as the power to determine under condition (b) is concerned, this does not include a power of re-entry or forfeiture for breach of any term or condition of the tenancy.[8] Thus the usual forfeiture clause will not prevent the tenancy from qualifying as an assured shorthold tenancy. The forfeiture clause cannot actually be operated, but its presence may enable the landlord to invoke certain grounds for possession during the fixed term.[9] Clearly a break clause which the landlord could operate within the six-month period would infringe the condition, although a tenant's break clause would not have this effect. Where a landlord's break clause can be operated after the first six months, presumably its operation will give rise to an assured shorthold statutory periodic tenancy.[10] It has been suggested that if the landlord's mortgagee has agreed to the creation of a shorthold tenancy which is to contain provisions enabling recovery of possession on the basis of Ground 2 (mortgagee exercising power of sale requires possession), the tenancy will not in fact be shorthold because the possibility of default by the landlord within the first six months means that section 20(1)(b) is not satisfied.[11] To avoid this problem the right to possession within the first six months should be excluded.

Prior notice

The court has no power to dispense with the landlord's obligation under section 20 to serve a shorthold notice before the grant of the tenancy. Failure to comply means

---

[5] This refers to the day on which the tenancy is entered into or, if later, the day on which, under the terms of any lease, agreement or other document, the tenant is entitled to possession: Housing Act 1988, s. 45(2). Where a lease is expressed to commence from a date already past, no part of the period before the date on which the tenancy is entered into can, therefore, be taken into account in calculating the six-month period under condition (b).

[6] Or by at least one of joint landlords: Housing Act 1988, s. 20(6).

[7] Housing Act 1988, s. 20(2); Assured Tenancies and Agricultural Occupancies (Forms) Regulations 1988 (S.I. 1988 No. 2203) (Form No. 7), as amended by S.I. 1990 No. 1532 and S.I. 1993 No. 654. See Appendix, p. 270.

[8] Housing Act 1988, s. 45(4). Unlike protected shorthold tenancies, there is no power for the tenant to determine prematurely. It has been held, however, that a tenancy terminates where the tenant accepts repudiation by the landlord. See *Hussein v. Mehlman* [1992] 2 E.G.L.R. 87 (county court), where a three year assured shorthold tenancy ended on acceptance by the tenant of repudiation arising from the landlord's serious breaches of repair obligations.

[9] Housing Act 1988, ss. 5(1), 7(6); above, p. 209.

[10] See (1991) 135 Sol. Jo. 728 (C. Rodgers), discussing the relationship between ss. 5(2) (the statutory periodic tenancy), 7(6) and the shorthold provisions.

[11] See correspondence at [1994] 08 E.G. 50–51.

that a full assured tenancy is created, assuming the requirements of such a tenancy are otherwise satisfied. Use of an outdated prescribed form will have this effect, unless the old form can be regarded as "substantially to the like effect" as the current one.[12] In *Panayi v. Roberts*[13] a tenancy was granted in November 1990 for 12 months, to end in November 1991. By mistake, the prior notice under section 20 stated that the date of termination was May 1991. The prescribed form requires a specification of the dates of commencement and termination of the shorthold tenancy. It was held that the landlord's notice was not substantially to the same effect as required by the regulations. The mistake was not an obvious slip[14] (which would not have invalidated the notice), as a prospective tenant might have been unsure whether the term was for six months or a year. It did not matter whether or not the tenant had actually been misled.[15] Thus the tenant had been granted a full assured tenancy in November 1990. In fact it had been renewed for six months in November 1991, purportedly as a new assured shorthold, but the finding that the original tenancy was not a shorthold meant that the renewal could not take effect as a shorthold either.[16]

The point which arose in *Bedding v. McCarthy*[17] was whether the section 20 notice had been served on the prospective tenant before the tenancy was entered into, as required by section 20(2)(b). The tenant was given the notice on the morning of December 18, 1990. Later the same morning he entered into the tenancy agreement, which granted a tenancy for six months from December 18, 1990. In the afternoon he went into possession. The tenant claimed that he had a full assured tenancy either because his tenancy fell short of the required six months minimum by a few hours, or because a notice given on the same day as the grant was not given *before* it. The Court of Appeal held that the tenancy was an assured shorthold. In computing the term, no regard was paid to fractions of a day. The term, therefore, was for six months. Whether the notice had been given before the grant was a pure question of fact. It must be served before the tenancy was "entered into", which must

[12] See Assured Tenancies and Agricultural Occupancies (Forms) (Amendment) Regulations 1993 (S.I. 1993 No. 654), in force April 1, 1993, requiring a statement that if the rent includes a payment for council tax, any rent determined by a rent assessment committee will be inclusive of council tax.
[13] [1993] 2 E.G.L.R. 51; [1993] Conv. 301 (P. Smith). See also *London and Quadrant Housing Trust v. Robertson* (county court), noted (1991) *Legal Action*, September, p. 17; *Lomas v. Atkinson* (county court), noted (1993) *Legal Action*, September, p. 16.
[14] For example if the termination date had been specified as November 1891.
[15] *Tegerdine v. Brooks* (1977) 36 P.&C.R. 261.
[16] See s. 20(3) below.
[17] (1995) 27 H.L.R. 103. Clearly a tenancy granted for a period of six months from a date already past would not satisfy s. 20(1)(a).

not be confused with the time when, as a matter of law, it was deemed to commence. The tenancy was entered into when the agreement was signed, even though it was deemed to commence some hours earlier.

Exceptions

Anti-avoidance

As an anti-avoidance measure, section 20(3) of the 1988 Act provides that a tenancy cannot be an assured shorthold tenancy (even if it satisfies the above conditions), if it is granted to a person[18] who immediately before the grant was a tenant under an assured tenancy which was not shorthold, where the new tenancy is granted by the person who was the landlord under the previous assured tenancy.[19] This provision applies whether or not the new tenancy is of the same dwelling-house.

By analogy with the similar provisions relating to protected shorthold tenancies under the Rent Act 1977, section 20(3) will not apply where the previous assured tenancy has been effectively surrendered prior to the grant of the new tenancy.[20]

Assured shorthold where usual conditions not satisfied

There are three cases where an assured shorthold tenancy may exist even though the conditions set out in section 20(1) are not satisfied.

First, section 20(4) provides that where a new tenancy of the same or substantially the same premises comes into

Where prior assured shorthold

being on the termination of an assured shorthold tenancy, having the same landlord and tenant, then if and so long as the new tenancy is an assured tenancy, it shall be an assured shorthold tenancy whether or not it fulfils the conditions of section 20(1).

The expression "comes into being" covers the case of a new grant and the case where an assured shorthold tenancy

Statutory periodic tenancy

expires but the landlord does not seek possession, so that a statutory periodic tenancy arises (as explained below). The landlord will still be able to rely on the special ground for possession applicable to assured shorthold tenancies, as in the case of the previous tenancy. Section 20(4) does not, however, apply if the landlord[21] serves notice on the tenant before the new tenancy is entered into (or, in the case of a

[18] If granted to more than one person, at least one must have been an assured tenant immediately before the grant.
[19] See *Panayi v. Roberts* [1993] 2 E.G.L.R. 51.
[20] *Dibbs v. Campbell* [1988] 2 E.G.L.R. 122; above, p. 140. See Appendix, p. 283.
[21] Or one of joint landlords: Housing Act 1988, s. 20(6).

statutory periodic tenancy, takes effect in possession), stating that the new tenancy is not to be a shorthold tenancy.[22]

Transitional provisions   The second case concerns the transitional provisions. As a general rule, a protected tenancy may still be granted after the commencement of the 1988 Act in favour of a person who immediately before the grant was a protected or statutory tenant, where the new grant is by the landlord under that tenancy.[23] This provision does not apply where the previous protected or statutory tenancy was shorthold.[24] Where, because of the latter exception, a tenancy entered into on or after the commencement of the 1988 Act is an assured tenancy, but would have been a protected tenancy but for the exception relating to shortholds, the new tenancy is an assured shorthold tenancy even though it does not fulfil the conditions of section 20(1), unless the landlord serves notice on the tenant before it is entered into, stating that it is not to be a shorthold tenancy.[25] The transitional provisions do not apply to the situation where a protected shorthold tenancy is converted to a statutory tenancy after the commencement of the 1988 Act. The statutory tenancy is not "entered into" within section 34 but arises automatically. Thus the tenancy does not become an assured shorthold and remains a shorthold tenancy under the Rent Act 1977.[26]

Succession   The third exception relates to the succession rules applicable on the death of a protected or statutory tenant under the Rent Act 1977 after the commencement of the 1988 Act. As a general rule, a successor other than a spouse takes an assured periodic tenancy.[27] Where, however, the landlord might have recovered possession under Case 19 of the Rent Act 1977 (relating to protected shorthold tenancies) immediately before the death of the predecessor, then the assured periodic tenancy to which the successor becomes entitled shall be an assured shorthold tenancy, whether or not it fulfils the conditions of section 20(1).[28]

The significance of these exceptional cases is the availability to the landlord of the special ground for possession applicable to assured shorthold tenancies. He is, accordingly, no worse off than under the previous tenancy, which in all of the exceptional cases was either an assured shorthold or a protected shorthold tenancy and hence subject to the special ground under the Housing Act 1988 and the Rent Act 1977 respectively.

---

[22] *ibid.* s. 20(5). Where no such notice is served, the tenant may not appreciate that the tenancy is shorthold.
[23] *ibid.* s. 34(1).
[24] *ibid.* s. 34(2). Likewise where the previous tenancy was subject to Case 19 of the Rent Act 1977 although not currently shorthold.
[25] *ibid.* s. 34(3).
[26] *Ridehalgh v. Horsefield* (1992) 24 H.L.R. 453.
[27] Housing Act 1988, s. 39(5). See Chap. 8.
[28] *ibid.* s. 39(7).

Recovery of possession

General grounds available

As the assured shorthold tenancy is a sub-category of assured tenancy, the grounds for possession applicable to assured tenancies generally (discussed in Chapter 13) are available. In addition, the landlord may invoke the special mandatory ground in section 21 of the 1988 Act. Therein lies the incentive to the landlord to grant such a tenancy.[29]

Fixed terms

Section 21(1) provides that, on or after the coming to an end of an assured shorthold tenancy which was a fixed-term tenancy, the court shall make an order for possession if it is satisfied:

(a)   that the tenancy has ended and no further assured tenancy (whether shorthold or not) is currently in existence, other than an assured shorthold periodic tenancy (whether statutory or not)[30]; and

(b)   the landlord (or at least one of joint landlords) has given the tenant not less than two months' notice stating that he requires[31] possession.

The notice referred to above may be given on or before the day on which the tenancy comes to an end, even though a statutory periodic tenancy then arises.[32] Obviously the possession order cannot take effect before the end of the fixed term.

Any possession order made under section 21 operates to terminate any statutory periodic tenancy which has arisen on the coming to an end of the assured shorthold tenancy, without further notice and regardless of the period. The tenancy ends on the day on which the order takes effect.[33]

Periodic tenancy

Where the assured shorthold tenancy is a periodic tenancy, section 21(4) provides that the court shall make a possession order if satisfied:

(a)   that the landlord (or at least one of joint landlords) has given the tenant a notice[34] stating that, after a date specified in the notice, being the last day of a period of the tenancy and not earlier than two months after the date the notice was given, possession is required by virtue of section 21; and

---

[29] As amended by Local Government and Housing Act 1989, Sched. 11, para. 103.

[30] It is difficult to envisage a situation where a non-statutory assured shorthold periodic tenancy could follow a fixed term assured shorthold save under s. 20(4). It is doubtful whether a tenancy granted for a fixed term and thereafter on a periodic basis could qualify as a shorthold tenancy; (1993) 143 N.L.J. 1271 (N. Hickman).

[31] By analogy with Case 11 of the Rent Act 1977, there is no element of reasonableness: *Kennealy v. Dunne* [1977] 1 Q.B. 837; above, p. 129. The court has no discretion to stay or suspend the order: s. 9(6); below, p. 244.

[32] Housing Act 1988, s. 21(2). See Appendix, p. 272.

[33] *ibid*, s. 21(3).

[34] See Appendix, p. 274.

(b) that the specified date is not earlier than the earliest day
     on which, apart from section 5(1),[35] the tenancy could
     be ended by notice to quit given on the same date as the
     notice under (a) above.

Statutory periodic tenancy

This provision will apply, for example, where the fixed-
term shorthold tenancy has already expired and been
replaced by a statutory periodic tenancy, or where a
successor has taken an assured shorthold periodic tenancy
before service of the notice, as mentioned above.[36] It will be
appreciated that the two months' notice is a minimum
period. If, for example, the tenancy is quarterly, a quarter's
notice must be given under paragraph (b). Section 21(4)
thus requires compliance with the technical common law
rules concerning the validity of a notice to quit. Amendment
has been suggested, to simplify the requirements of the
subsection.[37] The notice does not, however, have to be in a
prescribed form. Nor does a landlord who invokes section
21 have to serve a notice of proceedings for possession
under section 8,[38] as section 21 provides a self-contained
code for assured shorthold tenancies.[39]

Accelerated possession procedure

A landlord who has complied with the requirements of
section 21 may take advantage of the accelerated possession
procedure applicable to assured shorthold tenancies and to
certain mandatory grounds for possession relating to assured
tenancies, which came into force on November 1, 1993.[40]
This procedure requires a court order but not a court
hearing, and was designed as a further encouragement to
assured shorthold (and other assured) lettings and to reduce
delay in recovering possession in cases where the court has
no discretion. It may be utilised only if there is no other
claim for relief (such as rent arrears) beyond possession and
costs, and is applicable to both fixed term and periodic
assured shorthold tenancies.

The landlord must make an affidavit application in
prescribed form,[41] attaching copies of the tenancy
agreement, the statutory notices and any other documents
necessary to prove his claim. Service on the tenant may be
effected only by the court. If the tenant wishes to oppose
the order he must file a reply within 14 days of service. If he
does not reply, the landlord may file a written request for a
possession order. The district judge will consider the

---

[35] Providing that an assured tenancy cannot be ended by a landlord's notice
     to quit.
[36] See above, p. 221.
[37] (1993) 143 N.L.J. 1271 (N. Hickman).
[38] Below, p. 227.
[39] *Panayi v. Roberts* [1993] 2 E.G.L.R. 51.
[40] County Court (Amendment No. 3) Rules 1993 (S.I. 1993 No. 2175);
     C.C.R. Ord. 49, r. 6A. See (1993) 90 L.S. Gaz. No. 42, p. 19 (P.
     Walter), suggesting a drafting error in r. 6A(9).
[41] County Court (Forms) (Amendment No. 2) Rules 1993 (S.I. 1993 No.
     2174).

application and any reply and will either make a possession order (and an order for fixed costs) or will fix a date for an oral hearing, with at least 14 days' notice to the parties. A possession order made without a hearing can be set aside or varied on the tenant's application made on notice within 14 days of service of the order, but this time limit can be extended by the court.

Homelessness   It should be added that, for the purposes of the housing legislation, a tenant who vacates without waiting for a court order may be considered to have made himself intentionally homeless.[42] On another point, a local authority can discharge its duty to house the unintentionally homeless by arranging for a landlord to grant an assured shorthold tenancy with an expectation of renewal.[43]

Where possession not sought   Obviously the landlord is not obliged to seek possession at the earliest opportunity. If he does not do so, a statutory periodic tenancy arises in the ordinary way on expiry of the fixed term assured shorthold tenancy, although the special ground for possession in section 21 continues to be available. If the tenant under an assured shorthold periodic tenancy dies, not being himself a successor, then presumably his spouse may succeed to the tenancy under section 17.[44] Again, the special ground for possession would continue to be available.

---

[42] *R. v. London Borough of Croydon, ex p. Jarvis* (1994) 26 H.L.R. 194, reviewing the authorities.
[43] *R. v. Wandsworth London Borough Council, ex p. Crookes*, *The Times*, April 12, 1995.
[44] See above, p. 212.

13 RECOVERY OF POSSESSION

The scheme of the Housing Act 1988 is broadly similar to that of the Rent Act 1977 in relation to regulated tenancies. The landlord may not recover possession from an assured tenant save by means of a court order based on a ground for possession.[1] A landlord's notice to quit is of no effect in relation to a periodic tenancy.[2] The grounds bear some resemblance to those operating under the Rent Act 1977, but several are new. Under the 1977 Act there are ten discretionary grounds (including suitable alternative accommodation) and 10 mandatory grounds.[3] Under the 1988 Act there are eight mandatory and eight discretionary grounds applicable to assured tenancies.[4] The emphasis is on the mandatory grounds, which are set out first, and which include some which are only discretionary under the Rent Act. In addition, there is the special mandatory ground applicable to assured shorthold tenancies, which was dealt with in Chapter 12.[5]

Ground for possession required

Mandatory and discretionary grounds

The landlord may, of course, recover possession on termination of the tenancy without a ground for possession if it has by then ceased to satisfy the definition of an assured tenancy, as where, for example, the tenant no longer occupies the dwelling-house as his only or principal home.[6] A court order will still be required in such cases under section 3 of the Protection from Eviction Act 1977, if there is any person lawfully residing at the premises.[7]

Tenancy no longer assured

It will be noted that section 5 of the 1988 Act only prevents the *landlord* from bringing an assured tenancy to an end without a court order. Unlike the position under the Rent Act 1977, a periodic assured tenancy may be terminated by a *tenant's* notice to quit.[8] A fixed-term assured tenancy may be terminated by "a surrender or other action

Tenant's notice to quit or surrender

---

[1] Housing Act 1988, ss. 5, 7. The decision in *Appleton v. Aspin* [1988] 1 W.L.R. 410, above, p. 111, would be equally applicable here. As to consent orders, see above, p. 138.

[2] *ibid.* s. 5(1); *Love v. Herrity* (1991) 23 H.L.R. 217.

[3] See above, Chap. 7.

[4] Housing Act 1988, Sched. 2.

[5] *ibid.* s. 21; above, p. 222.

[6] *ibid.* s. 1; above, p. 195.

[7] See above, p. 47.

[8] As in the case of a secure tenancy under Housing Act 1985. The 1988 Act does not displace the rule that one of joint tenants may terminate the tenancy by notice to quit: *Hammersmith and Fulham London Borough Council v. Monk* [1992] 1 A.C. 478. The requirements of the Protection from Eviction Act 1977, s. 3, should also be considered here.

Anti-avoidance

on the part of the tenant."[9] However, as an anti-avoidance measure, it is provided that if the prospective tenant enters into an obligation to do any act which would cause the tenancy to come to an end or executes any surrender, notice to quit or other document which would bring the tenancy to an end at a time when it is an assured tenancy, the obligation, surrender and so forth shall be of no effect if entered into or executed on or before the tenancy is entered into or, in the case of a statutory periodic tenancy, on or before it arises.[10] An act such as a surrender or notice to quit by the tenant is, therefore, effective only if voluntary.

Grounds during fixed term

In the case of fixed-term tenancy, certain of the grounds for possession may be utilised during the fixed term where the terms of the tenancy make provision for it to be brought to an end on the ground in question, for example by means of a forfeiture clause or a provision for determination by notice.[11] As explained in Chapter 11, an assured tenancy cannot be terminated by forfeiture, but the inclusion of a forfeiture clause may enable the landlord to invoke a ground for possession in circumstances where, apart from the 1988 Act, forfeiture would have been possible. Subject to this, a fixed term will normally be replaced by a statutory periodic tenancy on expiry, which may then be ended by any relevant ground for possession.

Statutory periodic tenancy also terminated

Where a fixed-term tenancy has come to an end, any possession order operates to terminate also any statutory periodic tenancy which has arisen under section 5, without any notice and regardless of the period of the tenancy. The statutory periodic tenancy ends on the day on which the order takes effect.[12]

Tenant's mortgagee

It might be added that the provisions of the 1988 Act do not restrict the right of a mortgagee to bring possession proceedings where the security is an assured tenancy.[13]

Housing associations

Housing Association landlords will rely only on mandatory ground 7 (death of tenant) and discretionary grounds 9, 10 and 12 to 14.[14] Of course some grounds, such as ground 1 (owner-occupier) could not be satisfied by Housing Associations. Of those grounds which could be

---

[9] Housing Act 1988, s. 5(2). See *Dibbs v. Campbell* [1988] 2 E.G.L.R. 122; [1989] Conv. 98 (S. Bridge); Appendix, p. 283.

[10] *ibid.* s. 5(5). This is similar to the protection afforded to business tenants by Landlord and Tenant Act 1954, s. 24(2). It has been suggested that a contractual provision to increase the rent above the market level could be within s. 5(5); *Blundell Memorial Lecture* (1989) (N. Madge and J. Wilson). This seems doubtful.

[11] *ibid.* s. 7(6), referring to mandatory grounds 2 (mortgagee's power of sale) and 8 (three months' rent arrears) and the discretionary grounds other than 9 (suitable alternative accommodation) and 16 (employee). See above, p. 209.

[12] *ibid.* s. 7(7).

[13] *ibid.* s. 7(1). As to the mortgagee's position where the landlord's interest is the security, see Ground 2, below, p. 231.

[14] See the Model Tenancy Agreement issued by the National Federation of Housing Associations.

invoked by such landlords but will not be, most significant are ground 8, the mandatory ground relating to unpaid rent, and ground 11, the discretionary ground relating to persistent delay in paying rent.

Finally, there is a restriction on the grounds for possession applicable to assured periodic tenancies arising on the termination of long residential leases.[15]

Procedure for recovery of possession

Notice of proceedings

Dispensing power

In order to recover possession by means of a court order based on the various grounds for possession, the landlord[16] must first have served the appropriate notice under section 8 of the 1988 Act and must have begun proceedings within the relevant time limits. The court may dispense with the notice requirement if it considers it just and equitable to do so.[17] A similar provision applies in relation to notices under certain of the Rent Act grounds, for example, Case 11 (the owner-occupier ground). Authorities on the 1977 Act may afford some guidance, although arising in a different context.[18] The dispensing power does not apply where possession is sought on the basis of Ground 8 (three months' rent arrears).[19]

Ground stated in notice

Contents of notice

The ground (or grounds) which the landlord seeks to rely on, plus particulars,[20] must be specified in the notice, but the specified grounds may be altered or added to with the leave of the court.[21]

The notice must be in the prescribed form,[22] and must inform the tenant of three things:

(a) that the landlord intends to begin proceedings for possession on one or more of the grounds specified in the notice; and

Two-week rule

(b) that proceedings will not begin earlier than a date specified in the notice, which (subject to further limitations mentioned below) shall not be earlier than the expiry of two weeks from the date of service of the notice; and

(c) that proceedings will not begin later than 12 months from the service of the notice.[23]

---

[15] Housing Act 1988, s. 7(5A), inserted by Local Government and Housing Act 1989, Sched. 11, para. 101.
[16] Or at least one of joint landlords: s. 8(1)(a).
[17] s. 8(1)(b).
[18] See above, p. 130. A similar dispensing power exists in relation to protected shorthold tenancies: above, p. 79.
[19] s. 8(5).
[20] *i.e.* the amount owing in arrears cases: *Torridge D.C. v. Jones* (1985) 18 H.L.R. 107.
[21] s. 8(2).
[22] Assured Tenancies and Agricultural Occupancies (Forms) Regulations 1988 (S.I. 1988 No. 2203) (Form No. 3).
[23] s. 8(3).

Longer notice for certain grounds

The further limitations referred to in (b) above apply where the notice specifies any of the following grounds (whether with or without other grounds): Ground 1 (owner-occupier), Ground 2 (mortgagee's power of sale), Ground 5 (occupation required for minister of religion), Ground 6 (intention to demolish or reconstruct), Ground 7 (death of tenant), Ground 9 (suitable alternative accommodation) and Ground 16 (employee). In such cases the date specified in the landlord's notice must not be earlier than two months

Minimum two-month period

from the date of service of the notice, and, in the case of a periodic tenancy, must not be earlier than the earliest date on which the tenancy (but for section 5) could have been ended by notice to quit given by the landlord on the same date as the service of the notice.[24] It seems that, provided the

No notice to quit needed

landlord complies with the above procedure, no common law notice to quit is necessary in the case of a periodic tenancy.[25]

Fixed terms

In the case of a fixed-term tenancy, if the notice is served during the term or after it ends but in reliance upon events during the fixed term, then the notice has effect, notwithstanding that the tenant becomes or has become a statutory periodic tenant on termination of the fixed term.[26]

Accelerated possession procedure

The accelerated possession procedure applicable to assured shorthold tenancies applies also to the recovery of possession from assured tenants on the basis of mandatory grounds 1, 3, 4 and 5. This procedure, which is fully explained in Chapter 12,[27] enables a court order to be granted without a hearing, provided no other relief is claimed (such as rent arrears) beyond possession and costs.

Validity of notice

The requirements of the section 8 notice were fully examined by the Court of Appeal in *Mountain v. Hastings*.[28] The landlord, seeking to recover possession in the basis of Ground 8 (three months' rent arrears) and other grounds, served a notice which did not set out the full text of Ground 8 but merely stated "At least three months' rent is unpaid." Particulars were added as to the amount of the arrears and the last date of payment. The issue was whether this notice satisfied section 8, which requires the notice to be in prescribed form or "substantially to the same effect." It was held that the notice was invalid, and therefore there was no jurisdiction to make a possession order. A notice under section 8 need not use the exact statutory wording when specifying a ground (although it is preferable if it does), but it must set out fully the substance of the ground. The purpose of section 8 was that the tenant should be given the information required to enable him to consider what could

---

[24] s. 8(4).
[25] See s. 5(1). Presumably a notice to quit is needed if the tenancy ceases to be assured after service of the s. 8 notice, unless the latter complies with the common law rules.
[26] s. 8(6).
[27] Above, p. 223.
[28] (1993) 25 H.L.R. 427; [1994] Conv. 74 (S. Bridge).

be done to avoid a possession order. It was not enough to identify the ground. In the case of Ground 8, the notice must not only refer to three months' arrears, but must also refer to the requirement that the rent must be unpaid at the date of service of the notice and at the date of the hearing, and to the requirement that the rent must be lawfully due. The landlord argued that the defect could be cured under section 8(2), which allows the specified grounds to be altered or added to with the leave of the court. This was rejected on the ground that there must be a valid section 8 notice in existence before the court can consider giving leave to alter or add to the specified grounds. This was so whether or not the landlord's notice had included other correctly specified grounds. If it contained any defectively specified grounds, it was a bad notice. Of course, if a notice is defective the court might dispense with it under section 8(1)(b), but this cannot be done where the landlord relies on Ground 8.[29]

Mandatory grounds for possession

Schedule 2 of the 1988 Act contains eight mandatory grounds upon which the court must order possession.

Ground 1

"Not later than the beginning[30] of the tenancy the landlord[31] gave notice[32] in writing to the tenant that possession might be recovered on this ground or the court is of the opinion that it is just and equitable to dispense with the requirement of notice and (in either case):

Prior occupation
    (a)   at some time before the beginning[33] of the tenancy, the landlord who is seeking possession or, in the case of joint landlords seeking possession, at least one of them occupied the dwelling-house as his only or principal home[34]; or

---

[29] s. 8(5), above. Although there was no power to cure the defective specification of Ground 8, it was left open whether, in a case where other grounds were correctly specified, the court could strike out the reference to Ground 8 in the exercise of its dispensing power.

[30] By way of exception to s. 45(2), this means no later than the day on which the tenancy is entered into: Sched. 2, Part IV, para. 11, applying also to Grounds 2–5, below.

[31] Or at least one of joint landlords: *ibid.* para. 7, applying also to Grounds 2–5, below.

[32] For a "long stop" Ground 1 notice in cases where the occupier may not have an assured tenancy, see *Precedents for the Conveyancer*, Form 5-78A, Appendix, p. 276. Notices under Ground 1 (and Grounds 2 to 5) do not have to be in prescribed form. As to the requirements of a "notice", see *Springfield Investments Ltd v. Bell* (1990) 2 H.L.R. 440 (on Case 16 of the Rent Act 1977).

[33] See s. 45(2). The occupation need not have been immediately before the letting.

[34] See above, p. 196.

(b)   the landlord who is seeking possession or, in the
       case of joint landlords seeking possession, at least
       one of them requires the dwelling-house as his or
       his spouse's only or principal home and neither
Or requirement   the landlord (or, in the case of joint landlords, any
as a home   one of them) nor any other person who, as
       landlord, derived title under the landlord who
       gave the notice mentioned above acquired the
       reversion on the tenancy for money or money's
       worth."

This ground is a combination of the discretionary Case 9[35]
and the mandatory Case 11[36] under the Rent Act 1977, but
is different from both in significant respects and is easier to
Case 11   establish. Paragraph (a) is broadly equivalent to Case 11,
compared   but does not contain any requirement that the landlord
should be intending to reside at the premises himself (or
that the premises should be wanted for certain other
purposes specified by the 1977 Act). In another respect,
however, it is stricter than Case 11. The requirement that
Only or principal   the landlord must have occupied as his only or principal
home   home imports a stricter test than that applicable under Case
11.[37] Clearly the ground cannot be invoked by corporate
landlords.

Case 9 compared   Paragraph (b) is loosely based on Case 9 of the 1977 Act,
but again is easier to establish in most respects. First,
because it is mandatory. Secondly, because there is
apparently no requirement that the landlord's desire to
occupy should be reasonable.[38] Thirdly, because there is no
"greater hardship" rule.[39] In some other respects it is stricter
than Case 9, namely in that it is confined to residence by the
landlord or his spouse rather than for the wider class of
relatives envisaged by Case 9, and the "only or principal
home" requirement is stricter than "residence" under Case
9. Although the wording is different, cases on the "landlord
Purchase   by purchase"[40]aspect of Case 9 may afford
guidance on the "money or money's worth" element of
Ground 1. The latter formula is perhaps clearer. Case 9 may
also provide guidance on the question how far the
requirement as a home may relate to a future time.[41] As with
Case 9, no period of former residence need be

---

[35] See above, p. 122.
[36] See above, p. 127. In effect it covers also Cases 12 and 20: above, pp.
    132, 136. See (1989) 139 N.L.J. 252 (F. Webb), pointing out that,
    unlike Case 11, Ground 1 does not cover the case where the personal
    representative of a deceased landlord wishes to dispose of the property.
[37] See *Naish v. Curzon* (1986) 51 P.&C.R. 229; *Davies v. Peterson* [1989] 1
    E.G.L.R. 121; above, p. 128.
[38] *cf.* on Case 11, *Kennealy v. Dunne* [1977] 1 Q.B. 837; above, p. 000. The
    intention must, of course, be genuine.
[39] See above, p. 125.
[40] See above, p. 123.
[41] See above, p. 124.

Joint landlords   established. As far as joint landlords are concerned, it will be noted that Ground 1 adopts the principle of *Tilling v. Whiteman*[42] (one of joint landlords could invoke Case 11).

Dispensing power   The dispensing power in relation to the prior notice is similar to that applying to Case 11 under the Rent Act 1977, although the wording is not identical. No doubt the decisions in that context will be applicable here.[43]

Later tenancies   Where the landlord has granted a further tenancy to the same tenant, taking effect immediately on the coming to an end of the earlier tenancy, and of substantially the same dwelling-house, or where a statutory periodic tenancy subsequently arises, then the notice served in relation to the original tenancy has effect also in relation to the later tenancy, unless the landlord gives written notice to the contrary no later than the beginning of the later tenancy.[44]

Misrepres-   Where the landlord obtains a possession order but it
entation   subsequently appears that it was obtained by misrepresentation or concealment of material facts, the court may order the former landlord to pay to the former tenant compensation for damage or loss sustained by him as a result of the order.[45]

As mentioned above, the accelerated possession procedure is available.

Ground 2

Prior mortgagee exercising power of sale   "The dwelling-house is subject to a mortgage[46] granted before the beginning of the tenancy and:

(a)   the mortgagee is entitled to exercise a power of sale conferred on him by the mortgage or by section 101 of the Law of Property Act 1925; and

(b)   the mortgagee requires possession of the dwelling-house for the purpose of disposing of it with vacant possession in exercise of that power; and

(c)   either notice was given as mentioned in Ground 1 or the court is satisfied that it is just and equitable to dispense with the requirement of notice."

The points made in relation to Ground 1 concerning the dispensing power and the situation where a second tenancy is granted or a statutory periodic tenancy arises apply here also.[47]

It appears that the notice referred to in paragraph (c) above is actually a Ground 1 notice.[48] Ground 2 is, therefore

[42] [1980] A.C. 1; above, p. 130.
[43] See above, p. 130. See further (1989) 139 N.L.J. 252 (F. Webb).
[44] Housing Act 1988, Sched. 2, Part IV, para. 8, applying also to Grounds 2–5, below. See also para. 9.
[45] Housing Act 1988, s. 12.
[46] Or charge.
[47] See above.
[48] See correspondence at (1989) 139 N.L.J. 326.

linked to Ground 1 and cannot apply to a landlord (such as a corporate landlord) who cannot satisfy Ground 1. The purpose of linking Ground 2 to Ground 1, it has been suggested, was to encourage owner-occupiers to let and mortgagees to be more flexible in consenting to such lettings.[49]

Tenant's mortgagee

Of course, where the subject-matter of the mortgage is the assured tenancy itself, the mortgagee can take possession in the ordinary way, and is not affected by the Housing Act 1988.[50] Where a mortgage of the reversion is granted after the tenancy, Ground 2 is inapplicable; the mortgagee cannot sell with vacant possession, but only subject to the tenancy.[51]

Mortgage after tenancy

Under the general law, a tenancy granted after a mortgage is only binding on the mortgagee if the mortgagor's leasing power under section 99 of the Law of Property Act 1925 has not been excluded, or if the mortgagee has agreed to the tenancy or accepted the tenant.[52] If, on the other hand, the mortgagor's leasing power has been excluded, as is commonly the case, any lease granted binds the mortgagor by estoppel, but does not bind the mortgagee.[53] Presumably in the latter situation the mortgagee could still recover possession without regard to Ground 2, but the landlord himself could not bring possession proceedings without satisfying Ground 2. In the case where the tenancy was granted after the mortgage and is not binding on the mortgagee, a subsequent remortgage by the landlord should not alter the position.[54] Where, on the other hand, the tenancy is binding on the mortgagee, he will not be able to take possession unless the conditions of Ground 2 are satisfied. No doubt the mortgagee will insist on a Ground 1 notice being served and, in the case of a fixed term tenancy, will insist that it contains a provision enabling recovery of possession during the term on the basis of Ground 2.[55]

Where tenancy not binding on mortgagee

Although the Rent Act 1977 does not contain a separate ground equivalent to Ground 2, the latter is not in fact new. Case 11 of the 1977 Act (the owner-occupier ground)

Case 11 compared

---

[49] (1991) 135 Sol. Jo. 409 (J. Driscoll and I. Graham).
[50] s. 7(1).
[51] If, however, the tenancy was "granted" before the conveyance of the land to the landlord purchaser, the tenancy does not bind a mortgagee whose mortgage was in effect simultaneous with the conveyance: *Abbey National Building Society v. Cann* [1991] 1 A.C. 56, overruling *Church of England Building Society v. Piskor* [1954] Ch. 553.
[52] See also *Quennell v. Maltby* [1979] 1 W.L.R. 318, holding that a prior mortgagee cannot evict the tenant unless pursuant to a bona fide exercise of the right to possession.
[53] *Dudley and District Benefit Building Society v. Emerson* [1949] Ch. 707; above, p. 141. The definition of "landlord" in Housing Act 1988, s. 45(1) is similar to that in Rent Act 1977, s. 152. *cf. Appleton v. Aspin* [1988] 1 W.L.R. 410.
[54] By analogy with *Equity and Law Home Loans Ltd v. Prestidge* [1992] 1 W.L.R. 137.
[55] s. 7(6); above, p. 226. It has been suggested that in such a case the tenancy could not qualify as shorthold; above, p. 218.

includes the similar situation where the mortgage was granted before the tenancy and the mortgagee requires possession for the purpose of exercising the power of sale.[56]

Ground 3

Out of season lettings

"The tenancy is a fixed term[57] tenancy for a term not exceeding eight months and:
(a) no later than the beginning[58] of the tenancy the landlord[59] gave notice in writing to the tenant that possession might be recovered on this ground; and
(b) at some time within the period of twelve months ending with the beginning[60] of the tenancy, the dwelling-house was occupied under a right to occupy it for a holiday."

The position is the same as under Ground 1 where there is a second tenancy or where a statutory periodic tenancy arises.[61]

Case 13 compared

This ground is based on the mandatory Case 13 under the Rent Act 1977, which was explained in Chapter 7.[62] As holiday lettings are also excluded from protection under the 1988 Act,[63] landlords may continue to grant holiday lettings and out of season lettings without being unable to recover possession at any stage.

The accelerated possession procedure is available.[64]

Ground 4

Vacation lettings of student accommodation

"The tenancy is a fixed term[65] tenancy for a term not exceeding twelve months and:
(a) no later than the beginning[66] of the tenancy the landlord[67] gave notice in writing to the tenant that possession might be recovered on this ground; and
(b) at some time within the period of twelve months ending with the beginning[68] of the tenancy, the dwelling-house was let on a tenancy falling within paragraph 8 of the Schedule 1 to this Act."

Case 14 compared

Paragraph 8 excludes certain student lettings from protection.[69] Ground 4 is based on the mandatory Case 14 under the Rent Act 1977, which was explained in Chapter

[56] See above, p. 128. Likewise Cases 12 and 20, above, pp. 132, 136.
[57] See s. 45(1).
[58] The day on which the tenancy is entered into: Sched. 2, para. 11.
[59] Or one of joint landlords: Sched. 2, para. 7.
[60] See s. 45(2).
[61] See above, p. 231. See also Sched. 2, para. 10.
[62] See above, p. 132.
[63] Sched. 1, para. 9; above, p. 203.
[64] See above, p. 223.
[65] See s. 45(1).
[66] The day on which the tenancy is entered into: Sched. 2, para. 11.
[67] Or at least one of joint landlords: Sched. 2, para. 7.
[68] See s. 45(2).
[69] See above, p. 203.

7.[70] The purpose of Ground 4 is to allow landlords to grant vacation lettings of student accommodation with the certainty of being able to recover possession by the end of the vacation. Excluded student lettings may then be granted during term.

The position is the same as under Ground 1 where there is a second tenancy or where a statutory periodic tenancy arises.[71]

The accelerated possession procedure is available.[72]

Ground 5

Occupation by minister of religion

"The dwelling-house is held for the purposes of being available for occupation by a minister of religion as a residence from which to perform the duties of his office and:
(a) not later than the beginning[73] of the tenancy the landlord[74] gave notice in writing to the tenant that possession might be recovered on this ground; and
(b) the court is satisfied that the dwelling-house is required for occupation by a minister of religion as such a residence."

Case 15 compared

This is the same as the mandatory Case 15 of the Rent Act 1977, discussed in Chapter 7.[75] It appears that lettings of Church of England parsonages are excluded from assured tenancy status.[76] Other religions are not excluded, but Ground 5 provides a ground for possession.

The position is the same as under Ground 1 where there is a second tenancy or where a statutory periodic tenancy has arisen.[77]

The accelerated possession procedure is available.[78]

Ground 6

Intention to demolish or reconstruct

"The landlord[79] who is seeking possession or, if that landlord is a registered housing association or charitable housing trust,[80] a superior landlord intends to demolish or reconstruct the whole or a substantial part of the dwelling-house or to carry out substantial works on the dwelling-house or any part thereof or any building of which it forms part and the following conditions are fulfilled:

---

[70] See above, p. 133.
[71] See above, p. 231. See also Sched. 2, para. 10.
[72] See above, p. 223.
[73] The day on which the tenancy is entered into: Sched. 2, para. 11.
[74] Or at least one of joint landlords: Sched. 2, para. 7.
[75] See above, p. 133.
[76] See above, p. 200.
[77] See above, p. 231.
[78] See above, p. 223.
[79] Meaning all of joint landlords: s. 45(3); *cf.* Grounds 1–5.
[80] As defined in Ground 6.

(a) the intended work cannot reasonably be carried out without the tenant giving up possession of the dwelling-house because—

   (i) the tenant is not willing to agree to such a variation of the terms of the tenancy as would give such access and other facilities as would permit the intended work to be carried out, or

   (ii) the nature of the intended work is such that no such variation is practicable, or

   (iii) the tenant is not willing to accept an assured tenancy of such part only of the dwelling-house (in this sub-paragraph referred to as 'the reduced part') as would leave in the possession of his landlord so much of the dwelling-house as would be reasonable to enable the intended work to be carried out and, where appropriate, as would give such access and other facilities over the reduced part as would permit the intended work to be carried out, or

   (iv) the nature of the intended work is such that such a tenancy is not practicable; and

(b) either the landlord seeking possession acquired his interest in the dwelling-house before the grant of the tenancy or that interest was in existence at the time of that grant and neither that landlord (or, in the case of joint landlords, any of them) nor any other person who, alone or jointly with others, has acquired that interest since that time acquired it for money or money's worth."

This ground is not found in the Rent Act 1977. It is modelled on section 30(1)(f)[81] of the Landlord and Tenant Act 1954 (business tenancies), which applied also to "old-style" assured tenancies.[82]

Inapplicable to Rent Act successors It does not apply to tenants who have taken assured tenancies by way of succession under the Rent Act 1977 in the case of deaths after January 15, 1989.[83]

Removal expenses Where Ground 6 is established, the landlord must pay to the tenant, by way of compensation, a sum equal to the reasonable expenses likely to be incurred by the tenant in moving from the premises.[84] This sum is to be determined by the court in default of agreement. A similar rule applies to business tenants where the landlord recovers possession on the corresponding ground, although there it is intended to compensate them for loss of goodwill.[85] Compensation will also be payable if it subsequently appears that the order

[81] And s. 31A of the 1954 Act, inserted by Law of Property Act 1969. See also Housing Act 1985, Sched. 2, Ground 10.
[82] Housing Act 1980, s. 58.
[83] Ground 6, para. (c). As to such successors, see above, p. 147.
[84] Housing Act 1988, s. 11.
[85] Landlord and Tenant Act 1954, s. 37. This is based on a multiplier of the rateable value.

**Misrepres-
entation**

**Must not be
landlord by
purchase**

**Where tenancy
renewed**

was obtained by misrepresentation or concealment of
material facts.[86]

The effect of paragraph (b)[87] of Ground 6, set out above,
is that a landlord cannot invoke the ground if he purchased
the property subject to the tenancy. He is not debarred if he
purchased it and subsequently granted the tenancy. If he
acquired his interest after the grant, he can invoke Ground 6
only if neither he nor any other person becoming landlord
since the grant acquired the interest for money or money's
worth. For example, a person who inherits the property
subject to the tenancy from the original landlord may
succeed, but not a person who purchased the property
subject to the tenancy, nor anyone who inherited the
property from such a person.

If the current tenancy was granted to a person who,
immediately before the grant, was an assured tenant of the
dwelling-house, then the landlord may only rely on having
purchased the property before the grant if he purchased it
before the grant of the *earlier* tenancy.[88] (Likewise where he
relies on there having been no landlord by purchase since
the grant; the relevant grant is the earlier one.) This is to
prevent a person buying tenanted property with a view to
development, renewing the tenancy, and then invoking
Ground 6.

As Ground 6 is very similar to section 30(1)(f) of the
1954 Act, it is likely that decisions on the latter provision
will be relied upon here. The scheme of both grounds is that
a landlord who intends to do the specified works shall
succeed unless the tenant agrees to give him access and
facilities[89] (if this is practicable) or is willing to take a
tenancy of a smaller area so that the works may be carried
out on the remainder (where this is practicable). It is
established under the 1954 Act that a landlord who intends
to sell to a developer cannot invoke the ground, but that, as
the landlord does not have to do the work personally, it
suffices that he intends to grant a building lease to a new
tenant, normally a developer, who will do the work.[90]

The requirements of Ground 6 will now be examined in
the light of the case-law on the 1954 Act. The first element

---

[86] Housing Act 1988, s. 12.
[87] For minor amendments relating to former secure tenancies under the
"Change of Landlord" provisions of Part IV of the Housing Act 1988,
see Local Government and Housing Act 1989, Sched. 11, paras. 108,
109.
[88] Ground 6 (penultimate paragraph).
[89] It is an implied term of every assured tenancy that the tenant shall give
the landlord access and reasonable facilities for executing repairs:
Housing Act 1988, s. 16. The works envisaged by Ground 6, however,
go beyond "repairs".
[90] *P.F. Ahern & Sons Ltd v. Hunt* [1988] 1 E.G.L.R. 74 (125 year lease);
Spook Erection Ltd v. British Railways Board [1988] 1 E.G.L.R. 76 (99
year lease); *Turner v. Wandsworth L.B.C.* (1995) 69 P.&C.R. 433 (four
year lease).

Intention is that the landlord must "intend" to do the specified works. The authorities on the 1954 Act[91] indicate that the intention must be established at the date of the hearing.[92] The landlord must have gone beyond merely contemplating the works.[93] He should have taken some active steps towards implementing his intention, such as seeking planning permission and finance (where necessary). He must have evidence that would indicate to a reasonable man that there is a reasonable prospect of implementation, the test being objective.[94] Matters such as the drawing up of plans, quotations for work from builders and so on will be relevant. It has been held that intention to reconstruct need not be the primary purpose of seeking possession.[95]

Reconstruction "Reconstruction" means some substantial interference with the existing structure, and is a question of fact and degree.[96] The alternative of "substantial works" is not, however, confined to structural works, and could include major refurbishment.

Possession "Possession" means legal, not physical, possession.[97] In other words, it is not enough for the landlord to show that he needs physical possession to do the works. If the tenancy contains a sufficiently wide access term,[98]or if the tenant is willing to agree to a term giving access to the landlord (where practicable), possession will not be ordered. The reference to practicability means that the tenant cannot avoid the possession order by offering to give access or to take a tenancy of a reduced part if the landlord's proposed works inevitably involve the whole or most of the premises, or would interfere too greatly with the tenant's enjoyment of the premises.[99]

Ground 7

Death of periodic tenant "The tenancy is a periodic tenancy (including a statutory periodic tenancy) which has devolved under the will or intestacy of the former tenant and the

---

[91] Also s. 30(1)(g) (landlord intends to occupy for business or as a residence). See generally Yates and Hawkins, *Landlord and Tenant Law* (2nd ed., 1986) pp. 697 *et seq.*
[92] *Betty's Cafés v. Phillips Furnishing Stores* [1959] A.C. 20.
[93] *Cunliffe v. Goodman* [1950] 2 K.B. 237.
[94] *Poppett's (Caterers) Ltd v. Maidenhead B.C.* [1971] 1 W.L.R. 69. For a lenient decision where the landlord recovered possession even though the chances of his plans succeeding were doubtful, see *Cox v. Binfield* [1989] 1 E.G.L.R. 97.
[95] *Betty's Cafés v. Phillips Furnishing Stores*, above.
[96] See *Joel v. Swaddle* [1957] 1 W.L.R. 1094.
[97] *Heath v. Drown* [1973] A.C. 498.
[98] *ibid.*
[99] *Redfern v. Reeves* (1978) 37 P.&C.R. 364; *Leathwoods Ltd v. Total Oil (Great Britain) Ltd* (1986) 51 P.&C.R. 20; *Cerex Jewels Ltd v. Peachey Property Corpn. plc* (1986) 52 P.&C.R. 127; *Blackburn v. Hussain* [1988] 2 E.G.L.R. 77.

proceedings for the recovery of possession are begun
not later than twelve months after the death of the
former tenant or, if the court so directs, after the date
on which, in the opinion of the court, the landlord or,
in the case of joint landlords, any one of them became
aware of the former tenant's death.

No inference of new tenancy

For the purposes of this ground, the acceptance by
the landlord of rent from a new tenant after the death of
the former tenant shall not be regarded as creating a
new periodic tenancy, unless the landlord agrees in
writing to a change (as compared with the tenancy
before the death) in the amount of the rent, the period
of the tenancy, the premises which are let or any other
term of the tenancy."

Rent Act compared

This ground resembles Case G of the Agricultural
Holdings Act 1986.[1] It has no counterpart in the Rent Act
1977. In the case of a regulated tenancy, a successor may
have a claim to a statutory or assured tenancy.[2] If there is no
successor, a statutory tenancy will come to an end, whereas
a protected tenancy will devolve under the will or intestacy
of the tenant.

Where succession rights

In the case of an assured periodic tenancy, we have seen
that there are limited succession rights in favour of the
spouse or cohabitant.[3] In such a case the tenancy does not
devolve under the tenant's will or intestacy, and so Ground
7 will not be available (although it will become available on
the death of the successor).

Inapplicable to fixed terms

It will be noted that neither the succession rules nor
Ground 7 apply to an assured tenancy for a fixed term. On
the death of the tenant in such a case, the tenancy will
devolve under his will or intestacy. If the person upon whom
it devolves does not satisfy the requirements of an assured
tenancy,[4] for example if he does not occupy as his only or
principal home, then the tenancy will cease to be assured
and the landlord may recover possession at the end of the
tenancy. If the person who inherits the tenancy does satisfy
the requirements, then he will be the assured tenant. If he
continues to occupy, a statutory periodic tenancy will arise
on the termination of the fixed term. Ground 7 will be
subsequently available on his death, upon which no
succession under section 17 is possible.[5] Of course, if
nobody is occupying at that time, possession may be
recovered without recourse to Ground 7, as there will no
longer be an assured tenancy.

[1] Agricultural Holdings Act 1986, Sched. 23. There written notice of the
death must be served on the landlord.
[2] See above, p. 143.
[3] Housing Act 1988, s. 17: above, p. 212.
[4] *ibid.* s. 1; above, p. 195.
[5] s. 17(2)(a).

After expiry of time limits

Where Ground 7 is available but the landlord does not act within the specified time limits, the person upon whom the tenancy has devolved may continue in occupation as an assured tenant so long as he satisfies the conditions of section 1 of the 1988 Act, until some other Ground becomes available.[6]

Ground 8

"Both at the date of service of the notice under section 8[7] of this Act relating to the proceedings for possession and at the date of the hearing:

(a) if rent is payable weekly or fortnightly, at least thirteen weeks' rent is unpaid;

Three months' rent unpaid

(b) if rent is payable monthly, at least three months' rent is unpaid;

(c) if rent is payable quarterly, at least one quarter's rent is more than three months in arrears; and

(d) if rent is payable yearly, at least three months' rent is more than three months in arrears;

and for the purpose of this ground 'rent' means rent lawfully due from the tenant."

This is one of three grounds for possession relating to rent arrears, the other two being discretionary, as discussed below. This may be contrasted with the Rent Act, where there is only one (discretionary) ground relating to rent.[8]

Rent lawfully due

The reference to rent "lawfully due" means that the ground cannot be invoked if the rent which the tenant has failed to pay exceeds any figure determined by the rent assessment committee.[9]

No suspension powers

As the ground is mandatory, the court has no power to suspend or postpone the order subject to conditions relating to payment.[10] It is no defence that the arrears are due to delay in paying housing benefit.

It will be noted that if the arrears are discharged before the hearing, Ground 8 will no longer apply, although the discretionary grounds may be available. If the landlord wishes to invoke the latter grounds, he should include them in his section 8 notice. Otherwise he must get the leave of the court to amend his notice,[11] or serve a new one.

---

[6] The tenancy may not have been assignable. See Housing Act 1988, s. 15, above, p. 206.

[7] Above, p. 227. See *Mountain v. Hastings* (1993) 25 H.L.R. 427.

[8] See above, p. 117.

[9] Below, Chap. 14. There are other reasons why rent may not be lawfully due, for example non-compliance with Landlord and Tenant Act 1987, ss. 47, 48 (duty to provide information to tenant), or where the tenant has a valid set-off or counterclaim; see above, p. 117.

[10] Housing Act 1988, s. 9; below, p. 244.

[11] *ibid.* s. 8(2).

Discretionary grounds

Schedule 2 of the 1988 Act contains a further eight grounds upon which the court may order possession if it considers it reasonable to do so.[12]

Ground 9

Suitable alternative accommodation

"Suitable alternative accommodation is available for the tenant or will be available for him when the order for possession takes effect."

This ground, which changed from mandatory to discretionary during the passage of the Bill, is modelled upon section 98 of the Rent Act 1977.[13] As under the 1977 Act, the question whether the alternative accommodation is suitable and the question whether it is reasonable to make the order are two separate matters. As in the case of regulated tenancies, suitability depends on the fulfilment of statutory criteria. As under the 1977 Act, a local authority **Local authority certificate** certificate of willingness to provide suitable alternative accommodation is conclusive evidence of availability.[14] The statutory criteria relating to proximity to work, rental, extent **Needs of tenant** and character of the alternative accommodation[15] are identical to those laid down by the 1977 Act. These provisions, and the case-law upon them (which will be equally applicable here), were fully discussed in Chapter 7.[16] **Equivalent security** The criteria relating to security of tenure are modified in the light of the assured tenancy regime. In the absence of a local authority certificate, alternative accommodation can be suitable only if the premises are to be let as a separate dwelling on an assured tenancy which is neither an assured shorthold tenancy nor an assured tenancy to which any of the mandatory Grounds 1 to 5 applies. Alternatively, the accommodation can be suitable if the premises are to be let as a separate dwelling on terms which, in the opinion of the court, afford security reasonably equivalent to an assured tenancy of the kind described above.[17]

As in the case of Ground 6, a landlord who recovers possession on the basis of Ground 9 will be obliged to pay **Removal expenses** reasonable removal expenses to the tenant. This sum is to be determined by the court in default of agreement.[18]

---

[12] s. 7(4). For general principles as to "reasonableness" in the context of the discretionary grounds, see above, p. 117.
[13] See above, p. 112.
[14] Housing Act 1988, Sched. 2, Part III, para. 1.
[15] ibid. para 3.
[16] See above, p. 112.
[17] Housing Act 1988, Sched. 2, Part III, para. 2. As to "reasonably equivalent", see above, p. 113.
[18] ibid. s. 11.

Ground 10

Some rent unpaid

"Some rent lawfully due[19] from the tenant
(a) is unpaid on the date on which the proceedings for possession are begun; and
(b) except where subsection (1)(b) of section 8[20] of this Act applies, was in arrears at the date of the service of the notice under that section relating to those proceedings."

Unlike mandatory Ground 8, the rent need not be unpaid at the date of the hearing, and may be less than three **May be suspended** months in arrears. The possibility of the suspension or postponement of the order is dealt with below.[21] It will be seen there that an immediate possession order is unlikely to result from an isolated breach. Of course, in the case of a minor breach, the court may not consider it reasonable to make the order at all.

Ground 11

Persistent delay in paying rent

"Whether or not any rent is in arrears on the date on which proceedings for possession are begun, the tenant has persistently delayed paying rent which has become lawfully due."[22]

This ground resembles the business tenancy ground contained in the Landlord and Tenant Act 1954.[23] Authorities on the latter provision may be found useful here. The court may refuse the order if the tenant can explain his failures and satisfy the court as to the future.[24] As in the case of Ground 10, a possession order may be suspended if the court so directs.[25] The landlord may, of course, specify Grounds 8, 10 and 11 in his notice.

Ground 12

Other breaches

"Any obligation of the tenancy (other than one related to the payment of rent) has been broken or not performed."

This ground is based on Case I of the Rent Act 1977 (save that Case I includes rent breaches also). Illustrations may be found in Chapter 7, where the position as to waiver is also discussed.[26] Where the breach is not serious or is

[19] This was discussed in connection with Ground 8, above, p. 239.
[20] Where the court considers it just and equitable to dispense with the notice requirement.
[21] Housing Act 1988, s. 9; below, p. 244.
[22] See n. 19, above.
[23] s. 30(1)(b).
[24] *Hurstfell Ltd v. Leicester Square Property Co. Ltd* [1988] 2 E.G.L.R. 105 (business tenancy).
[25] See below, p. 244.
[26] See above, p. 118.

remediable, the order is likely to be either suspended or
refused.

Ground 13

**Condition of
dwelling-house**

"The condition of the dwelling-house or any of the
common parts[27] has deteriorated owing to acts of waste
by, or the neglect or default of, the tenant or any other
person residing in the dwelling-house and, in the case of
an act of waste by, or the neglect or default of, a person
lodging with the tenant or a sub-tenant of his, the
tenant has not taken such steps as he ought reasonably
to have taken for the removal of the lodger or sub-
tenant."

This ground resembles Case 3 of the Rent Act 1977,
which was discussed in Chapter 7.[28] The only distinction is
that Ground 13 extends to the condition of the common
parts. An immediate possession order is unlikely save in the
case of serious deterioration.

Ground 14

**Nuisance or
annoyance**

"The tenant or any other person residing in the
dwelling-house has been guilty of conduct which is a
nuisance or annoyance to adjoining occupiers, or has
been convicted of using the dwelling-house or allowing
the dwelling-house to be used for immoral or illegal
purposes."

This ground is based on Case 2 of the Rent Act 1977, of
which illustrations have been given in Chapter 7.[29] The only
difference is that the acts of persons other than the tenant
are included in Case 2 only if they are sub-tenants or
persons residing or lodging *with* the tenant. In Ground 14
such persons need only have been residing "in the dwelling-
house."[30]

Ground 15

**Condition of
furniture**

"The condition of any furniture provided for use under
the tenancy has, in the opinion of the court,
deteriorated owing to ill-treatment by the tenant or any
other person residing in the dwelling-house and, in the
case of ill-treatment by a person lodging with the tenant
or by a sub-tenant of his, the tenant has not taken such
steps as he ought reasonably to have taken for the
removal of the lodger or sub-tenant."

This ground is based on Case 4 of the Rent Act 1977,
considered in Chapter 7.[31] The point made in respect of

[27] As defined in the second paragraph of Ground 13.
[28] See above, p. 119.
[29] See above, p. 118.
[30] For a similar distinction, see the succession rules, above, p. 151.
[31] See above, p. 120.

Ground 14 above relating to the distinction between residing or lodging "with" the tenant and merely residing "in the dwelling-house" applies here also.

Ground 16

Former employee

"The dwelling-house was let to the tenant[32] in consequence of his employment by the landlord[33] seeking possession or a previous landlord under the tenancy and the tenant has ceased to be in that employment."

This ground differs from Case 8 of the Rent Act 1977, upon which it is based,[34] in one significant respect. Under Case 8, the dwelling-house must be needed for another employee, but there is no such requirement under Ground 16. No doubt the landlord is more likely to obtain possession if he does need the premises for a new employee or where the occupation of the premises was related to the duties of the former employee. For the purpose of Ground 16, employment by a health service body is to be regarded as employment by the Secretary of State where the latter is the landlord.[35] The effect of this provision is to facilitate recovery of possession by the Secretary of State.

Inapplicable Rent Act grounds

It will be noted that some of the Rent Act discretionary grounds have no counterpart under the 1988 Act. Case 5 (tenant's notice to quit) is not perpetuated because an assured tenancy terminates upon the tenant's notice to quit.[36] Case 6 (assignment or subletting of the whole without consent) does not apply, although Ground 12 would cover the case of an assignment or subletting in breach of covenant. Furthermore, a tenant who sublets the whole will cease to satisfy the residence requirement of section 1.[37] Finally, Case 10 (overcharging of sub-tenant) is also inapplicable.

Misrepresentation and concealment

Where a landlord obtains possession on one (or more) of the grounds for possession but it subsequently appears to the

---

[32] Meaning both or all of joint tenants: Housing Act 1988, s. 45(3).
[33] Meaning both or all of joint tenants: *ibid.*
[34] See above, p. 122.
[35] National Health Service and Community Care Act 1990, Sched. 8, para. 10.
[36] See above, p. 208.
[37] See above, p. 194. As to the sub-tenant's position, see s. 18, above, p. 214.

Compensation

court that the order was obtained by misrepresentation or concealment of material facts, the court may order the landlord to pay to the former tenant compensation for damage or loss resulting from the order.[38]

This provision is most likely to apply to those grounds which involve an intention on the part of the landlord to use the premises for some particular purpose, such as Ground 1 (residence) and Ground 6 (demolition or reconstruction).

Another possibility might be to claim that a notice served under section 8 of the 1988 Act specifying grounds which involve an intention to use the premises in a particular way is fraudulent and of no effect if the landlord in fact has no such intention.[39]

Suspension and postponement

Discretionary grounds only

The court has a discretion to adjourn possession proceedings, or, on the making of a possession order (and before its execution), to stay or suspend execution of the order or to postpone the date of possession for such a period as the court thinks just.[40] This provision has no application to the mandatory grounds, nor to recovery of possession against assured shorthold tenants under section 21 of the 1988 Act.[41] However, the court's ordinary power of

Ordinary adjournment

adjournment to control and direct the conduct of a trial is unaffected by the statutory provisions just mentioned. This power may be exercised, for example, where the tenant seeks an adjournment to bring evidence of a set-off defence, whether the ground for possession relied on is discretionary or mandatory.[42]

Conditions

Where the court exercises its discretion under section 9, it shall impose conditions as to the payment of any rent arrears or mesne profits, unless it considers that this would cause exceptional hardship to the tenant or would otherwise be unreasonable. It may also impose such other conditions as it thinks fit.[43] Where the tenant complies with conditions

---

[38] Housing Act 1988, s. 12. For equivalent provisions, see Rent Act 1977, s. 102 (Cases 8 and 9); Landlord and Tenant Act 1954, s. 55. As the tenant will have been paying a market rent, the damages are unlikely to be large.

[39] See *Rous v. Mitchell* [1991] 1 W.L.R. 469 (notice to quit agricultural tenancy containing fraudulent misrepresentation was invalid); [1991] Conv. 144 at 148 (C. Rodgers).

[40] Housing Act 1988, s. 9.

[41] See above, p. 222. As to the mandatory grounds, see Housing Act 1980, s. 89(1), above, p. 137. It has been held that s. 89(1) does not restrict the powers of the High Court: *Bain and Co. v. Church Commissioners for England* [1989] 1 W.L.R. 24.

[42] *Mountain v. Hastings* (1993) 25 H.L.R. 427. For the setting aside of possession orders, see (1992) *Legal Action*, November, p. 14 and (1995) *Legal Action*, April, p. 20 (C. Johnson).

[43] s. 9(3).

which have been imposed, the court may discharge or rescind the possession order.[44]

This is a jurisdiction which is likely to be exercised in relation to the discretionary rent arrears grounds, as is commonly the case under the similar provisions of the Rent Act 1977.[45] Reference should be made to Chapter 7, where the effect of conditional orders is considered.[46]

Rights of spouse   Where the tenant's spouse or former spouse, having rights of occupation under the Matrimonial Homes Act 1983, is in occupation at the time proceedings are brought, and the assured tenancy is terminated as a result of the proceedings, he or she has the same rights in connection with any adjournment, suspension or postponement, so long as he or she remains in occupation, as if those occupation rights were not affected by the termination of the tenancy.[47] This provision, which is similar to that applying to regulated tenancies,[48] means that the spouse may apply to court for the exercise of its powers of suspension and so forth.

Shared accommodation

Special provisions apply to the situation where there is a tenancy of some separate accommodation, but the tenant is **Sharing with** entitled to use other accommodation in common with **other tenants** another person or persons, not including the landlord.[49] The circumstances envisaged here include, for example, the case where the tenant has the use of a kitchen or bathroom in common with other tenants.

No possession   Section 10 of the 1988 Act provides that the landlord **order of shared** cannot obtain a possession order in respect of the shared **accommodation** accommodation unless an order is being (or has been) made **alone** in respect of the separate accommodation.[50]

The landlord may, however, apply to court for an order terminating the tenant's right to use shared accommodation **Permitted** which is not "living" accommodation,[51] or modifying his **modifications** right to use all or part of the shared accommodation (whether or not "living" accommodation), whether by varying the persons or increasing the number of persons entitled to use that accommodation or otherwise.[52] The

[44] s. 9(4).
[45] Rent Act 1977, s. 100; above, p. 137.
[46] See above, p. 137.
[47] s. 9(5). The provision is extended to cohabitants by the Family Homes and Domestic Violence Bill, Sched. 5, inserting s. 9(5A).
[48] See above, p. 138.
[49] See Housing Act 1988, s. 3(1); above, p. 199. A tenant who shares accommodation with his landlord is likely to be excluded from the assured tenancy code by the resident landlord rule; above, p. 204.
[50] The landlord, therefore, cannot seek variation of the terms of a statutory periodic tenancy under s. 6 in such a way as to terminate rights over the shared accommodation.
[51] As defined in s. 3(5). For the meaning of this term, see above, p. 63.
[52] s. 10(3).

court may make such order as it thinks just. No such order may be made unless the terms of the tenancy, apart from section 3(3),[53] permit such modification or termination of the tenant's rights.[54]

Section 10 is based on section 22 of the Rent Act 1977, which makes similar provision in relation to regulated tenancies.[55]

Termination apart from grounds for possession

As in the case of regulated tenancies under the Rent Act 1977, there are certain situations in which the landlord may recover possession from an assured tenant apart from the grounds for possession discussed above, or in which the tenancy ceases to be assured so that possession may be recovered under the general law or under some other statutory code.

Of course, the assured tenancy will end if the tenant gives notice to quit or surrenders the tenancy.[56] It has been held that an assured (or any other) tenancy terminates if the tenant accepts a repudiatory breach (such as serious disrepair) by the landlord.[57] If, however, the repudiatory breach was by the tenant, the landlord could not invoke this principle because it would be modified by the terms of the tenancy (such as a forfeiture clause) and by the statutory provisions concerning recovery of possession.

Where section 1 no longer satisfied If at any time the tenant ceases to satisfy the definition in section 1, the tenancy will not end, but will cease to be assured, so that possession may be recovered when permitted under the general law. This will be the case, for example, if the tenant ceases to occupy as his only or principal home, or if any of the exclusions in Schedule 1 become applicable, as where the reversion is transferred to the Crown,[58] or where the rules as to the level of rent cease to be satisfied.[59]

Bankruptcy There will be no automatic right to possession, however, upon the bankruptcy of an assured tenant, because the tenancy does not normally vest in the trustee in bankruptcy.[60] The tenant, therefore, may continue to satisfy the requirements of section 1.

Certain provisions of the Housing Act 1985, as amended by the 1988 Act, allow recovery of possession against an assured tenant in particular circumstances. For example,

(margin label) **Repudiation**

---

[53] See above, p. 199.
[54] s. 10(4).
[55] See above, p. 63.
[56] See above, p. 208.
[57] *Hussein v. Mehlman* [1992] 2 E.G.L.R. 87 (county court).
[58] Sched. 1, para. 11.
[59] *ibid.* paras. 2, 3.
[60] Housing Act 1988, s. 117, discussed further, above. p. 94.

Closing orders, etc. where the premises are subject to a closing or demolition order,[61] or where there is inadequate fire escape provision.[62]

Change of user Other circumstances discussed in Chapter 7 appear to apply equally to assured tenants. Thus if there is a change of user, for example from residential to business, the tenancy will cease to be assured (although recovery of possession may be restricted by the Landlord and Tenant Act 1954).[63] The assured tenancy code will similarly cease to apply if the

Change of status tenant's status is changed, for example in the rare case where he is held to have become a licensee.[64] If the premises

Destruction of premises are destroyed or become uninhabitable (other than temporarily) the tenancy could still exist under the general law, but assured tenancy status would be lost if the tenant could no longer satisfy the occupation requirement of section 1.

Mortgagee Finally, a mortgagee upon whom the tenancy is not binding may recover possession by exercising his powers as mortgagee without regard to the grounds for possession, as discussed above in the context of Ground 2.

---

[61] Housing Act 1985, Part IX, as amended by Housing Act 1988, Sched. 17, para. 47.

[62] Housing Act 1985, s. 368, as amended by Housing Act 1988, Sched. 17, para. 50. See also paras. 48, 60 and 63.

[63] See above, p. 139.

[64] See above, p. 140.

14 RENT CONTROL

Introduction

The objective of the Housing Act 1988 is to encourage letting in the private sector. The incentive to the landlord is the reduction in security of tenure, as explained in the previous chapters of Part III, combined with a reduction in rent control. The scheme of the Rent Act 1977 was to reduce rents below the market level, by means of the "fair rent" concept.[1] The scheme of the Housing Act 1988 in relation to assured and assured shorthold tenancies is merely to prevent excessive rents; in other words, to keep rents at the market level, and to prevent the tenant from being forced out by an extortionate rent after expiry of the original term. To this extent it bears more resemblance to the business tenancy code under the Landlord and Tenant Act 1954, Part II.

Premiums not prohibited

Unlike the position under the Rent Act 1977, there is no prohibition on premiums on the grant or assignment of an assured tenancy. Premiums are prohibited under the 1977 Act in order to prevent evasion of the rent control rules. Insofar as assured tenancy rents are basically governed by the market, this rationale is inapplicable. In one context, however, consequences flow from a requirement of a premium in respect of an assured tenancy. In the case of a periodic assured tenancy (other than a statutory periodic tenancy) where a premium[2] is required to be paid on the grant or renewal of the tenancy, section 15(1) of the 1988 Act[3] (implying a covenant against assignment or subletting without consent) does not apply.[4]

Rent books
Distress

Housing benefit

Other general points relating to rent include the application of the rent book requirement to assured tenants who pay their rent weekly,[5] and the restrictions on the remedy of distress for unpaid rent in the case of assured tenancies.[6] It should also be noted that housing benefit will not necessarily cover the whole rent.[7] Subject to certain exceptions, housing benefit is payable only in respect of such

[1] See above, Chap. 10.
[2] Defined in Housing Act 1988, s. 15(4).
[3] See above, p. 206.
[4] s. 15(3).
[5] Landlord and Tenant Act 1985, ss. 4–7, above, p. 171, as amended by Housing Act 1988, Sched. 17, para. 67. See the Rent Book (Forms of Notice) (Amendment) Regulations 1993 (S.I. 1993 No. 656).
[6] Housing Act 1988, s. 19, corresponding with Rent Act 1977, s. 147 (regulated tenancies).
[7] Housing Act 1988, s. 121; Rent Officers (Additional Functions) Order 1989 (S.I. 1989 No. 590) as amended by S.I. 1991 No. 426, S.I. 1993 No. 652 and S.I. 1994 No. 568.

part of the rent as is considered reasonable.[8] This benefit
shortfall can lead to arrears and harassment.[9]

Rent increases

**Increase by
notice where
periodic**

Section 13 of the 1988 Act provides a mechanism for
increasing the rent under a statutory periodic tenancy or any
other assured periodic tenancy having no express provision
for increasing the rent. The section does not apply to a
fixed-term assured tenancy, although the rent under such a
tenancy may be increased if there is a rent review clause.[10] It
is doubtful whether such an express review provision carries
over into a statutory periodic tenancy arising on termination
of the fixed term.[11]

Prescribed form

The procedure under section 13 is that the landlord may
serve on the tenant a notice in prescribed form proposing a
new rent to take effect at the beginning of a new period of

**Commencement
of new rent**

the tenancy specified in the notice.[12] This new period must
begin no earlier than:

(a) the minimum period after the date of service of the
notice; and
(b) except in the case of a statutory periodic tenancy, the
first anniversary of the date on which the first period of
the tenancy began; and
(c) if the rent has previously been increased under section
13 or upon a determination by the rent assessment
committee under section 14 (below), the first
anniversary of the date on which the increased rent took
effect.

The "minimum period" referred to in (a) above is six
months in the case of a yearly tenancy, one month where the
period is less than a month, and a period equal to the period
of the tenancy in any other case.[13]

The rent specified in the landlord's notice takes effect as
mentioned in the notice unless, before the beginning of the

[8] See *R. v. Manchester City Council, ex p. Baragrove Properties Ltd* (1991) 23
H.L.R. 337; *R. v. Manchester City Council, ex p. Harcup* (1994) 26
H.L.R. 402.
[9] See (1989) *Legal Action*, June, p. 14 (J. Luba); (1992) *Legal Action*,
October, p. 18 (R. East); *Forced Out*, Shelter Publications, noted [1990]
03 E.G. 14.
[10] See generally [1989] Conv. 111 (D.N. Clarke); *Precedents for the
Conveyancer*, Vol. I, 5–99, 5–100, 5– 103, 5–104, Appendix, pp.
279–282. For further precedents, see Clarke and Adams, *Rent Reviews
and Variable Rents* (3rd ed., 1990).
[11] See Megarry, *The Rent Acts* (11th ed.) Vol. 3, p. 198.
[12] s. 13(2); Assured Tenancies and Agricultural Occupancies (Forms)
Regulations 1988 (S.I. No. 1988 No. 2203); Assured Tenancies and
Agricultural Occupancies (Forms) (Amendment) Regulations 1989 (S.I.
1989 No. 146) and 1993 (S.I. 1993 No. 654). It is doubtful whether the
notice may be served before expiry of a fixed term, in relation to the
ensuing statutory periodic tenancy.
[13] s. 13(3).

Takes effect unless referred under section 14

new period specified in the notice, the tenant refers the notice to a rent assessment committee under section 14 by an application in the prescribed form, or the parties agree on a variation of the rent which is different from that proposed in the notice or agree that the rent should not be varied.[14] Obviously the increase will not be recoverable if the notice is in any way invalid.

Variation by agreement

The procedure in section 13 is without prejudice to the rights of the parties to an assured tenancy to vary by agreement any of its terms, including the rent.[15]

Initial rent not controlled

The rent initially payable under an assured tenancy is the contractual rent. This may be increased subsequently under any rent review or indexation clause. There is no machinery for controlling the rent initially agreed or increased under a review clause. The effect of section 13 is that the landlord may increase the rent under a periodic tenancy even though there is no rent review clause. This cannot be done during the first year except in the case of a statutory periodic tenancy arising on the termination of an assured tenancy, where the landlord is not obliged to wait for the anniversary of the termination. Nor may it be done within a year of any previous increase by notice or by the rent assessment committee. If the tenant does not accept the landlord's figure, he must apply to the rent assessment committee under section 14, as explained below.

Effect of section 13

Action by tenant

Determination by the rent assessment committee

Where the landlord invokes the notice procedure of section 13, the tenant may refer the notice to the rent assessment committee under section 14 by an application in prescribed form.[16] The committee must then determine the rent at which they consider that the dwelling-house concerned "might reasonably be expected to be let in the open market by a willing landlord under an assured tenancy."[17] It is assumed that this hypothetical assured tenancy is a periodic tenancy having the same periods as the actual tenancy; commencing at the beginning of the new period specified in the notice; having the same terms (other than as to rent) as the actual tenancy; and in respect of which the same notices, if any, have been given under any of Grounds 1 to 5 of

Assumptions in determining market rent

---

[14] s. 13(4).
[15] s. 13(5).
[16] Assured Tenancies and Agricultural Occupancies (Forms) Regulations 1988 (S.I. 1988 No. 2203) (Form No. 6).
[17] s. 14(1). The formula is similar to that which applies to business tenancies under Landlord and Tenant Act 1954, s. 34.

Schedule 2[18] as have been given in relation to the actual tenancy.[19]

Disregards

In assessing the market rent, three matters must be disregarded.[20] First, any effect on the rent attributable to the granting of a tenancy to a sitting tenant. Hence the level of rents fixed under section 14 will not differ from rents on initial grants of assured tenancies. Secondly, any increase in

Improvements

the value of the dwelling-house attributable to a relevant improvement[21] carried out by a person who was the tenant at the time it was carried out.[22] The improvement will not be disregarded if it was carried out in pursuance of an obligation to the immediate landlord,[23] but it will be disregarded if it was carried out pursuant to an obligation to the immediate landlord which did not relate to the specific improvement concerned but arose by reference to consent given to the carrying out of that improvement.[24] "Improvement" itself is not defined, but a "relevant improvement"[25] is one carried out either during the tenancy, or not more than 21 years before the service of the notice,[26] provided in the latter case, that the dwelling-house has been let under an assured tenancy at all times between the carrying out of the improvement and the service of the notice under section 13, and that on the coming to an end of an assured tenancy during that period, the tenant did not quit.[27]

Tenant's breach

The third matter to be disregarded in determining the rent is any reduction in the value of the dwelling-house attributable to a failure by the tenant to comply with any terms of the tenancy. The typical example would be failure to repair.[28] The value of the property might also be reduced

Former tenant's breach

by unauthorised alterations. The question which arose in *N. & D. (London) Ltd v. Gadsdon*[29] was whether disrepair by

---

[18] See above, pp. 229 *et seq.* (mandatory grounds).

[19] s. 14(1).

[20] s. 14(2).

[21] See below.

[22] See, on Rent Act 1977, s. 70(3), *Trustees of Henry Smith's Charity v. Hemmings* (1983) 265 E.G. 383 (improvements not disregarded when done before grant of lease). See generally [1987] 22 E.G. 963 (J. Martin).

[23] See the similar provision relating to business tenancies in Landlord and Tenant Act 1954, s. 34(2). For problems with such a disregard, see *Forte and Co. Ltd v. General Accident Life Assurance Ltd* (1987) 54 P.&C.R. 9.

[24] For example, where the tenant has an obligation to carry out any improvements for which the landlord gives consent.

[25] s. 13(3).

[26] See the similar provision relating to business tenancies in Landlord and Tenant Act 1954, s. 34(2). It is difficult to assess the effect on rental value of improvements done outside this period.

[27] This is also similar to the business tenancy provision in Landlord and Tenant Act 1954, s. 34(2). If the earlier tenant had quit, there would be no connection between the improvement and the tenant currently seeking to have it disregarded.

[28] Specifically disregarded in Rent Act 1977, s. 70(3).

[29] (1992) 24 H.L.R. 64; [1992] Conv. 272 (J. Martin).

a former tenant was to be disregarded. The present tenant had taken an assured tenancy as successor to his father's statutory tenancy. The father had let the premises fall into such disrepair that the rent assessment committee considered a rent of £5 a month to be appropriate. A fair rent of £30 a month had been registered under the Rent Act in 1988, before the father's death in 1989. The landlord, who proposed a rent of £500 a month, claimed that the disrepair should be disregarded. The disrepair could not be attributed save in very small measure to the present tenant. It was held that the disregard in section 14(2)(c), which refers to a failure by "the tenant" to comply with the terms of the tenancy, did not extend to a breach by a predecessor. The wording contrasts with section 14(2)(b), which provides for the disregard of any improvement by "a person who at the time it was carried out" was the tenant. The son's assured tenancy was a new tenancy, and not a continuation of his father's, albeit on the same terms as to repair. The landlord should have been more vigilant in enforcing the repair obligations against the father. Thus the nominal rent of £5 was upheld. It would still be open to the landlord to enforce the son's repair obligations, the extent of which would depend upon a consideration of the terms of the assured tenancy in the light of the condition of the premises when it commenced.

A similar point could be taken where a fixed term assured tenancy ends and is replaced by a statutory periodic tenancy, in circumstances where a breach of the repair obligation occurred during the fixed term. Even though the statutory periodic tenancy may be regarded as a new tenancy, no doubt the disregard would apply, either because "the tenant" is the same person throughout or because to hold otherwise would allow the tenant to take advantage of his own wrong.

Meaning of "rent" For the purpose of section 14, "rent" does not include a variable service charge,[30] but includes any sums payable by the tenant to the landlord for the use of furniture or for services, repairs, maintenance, insurance or management costs, even if payable under separate agreements.[31] This is an anti-avoidance provision, designed to prevent the landlord from diminishing the jurisdiction of the rent assessment committee by artificially separating the various components of the rent, and is similar to the provisions of the Rent Act 1977.[32] In the case of houses in multiple **Council tax** occupation, the landlord is liable to pay council tax.[33] Whether he can pass this on to the tenants depends on the terms of the tenancy. The tenancy will normally permit this

[30] Within the meaning of Landlord and Tenant Act 1985, s. 18. Such a service charge is within the control of the 1985 Act.
[31] s. 14(4).
[32] Rent Act 1977, s. 71(1); above, p. 178.
[33] Council Tax (Liability of Owners) Regulations 1992 (S.I. 1992 No. 551), as amended by S.I. 1993 No. 151.

if granted after the advent of council tax, which replaced the community charge (which itself replaced domestic rating). When a market rent is assessed under section 14, any such liability of the landlord is to be taken into account.[34]

It may be that a notice under section 6(2)[35] (relating to the fixing of terms of a statutory periodic tenancy) has also been referred to the rent assessment committee. If the date specified in the section 6(2) notice is not later than the first day of the new period specified in the section 13 notice, and the committee proposes to hear the two references together, then the committee shall make the determination under section 6 before that under section 13. Where the terms of a statutory periodic tenancy are to be varied, obviously this should be settled before assessing the market rent. When any variation has been established, the new terms will then be taken into account under section 14(1).[36]

Where section 6 notice also referred

Effective date

The rent determined by the rent assessment committee becomes the rent payable with effect from the beginning of the new period specified in the section 13 notice (unless the landlord and tenant agree otherwise). A later date (not being later than the date the rent is determined) may be substituted if it appears to the committee that the earlier date would cause undue hardship to the tenant.[37] There is no provision for the registration of the rent, although the figures determined by the committee are to be publicly available, as explained below. Unlike the position under the Rent Act 1977, a determination by the committee under section 14 (or under section 22, discussed below) does not operate *in rem* so as to bind future lettings. There is no appeal from the committee's determination except on a point of law.

No registration

Finally, nothing in section 14 affects the rights of the parties to vary the rent by agreement,[38] nor does it require the committee to continue with their determination if the tenancy has ended or if the parties give written notice that they no longer require such a determination.[39]

Discontinuance

Additional provisions relating to assured shorthold tenancies

Section 22 of the 1988 Act provides a procedure which may be invoked only by assured shorthold tenants. Such tenants

---

[34] Local Government Finance (Housing) (Consequential Amendments) Order 1993 (S.I. 1993 No. 651).
[35] See above, p. 211.
[36] See above.
[37] Housing Act 1988, s. 14(7).
[38] *ibid.* s. 13(5).
[39] *ibid.* s. 14(8).

may take advantage of the section 14 procedure where they fall within the qualifying conditions of section 13, in other words, where the tenancy is a periodic tenancy. A shorthold tenancy is normally for a fixed term, but on expiry will become a statutory periodic tenancy if the landlord does not recover possession; section 14 will then apply.

The main distinction between section 14 and section 22 is that the reference to the rent assessment committee under section 14 may only be made if the landlord has served a notice to increase the rent under section 13. There is no mechanism there for referring a rent initially agreed. Under section 22, on the other hand, the tenant may initiate the procedure, which operates to vary the agreed rent. The assured shorthold tenant, therefore, has in theory greater rights in relation to rent than an assured tenant, although less security.

Initial rent may be altered

Procedure

The tenant may apply in the prescribed form[40] for a determination by the rent assessment committee. The committee will determine the rent which, in their opinion, "the landlord might reasonably be expected to obtain under the assured shorthold tenancy."[41] Presumably a market rent is here envisaged.

Not available to statutory periodic tenants

The procedure may be invoked once only, and is not available to assured shorthold tenants falling within section 20(4) (where a new tenancy has been granted or a statutory periodic tenancy has arisen on the coming to an end of an assured shorthold tenancy).[42] The statutory periodic tenant may, however, invoke the section 14 procedure, as stated above.

No determination if lack of comparables or rent insufficiently excessive

Where an application is made under section 22, the committee is not to make a determination unless they consider that there is a sufficient number of similar dwellings in the locality let on assured tenancies (whether shorthold or not), and that the rent in question is *significantly* higher than the rent which the landlord might reasonably be expected to be able to obtain.[43] The committee has no power to increase the rent. Thus the tenant will not succeed if there are insufficient comparables, nor if his rent is not sufficiently excessive. In any event, he may be reluctant to apply because of the absence of security of tenure, unless he has a substantial fixed term.

Effective date

Where a determination is made under section 22, it has effect from such date as the committee may direct, not being

---

[40] Assured Tenancies and Agricultural Occupancies (Forms) Regulations 1988 (S.I. 1988 No. 2203) (Form No. 8), as amended by S.I. 1993 No. 654.

[41] Housing Act 1988, s. 22(1).

[42] *ibid*. s. 22(2). If the tenancy is renewed by way of a fixed term, neither s. 14 nor s. 22 will apply.

[43] *ibid*. s. 22(3). As far as comparables are concerned, private landlords are likely to charge higher rents than housing associations. See *Blundell Memorial Lecture* (1989) (N. Madge and J. Wilson).

earlier than the date of the application. Any excess above the rent so determined is irrecoverable from the tenant.[44]

Further increases   The landlord cannot subsequently serve a notice of increase under section 13 until after the first anniversary of the date on which the determination takes effect.[45]

A determination under section 22 is subject to the same provisions as one made under section 14 in respect of the meaning of "rent," and discontinuance of the determination if the tenancy has ended or if the parties so require by written notice.[46]

Termination of committee's functions   If the Secretary of State so provides by order made by statutory instrument, section 22 shall cease to apply to such cases, areas or in such circumstances as may be specified, subject to such transitional provisions as appear desirable.[47]

Information powers of rent assessment committee

Where reference is made to the rent assessment committee under the above provisions relating to assured or assured shorthold tenancies, section 41 of the 1988 Act gives the committee power to serve notice (in prescribed form)[48] upon the landlord or tenant, requiring him to give the committee such information as they may reasonably require, within a specified period of not less than 14 days from the service of the notice. Failure to comply without reasonable excuse is punishable by fine.

Public availability of information as to rents

Information as to rents under assured tenancies which have been the subject of applications to rent assessment committees is to be kept and made publicly available by the President of every rent assessment panel.[49] The purpose of this provision is to assist in the building up of a body of comparables. As previously noted, there is no provision for the registration as such of any rents.

---

[44] *ibid.* s. 22(4). There is no such provision in relation to s. 14.
[45] *ibid.*
[46] *ibid.* s. 22(5); above, pp. 254.
[47] *ibid.* s. 23.
[48] Assured Tenancies and Agricultural Occupancies (Rent Information) Order 1988 (S.I. 1988 No. 2199); Assured Tenancies and Agricultural Occupancies (Rent Information) (Amendment) Order 1993 (S.I. 1993 No. 657).
[49] Housing Act 1988, s. 42; Assured Tenancies and Agricultural Occupancies (Rent Information) Order 1988 (S.I. 1988 No. 2199). See also s. 43, authorising the publication of information by local authorities concerning assured tenancies for the benefit of landlords and tenants.

APPENDIX: FORMS
AND PRECEDENTS

CONTENTS

Forms and Precedents

AGREEMENT

for letting furnished dwellinghouse
on an assured shorthold tenancy
under Part I of the Housing Act 1988.

DATE   19

PARTIES   1.   THE Landlord

2.   THE Tenant

PROPERTY   The dwelling-house situated at and being

Together with the Fixtures Furniture and Effects therein and more
particularly specified in the Inventory thereof signed by the parties

TERM   A term certain of   *months/year(s) from   19

RENT   £   per   †(subject
                   nevertheless as hereinafter provided)

PAYABLE   in advance by equal   payments on

First payment to be made on the   day of   next

1. **THE** Landlord lets and the Tenant takes the Property for the Term at the Rent
    payable as above

2. **THIS** Agreement is intended to create an assured shorthold tenancy as defined in
    section 20 of the Housing Act 1988 and the provisions for the recovery of possession
    by the Landlord in section 21 thereof apply accordingly

3. WHERE the context admits —

(a) "The Landlord" includes the persons for the time being entitled in reversion expectant on the tenancy

(b) "The Tenant" includes the persons deriving title under the Tenant

(c) References to the Property include references to any part or parts of the Property and to the Fixtures Furniture and Effects or any of them

4. THE Tenant will —

(a) Pay the Rent at the times and in the manner specified

(b) Pay for all gas and electric light and power which shall be consumed or supplied on or to the Property during the tenancy and the amount of the water rate charged in respect of the Property during the tenancy and the amount of all charges made for the use of the telephone (if any) on the Property during the tenancy or a proper proportion of the amount of the rental or other recurring charges to be assessed according to the duration of the tenancy

(c) Not damage or injure the Property or make any alteration in or addition to it

(d) Preserve the Fixtures Furniture and Effects from being destroyed or damaged and not remove any of them from the Property

(e) Yield up the Property at the end of the tenancy in the same clean state and condition as it was in the beginning of the tenancy and make good pay for the repair of or replace all such items of the Fixtures Furniture and Effects as shall be broken lost damaged or destroyed during the tenancy (reasonable wear and damage by fire excepted)

(f) Leave the Furniture and Effects at the end of the tenancy in the rooms or places in which they were at the beginning of the tenancy

(g) Pay for the washing (including ironing or pressing) of all linen and for the washing and cleaning (including ironing and pressing) of all counterpanes blankets and curtains which shall have been soiled during the tenancy (the reasonable use thereof nevertheless to be allowed for)

(h) Permit the Landlord or the Landlord's agents at reasonable hours in the daytime to enter the Property to view the state and condition thereof

(i) Not assign sublet or otherwise part with possession of the Property

(j) Not carry on on the Property any profession trade or business or let apartments or receive paying guests on the Property or place or exhibit any notice board or notice on the Property or use the Property for any other purpose than that of a strictly private residence

(k) Not do or suffer to be done on the Property anything which may be or become a nuisance or annoyance to the Landlord or the Tenants or occupiers of any adjoining premises or which may vitiate any insurance of the Property against fire or otherwise or increase the ordinary premium for such insurance

(l) Permit the Landlord or the Landlord's agents at reasonable hours in the daytime within the last twenty-eight days of the tenancy to enter and view the Property with prospective Tenants

(m) Perform and observe any obligation on the part of the Tenant arising under the Local Government Finance Act 1992 or regulations made thereunder to pay council tax and indemnify the Landlord against any such obligation which the Landlord may incur during the tenancy by reason of the Tenant's ceasing to be resident in the Property

5. **PROVIDED** that if the Rent or any instalment or part thereof shall be in arrear for at least fourteen days after the same shall have become due (whether legally demanded or not) or if there shall be a breach of any of the agreements by the Tenant the Landlord may re-enter on the Property (subject always to any statutory restrictions on his power so to do) and immediately thereupon the tenancy shall absolutely determine without prejudice to the other rights and remedies of the Landlord

6. **THE** Landlord agrees with the Tenant as follows —

    (1) To pay and indemnify the Tenant against all assessments and outgoings in respect of the Property (except the water rate and any council tax payable by the Tenant under clause 4 above and except charges for the supply of gas or electric light and power or the use of any telephone)

    (2) That the Tenant paying the Rent and performing the agreements on the part of the Tenant may quietly possess and enjoy the Property during the tenancy without any lawful interruption from the Landlord or any person claiming under or in trust for the Landlord

    (3) To return to the Tenant any rent payable for any period while the Property is rendered uninhabitable by fire the amount in case of dispute to be settled by arbitration

7. **THIS** Agreement shall take effect subject to the provisions of section 11 of the Landlord and Tenant Act 1985 if applicable to the tenancy

8. **NOTICE** under section 48 of the Landlord and Tenant Act 1987

    The Tenant is hereby notified that notices (including notices in proceedings) must be served on the Landlord by the Tenant at the following address‡:

‡This must be an address in England and Wales

AS WITNESS the hands of the parties hereto the day and year first above written

SIGNED by the above-named
(the Landlord)

in the presence of

SIGNED by the above-named
(the Tenant)

in the presence of

DATED   19

and

AGREEMENT

for letting furnished dwellinghouse at

on assured shorthold tenancy

Rent £

© 1993 **OYEZ** The Solicitors' Law Stationery Society Ltd, *1993 Edition*
Oyez House, 7 Spa Road, London SE16 3QQ 6.94 F27332

5004384

(All rights reserved)   **Agreement 20**   ★ ★ ★

AGREEMENT

for letting an unfurnished dwellinghouse
on an assured shorthold tenancy
under Part I of the Housing Act 1988

This is a form of legal document and is not produced or drafted for use, without technical assistance, by persons unfamiliar with the law of landlord and tenant.

Note that the notice condition in the Housing Act 1988, s.20(1)(c), requires prior service of notice in the prescribed form.

This form should not be used for granting a tenancy to a person who is already a protected or statutory tenant or a protected occupier: see Housing Act 1988.

DATE   19

PARTIES   1. **THE** Landlord

                   2. **THE** Tenant

PROPERTY   The dwelling-house situated at and being

TERM   A term certain of   *months/year(s) from   19

*The number of months must not be less than six: Housing Act 1988, s.20(1)(a).

RENT   per   †(subject
                   nevertheless as hereinafter provided)

†The period mentioned here will form the basis of any subsequent periodic tenancy.

PAYABLE   [in advance] by equal   payments on

FIRST payment to be made on the   day of   next

1. **THE** Landlord lets and the Tenant takes the Property for the Term at the Rent payable as above

2. **THIS** Agreement is intended to create an assured shorthold tenancy as defined in section 20 of the Housing Act 1988 and the provisions for the recovery of possession by the Landlord in section 21 thereof apply accordingly

3. **IF** the property shall be burnt down or rendered uninhabitable by fire the Rent shall from that date cease to be payable until the Property is reinstated and rendered habitable and in case any dispute arises under this provision it shall be submitted to arbitration pursuant to the Arbitration Act 1950

4. THE Tenant agrees with the Landlord —

(1) To pay the Rent at the times and in the manner aforesaid

(2) (a) To perform and observe any obligation on the part of the Tenant arising under the Local Government Finance Act 1992 or regulations made thereunder to pay council tax and indemnify the Landlord against any such obligation which the Landlord may incur during the tenancy by reason of the Tenant's ceasing to be resident in the Property

(b) To pay all other taxes duties assessments impositions and outgoings which are now or which may at any time hereafter be assessed charged or imposed upon the Property or on the owner or occupier in respect thereof

(3) To pay for all gas and electric light and power which shall be consumed or supplied on or to the Property during the tenancy and the amount of all charges made for the use of the telephone (if any) on the Property during the tenancy or a proper proportion of the amount of the rental or other recurring charges to be assessed according to the duration of the tenancy

(4) To keep the drains gutters and pipes of the Property clear the chimneys swept and the garden neat

(5) To keep in good and complete repair order and condition (damage by accidental fire only excepted) the interior of the Property and the painting papering and decorations thereof and the fixtures fittings and appliances therein (except installations and things which the Landlord is liable hereunder or by law to repair)

(6) That the Landlord or any person authorised by the Landlord in writing may at reasonable times of the day on giving 24 hours' notice in writing to the occupier enter the Property for the purpose of viewing its condition and state of repair

(7) To use the Property as and for a private dwellinghouse only and not to carry on or permit to be carried on upon the Property any profession trade or business whatsoever

(8) Not to make any alteration in or addition to the Property or do or suffer any act or thing to be done thereon whereby the fire insurance premium might be increased

(9) Not to do or suffer to be done in or upon the Property any act or thing which may be a nuisance damage or annoyance to the Landlord or the tenants or occupiers of any of the adjoining premises

(10) Not assign sublet or otherwise part with possession of the Property

(11) At the expiration or sooner determination of the tenancy to deliver up the Property to the Landlord in such order condition and state as shall be consistent with the due performance of the obligations of the Tenant herein contained

5. **PROVIDED** that if the Rent or any part thereof shall be in arrear for fourteen days after the same shall have become due (whether legally demanded or not) or in the event of the breach of any of the agreements on the part of the Tenant herein contained the Landlord may re-enter upon the Property and immediately thereupon the tenancy shall absolutely determine but without prejudice to the other rights and remedies of the Landlord

6. **THE** Landlord agrees with the Tenant that the Tenant paying the rent and performing and observing all the agreements herein contained may quietly possess and enjoy the Property during the tenancy without any lawful interruption from or by the Landlord or any person claiming through or under or in trust for the Landlord

7. **THIS** Agreement shall take effect subject to the provisions of section 11 of the Landlord and Tenant Act 1985 if applicable to the tenancy

8. **WHERE** the context admits—

   (i) ''The Landlord'' includes the persons for the time being entitled in reversion expectant on the tenancy

   (ii) ''The Tenant'' includes the persons deriving title under the Tenant

   (iii) References to the Property include references to any part or parts of the Property

‡This must be
an address in
England and Wales.

9. **NOTICE** under section 48 of the Landlord and Tenant Act 1987

   The Tenant is hereby notified that notices (including notices in proceedings) may be served on the Landlord by the Tenant at the following address‡:

AS WITNESS the hands of the parties hereto the day and year first above written

SIGNED by the above-named
(the Landlord)
in the presence of

SIGNED by the above-named
(the Tenant)
in the presence of

DATED _____ 19 _____

and

AGREEMENT

for letting unfurnished dwellinghouse at

on assured shorthold tenancy

Rent £

©1993 **OYEZ** The Solicitors' Law Stationery Society Ltd, *1993 Edition*
Oyez House, 7 Spa Road, London SE16 3QQ 11.93 F25927

5004376

Agreement 19 *

©1993 **OYEZ** Form No. 7 of the Assured
Tenancies and Agricultural Occupancies
(Forms) Regulations 1988 (as amended)

HOUSING ACT 1988

Section 20

Notice of an Assured Shorthold Tenancy

- Please write clearly in black ink.

- If there is anything you do not understand you should get advice from a solicitor or a Citizens' Advice Bureau, before you agree to the tenancy.

- The landlord must give this notice to the tenant before an assured shorthold tenancy is granted. It does not commit the tenant to take the tenancy.

- **THIS DOCUMENT IS IMPORTANT, KEEP IT IN A SAFE PLACE.**

(1) Name of proposed tenant. If a joint tenancy is being offered enter the names of the joint tenant(s).

To(¹):

1. You are proposing to take a tenancy of the dwelling known as:

(2) The tenancy **must** be for a term certain of at least six months.

(²) from the   day of   19
    to the   day of   19

2. This notice is to tell you that your tenancy is to be an *assured shorthold tenancy*. Provided you keep to the terms of the tenancy, you are entitled to remain in the dwelling for at least the first six months of the fixed period agreed at the start of the tenancy. At the end of this period, depending on the terms of the tenancy, the landlord may have the right to repossession if he/she wants.

3. The rent for this tenancy is the rent we have agreed. However, you have the right to apply to a rent assessment committee for a determinaton of the rent which the committee considers might reasonably be obtained under the tenancy. If the committee considers (i) that there is a sufficient number of similar properties in the locality let on assured tenancies and that (ii) the rent we have agreed is significantly higher than the rent which might reasonably be obtained having regard to the level of rents for other assured tenancies in the locality, it will determine a rent for the tenancy. That rent will be the legal maximum you can be required to pay from the date the committee directs. If the rent includes a payment for council tax, the rent determined by the committee will be inclusive of council tax.

[P.T.O.

To be signed by the landlord or his/her agent (someone acting for him/her). If there are joint landlords each must sign, unless one signs on behalf of the rest with their agreement.

Signed:

Name(s) of
landlord(s):

Address of
landlord(s):

Telephone:

If signed by agent, name and address of agent

Telephone: Date: 19

SPECIAL NOTE FOR EXISTING TENANTS

- Generally, if you already have a protected or statutory tenancy and you give it up to take a new tenancy in the same or other accommodation owned by the same landlord, that tenancy cannot be an assured tenancy. It can still be a protected tenancy.

- But if you currently occupy a dwelling which was let to you as a protected shorthold tenant, special rules apply.

- If you have an assured tenancy which is not a shorthold under the Housing Act 1988, you cannot be offered an assured shorthold tenancy of the same or other accommodation by the same landlord.

© 1993 **OYEZ** The Solicitors' Law Stationery Society Ltd, Oyez House, 7 Spa Road, London SE16 3QQ

1993 Edition
2.94 F26522

5045316

HA 35

© 1988 *OYEZ*

HOUSING ACT 1988
Section 21(1)(b)

Assured Shorthold Tenancy : Notice Requiring Possession:

Fixed Term Tenancy
(Notes)

(1) Name and address of tenant.

To(¹)

of

(2) Name and address of landlord (Note 2 overleaf).

From(²)

of

(3) Address of dwelling.

I give you notice that I require possession of the dwelling house known as(³)

(4) Date of expiry (Note 3 overleaf).

after(⁴)

(5) Note 3 overleaf.

Dated(⁵)   19

Landlord

(6) Name and address.

[Landlord's agent](⁶)

[P.T.O.

NOTES

1.   On or after the coming to an end of a fixed term assured shorthold tenancy, a court must make an order for possession if the landlord has given a notice in this form.

2.   Where there are joint landlords, at least one of them must give this notice.

3.   The length of the notice must be at least two months and the notice may be given before or on the day on which the fixed term comes to an end.

© 1988 *OYEZ* The Solicitors' Law Stationery Society Ltd, Oyez House, 7 Spa Road, London SE16 3QQ

11.94 F28220
5045201
★ ★ ★ ★ ★

© 1989 *OYEZ*

HOUSING ACT 1988
Section 21(4)(a)

Assured Shorthold Tenancy : Notice Requiring Possession: Periodic Tenancy
(Notes)

(1) Name and address of tenant.

To(¹)

of

(2) Name and address of landlord (Note 2 overleaf)

From(²)

of

(3) Address of dwelling.

I give you notice that I require possession of the dwelling house known as(³)

(4) Date of expiry (Note 3 overleaf).

after(⁴)

(5) Note 3 overleaf.

Dated(⁵)   19

Landlord

(6) Name and address.

[Landlord's agent](⁶)

[P.T.O.

NOTES

1.   Where an assured shorthold tenancy has become a periodic tenancy, a court must make an order for possession if the landlord has given proper notice in this form.

2.   Where there are joint landlords, at least one of them must give this notice.

3.   This notice must expire:

(a)   on the last day of a period of the tenancy.

(b)   at least two months after this notice is given.

(c)   no sooner than the earliest day on which the tenancy could ordinarily be brought to an end by a notice to quit given by the landlord on the same day.

© 1989 **OYEZ** The Solicitors' Law Stationery Society Ltd, Oyez House, 7 Spa Road, London SE16 3QQ   7.94 F27608

5045332

★ ★ ★ ★

HA 21A

Notice by Owner Designed to Protect His Position under the Housing Act 1988 Without Conceding that the Act Applies.*

To: — — [*intended occupier(s)*]
I/We of — — [*the owner(s)*] notify you that I/we own [and have occupied as my/our only or principal home] the property known as — — and if the agreement intended to be made between us creates an assured tenancy within the meaning of section 1 of the Housing Act 1988 possession of the property may be recovered under Ground 1 in Schedule 2 to the Act.

Dated — 19—

Signed:-

Received on — 19— a notice of which the above is a true copy.

Signed:-

Notes

This Form replaces an earlier form first published in June 1982 based on a draft supplied by A. A. Preece, Solicitor. That Form dealt with the position under the Rent Acts, where an owner-occupier might seek possession under a regulated tenancy under Case 11 or for a restricted contract under section 105 of the 1977 Act if prior notice was given.

The following note explaining the rationale of the Form reproduces the note to the earlier Form adapted to relate it to the 1988 Act:–

> "This notice is designed for use in the not uncommon situation where a person intends to allow another person to use residential property for a consideration without wishing the arrangement to attract statutory protection. The circumstances may be that it is uncertain whether a Court would hold that the arrangement constituted a licence or a tenancy, but, if the latter, Ground 1 is applicable, because the grantor is either an owner-occupier, within the meaning of the Housing Act provisions or is an owner who has not occupied but might wish to do so in the future. The optional wording in line 2 only applies to the former.
>
> It seeks to avoid the need to choose finally between trying to avoid the Housing Act by employing a licence and granting a tenancy with reliance on Ground 1 by leaving open the possibility of the transaction being upheld as a licence whilst serving notice, as a long stop, in case the agreement should be held to be a tenancy."

Similarly, this form of notice may be useful where it is uncertain whether or not the tenant occupies the premises as his only or principal home (see section 1(1)(b) of the Act). If he does not, there is no protection except possibly the Protection from Eviction Act 1977.

The continuing problems in drawing the line between licence and tenancy are well illustrated by the line of cases following *Street v. Mountford* [1985] A.C. 809 and especially *Duke v. Wynn* [1989] 38 E.G. 109. Of course, by serving even a protective notice such as this, the owner may be weakening his own position to argue that he has created a licence or may alert the occupier to the opportunity to claim a tenancy. However, litigating a possession claim under Ground 1 of the Housing Act, especially under the first owner-occupier limb, differs from seeking possession from a licensee unwilling to leave only in terms of

* Precedent and Notes first published in *Precedents for the Conveyancer*. Reproduced here by kind permission of John Adams.

some delay and probable extra expense. The benefit of thus being able to rely on Ground 1, with the relaxed conditions compared to Case 11 or, especially, Case 9 of the Rent Act, can be set against those disadvantages.

Other Grounds

Ownership of the property may be turned to advantage by adding wording based on this Form to notices under Grounds 3 or 4 where there is uncertainty over whether prior occupation for a holiday or a relevant student letting could be established. Moreover, in so far as the wordings of Ground 2 requires a notice under Ground 1 to have been served, this Form could be used, in appropriate circumstances, where the individual owner has created an earlier mortgage, provided the tenancy permits termination because a mortgagee needs vacant possession for purposes of a sale (see Ground 2 in Schedule 2 of the 1988 Act and the wording of section 7(6)).

Co-Owners

Recovery by one of two owners is now possible under the express wording of Ground 1, so eliminating the contrast between Case 11, where the same applied (*Tilling v. Whiteman* [1980] A.C. 1) and Case 9, where it did not (*McIntyre v. Hardcastle* [1948] 2 K.B. 82).

Provision in Tenancy to Permit Landlord Unilaterally to Reduce Rent to a Level on which Rent Act (or Housing Act) Protection is Removed*

Usual form of tenancy agreement save for habendum in following form:

At the rent (unless and until any notice of reduction under the following provision takes effect) of £____ per [week][month] payable [weekly][monthly] in advance but upon expiry of written notice of not less than ____ [days] [weeks] served by the Landlord [not earlier than ____ [weeks][months] after the commencement of the tenancy] of such lower sum as shall be specified in such notice payable [weekly][monthly] in advance from the date specified in such notice.

Notes

The efficacy of this avoidance device derives from two propositions: — (a) that rent can be varied by notice given by a landlord unilaterally and (b) that the relevant time for deciding if the rent is less than two-thirds of the rateable value, so taking the tenancy outside the scope of the Rent Act 1977 by virtue of section 5, is the time when the issue of protection arises and the applicability of the sections falls to be tested. Authority for the first proposition will be found in *G.L.C. v. Connolly* [1970] 2 Q.B. 100, C.A. (where, in fact, the notice was to increase the rent) and for the second in *J. & F. Stone Lighting and Radio Ltd v. Levitt* [1947] A.C. 209, H.L. Even if a fair rent were registered it only provides a maximum and not a minimum and the exercise of the power to reduce the rent is not attended by the problems of the meaning of "rent payable" when registration of a fair rent restricts the rent recoverable, as discussed at [1981] Conv. 325. The reduced rent is that payable.

The landlord will have to forego the economic rent for the period from expiry of the notice of reduction until the recovery of possession, for which proceedings will be necessary by reason of section 3 of the Protection from Eviction Act 1977, following a minimum of four weeks' notice as required by section 5 of the same Act, but may regard this as a small price to pay for the ability to remove Rent Act protection virtually at will. Exercise of that power could be postponed for an initial period, as provided for in the optional phrase beginning "not earlier" in the form, which should otherwise be omitted.

Position under Housing Act 1988

The Form is equally effective to remove protection from assured tenancies under the 1988 Act, whether the test is for a pre-April 1990 tenancy rent less than two-thirds of the March 31, 1990 rateable value or for a later tenancy rent of £1,000 p.a. or less in Greater London or £250 p.a. elsewhere.

---

* Precedent and Notes first published in *Precedents for the Conveyancer*. Reproduced here by kind permission of John Adams.

Indexation of Rent Clause for Assured Tenancy*

(a) On every anniversary of this tenancy the rent will be revised.

(b) If the base date for the Retail Prices Index has not changed from the current base date the rent will be the initial rent increased by the same proportion as the RPI last published before the relevant anniversary has increased over the RPI last published before the date of this agreement [which figure is noted below].

(c) If the base date for the RPI has changed the rent will be increased to the figure of the revised rent at the date of the change increased by the same proportion as the RPI last published before the relevant anniversary has increased over 100.

(d) The process in (c) will apply after the second or later change in the base date.

[(e) All revised rents will be rounded up or down to the nearest figure that gives a monthly payment in full pounds without pence.]

Notes

In the interests of brevity, the clause does not provide for the eventuality of abandonment of the RPI. Should that happen then, in the absence of agreement, the Landlord could offer the Tenant a new tenancy of the premises on identical terms, except for the basis of rental adjustment, and seek possession on the suitable alternative accommodation ground if the Tenant declines. Alternatively the Landlord could invoke the jurisdiction of the court demonstrated in *Pole Properties Ltd v. Feinberg* (1981) 41 P. & C.R. 121 to rewrite the contract to reflect a fundamental change of circumstances.

---

* Precedent and Notes first published in *Precedents for the Conveyancer*. Reproduced here by kind permission of John Adams.

Rent Review Clause for an Assured Tenancy by Agreement between the Parties, with Independent Valuation in Default*

(a) The Rent Revision Date shall be —— 19– and every anniversary thereafter.

(b) On each Rent Revision Date the rent may be revised to such sum as is agreed [in writing] between the parties. [Any sum so agreed shall be endorsed on this tenancy agreement].

(c) If the parties fail to agree on the rent payable from any Rent Revision Date then either party may refer the issue of the revised rent to the decision of the Nominated Valuer.

(d) The Nominated Valuer shall be a valuer agreed upon by the parties or, in default of agreement, appointed on the application of either party by the President or senior officer of the local [Law Society] [branch of the RICS].

(e) The Nominated Valuer shall determine the revised rent at that at which he considers the [property] might reasonably be expected to be let in the open market by a willing landlord under an assured [shorthold] tenancy–

(i)   which is a tenancy of the same fixed term or having the same periods as this tenancy;

(ii) which begins on the Rent Revision Date;

(iii) the terms of which (other than relating to the amount of the rent) are the same as those of this tenancy;

but disregarding those matters set out in sections 14(2) and 14(3) of the Housing Act 1988.

(f) The revised rent as so agreed or so determined shall take effect from the Rent Revision Date [save that if the reference to an agreed Nominated Valuer, or application for appointment of a Nominated Valuer, occurs more than [three] months after the Rent Revision Date then the revised rent shall take effect at the first rent date following such reference or application].

(g) The [Nominated Valuer shall have power to provide for the payment of his fees by only one party if he considers that that party has acted unreasonably in not agreeing a rent proposed by the other party but otherwise the] fees of the Nominated Valuer shall be borne equally by the parties.

Notes

It is anticipated that the Form will be used primarily in fixed term assured tenancies. Periodic tenancies may have the rent revised under section 13 of the Housing Act 1988, but those provisions, with the possible intervention of the Rent Assessment Committee, do not apply where the tenancy agreement itself provides for variation and there is no objection in principle to such a provision in a periodic tenancy.

The Form avoids notices and is designed to encourage rent revision by informal agreement. Where reference to a valuer is necessary, the basis of valuation is designed to mirror the statutory formula set out in section 14 of the Housing Act. The disregards referred to in clause (e) may be set out in full if it is so desired.

* Precedent and Notes first published in *Precedents for the Conveyancer*. Reproduced here by kind permission of D. N. Clarke.

Rent Review Clause for an Assured Tenancy by Lessor's Unilateral Notice*

(a) The landlord may by written notice (a "Rent Revision Notice") served on the tenant revise the rent payable under this agreement.

(b) The Rent Revision Notice shall specify the [monthly] [weekly] rent which is to become payable and the date on which it is to take effect (the "Rent Revision Date").

(c) The Rent Revision Date so specified in the Rent Revision Notice for the new rent to become payable shall in no event be earlier than the anniversary of the start of the tenancy or the last Rent Revision Date, as the case may be; it must also be at least four weeks after the service of the Rent Revision Notice.

[(d) In the four week period following the service of the Rent Revision Notice, the tenant may serve on the landlord a four weeks notice to quit and if the tenant so terminates the tenancy, the Rent Revision Notice shall be of no effect].

Notes

Use of this Form avoids the expense and delay of (possible) reference to a third party.

The validity of varying a rent by unilateral notice was upheld by the Court of Appeal in *Greater London Council v. Connelly* [1970] 2 Q.B. 100.

This Form seeks to ensure that a landlord can give notice of an annual increase of rent. A retrospective increase is not possible; there is no obstacle to revision more frequently than once a year, but that might create "consumer resistance".

The inclusion (especially in a fixed term tenancy) of sub-clause (d), allowing a tenant to quit is recommended. A court might shrink from allowing a tenant to be burdened with a unilaterally imposed increase in a situation where he is left without the option of leaving.

---

* Precedent and Notes first published in *Precedents for the Conveyancer*. Reproduced here by kind permission of D. N. Clarke.

Rent Review Provision for Assured Tenancy*

(a) The landlord may serve a notice stating a revised rent to take effect not less than four weeks after service and not earlier than one year from the later of the start of the tenancy or the last revision date. The revised rent stated in that notice is "the Landlord's Figure."

(b) The tenant within two weeks of service of the landlord's notice may serve a counter notice stating a different revised rent. The revised rent stated in that notice is "the Tenant's Figure."

(c) If the tenant does not serve a counter notice the landlord's notice takes effect at the revision date stated in it to revise the rent to the Landlord's Figure. If the landlord accepts the Tenant's Figure the tenant's counter-notice takes effect at the revision date stated in the landlord's notice to revise the rent to the Tenant's Figure.

(d) If the Tenant's Figure has not been accepted by the revision date either party may refer the issue of the revised rent to the decision of the Nominated Valuer. The Nominated Valuer is the valuer named in the landlord's notice or, if none is named in that notice, named in the tenant's counter-notice but if a different valuer is named in both the notice and the counter-notice a valuer shall be appointed at the request of either party by the senior officer of the local [Law Society] [branch of the RICS]. The Nominated Valuer must invite each party to make written representations in support of their respective Figures and must then notify the parties which of the Landlord's Figure and Tenant's figure is in his opinion as an expert the nearer to the market rent for the premises (assuming full performance of the Tenant's obligations) in the light of the terms of this agreement at the revision date and the figure so chosen is the revised rent from the revision date. The parties must each pay one half of the Valuer's fees [unless the Valuer decides that one party has acted unreasonably in not agreeing the other party's figure when he may decide the former must meet the whole fees].

(e) Pending the notification of the Nominated Valuer's decision the Tenant must pay rent at a figure half-way between the Landlord's Figure and the Tenant's Figure. On the next rent day after notification the payment must reflect the amount due to either party as a consequence of the decision in the light of the interim payments.

(f) All time limits in this clause must be strictly observed.

Notes

If an assured tenancy contains provisions for adjustment of the rent the provisions of the Housing Act 1988 ss. 13, 14 for service of a rent revision notice and the tenant's right to refer it to a Rent Assessment Committee do not apply.

Although the third party is to act as an expert and not an arbitrator, the process to be followed is based on the notion of the so-called "flip-flop" or "pendulum" arbitration whereby the referee chooses between the two figures put forward, so reducing the cost of the decision and putting each party under pressure to put forward a realistic figure. The optional provision at the end of sub-clause (d) will be a further sanction, if it is included, against putting in a figure too low or too high to an unreasonable extent.

---

* Precedent and Notes first published in *Precedents for the Conveyancer*. Reproduced here by kind permission of John Adams.

Surrender of Existing Tenancy and all Statutory Rights in preparation for New Assured Tenancy*

BY THIS DEED made _____ 19__ I AB of_____ [as beneficial owner] SURRENDER to you XYZ PROPERTIES LIMITED of_____all my rights title and interest arising at law or in equity or under any statutory provision in relation to the premises known as _____ so that the tenancy arising under an agreement made between us on _____ 19__ shall immediately merge and be extinguished in your [freehold] estate in the premises and all other rights shall immediately determine and I WAIVE all rights, claims and demands arising against you under or by virtue of the agreement and RELEASE you from all claims, demands or liabilities under it.

[*Executed by the Tenant*]

Notes

This Form is based closely, though in a less wordy style, on that litigated in *Dibbs v. Campbell* [1988] 2 E.G.L.R. 122. That case illustrates one of the sets of circumstances where the intended grant of a protected shorthold tenancy was vitiated by errors over prior service of the statutory notice, but similar mistakes have been made with assured shorthold tenancies. Other errors can include granting a tenancy for less than the minimum six month period caused by a delay (possibly brief) in signing the agreement (see, for a comparable error in agricultural tenancies, *Keen v. Holland* [1984] 1W.L.R.251). Once an assured tenancy has thus been inadvertently created, any purported assured shorthold tenancy immediately following it will fall foul of section 20(3) of the Housing Act 1988 and itself take effect as an assured tenancy. The former tenancy will be surrendered by operation of law (*Fenner v. Blake* [1900] 1 Q.B. 426).

Dibbs v. Campbell held that an express surrender effectively "cleared the decks" of both the earlier tenancy and the statutory rights of the tenant. It was intended, in that case, that the tenant should move out for a brief period and that is desirable (for a weekend, perhaps, even paid for or subsidised by the landlord), but the court ruled it was not essential. Even handing over all the keys for a short time might help.

The Form can be used for other transactions, *e.g.* the surrender of a protected tenancy of one property to permit the grant of an assured (but not necessarily shorthold) tenancy of other property belonging to the same landlord, thereby side-stepping section 34(1) of the 1988 Act, or to end an assured tenancy and replace it with one outside the Act where a change of circumstances permits that. For example, such a step could preclude arguments on whether the tenant any longer occupied the premises as the only or principal residence.

Care must be taken, in all these circumstances, to avoid any step or statement which will give credence to later allegations of a sham or pretence, and full and independent legal advice to the tenant is highly desirable. The position *vis-à-vis* any mortgagee must also be safeguarded so that it remains bound by the new tenancy if bound by the old.

* Precedent and Notes first published in *Precedents for the Conveyancer*. Reproduced here by kind permission of John Adams.

Tenancy Agreement for Letting by Educational Body with Provision for sharing with Named Non-Student*

TENANCY AGREEMENT made _____ 19__ between the College _____ COLLEGE and ___ the Student _____ a registered student of the College.

1. The College lets to the Student:

  (a) the furnished room numbered _____ in _____ the building known as _____
  (b) the furniture and equipment listed in the inventory signed by the Student and attached.

2. The tenancy runs from _____ 19__ to_____ 19__ but:

  (a) the Student may end it earlier by one calendar month's notice given to the College not later than _____ 19__
  (b) the College may end it immediately if any rent is in arrear for two weeks (without the need for formal demand) or if the Student breaks any of the Student's obligations in this Agreement.

3. The Student must pay the rent by instalments:—
  by_____ 19__ £__
  by_____ 19__ £__ and
  by_____ 19__ £__
and must also pay a surcharge of £ for each week (or part week) the rent is in arrear.

4. The Student must:

  (a) occupy the room personally and not assign sub-let share or part with possession nor permit use or occupation by anyone else except for (i) subletting with consent to another named College student for all or part of the vacations or (ii) sharing occupation with the Second Occupier named in the Appendix who has signed that Appendix
  (b) (i) keep the room clean and in reasonable condition allowing for fair wear and tear
      (ii) not move any furniture and equipment out of the room
      (iii) keep the furniture and equipment in as good condition as at the start of the tenancy allowing for fair wear and tear
  (c) leave the room clean and free of all items (except the listed furniture and equipment) and rubbish at the end of the tenancy
  (d) except with consent
      (i) not carry out redecorations or alterations to the room
      (ii) not change the locks or instal additional locks

---

* Precedent and Notes first published in *Precedents for the Conveyancer*. Reproduced here by kind permission of John Adams.

(iii) not instal or use additional heaters or refrigerators or any aerial

(e) not bring motor-cycles or vehicle parts into the room or any part of the building

(f) not create any nuisance in the room or anywhere else in the building nor permit the Student's visitors to do so and in particular not keep any pets or play radios TV sets tape machinery record players or musical instruments to cause annoyance or in any event after 11.00 p.m.

(g) report any damage loss or malfunction to the College Assistant Secretary (Student Accommodation)

(h) use electricity in a reasonable manner and switch off heaters when the room is empty

(i) abide by the fire regulations for the building.

5. The college may
   (a) enter the room at any time for inspection or to carry out work to the room the furniture and equipment or the building
   (b) use the deposit of £___ made by the Student to cover rent arrears or to make good the Student's responsibilities for any loss or damage to the room to any part of the building damaged by the Student the Second Occupier or the Student's visitors or to the listed furniture and equipment to clean the room if left dirty on leaving or to pay for excessive use of electricity.

6. "Consent" in this agreement means the College's written consent before the act or event in question.

7. This is a student letting under para 8, Schedule 1 to the Housing Act 1988 and therefore not an assured tenancy.

Signed for the College by:

Signed by the Student:

Notes

(a) Tenants are responsible for the safety of their own and College belongings and should never leave the room unlocked.

(b) College Regulations and University Regulations impose certain severe penalties where a student owes money to the College.

Appendix

I _____ acknowledge that I am the Second Occupier for the purposes of Clause 4(a). I understand that no tenancy or sub-tenancy has been or can be created in my favour and I agree to vacate the room when the Student's right to occupy it ends. I also agree to abide by the provisions of the Tenancy Agreement.

Signed by the Second Occupier.

Notes:

This is a "Plain English" style of tenancy agreement for use in a hall of residence, hostel or student house by a specified educational institution formerly within section 8 of the Rent Act 1977 and now paragraph 8, Schedule 1 to the Housing Act 1988. It can, however, be readily adapted for more general use.

Although not cast in traditional form, it is accepted that the power in Clause 2(b) to terminate the tenancy in certain circumstances is a forfeiture provision (*Richard Clarke & Co. Ltd v. Widnall* [1976] 1 W.L.R. 858) and so within section 146 of the Law of Property Act (except for unpaid rent) and the various statutory and common law powers for rent arrears. In the student letting context, with a letting period covering an academic year, it is perhaps unlikely that the procedure would be invoked and other disciplinary measures may be available. In a general tenancy, where Rent Act or Housing Act protection applies, then, provided the initial fixed period is not too long, the value of a forfeiture provision is doubtful, for it involves the giving of reasonable notice, the length of which is uncertain and which may even for a serious breach be longer than the statutory minimum period of notice, and does not avoid the need to prove a Rent Act or Housing Act ground, and reasonableness, for a possession order. Accordingly, the Editor would omit the provision. That also avoids problems over waiver.

The provisions in Clause 4(a) and the Appendix for a second occupier cater for, say, a spouse or other non-student consort, who might legitimately occupy under a tenancy, not containing the wide prohibition in that Clause, without necessarily obtaining tenancy rights. The machinery of the Appendix is designed, nevertheless, to strengthen the landlord's position. Conceivably a spouse might exercise Matrimonial Homes Act rights if the student spouse left but only for the balance of the fixed term, and subject to termination under Clause 2(b) for breach of the obligation placed on the student to occupy personally — see *Sumnall v. Statt* (1984) 49 P. & C.R. 367.

The obligation not to share may also, incidentally, bolster the landlord's right to claim possession if unauthorised sharing produces statutory over-crowding — see section 101(1) Rent Act 1977.

Note the landlord's duties:

(a) to notify overcrowding to the local authority (section 333 Housing Act 1985)

(b) and to give details of permitted numbers in any rent book (section 332 of that Act)

both of which may be frequently overlooked in practice.

Obligations requiring consent

The Editor feels that, in view of the nature of the letting, the implication of consent not being unreasonably withheld, would not be made for Clause 4(d) even where a different result might be reached for comparable prohibition in other contexts.

INDEX